PORTRAITS

of the

AMERICAN UNIVERSITY

1890-1910

❧❧❧❧❧❧❧❧❧❧❧❧❧❧❧❧❧❧❧❧❧

Being a Facsimile Collection of *authentic* Articles,
written by such *great* Educators and/or Writers as
DAVID STARR JORDAN, CHARLES WILLIAM ELIOT,
LINCOLN STEFFENS, BENJAMIN IDE WHEELER,
and many more,
and encompassing such *diverse* Subjects as
expansion of the Universities,
educational Ideals, college Democracy,
as well as
Architecture, undergraduate Life, and Fraternities,
with a
Foreword by **Clarence Faust,**
and a
Prologue by **Algo D. Henderson.**
COMPILED FOR PUBLICATION BY
James C. Stone and **Donald P. DeNevi.**
Lavishly *illustrated* by some of the most Prominent
Photographers of the Day.

COMPILED BY

James C. Stone
and
Donald P. DeNevi

FOREWORD BY
Clarence Faust

PROLOGUE BY
Algo D. Henderson

PORTRAITS
of the
AMERICAN
UNIVERSITY
1890-1910

Jossey-Bass Inc., Publishers
615 Montgomery Street · San Francisco · 1971

PORTRAITS OF THE AMERICAN UNIVERSITY 1890–1910
James C. Stone and Donald P. DeNevi

Copyright © 1971 by Jossey-Bass, Inc., Publishers

Copyright under Pan American and Universal Copyright
Conventions. All rights reserved. Address all inquiries to:

Jossey-Bass, Inc., Publishers
615 Montgomery Street
San Francisco, California 94111

Library of Congress Catalog Card Number 72–146783

International Standard Book Number ISBN 0–87589–087–3

Manufactured in the United States of America
Printed by Hamilton Printing Company
Bound by Chas. H. Bohn & Co., Inc.
Jacket design by Image and Design

FIRST EDITION

Code 7105

FOREWORD

by
Clarence Faust

The closing years of the nineteenth century and the opening years of the twentieth were peculiarly important in the development of higher education in America. New institutions destined to become large and influential were established and given their character—the University of Chicago, Johns Hopkins, and Stanford, for example. Important new ideas were put into effect in older institutions such as Columbia, Harvard, Yale, and Princeton. Significant developments were taking place in the land-grant colleges and universities—the University of California and the University of Wisconsin, to name only two. Masterful presidents were at the helms of these developing institutions— Gilman of Johns Hopkins, Wilson of Princeton, Eliot of Harvard, Jordan of Stanford, Harper of Chicago, and so on.

These men and the institutions they headed were grappling with problems many of which are still not resolved, such as the purpose of an undergraduate education, the character of graduate study, the role of science and technology in higher education, the relation of education to the practical problems of our productivity as a people, the education of women, the elective system, the place of athletics in colleges and universities, democracy in college life, and student activism.

All these matters and more are dealt with in Portraits of the American University 1890–1910, *but they are not presented as just another history of higher education at the turn of the century or as merely comprehensive source material for such a history. Rather, this is a collection of contemporary journalistic pieces about institutions of higher education and about leading men and their ideas, as well as descriptive articles on student life. The collection represents first-rate, responsible journalism. A certain quaintness of language and tone and a timely vividness make the reading of these republished pieces interesting, exciting, and rewarding. They were carefully selected to reveal the early stages of current and perhaps abiding problems. A few set forth situations no longer of concern and thus convey some idea of the pace of change in higher education and some reassurance in a time when many problems are seen as matters of life and death to education or even to civilization itself.*

The scholar who deals with the history of higher education, the professor or administrator spending his life in the college and university world, and the layman interested in the development of higher education will each find this unusual collection interesting, sometimes amusing, and very often illuminating in its insights and its vividness.

Claremont, California
January 1971

To
John Ellis
Simon Fraser University

William A. Brownell
University of California

PREFACE

by

James C. Stone

Donald P. DeNevi

What should be the relationship between a university and the society it serves? How should it be governed, organized, and financed? What physical facilities are needed, where, and for whose use? Who should be admitted, what shall they be taught, where, when, how, and by whom? With what freedom shall ideas be dealt with, and whose ideas? What voice shall the students have in deciding their own education? What voice shall the faculty have? What experiences outside the classroom and off campus shall be included as a legitimate part of a college education? What scheme of rewards and sanctions shall prevail for students and faculty and by whom shall they be administered?

These are crucial issues in higher education today. They are universals. They are persistent. They began with the founding of American colleges and universities, and their answers have been sought since. Some answers have been found and some traditions established—the same traditions that are seriously in question today. We need perspective, a closer look at origins and history.

In the early 1920s Upton Sinclair wrote that, "the thousands of young attending colleges and universities in America . . . are the pick of our coming generation; they are the future of our country. If they are wisely and soundly taught, America will be great and happy; if they are misguided and mistaught, no power can save us." [1] Sinclair distilled our list of the universal issues of higer education into two fundamental questions: "What is the so-called 'higher education' of these United States? Do the men charged with the responsibility for administering it possess the kind of knowledge and understanding required in an age of disaffection?" [2] After posing his first fundamental question, Sinclair said that his program for colleges was

> to discuss the vital ideas, the subjects that men are arguing and fighting over, the problems that must be solved if our society is not to be rent by civil war. Everybody is interested in these questions, old and young, rich and poor, high and low, and if you deal with them you solve several vexing problems at once. You solve the problems of getting the students to study and also the problem of student morals; you turn your college from a country club to which elegant young gentlemen come to wear good clothes and play games and more or less in secret to drink and carouse—you turn it from that into a place where ideas are taken seriously. . . . When you understand this . . . you are no longer afraid of the specters and the goblins, the dragons and devils and other mon-

[1] *U. Sinclair, The Goose-Step, A Study of American Education (published by the author, Pasadena, California; distributed by the Economy Book Shop, Chicago, 1922), p. ix.*
[2] Ibid.

sters which haunted the imagination of our racial childhood. You know;
you know precisely, and you know certainly, and so you are free from fear;
you go out into life as a young warrior with an enchanted sword, all powerful
against all enemies. To forge that sword and train you in the care of it and the
use of it—that is the true task of our institutions of higher education.[3]

In the turmoil and transition today, when new economic and social demands are
being made upon higher education and when instructional developments encourage reorganization of old institutions and creation of new institutions, Sinclair's two questions
are more relevant than ever before. They are the concern of this anthology—considered
in the perspective of seventy-five to one hundred years ago. A reexamination of the
slow-maturing system of higher education as it entered the mainstream of American
culture provides fresh light on the vision, hope, and history of this system as recorded
in the original publications of early educators themselves. Surprisingly fresh, enthusiastic,
and passionate, these writers weave a coherent explanation of the painful confusion
involved in the first attainments of higher education. With the end of these great
traditions in sight, we invite both the serious student as well as the nostalgic educator
to pause a few moments to rediscover those events and institutions which supposedly made
every man they touched a scholar and gentleman.

Because the major thoughts and actions in those early days grow dimmer with every
passing year while the issues become more relevant, we have fashioned this anthology.
It contains nearly twenty-five original and complete articles which appeared in the
leading journals of the day and preserves the full flavor and color of each article's script,
titles, subtitles, illustrations, and captions. We are particularly excited about the collection because it provides in a single source a number of original writings not commonly
available in libraries with limited or specialized holdings. All the selections, chosen from
several hundred similar articles, are in some measure philosophic since all deal with
the values of higher education, the nature of knowledge at that time, the goals of a rapidly
expanding economy and society, and the question of universal education. Strictly speaking,
however, the selections might well be called a collage, providing primary sources of
information long buried and forgotten.

Many of these early writers recognized the frontiers of higher education long before
doing so became an industry. The men and their visions were strong, often humble, and
certainly omniscient. Most of them, as their writings so vividly illustrate, waged one-man
wars against dangers to the right and universality of higher education for all Americans.
As you read these selections, you will be impressed with the spirited arguments that
higher education should have one overriding goal: to foster a reverence for life coupled
with a philosophical and emotional commitment to learning.

Pressures were commonly exerted upon many professors forcing them to compromise
these ideals. The contributors undoubtedly agreed to whatever demands were made by
administrators, boards, or committees, and returned to their classrooms, closed the doors,
agonized over the difficult realism of the day, and then fought madly, tooth and nail, for
those views which relate man to man. In a sense, each of the early writers argued, "This
is what higher education is all about—relating man to man. This is what we feel to be
correct for your sons and daughters—what your sons and daughters should think about it,
what faculty should think about it, and what taxpayers should feel about it. Make up
your own mind whether this situation suits you or whether you want it changed. But

[3] Ibid., *pp. 477–478.*

PREFACE

know that in another seventy years, the 1970s will be upon our graduates and their children. Will we have succeeded in sending into the world resourceful, inquiring, and imaginative human beings motivated in redefining and justifying every step in the processes of democracy?" If the answer is yes, then what have we learned over the past seventy years which is applicable to the present?

Berkeley, California
Oakland, California
January 1971

CONTENTS

CONTENTS

CONTENTS

CONTENTS

CONTRIBUTORS

A few words are found below about the most prominent of those men whose contributions are in this book. In several instances identity of author or specific reference in literature could not be unearthed since all we had was the original article clipped at some point around the turn of the century.

CLAYTON SEDGWICK COOPER was an author and lecturer. He served as a regent of the University of Miami and on the President's Committee of One Hundred. He is best known for his writings on foreign trade markets and their methods. He died in 1936.

JOHN CORBIN was an author, drama critic, and lecturer. He wrote for the *Harper's Magazine* and the *New York Times* and contributed stories and articles to a variety of different journals. He died in 1959.

CHARLES W. ELIOT was an educator, author, and university president. He served as president of Harvard between 1869 and 1909. He died in 1926.

DANIEL C. GILMAN was an educator and author and served as the first president of Johns Hopkins University from 1875 to 1901. Gilman died in 1908.

DAVID STARR JORDAN was an educator, author, and naturalist. He was the president of Stanford University from 1891 to 1913 and served as an emeritus chancellor from 1913 to 1916. Jordan died in 1931.

EDWARD S. MARTIN was an author. Founding the Harvard *Lampoon* in 1876, he went on to become the first editor of *Life* as well as a contributor to *Harper's Magazine*. He died in 1939.

LINCOLN STEFFENS was a writer and lecturer. He served as assistant city editor of the *New York Evening Post*, managing editor of *McClure's Magazine, American Magazine,* and *Everybody's Magazine.* Among his books are *The Shame of the Cities* (1904) and *The Struggle for Self-Government* (1906). He died in 1936.

CONTRIBUTORS

MARK SULLIVAN was an author, lecturer, and commentator for the *Overseer* at Harvard between 1928 and 1934. He was a Bromley lecturer at Yale in 1929. His best known book is *Education of an American* (1938). Sullivan died in 1952.

ETHELBERT D. WARFIELD was the president of Miami University from 1888 to 1891; president of Lafayette College from 1891 to 1914; and president of Wilson College in 1915. He was also an author and became an ordained Presbyterian minister before his death in 1936.

BENJAMIN IDE WHEELER was an educator and author and was president of the University of California from 1899 to 1919. He wrote *Organization of Higher Education* in 1896. Wheeler died in 1927.

JESSE LYNCH WILLIAMS was an author who wrote among other things *Princeton Stories* (1895), *History of Princeton University* (1898), and *The Adventures of a Freshman* (1899). He was awarded a Pulitzer Prize by Columbia University for the best American play produced in 1917. He died in 1929.

PORTRAITS
of the
AMERICAN UNIVERSITY
1890-1910

PROLOGUE

PORTRAITS
of the
AMERICAN UNIVERSITY
by
Algo D. Henderson

College students of today should enjoy this volume, because a glance at the portraits of the distinguished presidents of a few decades ago shows that they wore flowing side burns, drooping moustaches, and beautiful beards! They also had ideas for changing the university: the elective system, graduate education, extension programs to bring the university to the people, and expanding the concept of *profession* by establishing many new professional schools.

These presidents had a style of leadership that made them educators rather than mere managers. They wrote vigorously about higher education, they chaired their faculties, they coupled the objectives of the growing university with the coming greatness of the state. Jordan of Stanford was not only visible to the students, he tipped his slouch hat to them as he walked across the campus. On one occasion Eliot of Harvard spent a half a day helping a student find the Latin book he needed. Mark Sullivan, a distinguished journalist of the time, described Eliot as scorning a middle course by "his taking up the lance in fields far remote from his chosen path of education, his virile, uncompromising partisanship on questions of politics, of religion, of labor and capital, concerning which public prejudice is sensitive to the quick." But these men also rode the crest of a running tide. The industrial revolution was coming into its maturity. This was an era of expansion, of population growth, of building, of harnessing the frontier, and—unfortunately for the later consequences—of the exploitation of our minerals, our water, our air. Higher education was beginning to provide the educated men, the theories, the research findings that were being hungrily absorbed by commerce, industry, agriculture, and the government.

The colleges and universities, in turn, were nourished by those who had achieved great wealth—as the names of the private institutions reveal. This was before the day of the income tax and diminishing disposable income. And the demands of the colleges were more modest. We are reminded that a century earlier all the plant that a college needed was a chapel and four recitation rooms. By 1900, plants had expanded considerably to include scientific laboratories, larger libraries, more classrooms, administration buildings, and dormitories; but there was an abundance of self-made men and women, as well as loyal alumni who wanted to erect memorials to themselves. Today, the cultivation of alumni and legislators, and the highly organized drives for funds, by contrast, almost stagger the imagination. Poor Horace Mann, whose college was sold at auction to pay its debts, had to write his appeals for money to his Boston friends in long hand.

During the interval since these essays were written the status of students has changed. Students had been objects to be manipulated—to be filled with certain knowledge, inculcated with religious precepts, and polished in their manners. A writer of 1897 repeatedly calls the boys "lads," which suggests the paternalistic attitude that generally had prevailed. The penalties at Harvard had included "marks of censure, parental admonition, private admonition, public admonition, special probation, suspension, dismission, and expulsion." An alumnus wrote that proctors "dogged our footsteps at night and stalked between the tables on examination day." Vice-President Spiro Agnew would have approved. But the courts have been gradually applying the concepts of civil rights to students' rights, and students today are entitled to have orderly hearings on charges made against them. Youth at ages eighteen to twenty are more mature than formerly, and the average age of the enrollees at the larger institutions today is usually well into the twenties. Students today contend that they are consumers of education, and hence should participate in decision making.

At Wellesley in 1898, women students had to be "under the direct care of the college authorities." This accords with advice given by Mann to a faculty committee at the University of Michigan, which a half century earlier was toying with the idea of admitting women to the university. Mann cautioned Michigan not to let the young ladies board promiscuously in the village. He revealed that at Antioch College, which did have coeducation, they had avoided having any incidents (commonly called "accidents") by having the faculty diligently oversee the young ladies day and night. As of 1970, the pill has played havoc with this whole mode of behavior. And what would Jordan, who was an advocate of coeducation, think if he could see the coed dorms of Stanford today! The colleges have, of course, established professional counseling services to replace paternalistic supervision, a move not as yet fully accepted by parents and the public.

These earlier educators were great travelers, especially for observing education in Britain and on the continent. A major consequence was the emulation of the German university in launching graduate level programs. Graduate study with accompanying research found a ready home in American universities. Today, a brief century after their founding, the graduate schools are enormously influential in the American scene. Interestingly, the typical graduate school has neither a budget nor control over the appointments of faculty. The graduate school is in the hands of the departments, mostly in the arts and sciences. It just grew up that way. These departments, each with its own specialized interest, dominate the educational scene. Now, after this period of rapid, spontaneous growth, the graduate school deserves reconsideration and reorganization. It needs fresh design, one that takes account of new programs that are not in the liberal arts and sciences, that recognizes the impact of fragmentation on undergraduate teaching, and that assumes responsibility for training college teachers.

Two influences have profoundly affected faculty interests and behavior during the past seventy years. The elective system opened the way for the sciences to come into the curriculum, and the graduate school stimulated the growth of research. The trend was away from the classical, united curriculum, in favor of specialization. As the movement swelled, the universities became focused on scholarship and gave rewards accordingly. The societies of scholars grew rapidly in size and won the loyalties of faculty. The professional association was where the professor got the recognition that he craved. Rewards and recognition became the twin magnets that gradually drew him away from undergraduate teaching and, indeed, from the old fashioned kind of loyalty he had had for his college. The other influence was the growth in size of the institution. In 1900, and much later, faculties could still meet in town-meeting fashion and thus enjoy a high degree of communication about the purposes and programs of the institution. Later, the facultly began to departmentalize and disintegrate. The departmental chairman became the influential educational leader, supervised to a degree by an academic dean or a vice-president. But the chairman had a worm's eye view of the university and had his own empire to build. His department would become distinguished only through publications.

The growth in the number of students in classes and the shift in the professor's interests are two of the factors that make the student feel that he has become a computer number. They also have had a strong impact upon the leadership style of the president. One may feel considerable nostalgia for the days of devotion to teaching, personal acquaintance with students, and small faculties of comprehensive interests. In the belief that these characteristics may be partially regained, some institutions are experimenting with cluster colleges.

Fragmentation has also gripped the study for the professions. As recently as a century ago, most universities had only four faculties: liberal arts (or philosophy), law, medicine, and theology. The land-grant university reform, of course, had added in some institutions agriculture and the mechanic arts, although these subjects were by no means widely accepted by the academic community. It took a relatively new university, one stimulated by its land grant, the University of California, to break out of the mold in a grand way. It founded, for instance, the first college of commerce. As early as 1899, it had colleges of letters, social science, natural science, agriculture, mechanics, mining, civil engineering, chemistry, commerce, and law, and also an institute of art, the Lick Observatory, and departments of medicine, dentistry, pharmacy, and veterinary medicine. Elmer E. Brown, in 1899, expressed well the new philosophy of education being implemented at California: "The endeavor is made continually to avoid anything like isolation from the vital interests of the state."

It was the capacity of business and industry to provide diversified employment that brought the enormous expansion in the applied areas such as business and engineering. Since 1900, law, medicine, and theology have increased in enrollments very slowly, but in the applied arts and technology, and in the much newer social sciences, the enrollments have skyrocketed. Also, in these fields the training of technicians, often on a two year basis, has become a major educational undertaking.

One of the most profound changes has been a shift in values. When Thomas Huxley lectured at Johns Hopkins in 1876 there was an outburst of public protest. His speech on the "new biology" was compounded in evil by the failure of the university to begin the meeting with prayer. The theory of evolution was directly contradictory, so it was thought, to the teachings of the Bible. Why should the university tolerate such blasphemy?

To me, the most interesting and relevant essay in this book is the one by Harold Bolce, in which he reveals the shocking things that were being taught in the universities in 1909. The institutions no longer had any "God-established convenants." "There are no absolute evils." The "highest ethical life consists at all times in the breaking of rules which have grown too narrow for the actual case." Standards of right vary from race to race, and change from time to time. Faculty were raising questions about the family, labor and capital, immigration, social welfare, and the social basis for ethics. "Whether the subject be a God or a gas, a matter of morals or volcanic mud, a syllogism or a star, the professor approaches it impersonally, critically determined to know the truth."

So much water has flowed over the dam that it is difficult for us to realize how religious the earlier colleges were. They were universally presided over by clergy—a practice the Catholics are only now abandoning. Daily prayers were compulsory, and chapel continued to be compulsory down into the twentieth century. What a shock it must have been to have science move into the curriculum and nudge religion out of its dominant position. Eliot was insisting that science be admitted on a par with other subjects—although, at both Harvard and Yale, the first courses were given in separate schools. Van Hise called this an appendix to the college, and at Wisconsin he brought the sciences right in on the ground floor. And here they have remained. Indeed, with the tremendous opportunities given to science through grants from government and industry, these subjects have almost driven all of the humanities into a corner.

To return to the professors and their radical ideas, they were of course beginning to use the scientific method of investigation. The quantities of fresh knowledge that they discovered have overwhelmed the curriculum and most of all the libraries. The amount of knowledge that is available for use in instruction and its tendency quickly to become obsolete have been forcing a revision of teaching theory. Science initially introduced the laboratory, and thus didactic forms of teaching were reduced. But today, especially in professional schools such as medicine, it is unsafe merely to fill the student with facts. Facts in engineering are said to have a half-life of only five years. Instead, it is essential that the professional man be trained as a problem solver and given incentive to continue his education after he gets his degree. In 1900, the degree, much valued, was a certificate of completion; today, it is still a badge but is diminishing in importance as a test of the education of the possessor.

The University of Wisconsin launched the universities into continuing education for adults. Van Hise believed that the university belonged to the people and should serve their needs. Farm boys were induced to come to the campus for short courses in agriculture even though they had cow dung on their boots; the short course was a clever way to demonstrate what knowledge could do for agriculture. So the short course quickly led to longer ones, until presently the farm boys were joining those from the cultured families in attending the university. The university did not hesitate to engage in very practical research—it found a treatment for oat smut, invented a milk separator, discovered how to improve the quality of cheese. The oat smut cure alone saved the farmers of the state over five million dollars a year. Now, a half century later, we look to Wisconsin as a great dairy and cheese state, forgetting that it was the university that gave it its eminence. Perhaps at this point James, Dewey, and the other pragmatists should take a bow. They began to formulate a new philosophy, nonauthoritarian in character, based upon observations of human experience, just as the professors were shaking off the more constricting of the religious teachings and beginning to perfect the scientific method. The public universities that arose and grew at this time were founded on pragmatic philosophy. They were ready to make full use of inductive reasoning.

As of 1900, people were still committed to the ideal of free public education. The Kalamazoo case in 1874 had decided once and for all that public boards of education could use public funds to establish free high schools. The high school became the comprehensive high school and grew by leaps and bounds. The public universities were the next step upward for young men and women. Though academic men were still elitist minded, students of good ability and intellectual curiosity began to flow into the colleges and universities. It was not until after World War II, however, that the total enrollments of public colleges began to rise above those of private colleges. Today the private-public balance is the reverse of what it was a few decades ago. And, unfortunatly, the public seems to be in a mood to abandon the ideal of free education. But at least higher education is no longer treated as a charity.

The egalitarian movement in higher education came into its own with the report of the President's Commission on Higher Education in 1948. This report advocated that a nation should not merely provide facilities for those youth with ambition to attend college; it should also inventory the talents among young people, search them out, and see that they have opportunity in education. As of 1970, we see that this principle applies to blacks and other disadvantaged persons as well as to WASPS. Although there were a half dozen private junior colleges before 1900, the public community-junior college movement began a few years later. It seems destined to provide universal access to higher education. In 1900, only about 11 per cent of the youth attended high school. Now nearly everyone does, and half of the graduates go on to college.

By 1888, fraternities were well entrenched on the campuses. Some presidents tried to get rid of them, but they did not succeed. They were thought to be natural groupings, a release from the stuffy classrooms, and a place where boys became men. The fraternities, and more especially the clubs at Ivy League schools, were also the route to social prestige. There was much "swiping" at Harvard, "heeling" at Yale, and "getting into a following" at Princeton—struggles to get into the right club. The members became the social aristocracy of the campus; other men were barbs (barbarians). There was a sharp division between the ins and the outs. Just as the badge of social class and the key to the civil service in England was the school tie, so in informal America the way to get ahead in the professions and in society was to be a pinned man.

Students were also disorderly in the good old days. They had their pranks, such as putting a cow in the belfry, their outlandish and sometimes sadistic initiations, their wine carousals, and their hooligan marching after games. Harvard, fortunately, had been able to abolish "bloody Monday" in 1870. Student smokers filled the rooms with foul air. And occasionally students protested bad teaching, such as by leaning their heads on the palms of their hands. These interests and activities were different from many of those of today, however, in that they were adolescent, indulged in for pleasure, or aimed to help the individual climb the social ladder. The protests and the disorders of the students of today, however destructive some of them may be, are initiated to get a hearing by the establishment concerning reforms that the students believe to be needed.

The early days also witnessed some well-intended actions. In 1910, six hundred college graduates left to fill religious mission posts in the Levant, India, China, and elsewhere. The zeal to bring to others in the world the saving graces of the Christian religion was strong. Perhaps an equivalent urge but with different motivation today is to join the Peace Corps. Clayton S. Cooper described as goals for the undergraduate, "gentlemanliness, open-mindedness, originality, honor, patriotism, truth." "College training must give a man permanent idealism." This reasonable sounding statement leaves open the question of whether the idealism relates to some perception of the puritanical life or whether instead it relates to the good of man.

Students now are very deeply concerned about the persistence of war, the threat of population growth, the polarizations in human relations, the disparities in health services provided the affluent and the poor, the pollution of our air and water, the grossness of materialistic incentives, the power of the military-industrial complex. They believe that the universities have contributed to these social blemishes. They sense that the industrial revolution has run its course and that we need to begin to build a new society. They engage in political action in ways and degrees formerly never dreamed of. The outcomes of these disturbances to our academic urbanity are still not clear, but the students exhibit motivations that could be harnessed in education. And if the students, not merely in the United States but in the world (for this is a worldwide movement), could find ways to organize the people of the world and to slough off some of the unhealthy and unsavory activities and habits of man, the world could easily become a better place than it now is. The students fear that shortly we may not have a world. These concerns seem much more vital and meaningful than do football, fraternities, playboy pranks, and social climbing.

The universities of today need reform much as did those of the earlier period. Liberal education over the centuries has gone through several transformations—the trivium and quadrivium, the Greek and Latin classics, the distribution of courses among the major divisions of knowledge, general education. Now we are faced with the issue of whether a liberal education that is based so heavily upon Western civilization is sufficient, especially in this nation of a plurality of cultures. The blacks ask why they should be subjected to a stream of thought that stems from a society, Greece, that was erected upon slavery. Orientals ask why we neglect so much the great religions, art, literature, and history of Asia. But the professors should ask whether we provincially minded Americans should not become more aware than we now are of other cultures. And should we not eliminate such indoctrinations as the glories of war, the superiority of the white race, and the infallibility of the Christian religion that are embedded in Western thought and literature? Our whole value system needs restudy and with it should be undertaken a redesign of liberal education based upon the best experience and wisdom of man wherever they can be found.

The professions, too, need a thorough overhaul. They need to be less occupation directed, less materialistic in orientation, more concerned with man and his well-being. The schools of engineering of the University of California recently have pointed out that the earlier role of engineers was to exploit the natural resources of the country, but that their future role should be to learn how to manage resources in the social interest. Mining, which occupied the prize building provided by Phoebe Hearst in 1901, has almost finished its role as exploiter. It is being phased out as a study at the university. Medical education was one of the professional fields that the distinguished presidents of the 1900s took for granted. Most medical schools were unrelated to universities. They were technician-training schools where practitioners trained future practitioners by apprentice methods. These schools had to wait until Abraham Flexner in 1910 shook them up. Once again medical education needs to be shaken up, for its policies and those of the professional associations in medicine have brought health services to a new crisis.

One of the professors whom Bolce identified as a teacher of dangerous ideas was Edward A. Ross of the University of Wisconsin. His case is instructive. In 1900, Ross had been fired by Stanford University because of his attacks on big capitalists who he contended were exploiting the country. Among his many publications was a pamphlet entitled "Honest Dollars," which had been used by a political party during the Bryan-McKinley election campaign. The dismissal was demanded in a letter from Mrs. Stanford to Jordan, and such was the power of the sugar-daddy that an otherwise good president, after much vacillation, yielded. Ross subsequently became employed at the University of Wisconsin, where he continued his vigorous analysis of contemporary social, economic, and political problems. He became a genuinely distinguished scholar. But in 1910 he was censured by the board of regents of the university for the views in his book *Sin and*

Society; and in 1935 he was investigated by the legislature for "alleged Communistic activities." The university, under strong leadership, managed to retain him on the faculty.

There were interesting sequels to these events. The Stanford case became a cause célèbre and directly resulted a few years later in the organization of the American Association of University Professors, which over the years has valiantly defended academic freedom. A second significant result was the formal action by the regents in 1958 in naming a building at Wisconsin the Edward Alsworth Ross House. In the lounge was placed a memorial plaque, the opening sentence of which reads: "Out of the University of Wisconsin tradition of scholarly attainment through freedom to inquire, Edward Alsworth Ross emerges, a giant figure," and near the end, the plaque continues: "Wherever men live together and ponder shared problems, the majestic thought of this great educator attends." Ross was right; Mrs. Stanford, the legislators, and the public acted from ignorance and prejudice in trying to protect the status quo; a distinguished private university failed to protect academic freedom, but a public one had the courage to withstand temporary hostility and later, when tempers had cooled, to honor a great professor.

The Ross incident and those of other professors who advocated such radical ideas as the theory of evolution, the organization of labor, and the institution of a federal income tax show how, with the passage of time, fear and protest over new ideas are replaced with acceptance. We are once again in a period of the generation of fresh ideas and of rapid social change. At the same time, higher education has become increasingly dependent upon public funds and hence upon public goodwill. Yet the gap in mutual understanding grows. The universities need to make changes in their programs. They should be ever ready to serve the public good and thereby help to effect the social changes that they foresee as bringing advances to civilized man. Will leaders emerge who can do this? Now that the students have made clear the bases for their protests, will they drop their violence and work constructively for needed change? Can the universities tide themselves successfully through the period of public distrust? These are among the unanswered questions that face the universities—and the public—today.

FIRST

COMING
of the
GREAT UNIVERSITIES

A growing number of students believe that regents, boards, and administrators view the collegiate structure as nothing but a production system, a gigantic machine consuming billions of dollars as well as the creative potential, tenderness, and beauty of youth. Students insist that much of the current violence, drug usage, and revolutionary movements on campus is in part a reaction to this machine.

Such views of the university as nothing but a system which suppresses feelings, awareness, and self-actualization are oversimplifications. True, the growing application of a systems approach to the development of higher education found in program budget literature should be taken seriously. Boards, regents, and state governors, impressed with the demonstrated utility and apparent success of these procedures, are turning more and more to such terms as output (graduates) and characteristics of output (curriculum), and programing them at the cheapest possible cost. True, the genius of American higher education has been due to the systematic way in which college leaders achieved their goals with the limited resources available to them.

Today, questions of the analytical and managerial type for maximizing the effectiveness and efficiency of the university are becoming increasingly crucial. A thorough understanding is needed of the interactions among programs, the costs and attributes of each of those programs, and the trade-offs among programs. In terms of specific instructional programs, colleges and their faculties are at the same time concerning themselves with requirements and breadth of courses. Students who argue that these are sometimes poorly articulated demand that such carry-overs from the nineteenth century be abolished and serious inquiry be given to the meaning of general and liberal education.

The following selection of writings partially satisfies the demand for historical and philosophical perspectives. In compiling the following part, the editors believed that an exploration of past successes and failures in higher education and the exhumation of family skeletons would provide for examination the guidelines once followed by ener-

getic and innovative men. The consensus of these men, sometimes filled with melo-dramatics and clichés dormant for decades, provides general principles which might be gleaned for humanistic approaches in the design of higher education.

Dealing with the creation, structure, and financing of higher education, then, Part One employs writers such as David Starr Jordan, Daniel C. Gilman, Benjamin Ide Wheeler, and twelve other college presidents and writers. The time was yesterday. Today, all of us teach in the shadow of their efforts. The few ironies which crop up are severe. Part One, at its best, is a polemic: a polemic worded by the contributors and arranged by the editors to dramatize the perspectives. Writing somewhat lyrically, the contributors use spare dialogue with very few euphemisms and metaphors.

According to traditionalist historians, there is no history, only biography. This part reaffirms that proposition. Men, not forces, shaped American universities. In their writings, one senses involvement, commitment, conviction, and compassion—not loftiness or arrogance. One also senses that it was primarily their skill as teachers and administrators rather than their skill with words which paved the way.

The first selection is a remarkably fresh one entitled "Expressions: Knowing Real Men" by David Starr Jordan, who presented this address to the graduating class of 1908 at Stanford. The words, human and passionate, provide each of us with an echo chamber of advocacy. Such can also be said of the other writings in this part.

KNOWING REAL MEN*

By David Starr Jordan

In a recent address, Professor William James has told us that the best result of a college education should be that you should "know a good man when you see him." In other words, it should teach something of the relative value of aims in life; to know good work from bad, and to ensure for ourselves, in some one direction at least, a grasp on a worthy ideal.

Our next question is this: Has your college education given this power to you? A recent writer in the American Magazine maintains that his college course never gave it to him. He did not know good work when he saw it. Many others would admit the same thing if the question ever occurred to them. The writer just mentioned claims that from his college course he gained no perspective. Near things bank larger than distant ones; accidents of the day outrank the great things of the past and the future. This he finds true from every point of view. For example, as a college graduate, Mark Hanna seemed to him a bigger man than Charlemagne. Later in life when the perspective became clearer he saw the difference and wished that he had made Charlemagne's acquaintance earlier. In his geography he says the map of Indiana and that of Montana covered each a page, and the one was as large as the other. New Jersey was as big as California and Maine as large as Australia. Later, when he crossed the Rocky Mountains, he found that the map did not do Montana justice. It's territory would make six states of the size of Indiana. This didn't matter much in this particular case, but the same distortion of values appeared in every thing he thought he knew. From this he concluded that his own college education was largely a failure. It did not meet Professor James' definition. He did not learn to know a good man when

he saw him. He did not know things as they really are in their relations, one thing to another.

When a wise man says a true thing, we can all say it after him. We wonder why we had not said it before ourselves. We see at once how hard it is to know a good man anyhow. If you as students take this matter to heart you will see the faults in your own education; you cannot tell the best that lies about you. The graduates of other colleges have the same defect of vision, and our whole system of higher education is perverted in the same way.

There was once a banker in the days of wildcat currency who had a wonderful skill in detecting counterfeits. He acquired this skill not by studying counterfeits; he studied good money. Whatever was not good money was not money at all to him. It was mere waste paper, not worth even the name of counterfeit. So to detect error one must study truth; the rest is waste and rubbish. To know a good man when you see him, you must study good men. All short of this is bad. To know good work you must study good work. The rest is frivolity and commonplace.

This is a time to search our own hearts, to size up our own promise of the future. Do you know a good man when you see him? Do you, after four years at Stanford, know what is really worth while? For example, some of you know, I presume, the best record for a quarter mile dash, for a race over hurdles, the record distance of a broad jump or a hammer throw. Some of you know a winning hand at poker, some how to tune up a rollicking song, some the manipulation of a skirt dance, some the framing of a sonnet, some the ideals of a Greek philosophy, some the art of inventing dynamos, some the theory

*Graduating Address to the Class of 1908, Stanford University.

of ions and electrons, some the measurement of electric charges, some the secret of knowing equities, some the investigation of the energies of life. Some are prepared for the next ball, some for entrance into a profession; some to break into politics, some, perhaps, to adorn the front of a tobacco store. Can you tell which of these is worth while?

There is an abundance of good work done at Stanford all the time. How many of us know the best thing, the ten best things, or any of the ten best things done by any Stanford man in the last ten years? How many of you know the best things done here at Stanford in the year just past? Can you tell which of your number is best worth while; which one will be wise, sound, clean and efficient, after the struggles and roundups of twenty or thirty years? Which one will then be leader of your class, not by the ballot, which is an emotional test, when it is not a selfish one, but by virtue of his crystallized character, of his own innate strength, of his being through and through a good man and a man who makes good? Sooner or later you should know a good man when you see him, do you know this same man now? If you do, it is well and good; this homily is wasted. If you do not, whose fault is it? Is it yours or ours? Or shall we modestly and justly divide the blame between our students and our teachers? Surely all share in the responsibility, as we all suffer in the failure in result.

There are many factors which tend to destroy the perspective in college life. These two bulk largest: the intrusion of the outside world—and the exaltation of side issues, the minor incidents, the by-play of boyhood, to the injury of the real business of the college.

The outside world intrudes through its vulgar standards of morality, its eagerness for money-getting, its instinct for sensationalism, its chase for vulgar pleasures and unearned and unreal joys. We cannot claim in fact that the standard of the average college man is continuously higher than that of other men; that he bears a price so high that the politician and the bribe-giver cannot reach him. We cannot claim that the average college man bears a loftier standard of ideals than other men of equal native ability. Here and there is one in whom our best ambitions are made real. Such a one stands out above other college men and in him is our hope and our justification. But he must have been a rare man to begin with and only the rare man can grow to be a better man after he leaves the college. A man can go through college and receive nothing of University ideals. There are many men who perform our college tasks, who meet our requirements, who pass our examinations, who receive our degrees, and yet who never know at all what it is all about. The finest poetry, the noblest philosophy, the loftiest enthusiasm, finds them dumb and cold. Their heart is in the market place, or worse, in the vaudeville theater, not in the Academy. The outside world, through its worst phase, the call for pleasure, holds them in its grasp. Perhaps we cannot help this. The very usefulness of the college, its popularity, its respectability, all growing by leaps and bounds, are sources of danger. They appeal to the unfit as well as to the fit; they all extend invitations to the degenerate as well as to the genius. And too often the college itself is deceived in this matter. It mistakes wealth and popularity and populousness for success. Why should we care for numbers, we University men? Why should we rejoice in popularity? Why should we welcome advertising? Surely none of these help the college, none of them strengthen the hold of the college on the lives of men.

In another way, less dangerous but still often disastrous, the outside world infringes. This is through the spirit of money-getting. What will the college do for me? It must raise my salary or I will have nothing of it. Training for live work does increase a man's salary. Thus it often becomes a means to this alone. Standing all alone, this is a petty end. To be sure, some source of income is the scholar's necessity. Every man worth while should earn his own living and enough more to pay his taxes and to do his part in the life of the community. The world owes no man a living so far as I know, and those who think it does and depend on collecting it, as a rule, have a deservedly hard time. But for the rest, money does not mean success. Stanford has stood from the first for preparation for success in life, but of this success a financial surplus is only an incident—a minor factor—the smallest part of the whole.

Again, the world, as we all see it, with its traditional associates, the flesh and the devil, makes its encroachments on the academic life in other guises, some more dangerous than the hope for financial gain. College spirit, like the mantle of charity covers its multitude of sins. Much that passes as college spirit is the poorest kind of vulgarity, the inspiration of the street, the bleachers, the saloon.

If your college spirit is not the real thing, if it is counterfeit, it is no spirit at all. It is nothing at all but a bit of noisy shaming. There is no counterfeit money; what is not money is not money at all. So with college spirit, what is not genuine is nothing. So with one's efforts in life; what is not honest, what is not real, has no existence.

For part of your shortcomings, if you have any, the college teachers are to blame. We have been too worldly, too little serious. We have let in too much of the outside world and introduced you too often to its agents. We have let Mark Hanna displace Charlemagne. We have made of science a railroad map in which our own line shows straight and large among feeble and meandering rivals.

The other great source of loss of perspective is in the exaltation of what we call student activities. By this we mean not the activities of the student, nor even the student's natural and normal by-play, but professionalism, with students as performers. Twenty years ago all of us welcomed football, track meets, and all other forms of intercollegiate athletics because it seemed to lay stress on physical betterment. We believe in sound minds, in sound bodies, and the encouragement of all out-of-door sports seemed to tend in that direction. But the outcome has been very different from the anticipation. In each college two or three dozen of racers and gladiators, trained out of all proportion, professionals in every sense, save that they are paid in gratitude and notoriety instead of money, practically monopolize our athletics. The rest of us as scrubs and weaklings worship from afar with noisy resonance. Our heroes of the day in the fierce light of publicity are exposed to praise or blame out of all proportion to their faults, their merits, or their achievements. Their duty is to win games, ours to show loyalty, and that by talk and yelling. And the tumult and the shouting has been organized into a concerted system as foolish as it is futile. I have never heard of a game ever won by the rooters, and it would not be honest sport if such were the case.

I believe in athletics, in sturdy, virile athletics, even in intercollegiate athletics, as means to an end—the great end of making one's brain and body work in unison. There is no training much more essential than training in physical manliness, but no part of our present system contributes much to this end, while manifold evils appear on every hand, and most notably in the distortion of ideals in college life. As the redcoat bully in his boots kept Thackeray from seeing the queen of England, so does the figure of the stalwart athlete keep us from recognizing the real college man. We don't know a good man when we see him because we don't see him. Figures of exaggerated mediocrity fill the center of the stage.

It is no answer to this to say that the same conditions exist in all our colleges, that your higher education is all in the same boat, and these evils are less in the California Universities than in any other of our great colleges. If this is true, but the more is the pity, the greater the need of a new revival of learning, a new revival of religion in the true meaning of the word, in the very heart of wisdom's chosen centers.

The great Eastern colleges are feeling this. They are trying their best to exalt the real college men. They print names of honor students in larger and larger letters. It is the dig and the grind, after all, the man who does his work when the work is due, who stands for the college of the future. The athlete counts only as brains and courage are counted. Fortunately brains and courage often go with athletic skill and strength—but not always. The alumnus who does things worth while, who lives a gentle and a sturdy life, is the man who gives joy to his alma mater. Only the force of tradition, the inertia of institutions, can excuse a college for granting its degrees to any inferior kind. A man is either a man or else he is not much of anything. There is nothing worth notice in a counterfeit. No institution can live, none deserves to live, unless from time to time it can be born again; Stanford is ready today for a new birth and a new dedication. It is for you to help give it. It is for all of us to agonize toward it, and when our young University, already too old, is reborn, you will know and I shall know, and every true Stanford man and woman will know a good man when he sees him.

2

THE LAUNCHING OF A UNIVERSITY

By Daniel C. Gilman

DURING the last five decades, American universities have grown up with unprecedented rapidity. It is not necessary to fix an exact date for the beginning of this progress. Some would like to say that the foundation of the Lawrence Scientific School in Harvard University, and, almost simultaneously, the organization of the School of Science in New Haven were initial undertakings. These events indicated that the two oldest colleges of New England were ready to introduce instruction of an advanced character, far more special than ever before, in the various branches of natural and physical science. An impulse was given by the passage of the Morrill Act, by which a large amount of scrip, representing public lands, was offered to any State that would maintain a college devoted to agriculture and the mechanic arts, without the exclusion of other scientific and literary studies. The foundation of Cornell University was of the highest significance, for it fortunately came under the guidance of one who was equally devoted to historical and scientific research, one whose plans showed an independence of thought and a power of organization then without precedent in the field of higher education. The changes introduced in Harvard, under masterful leadership, when the modern era of progress began, had profound influence. The gifts of Johns Hopkins, of Rockefeller, of Stanford, of Tulane, promoted the establishment of new institutions, in sympathy with the older colleges, yet freer to introduce new subjects and new methods. The State universities of the Northwest and of the Pacific coast, as population and wealth increased, became an important factor. These multiform agencies must all be carefully considered when an estimate is made up of the progress of the last half-century.

The theme is too large for discussion in these pages. No such task has been given to me. But I have been requested to put in form some reminiscences of events and persons. I was a close observer of the changes which were introduced at Yale in the fifties and sixties, the grafting of a new branch—" a wild olive," as it seemed—upon the old stock. Then I had some experience, brief but significant, in California, as the head of the State University, at a time when it was needful to answer the popular cry that it should become chiefly a school of agriculture, and when it was important to show the distinction between a university and a polytechnic institute. Then came a call to the East and a service of more than a quarter of a century in the organization and development of a new establishment. These are three typical institutions. Yale was a colonial foundation, wedded to precedents, where an effort was made to introduce new studies and new methods. California was a State institution, benefited by the so-called agricultural grant, where it was necessary to emphasize the importance of the liberal arts, because the practical arts were sure to take care of themselves. Baltimore afforded an opportunity to develop a private endowment free from ecclesiastical or political control, where from the beginning the old and the new, the humanities and the sciences, theory and practice, could be generously promoted.

In looking over this period, remarkable changes are manifest. In the first place, science receives an amount of support unknown before. This is a natural consequence of the wonderful discoveries which have been made in respect to the phenomena and laws of nature, and the improvements made in scientific instruments and researches. Educational leaders perceived the importance of the work carried on in laboratories and observatories under the impulse of such men as Liebig and Faraday. With this increased attention to science, the old-fashioned curriculum disappeared, of necessity, and many combinations of studies are permitted in the most conservative institutions.

Absolute freedom of choice is allowed in many places. Historical and political science has come to the front, and it is no longer enough to learn from a text-book long lists of names and dates ; reference must be made to original sources of information, or at any rate many books must be consulted in order to understand the progress of human society. Some knowledge of German and French is required of everyone. English literature receives an amount of attention never given to it in early days. Medicine is no longer taught by lectures only, but the better schools require continued practice in the biological laboratories and the subsequent observation of patients in hospitals and dispensaries. The admission of women to the advantages of higher education is also one of the most noteworthy advances of the period we are considering.

The historian that takes up these and allied indications of the progress of American universities, will have a difficult and an inspiring theme. It has been a delightful and exhilarating time in which to live and to work, to observe and to try. All the obstacles have not been overcome, some mistakes have been made, much remains for improvement, but on the whole the record of the last forty or fifty years exhibits substantial and satisfactory gains. The efforts of scholars have been sustained by the munificence of donors, and more than one institution now has an endowment larger than that of all the institutions which were in existence in 1850.

In the middle of the century, the word "university" was in the air. It was cautiously used in Cambridge and New Haven, where a number of professional schools were living vigorous lives near the parental domicile, then called "the college proper," as if the junior departments were colleges improper. To speak of "our university" savored of pretence in these old colleges. A story was told at Yale that a dignitary from a distant State introduced himself as chancellor of the university. "How large a faculty have you?" asked Dominie Day. "Not any," was the answer. "Have you any library or buildings?" "Not yet," replied the visitor. "Any endowment?" "None," came the monotonous and saddening negative. "What have you?" persisted the Yale president. The visitor brightened as he said, "We have a very good charter."

Among enlightened and well-read people, the proper significance of a university was of course understood. Students came home from Europe, and especially from Germany, with clear conceptions of its scope. Everett, Bancroft, Ticknor, Hedge, Woolsey, Thacher, Whitney, Gildersleeve, and many more were familiar with the courses of illustrious teachers on the Continent. European scholars were added to the American faculties — Follen, Beck, Lieber, Agassiz, Guyot, and others less distinguished. But the American colleges had been based on the idea of an English college, and upon this central nucleus the limited funds and the unlimited energies of the times were concentrated, not indeed exclusively, but diligently. Any diversion of the concentrated resources of the treasury to "outside" interests, like law, medicine, and theology, was not to be thought of. Even now, one hears occasionally the question, "After all, what *is* the difference between a university and a college?" To certain persons, the university simply means the best place of instruction that the locality can secure. The country is full of praiseworthy foundations which ought to be known as high-schools or academies or possibly as colleges, but which appear to great disadvantage under the more pretentious name they have assumed. Just after the war the enthusiastic sympathy of the North for the enfranchised blacks led to the bestowal of the highest term in educational nomenclature upon the institutes where the freedmen were to be taught. Fortunately, Hampton and Tuskegee escaped this christening, but Fiske, Atlanta, and Howard foundations were thus named. It was much nearer the truth to say that the complete university includes four faculties—the liberal arts or philosophy, law, medicine, and theology. Sometimes a university is regarded as the union, under one board of control, of all the highest institutions of a place or region. There is one instance where the name "university" is given to a board which in a general way supervises all the degree-giving institutions in the State.

When the announcement was made to the public, at the end of 1873, that a wealthy merchant of Baltimore had provided by his will for the establishment of a new university, a good deal of latent regret was felt because the country seemed to have already more higher seminaries than it could supply with teachers, students, or funds. Another "college" was expected to join the crowded column, and impoverish its neighbors by its superior attractions. Fortunately, the founder was wise as well as generous. He used the simplest phrases to express his wishes; and he did not define the distinguished name that he bestowed upon his child, nor embarrass its future by needless conditions. Details were left to a sagacious body of trustees whom he charged with the duty of supervision. They travelled east and west, brought to Baltimore experienced advisers, Eliot, Angell, and White, and procured many of the latest books that discussed the problem of education. By and by they chose a president, and accepted his suggestion that they should give emphasis to the word "university" and should endeavor to build up an institution quite different from a college, thus making an addition to American education, not introducing a rival. Young men who had already gone through that period of mental discipline which commonly leads to the baccalaureate degree, were invited to come and pursue those advanced studies for which they might have been prepared, and to accept the inspiration and guidance of professors selected because of acknowledged distinction or of special aptitudes. Among the phrases that were employed to indicate the project were many which then were novel, although they are now the commonplaces of catalogues and speeches.

Opportunities for advanced, not professional, studies, were then scanty in this country. In the older colleges certain graduate courses were attended by a small number of followers—but the teachers were for the most part absorbed with undergraduate instruction, and could give but little time to the few who sought their guidance. Probably my experience was not unusual. After taking the degree of Bachelor of Arts, in Yale College, I was undecided what profession to follow. The effect of the collegiate discipline, which " introduced " me, according to the phrase

of the day, to not less than twenty subjects in the senior year, was to arouse an interest of about equal intensity in as many branches of knowledge. I remained a year at New Haven as a resident graduate. President Woolsey, whom I consulted, asked me to read Rau's political economy and come and tell him its contents ; I did not accept the challenge. I asked Professor Hadley if I might read Greek with him ; he declined my proposal. Professor Porter did give me some guidance in reading, especially in German. I had many talks of an inspiring nature with Professor Dana—but on the whole I think that the year was wasted. The next autumn I went to Cambridge and called upon President Sparks, to learn what opportunities were there open. " You can hear Professor Agassiz lecture," he said, " if you want to ; and I believe Mr. Longfellow is reading Dante with a class." I did not find at Cambridge any better opportunities than I had found at New Haven—but in both places I learned to admire the great teachers, and to wish that there were better arrangements for enabling a graduate student to ascertain what could be enjoyed and to profit by the opportunities. The day has now come when there is almost a superfluity of advanced courses. Let me tell some of the conditions which brought the Johns Hopkins foundations into close relations with the upward and onward movements in American universities, during the period from 1876 to 1901.

Before a university can be launched there are six requisites : An idea ; capital, to make the ideal feasible ; a definite plan ; an able staff of coadjutors ; books and apparatus ; students. On each of these points, I shall briefly dwell, conscious of one advantage as a writer—conscious, also, of a disadvantage. I have the advantage of knowing more than any one else of an unwritten chapter of history ; the disadvantage of not being able or disposed to tell the half that I remember.

" The idea of the university " was early accepted by the trustees. This was a phrase to which Cardinal Newman had given currency in a remarkable series of letters in which he advocated the establishment of a Catholic foundation in Dublin. At a time when ecclesiastical or denominational colleges were at the front, and were considered by many people the only defensible places for the education of young men, his utterances for academic freedom were emancipating; at a time when early specialization was advocated, his defence of liberal culture was reassuring. The evidence elicited by the British university commissions was instructive, and the writings of Mark Pattison, Dr. Appleton, Matthew Arnold, and others were full of suggestions. Innumerable essays and pamphlets had appeared in Germany discussing the improvements which were called for in that land of research. The endeavors of the new men at Cambridge and New Haven, and the instructive success of the University of Virginia, were all brought under consideration. It is safe to say that the Johns Hopkins was founded upon the idea of a university as distinct from a college.

The capital was provided by a single individual. No public meeting was ever held to promote subscriptions or to advocate higher education; no speculation in land was proposed; no financial gains were expected; no religious body was involved, not even the Society of orthodox Friends, in which the founder had been trained, and from which he selected several of his confidential advisers. He gave what seemed at the time a princely gift; he supplemented it with an equal gift for a hospital. It was natural that he should also give his name. That was then the fashion. John Harvard and Elihu Yale had lived long ago, and they never sought the remembrance which their contemporaries insured; but in late years Girard, Smithson, Lawrence, Cornell, and Cooper, had all regarded their foundations as children entitled to bear the parental name. Their follower in Maryland did likewise.

It is always interesting to know the genesis of great gifts. Johns Hopkins, who had never married, was in doubt, when he grew old, respecting the bestowal of his acquisitions. The story is current that a sagacious friend said to him, "There are two things which are sure to live—a university, for there will always be the youth to train; and a hospital, for there will always be the suffering to relieve." This germ, implanted in a large brain, soon bore fruit. The will was drawn, and after provision for the nearest of kin, the fortune was divided between the two institutions which bear the founder's name. It was his wish that they should be united in the promotion of medical science, and this wish has controlled all subsequent proceedings.

There is another story which is worth repeating, for it shows the relation of one benefaction to another. When George Peabody, near the end of his life, came to Baltimore, the place of his former residence, he was invited to dine by Mr. John W. Garrett, and Mr. Hopkins was invited to meet him. It is my impression that they were alone at the table. The substance of Mr. Peabody's remarks has thus been given by the host:

"Mr. Hopkins, we both commenced our commercial life in Baltimore, and we knew each other well. I left Baltimore for London, and from the commencement of my busy life I must state that I was extremely fond of money, and very happy in acquiring it. I labored, struggled, and economized continuously and increased my store, and I have been very proud of my achievements. Leaving Baltimore, after a successful career in a relatively limited sphere, I began in London, the seat of the greatest intellectual forces connected with commerce, and there I succeeded wonderfully, and, in competition with houses that had been wealthy, prosperous, and famous for generations, I carved my way to opulence. It is due to you, Mr. Hopkins, to say, remembering you so well, that you are the only man I have met in all my experience more thoroughly anxious to make money and more determined to succeed than myself; and you have enjoyed the pleasure of success, too. In vigorous efforts for mercantile power, capital, of course, and large capital, was vital. I had the satisfaction, as you have had, of feeling that success is the test of merit, and I was happy in the view that I was in this sense, at least, very meritorious. You also have enjoyed a great share of success and of commercial power and honor. But, Mr. Hopkins, though my progress was for a long period satisfactory and gratifying, yet, when age came upon me, and when aches and pains made me realize that I was not immortal, I felt, after taking care of my relatives, great anxiety to place the millions that I had accumulated so as to accomplish the greatest good for humanity. I looked about me and formed the conclusion that there were men who were just as anxious to work with integrity and faithfulness, for the comfort, consolation, and advancement of the suffering and the struggling poor, as I had been to gather fortune. After careful consideration, I called a number of my friends in whom I had confidence to meet me, and I proposed that they should act as my trustees, and I organized my first scheme of benevolence. The trust was accepted, and I then for the first time felt there was a higher pleasure and a greater happiness than accumulating money, and that was derived from giving it for good and humane purposes ; and so, sir, I have gone on, and from that day realized, with increasing enjoyment, the pleasure of arranging for the greatest practicable good for those who would need my means to aid their well-being, progress, and happiness."

Given the idea and the funds, the next requisite was a plan. I remember very well my first interviews with the trustees at their office in North Charles Street, and subsequently at the Mount Vernon Hotel. They were men of intelligence, dignity, and public spirit, devoid of personal, political, or ecclesiastical bias. I was strongly impressed by their desire to do the very best that was possible under the circumstances in which they were placed.

We quickly reached concurrence. Without dissent, it was agreed that we were to develop, if possible, something more than a local institution, and were at least to aim at national influence ; that we should try to supplement, and not supplant, existing colleges, and should endeavor to bring to Baltimore, as teachers and as students, the ablest minds that we could attract. It was understood that we should postpone all questions of building, dormitories, commons, discipline, and degrees ; that we should hire or buy in the heart of the city a temporary perch, and remain on it until we could determine what wants should be revealed, and until we could decide upon future buildings.

We were to await the choice of a faculty before we matured any schemes of examination, instruction, and graduation.

I was encouraged to travel freely at home and abroad. Among many men of distinction whom I met on these journeys, it may be invidious to make a selection, but a few must be named. Foremost was President Eliot *facile princeps* among the college presidents of that day, whose encouragement and counsel have never been wanting. At New Haven, among many former colleagues, there were two, Professors Whitney and Brush, whom it was natural to consult in the confidence of friendship, and through them I came into closer relations with Dr. Wolcott Gibbs, the renowned chemist. With the president of Cornell University, now the United States ambassador in Germany, I had been on intimate terms since our undergraduate days, and his recent experiences in the development of an original project made him a very valuable adviser. In Oxford, Cambridge, Glasgow, Dublin, and Manchester much interest was shown in our new undertaking. I remember vividly and with special pleasure my visit to Lord Kelvin in his laboratory, and a dinner with the X Club in London, to which Professor Tyndall invited me, and where I met Spencer, Hooker, Huxley, Frankland, and other leaders of science. The story of this club is given in Huxley's memoirs. To many leaders in the profession of medicine I was introduced by Dr. John S. Billings. On the Continent I visited Paris, Berlin, Heidelberg, Strasburg, Freiburg, Leipsic, Munich, and Vienna. In all these places the laboratories were new and even more impressive than the libraries. Everywhere the problems of higher education were under discussion ; everywhere, readiness to be helpful and suggestive was apparent. One Sunday afternoon I sat for a long while on the vine-clad hill of Freiburg, looking at the beautiful spire of the cathedral and talking with the historian, Professor Von Holtz — already well acquainted with American conditions. He became one of our lecturers, and afterward took part in the development of the University of Chicago. He gave me an inside view of the workings of the German University system. Professor James Bryce was a most serviceable interpreter of the intricacies of Oxford and Cambridge. Through a college classmate who had become an agrégé in the University of France, I had a similar introduction to the methods of the French. Among my note-books I think there is one in which, while at Oxford, in the autumn of 1875, I drew up an outline of the possible organization of our work in Baltimore. It was brief, but it was also comprehensive.

The first real difficulty was the selection of a faculty. The announcement was boldly made that the best men who could be found would be first appointed without respect to the place from which they came, the college wherein they were trained, or the religious body to which they belonged. The effort would be made to secure the best men who were free to accept positions in a new, uncertain, and, it must be acknowledged, somewhat risky organization. I will not recall the overtures made to men of mark, nor the overtures received from men of no mark. Nor can I say whether it was harder to eliminate from the list of candidates the second best, or to secure the best. All this it is well to forget. When I die, the memory of those anxieties and perplexities will forever disappear. It is enough to remember that Sylvester, Gildersleeve, Remsen, Rowland, Morris, and Martin were the first professors. As a faculty " we were seven." Our education, our antecedents, our peculiarities were very different, but we were full of enthusiasm, and we got on together without a discordant note. Four of the six are dead ; one is still as vigorous and incisive as ever ; one is now president. An able corps of associates, lecturers, and fellows was appointed with the professors, and they were admirable helpers in the inception of the work. This is not the place, and perhaps I am not the person to give the characteristics of this corps.

One incident only I will tell, for the recent death of Professor Rowland has brought his name before the public, and I have often been asked how at the age of twenty-eight he was selected for the important chair of physics. The facts are these.

While on service as a member of the Board of Visitors at West Point in the summer of 1875, I became well acquainted with General Michie, then professor of physics in the United States Military Academy. I asked him who there was that could be considered for our chair of physics. He told me that there was a young man in Troy, of whom probably I had not heard, whom he had met at the house of Professor Forsyth and who seemed to him full of promise.

" What has he done ? " I said.

" He has lately published an article in the *Philosophical Magazine*," was his reply, " which shows great ability. If you want a young man you had better talk with him."

" Why did he publish it in London," said I, " and not in the *American Journal ?* "

" Because it was turned down by the American editors," he said, " and the writer at once forwarded it to Professor Clerk Maxwell, who sent it to the English periodical."

This at once arrested my attention and we telegraphed to Mr. Rowland to come from Troy, where he was an assistant instructor in the Rensselaer Polytechnic Institute. He came at once, and we walked up and down Kosciusko's Garden, talking over his plans and ours. He told me in detail of his correspondence with Maxwell, and I think he showed me the letters received from him. At any rate, it was obvious that I was in confidential relations with a young man of rare intellectual powers and of uncommon aptitude for experimental science. When I reported the facts to the trustees in Baltimore they said at once, " Engage that young man and take him with you to Europe, where he may follow the leaders in his science and be ready for a professorship." And so we did. His subsequent career is well known.

The purchase of books and apparatus is of but little interest to the public, so I pass that subject by, and will proceed at once to the sixth requisite. After plans had been formed and teachers installed, the question was still open, Where are the students ? We were very fortunate in those that came to us. They were not many at first, and it was comparatively easy to become acquainted with every one. Among the pleasantest recollections of my life are the relations which I have held with the young men among whom my lot has been cast. In later years the numbers have been large, the helpers many, so that I have not been quite as fortunate, but for a long while I was brought into close acquaintance with every student. This half-official, half-fraternal intercourse has ripened into life-long friendships. In Baltimore, I have always regarded the original body of fellows as the advance-guard, carefully chosen, well taught, and quickly promoted. Without exception these twenty men soon won distinction. Most of them are happily living—so I will not dwell upon their merits ; but of two who have lately passed away I will say a few words.

Professor Adams came to us at the very opening of the university, fresh from his studies under Bluntschli in Heidelberg. He quickly showed the rare qualities which were manifest through his life—enthusiasm, application, versatility, and a generous appreciation of others. His mind was suggestive, capable of forming wise plans, and quick in devising the methods by which those plans could be carried out. A remarkable trait was the power of perceiving the adaptation of his scholars to such posts as were open. He could almost always suggest the right man for a given vacancy ; and he was just as ready to deter one that he thought unsuitable from seeking a place beyond his powers.

He began at an early day what was not exactly an association nor a seminary, but a weekly reunion of the teachers and scholars in the department of historical and political science. These meetings were stimulating to all who took part in them, and while the leadership fell upon Dr. Adams, many men of distinction came to the gatherings and did their part in making them of interest. He also initiated that remarkable series of publications, which continued under his editorship until his death—a repository of memoirs, longer and shorter, pertaining to American institutional history. He edited for the Bureau of Education a series of monographs on instruction in the various States of the Union. To his bright mind (I suspect), the idea of forming an American historical association is due. Cer-

tainly he was in its early days the most efficient promoter of that society, and he continued to be, until his health broke down, the secretary and the editor of the annual reports.

After all, surely, his highest service was in the art of inspiring others ; and when I think of those who came under his influence, Woodrow Wilson, Albert Shaw, J. F. Jameson, Charles H. Levermore, D. R. Dewey, F. W. Blackmar, B. C. Steiner, W. W. Willoughby, C. H. Haskins, F. J. Turner, J. M. Vincent, and many more, it seems to me that no higher achievement could have been attained by him, no greater reward secured.

Before it was publicly known that Professor Sylvester was to have charge of our mathematical work, Thomas Craig, from Lafayette College, inquired of me whether Sylvester was coming to us. Now, Sylvester had no popular reputation. His writings were diffused through a multitude of scientific journals, and he had never published them in separate volumes. I was surprised by the inquiry of a youthful schoolmaster from the country, and said, " What do you know about Professor Sylvester? " His reply was, " Not to know the name of Sylvester, is to know nothing of modern mathematics." I said, " Very true, but is that all you know of him? " He then acknowledged that he had read some of the memoirs of this illustrious geometer. Then I asked what made him think that Sylvester was coming. He said that Professor Peirce, of Harvard, had told him. " Do you know Professor Peirce? " said I. " Not personally," was his reply, " but I have had several letters from him, and in one of them he told me that I ought to go to Baltimore and study with Sylvester." So I took the young man into confidence and told him that, although the arrangements were not quite perfected, we did expect the co-operation of this English savant. The young man came to us and accepted one of the fellowships, and from that time onward until his health gave way he was a brilliant member of our mathematical corps. He became the successor of Sylvester and the associate of Newcomb in the editorial control of the *American Journal of Mathematics* and was thus brought into personal relations with most of the renowned mathematicians of Europe, whose letters as they lie before me indicate their respect for this American correspondent. His text-books were used at one time in the University of Cambridge, England, and his other mathematical writings were of distinct value, though they were not numerous.

Among the early students one of the most brilliant was Dr. Keeler, later director of the Lick Astronomical Observatory, in California. He came of good New England stock, but had been far away from all opportunities of superior education at his home in Florida. One day he appeared in Baltimore and asked leave to be received as a student in optics. A visitor in Florida, Mr. Charles H. Rockwell, had seen him engaged in surveying land with a theodolite of his own construction, and had asked the future astronomer what career he wished to follow. Keeler replied, " I should like to be an optician." With remarkable insight Mr. Rockwell encouraged him to go to Cambridge and consult with Alvan Clark. This maker of telescopes said : " I cannot receive you as a student ; go to the Sheffield School in New Haven and see what they will do for you." At New Haven they told him, " Go to Baltimore and work with Dr. Hastings." So he came to us. His means were very small, and he was glad to earn a little money by the making of diagrams, by drawing a plot of our grounds, and in other ways. He showed so much ability that he was encouraged to clear off our requirements for matriculation, and subsequently he proceeded to the degree of Bachelor of Arts. Not long afterward, he went to California with Professor Langley and aided him in original investigations respecting the heat of the sun, on the summit of Mount Whitney He became an assistant in the Allegheny Observatory, and finally he ended his career while in charge of the great instrument at Mount Hamilton, California, having won the highest recognition from all the astronomers of his day.

These are by no means the only examples that occur to me of brilliant young men whom we were at once able to encourage. The list is long. Fortunately most of them are still winning reputation. Whatever service we have rendered them is largely due to the freedom of our methods, and to the close contact which has prevailed between the leading scholars and those that have come under their guidance, and above all to the brilliant and learned minds whose influence, often unconscious, has been the most potent factor in the university at Baltimore. Thus with the six requisites, an idea, a plan, an endowment, a faculty, apparatus and students, we proceeded to launch our bark upon the Patapsco.

As the day drew near for the opening of our doors and the beginning of instruction the word reached us that Professor Huxley, of London, was coming to this country. We had already decided that, in view of the attention which was to be given to medicine, biology should receive a large amount of attention, more than ever before in this country. That meant the study, in the laboratory, of vegetable and animal forms and functions, so that the eyes and hands and brains of the students might be well prepared for the study of the human body in health and in disease. Huxley, among English-speaking people, was the leader in these studies. His repute as an investigator was good, and as the popular interpreter and defender of biological investigations he was without a peer. His acquaintance with the problems of medical education was also well known. He had rendered us a service by nominating Dr. Martin to the professorship of biology. The moment was opportune for informing the public, through the speech of this master, in respect to the requirements of modern medicine and the value of biological research. I do not suppose that anyone connected with the university had thought of the popular hostility toward biology. We did not know that to many persons this mysterious term was like a red flag of warning. The fact that some naturalists were considered irreligious filled the air with suspicions that the new foundation would be handed over to the Evil One. The sequel will show what happened. Professor Huxley was invited ; he accepted, he came to Baltimore, he addressed a crowded assembly—then came a storm.

An amusing incident in this visit has been told by his biographer; but as my recollections differ in slight details, I will tell the story in my own way.

On his arrival in Baltimore, Professor Huxley was driven to the country seat of Mr. Garrett, who had offered him hospitality and had invited a large company to meet him in an afternoon party. There was but one intervening day between his arrival, tired out by a long journey in the interior, and his delivery of the address. He had hardly reached the residence of his host, before the reporters discovered him and asked for the manuscript of his speech. "Manuscript?" he said, "I have none. I shall speak freely on a theme with which I am quite familiar." "Well, professor," said the interlocutor, "that is all right, but our instructions are to send the speech to the papers in New York, and if you cannot give us the copy, we must take it down as well as we can and telegraph it, for the Associated Press is bound to print it the morning after it is spoken." This was appalling, for in view of the possible inaccuracy of the short-hand, and the possible condensation of the wire-hand, the lecturer was afraid that technical and scientific terms might not be rightly reproduced. "You can have your choice, professor," said the urbane reporter, "to give us the copy or to let us do the best we can; for report the speech we shall." The professor yielded, and the next day he walked up and down his room at Mr. Garrett's, dictating to a stenographer, in cold and irresponsive seclusion, the speech which he expected to make before a receptive and hospitable assembly.

I sat very near the orator as he delivered the address in the Academy of Music, and noticed that, although he kept looking at the pile of manuscript on the desk before him, he did not turn the pages over. The speech was appropriate and well received, but it had no glow, and the orator did not equal his reputation for charm and persuasiveness. When the applause was over, I said to Mr. Huxley, "I noticed that you did not read your address; I am afraid the light was insufficient." "Oh," said he, "that was not the matter. I have been in distress. The reporters brought me, according to their promise, the copy of their notes. It was on thin translucent paper, and to make it legible, they put clean white sheets between the leaves. That made such bulk that I removed the intermediate leaves, and when I stood up at the desk I found I could not read a sentence. So I have been in a dilemma—not daring to speak freely, and trying to recall what I dictated yesterday and allowed the reporters to send to New York." If he used an epithet before the word "reporters" I am sure he was justified, but I forget what it was.

Those of us who wanted guidance and encouragement from a leading advocate of biological studies were rewarded and gratified by the address, and have often referred to it as it was printed in his American discourses and afterward in his collected works.

We had sowed the wind and were to reap the whirlwind. The address had not been accompanied by any accessories except the presentation of the speaker, no other speech, no music, no opening prayer, no benediction. I had proposed to two of the most religious trustees that there should be an introductory prayer, and they had said no, preferring that the discourse should be given as lectures are given at the Peabody Institute, without note or comment.

It happened that a correspondent of one of the religious weeklies in New York was present, and he wrote a sensational letter to his paper, calling attention to the fact that there was no prayer. This was the storm-signal. Many people who thought that a university, like a college, could not succeed unless it was under some denominational control, were sure that this opening discourse was but an overture to the play of irreligious and anti-religious actors. Vain it was to mention the unquestioned orthodoxy of the trustees, and the ecclesiastical ties of those who had been selected to be the professors. Huxley was bad enough; Huxley without a prayer was intolerable.

Some weeks afterward, a letter came into my hands addressed to a Presbyterian minister of Baltimore, by a Presbyterian minister of New York. Both have now gone where such trifles have no importance, so I venture to give the letter, quoting from the autograph. The italics are mine

" NEW YORK, 3 Oct. '76.

" Thanks for your letter, my friend, and the information you give. The University advertised Huxley's Lecture as the ' Opening ' and so produced the impression which a Baltimore correspondent increased by taking the thing as it was announced. *It was bad enough to invite Huxley. It were better to have asked God to be present. It would have been absurd to ask them both.*

" I am sorry Gilman began with Huxley. But it is possible yet to redeem the University from the stain of such a beginning. No one will be more ready than I to herald a better sign."

It was several years before the black eye gained its natural color. People were on the alert for impiety, and were disappointed to find no traces of it—that the faculty was made up of just such men as were found in other faculties, and that in their private characters and their public utterances there was nothing to awaken suspicion or justify mistrust. It was a curious fact, unobserved and perhaps unknown, that four of the first professors came from the families of gospel ministers, and a fifth of the group of six was a former Fellow of Oriel and a man of quite unusual devoutness. The truth is that the public had been so wonted to regard colleges as religious foundations, and so used to their control by ministers, that it was not easy to accept at once the idea of an undenominational foundation controlled by laymen. Harvard and Cornell both incurred the like animosity. At length the prejudice wore away without any manifesto or explanation from the authorities. From the beginning there was a voluntary assembly daily held for Christian worship ; soon the Young Men's Christian Association was engrafted ; the students became active in the churches and Sunday-schools and charities of Baltimore ; some graduates entered the ministry, and one became a bishop, while the advanced courses in Hebrew, Greek, history, and philosophy were followed by ministers of many Protestant denominations, Catholic priests and Jewish rabbis. It is also gratifying to remember that many of the ministers of Baltimore, Presbyterian, Episcopalian, Methodist, and Baptist, have intrusted their sons to the guidance of the local seminary whose influence and instructions they could readily watch and carefully estimate. As I consider the situation in these days of reconstruction, I wish it were possible for religious people to agree upon what should be taught to the young, in respect to religious doctrine or at least to agree in religious worship, yet I cannot forget that, in ages and in countries where one authority has been recognized and obeyed, neither intellect nor morals have attained their highest development.

EVERING IN MARCH

By Albert Bigelow Paine

FAR-LYING leas where grows the wild night wind.
Dun, sodden earth beneath a starless sky.
Chill gusts of rain that drown relentlessly
The few dim lights along the distant town ;
And then the sunless, dreary day goes down,
And oh, the long night waste that lies behind !

3

The Expansion of Our Great Universities.

BY ETHELBERT D. WARFIELD, LL.D.,
PRESIDENT OF LAFAYETTE COLLEGE.

THE ORIGINAL PURPOSES OF HIGHER EDUCATION IN AMERICA, THE LINES ON WHICH OUR SYSTEM HAS GROWN, AND ITS MARVELOUS EXTENSION IN RECENT YEARS—A SPLENDID DEVELOPMENT THAT IS NOT WITHOUT ITS PROBLEMS AND ITS WEAKNESSES.

NO phase of social progress is more characteristic of the development of the United States in the nineteenth century than the growth of our universities. Indeed, the whole field of education has been so fertile in ideas and undertakings that European critics, and especially English critics, have declared that America is " education mad." The fact is that the growth of democracy demanded a leveling principle, and the growth of wealth made this a leveling up and not a leveling down, as it rendered it possible for the poor boy to work his way to an education, and the educated man to become a leader in political and —which is true of America almost alone —in social life.

One of the most marked features of our educational growth has been its spontaneousness. It has sprung from the people, from local needs and, even more, from local aspirations. On this account it has lacked unity and system; but it has gained something far better than either unity or system—vitality. It has been a part of the social life of the people, and the divergence in the social life of Massachusetts and of Georgia, of Pennsylvania and of California, has been no less than the difference in the school and college growth of those States.

As the educational institutions were the outgrowth of local needs, they were nearly always adapted to the field i⸱

A GENERAL VIEW OF THE BUILDING PLAN ADOPTED BY THE UNIVERSITY OF CALIFORNIA, AT BERKELEY, CALIFORNIA—THE PLAN WAS DESIGNED BY E. BÉNARD, OF PARIS, AND WON THE PRIZE OFFERED FOR COMPETITION TO THE ARCHITECTS OF THE WORLD.

which they sprang up; as they were not less the progeny of local aspirations, they were often vastly ambitious in plan and name. Fortunately those ambitions were allowed to slumber in the charter

CORNELL UNIVERSITY, ITHACA, NEW YORK—THE UPPER ENGRAVING SHOWS BARNES HALL, THE CHRISTIAN ASSOCIATION BUILDING; IN THE CENTER IS THE ARMORY, AND BELOW A GENERAL VIEW OF THE UNIVERSITY AND CAYUGA LAKE. THE PORTRAIT IS THAT OF THE PRESIDENT, JACOB GOULD SCHURMAN.

till the time was ripe for their prophecy to be fulfilled in fact.

THE FIRST AMERICAN UNIVERSITIES.

The early colonists were jealous of their position as educated men, and determined that their children should not decline in knowledge and intelligence. Yet few of the colonies made permanent foundation of schools upon such a liberal basis as insured a proportionate growth with the colony. The notable exceptions are Harvard, founded in 1636; Yale, in 1701, and William and Mary, in 1693. Among the colonial institutions still in existence, nearly all have had a more or less broken continuity. They are Bowdoin (Maine), Brown University (Rhode Island), Kings, now Columbia (New York), Dartmouth (New Hampshire), Prince-

ton and Rutgers (New Jersey), the University of Pennsylvania, and Washington, now Washington and Lee (Virginia). Of these, Harvard and Yale, of the earlier group, have grown with each generation and are typical American universities, and the same is true of Columbia, Princeton, and the University of Pennsylvania in the second group.

Immediately after the Revolution there was a movement for the founding of academies and colleges, a movement which spread rapidly into the new West. There, in Kentucky, Tennessee, and Ohio,

it gave birth to academies which somewhat prematurely set up the curriculum of colleges, and in the largeness of expectation which has ever characterized the West—whether trans-Appalachian, trans-Mississippi, or transcontinental, first flung out the banner of the "university." Thus Transylvania University burst its chrysalis on January 1, 1799, while Harvard and Yale, long after they had become universities in fact, clung to the time honored name of college.

A GENERAL VIEW OF THE NEW BUILDINGS OF COLUMBIA UNIVERSITY, WITH THE LIBRARY IN THE CENTER—THE PORTRAIT IS THAT OF THE PRESIDENT, SETH LOW.

From a copyrighted photograph by Sidman, New York—The portrait of President Low from a photograph by Rockwood, New York.

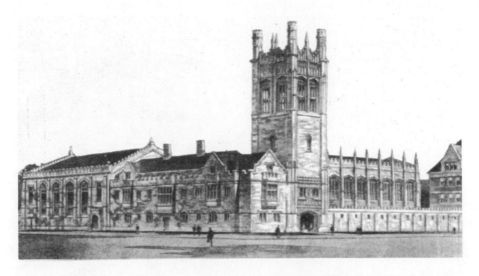

PART OF THE NEW BUILDINGS OF THE UNIVERSITY OF CHICAGO—ON THE LEFT IS MANDEL HALL; IN
THE CENTER, A STUDENTS' CLUBHOUSE; TO THE RIGHT, BEYOND THE TOWER,
THE COMMONS, OR DINING HALL.

The early type was based upon the colleges of the English universities, especially Cambridge, in which the American clergy had largely had their academic training. The instruction was relatively upon a low standard, and tended to gravitate rather to the type of the so called English colleges, or public schools, of Eton and Winchester. The chief subjects of instruction long remained elementary mathematics, Latin, and Greek. The impulse in the founding of the earlier schools having been given very largely by the clergy, there was always some instruction in mental and moral philosophy, and generally in history, which was really treated more as applied philosophy than as pure history. The practical demands of the pulpit and the controversial atmosphere of the times put a high value on what now appear to have been very dry and formal courses in rhetoric and logic. The sciences were in their infancy, but the claims of chemistry, physics, and astronomy were not wholly neglected. Indeed, the fact that they early found a place in the American curriculum shows the relative liberality of our colleges as compared with most European schools of the same grade and purpose.

It was unfortunate for the American people that, while they were struggling with high ambitions and keen practical vision for some basis for their educational system, they had so little to aid them in the mother country. The English universities had fallen into a sleepy old age in the eighteenth century, from which they have even yet but half aroused themselves. Jefferson saw this, and invoked the French influence in his foundation of the University of Virginia, in 1825, setting an example which affected many Southern institutions.

About 1840 England turned to Germany for more vital methods; the leaders of thought in New England took the same course at a somewhat earlier time. Gradually German influence brought about radical changes. The new suggestions fell upon a rich field. The time was fully come for American educational growth. Many ideas of native origin were stirring, such as those associated with the personality and work of Horace Mann, which embraced the thorough organization of the public schools, a normal school system, and the coördination of the education of women with that of men.

THREE GREAT FACTORS IN OUR UNIVERSITY DEVELOPMENT.

Two or three definite ideas became clearly marked in American education in the first half of the nineteenth century. They were not always properly connected, but as they were more and more widely accepted, it became necessary for educational reformers to unite them.

The first to become really dominant was the necessity of a college education. It was somewhat on the economic principle that in the progress of civilization luxuries precede necessities. Where few enjoyed

most unusual knowledge acquired was the most highly valued. Hence, instead of the colleges being degraded to the

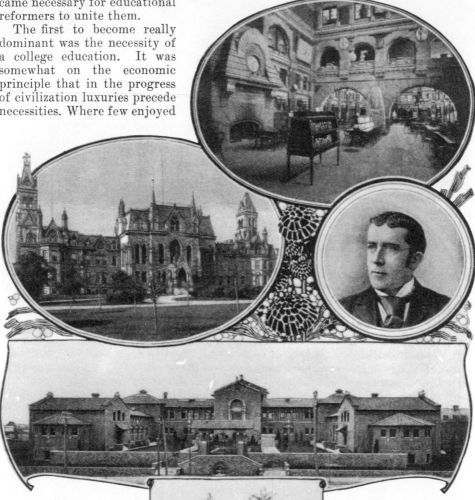

THE UNIVERSITY OF PENNSYL-VANIA, PHILADELPHIA—THE UPPER ENGRAVING SHOWS THE INTERIOR OF THE LI-BRARY; BELOW, ON THE LEFT, IS COLLEGE HALL; NEXT IS THE BUILDING—

—PRESENTED TO THE SCIENTI-FIC DEPARTMENT BY GEORGE W. DAWSON; BELOW, THE NORTH END OF COLLEGE HALL. THE PORTRAIT IS THAT OF THE PROVOST, CHARLES C. HARRISON.

this distinction, it was highly valued. The energies of an entire family were devoted to the proud purpose of giving the most promising son the privilege of "going to college." As the privilege was rare, the

practical requirements of a new country, they were stimulated to maintain an honorable eminence as intellectual leaders in communities that were rapidly advancing in wealth and material progress.

YALE UNIVERSITY, NEW HAVEN, CONNECTICUT—THE
WHITE AND BERKELEY DORMITORIES.

YALE UNIVERSITY—VANDERBILT HALL, THE FINEST COLLEGE DORMITORY BUILDING IN AMERICA. ABOVE
IS A PORTRAIT OF THE PRESIDENT OF YALE, ARTHUR TWINING HADLEY.

From photographs by Pach, New York, and Randall, New Haven.

THE UNIVERSITY OF WISCONSIN, MADISON, WISCONSIN
—THE LIBRARY BUILDING.

THE UNIVERSITY OF WISCONSIN—THE AGRICULTURE AND DAIRY BUILDINGS, WITH THE POWER HOUSE.
ABOVE IS A PORTRAIT OF THE PRESIDENT OF THE UNIVERSITY, CHARLES KENDALL ADAMS.

The portrait of President Adams from a photograph by Curtiss, Madison.

THE EXPANSION OF OUR GREAT UNIVERSITIES

HARVARD UNIVERSITY, CAMBRIDGE, MASSACHUSETTS—THE LAW SCHOOL.

The second was the growth of professional schools, often independent of college connection, sometimes connected with colleges. The early training in the professions was obtained by the sending of young men to study under preceptors. The clergy first departed from this method, to establish theological professorships, which grew into separate seminaries. Always the leaders in intellectual movements, they first insisted on a thorough college preparation before the commencement of the studies embraced in the theological course. Gradually independent schools were affiliated or absorbed, and the American colleges began to be universities—at least, so far as mere groups of faculties can constitute such institutions.

The third of these ideas was that of the public obligation to provide free schools—an idea of vast possibilities, many of which have been realized, and the end is not yet. It flourished first in New England. Gradually it carried the free school over the Northern States and made steady conquests in the South. From primary it advanced to secondary education, then to normal training. From time to time it showed its power in this State and that by leading to the State taking up collegiate work; then, in the Act of 1862, it invaded national legislation, and gave birth to the great system of land grant colleges, originally planned for education in agriculture and the mechanical arts, but which have assumed many and various forms and proportions undreamed by their founders.

These three ideas may be said to have

HARVARD UNIVERSITY—THE COLLEGE YARD AND TWO OF THE OLDER BUILDINGS, STOUGHTON AND HOLWORTHY HALLS.

been the great shaping influences that have given form to American university development. They have been combined in endless variety; they have been reinforced by many other influences; yet these have been fundamental. In general, we may say that university growth has been due to a wide spread popular estimate of the value of a college educa-

higher education which has faculties of arts, law, medicine, and theology. This is a poor definition, setting form above substance, and the body above the spirit; yet it has had a great influence in university growth. Thus Harvard, chartered in 1636, maintained its faculty of arts alone till 1783, when it first added a medical faculty. The law department

HARVARD UNIVERSITY—THE LIBRARY, WHICH IS THE BEST COLLEGE LIBRARY IN AMERICA, CONTAINING MORE THAN HALF A MILLION VOLUMES.

tion, to the bringing together into a single system of independent schools, and to a great public system of free education, which has prepared students for collegiate and professional courses, and has set up rivals for the older institutions in a great number of State colleges and universities.

WHAT CONSTITUTES A UNIVERSITY?

But university expansion in America has had some very unique features, which need to be especially noted. Those under the influence of the more formal type of German thought are wont to define a university as an institution of

dates from 1817, and the divinity school from 1819. The sister university in Connecticut, in many ways a contrast to Harvard, developed in this direction more slowly, and always with great conservative loyalty to the arts course as the center of Yale life. Yet Yale entered, by affiliation, into the medical field in 1814, into law in 1843, and divinity in 1867.

It is interesting to note that Columbia, situated in the metropolis, while following a similar course with the opportunity of affiliation almost thrust upon it, did not incorporate departments of law and medicine till so late as 1858 and 1891, and has now only very slender ties with the nominally affiliated theological faculties. The University of Pennsylvania only recently provided a

progress of science and invention, and the material wealth which has come forth from it since the middle of the century. Before it began to be felt, the

WILLIAM R. HARPER, PRESIDENT OF THE UNIVERSITY OF CHICAGO.

From a photograph by Gibson, Chicago.

BENJAMIN IDE WHEELER, PRESIDENT OF THE UNIVERSITY OF CALIFORNIA.

From a photograph by Wilcox, Berkeley.

CHARLES WILLIAM ELIOT, PRESIDENT OF HARVARD UNIVERSITY.

From a photograph by Notman, Boston.

law school, and is still without any sort of theological faculty. It is yet more striking to observe that, of the three great American colleges, Princeton has steadily resisted the temptation to add professional faculties, and has advanced to the university rank and name by virtue of its claim to do university work in intention rather than in extension, in spirit rather than in form.

THE ASCENDANCY OF SCIENCE.

Perhaps the most potent influence in that university expansion which appeals to the eye, and which has found expression in the magnificent buildings that adorn so many of the college grounds, has yet to be mentioned. This is the

> AFTER GOD HAD CARRIED VS SAFE TO NEW ENGLAND
> AND WEE HAD BVILDED OVR HOVSES
> PROVIDED NECESSARIES FOR OVR LIVELI HOOD
> REARD CONVENIENT PLACES FOR GODS WORSHIP
> AND SETLED THE CIVILL GOVERNMENT
> ONE OF THE NEXT THINGS WE LONGED FOR
> AND LOOKED AFTER WAS TO ADVANCE LEARNING·
> AND PERPETVATE IT TO POSTERITY
> DREADING TO LEAVE AN ILLITERATE MINISTERY
> TO THE CHVRCHES WHEN OVR PRESENT MINISTERS
> SHALL LIE IN THE DVST.
> NEW ENGLANDS FIRST FRVITS.

THE INSCRIPTION ON HARVARD HALL, HARVARD UNIVERSITY, RECORDING THE ORIGINAL AIM OF HIGHER EDUCATION IN NEW ENGLAND.

colleges were largely classical and philosophical. The branches of science taught were dealt with in the most elementary way; the instruction was from text books, there were few experiments and no laboratory work. As science began to advance, provision was gradually made for its teaching. A few feeble polytechnic schools came into existence to meet the practical demand for civil engineers. Men of practical taste and adequate wealth, finding an illiberal spirit in the college faculties of instruction, offered to endow coördinate faculties for scientific teaching. Thus the Lawrence School was established at Harvard by a gift of a hundred thousand dollars in 1847, and a similar school, afterwards the Sheffield School of Science, at Yale, the same year. In due time, as the various forms of engineering and applied science grew in importance, these schools began to take on the distinctly polytechnic type, and similar schools were added in many places, as the John C. Green School, at Princeton (1873); the School of Mines, at Columbia (1864); and the Pardee School, at Lafayette (1866).

This marked the adoption, in the fullest sense, of scientific thought and purpose into the academic field. As yet it was as a separate faculty, and, from the European point of view, one out of place

PRINCETON UNIVERSITY, PRINCETON, NEW JERSEY, AND ITS PRESIDENT, FRANCIS LANDEY PATTON—ABOVE, ON THE LEFT, IS ALEXANDER HALL; ON THE RIGHT, CLIO HALL, THE BUILDING OF A LITERARY SECRET SOCIETY. BELOW, ON THE LEFT, IS NASSAU HALL ("OLD NORTH"); ON THE RIGHT, BLAIR HALL, AND THE MAIN GATEWAY LEADING TO THE COLLEGE GROUNDS FROM THE RAILWAY STATION.

The portrait of President Patton from a photograph by Rose, New York.

in a university. Indeed, the complete assimilation of the departments of applied science is far from adjusted now. Yet the claims of these practical callings of engineering and chemistry, supported who seeks classical and historical training may find it there, vital and in touch with contemporary scholarship, but the college knows nothing of the culture and the force to be gained from the

LELAND STANFORD JUNIOR UNIVERSITY, PALO ALTO, CALIFORNIA—THE CENTRAL ENGRAVING SHOWS THE LIBRARY, ASSEMBLY HALL, AND MEMORIAL ARCH; ABOVE AND BELOW ARE VIEWS OF THE INNER QUADRANGLE. THE PORTRAIT IS THAT OF THE PRESIDENT, DAVID STARR JORDAN.

as they were by the wealth that they had brought to their votaries, accompanied by gifts for laboratories and endowments for professorships, took precedence over the pure sciences in receiving university recognition.

natural and the physical sciences. It is proud of the careers of such sons as Sydenham and Wren, but has established no school of chemistry and biology in memory of the one, or of architecture in honor of the other.

The American mind is at once practical and liberal. The English are less open minded. Conservatism, to them, is not a means to an end; it is, as often as not, an end in itself. So Oxford has failed to identify itself with the greater England of today, and is content to influence that part of English thought which it molded in the seventeenth century. The college of which I was a member in my student days has now the same buildings and the same plan of instruction it had when William Penn obtained his grant of Pennsylvania. He

As soon as graduates of American colleges realized that they had failed to get what they needed for their work in the dear old college days, they set about securing for others what they had missed. It was not long before there was a response from the professors of pure science, and, in due time, chairs were established and equipments purchased.

THE ELECTIVE SYSTEM.

Then a new and difficult question presented itself. The old college course was a well tested and closely articulated curriculum. Every part was nicely adjusted to every other part. The great staple was the historic humanities—the classical languages, with their literatures, embracing philological, philosophical, and historical teaching. The modern languages, some little physical science in a more or less narrow place, mathematics, enjoying considerable favor as far as the elements of calculus, and very humble applications in simple mechanics and surveying, completed the curriculum. The course was planned for boys, and was well adapted to develop them into strong men. It was not fitted to make scholars, and the new ideas demanded more knowledge as well as a wider curriculum.

An intense struggle began and is still going on. President Eliot, of Harvard, became the leader of the party which demanded the admission of the sciences on an equal footing with the old subjects. The practical method by which this was to be secured was the so called elective system, which allowed the student to choose from large groups what courses he would pursue. At first this choice was confined to the last year of the college course. Then time was gained by raising the entrance requirements, and the choice was extended into the junior year. From year to year the program of this school of educators became more and more radical, until it has finally taken up a position which practically asserts that all branches have an equal educative value if pursued for equal periods with equal earnestness. The result has been that Harvard practically asks nothing of its students in the college department, when once admitted, except a fairly definite purpose in the choice of studies made from its various and highly diversified courses. This tendency was met elsewhere by a more moderate use of the elective system, and by the arrangement of a number of parallel courses, definite in conception and leading to different degrees.

Two things have grown out of the elective system everywhere. The newer sciences have come into the colleges with a growing demand for more teachers, more time, more equipment, and the amount of study given to each subject

has greatly increased. This has reacted on all the teaching in all the departments, creating a demand for more Greek and more Latin, and better teachers of both.

SPECIAL KNOWLEDGE AND GENERAL CULTURE.

In the older days a single professor taught Greek and Latin, and often some other subject, such as philosophy. In the department of science, the natural and physical sciences were sometimes all in a single teacher's charge. While the teaching was often admirable, most of the sciences were but half developed, and all the instruction was elementary. But when the whole field of learning was being worked with marvelous results, specialists were naturally produced, and even humble students, who had no room in a busy life for research, were kept alert and active in merely following the researches of others. The teacher became a living worker, and longed to impart what he was daily learning. In consequence, the colleges gave themselves heartily to the movement for higher entrance requirements, and more extensive courses in every branch of learning.

It was plain to many wise teachers that this too eager pursuit of special knowledge was breaking up the power that had so long worked through a broad and thorough curriculum, without replacing it by a real mastery of special subjects. The true nature of the university became a great subject of discussion. It was made plain that the American college was not the equivalent of the philosophical faculty of the German university, and that the too eager Germanizers were wrecking the most vital factor in American education in a rash attempt to bend it to a new and alien end. These leaders began the advocacy of graduate courses, conducted on the true university principle of high specialization, extended investigation, and absolute freedom of choice. In 1876 Johns Hopkins University was opened. Working on this plan of supplementing, instead of supplanting, the admirable college course, it has done a splendid service to American education. It has become clear that the university purpose is best fulfilled in this country through the professional schools, on the one hand, and the graduate courses on the other. These courses are now conducted by the ablest specialists in America. They cover the widest possible range of scholarship, and are well supported by endowments and admirably supplied with laboratories and libraries. Professor Munsterberg of Harvard, looking through German glasses, thinks they do not as yet possess much fruit in " productive scholarship," but he has his eyes too much on books and academic performances, too little on men and economic and social forces. Though in their first age, and in some things too conscious of their own importance, the graduate faculties of American universities have accomplished a great deal in making plain the value of research and specialization as the real university work, and in discrediting the imitation of university work which has in some places been palmed off on a too credulous public in connection with the teaching of boys in colleges.

THE EDUCATIONAL DEPARTMENT STORE.

It remains to note the extension of universities by the addition to them of other faculties not historically connected with them, and the final extension of the name to cover the great " department store idea " in education. Thus, the medical school in this country early developed a very useful offshoot in the school of dentistry. A school of pharmacy followed, and the science and its application went a step farther in the school of veterinary medicine.

Some of the newer institutions, catching the popular feeling in favor of the combination suggested in the development of the medical field, at once began to make the standard of the university the old but somewhat discredited one, of a *studium generale*, in the sense that any one could learn in it anything conceivable. Thus, the prospectus of the Leland Stanford University announced that provision would be made for the instruction of any one in any subject demanded, and that the only qualification required would be a letter setting forth clearly what the writer wished to learn. This can scarcely be regarded as

a step in university expansion. It was rather university degradation.

The University of Chicago has taken up the idea of making a university a universal educational institution, and has achieved a popular success. It has had enormous financial resources, a remarkable executive, and a great field. At present its organization consists of five divisions. The first of these contains the professional schools, graduate schools and colleges of arts and science, and also an academy. The fourth contains the natural adjuncts to the schools and colleges, the libraries, laboratories, and museums. When we pass beyond these divisions we are in a position of doubt as to the attitude the remaining divisions bear to the university idea, or, indeed, to any sound educational scheme. The second division, for example, is that of "university extension," and includes a correspondence study department; the fourth is " the University Press," with a " department of purchase and sale "; the fifth consists of " the university affiliations," and includes " the work done in institutions which, although not forming an organic part of the university, have entered into the relationship of affiliation."

The wide scope of such an institution makes it possible for it to give great service, but it may be doubted whether the highest service of university leadership is not lost in an attempt to carry on too many of the departments of approved and unapproved educational work.

THE NEED OF A MORE PERFECT SYSTEM.

And here is the great weakness in the university development in America. On the foundation of the college and the " land grant " school of agriculture and mechanics we have erected splendid groups of buildings, and have peopled them with capable professors and eager students; but each in turn has followed a policy of rivalry instead of coöperation, of repetition instead of supplement. Clark University stands out as a lonely attempt to do a few things supremely well. Why is it not possible to avoid the endless repetition of costly equipment, and secure a cordial coöperation? Some work admirably done in one university may well be supplemented in another. A system of migration, such as is common in Germany, would enable a graduate student at Princeton to spend part of his time at Columbia or Johns Hopkins with due credit. An eminent foreigner, who is now a professor in one of our universities, made this experiment not long ago. The trustees deemed his act a blow at their claim to absolute and final possession of all knowledge, and made it the subject of a formal rebuke.

The growth of the past half century is remarkable from every point of view. It is to be hoped that the next half century will place a higher value on the university spirit in all forms of work, will more clearly recognize the limitations of the university as an institution, and of individual universities as effective forces, and develop a spirit of coöperation which will place learning above local reputation, and productive scholarship above the number of students.

4

CAMBRIDGE ON THE CHARLES

THE WASHINGTON ELM.

advantages save its excellent harbor, had not at that time been fixed upon as the seat of government; and one day in 1630, accordingly, Governor Winthrop and Lieutenant-Governor Dudley jumped on horseback and explored the plains and swamps and forests to the westward in search of a capital. The spot they finally picked out, with the help of some assistant magnates, lay about three miles west of Charlestown, on the banks of the tortuous little river since sung by poets, and already named the Charles by Captain John Smith, who never saw it. The elect location seemed to Winthrop "a fit place for a beautiful town;" and accordingly, on the 29th day of December a goodly number of persons bound themselves to build houses there early in the spring of the following year. The village they named Newtown, and laid out regularly in squares, the streets bearing such simple names as Creek, Wood, and Water, while there were, as lesser ways, Marsh Lane, Back Lane, and Crooked Lane. That was before the days of aristocratic thoroughfares like Brattle and Craigie and Ellery and Fayerweather streets.

Early in 1631 the houses began to rise, and Governor Winthrop set up the frame of his dwelling on the very spot where he had first pitched his tent. But the people of Boston had been promised by the Governor at the very first that he would never move away any where unless they accompanied him, and of this promise they now reminded him in pretty strenuous terms. Bound by two solemn agreements, and under the necessity of breaking one of them, Winthrop's conscience gave preference to the one first made; and so in the fall of 1631 he disap-

THE English colonists, Puritan and Cavalier, who peopled our coast in the early part of the seventeenth century were always shrewd in the selection of sites for their little towns and cities. Commercial or agricultural advantages guided their choice, as a rule; but once in a while they picked out some select location for the express purpose of making it a colonial capital. Something of the sort was the case with the Massachusetts village of Newtown, which has since developed into the American Cambridge. It was not exactly born great, but Governor Winthrop and his associates early tried to thrust greatness upon it. A scholar generally calm and discreet lately declared that the pre-Revolutionary Cambridge was "the first capital of our infant republic, the cradle of our nascent liberty, the hearth of our kindling patriotism." At any rate, this is just what, in a different sense, the Puritans of 1630 wanted it to be. Boston, then a small town with no special

GOVERNOR WINTHROP.

By 1634 the Newtown people began to complain of being overcrowded, and loudly talked, some of them, of moving to Connecticut. To that region the original Braintree settlers, to the number of one hundred, accordingly departed two years later, headed by their minister, the Rev. Thomas Hooker, and driving with them 160 cattle. The same year, 1636, this migratory church was replaced in Newtown by a permanent organization under the Rev. Thomas Shepard, a recent arrival from England; and the fortunes of the town were also bettered by the establishment in it of the colony's first school, endowed by the General Court with £400. Nearly all the ministers of the colony happened to be from the University of Cambridge in England, and the most of them, too, from a single one of its colleges, Emanuel. The neighboring Charlestown clergyman, the Rev. John Harvard, a scholarly and gentle graduate of Emanuel, took from the first a hearty interest in the Newtown school; and dying in 1638, he left to it his well-selected library of three hundred volumes and half his fortune. This bequest amounted, it is supposed, to nearly £800, or twice as much as the original gift of the General Court; and such was the effect of so magnificent a gift that the colonists determined to raise the school to the grade of a college, and to give to it the name of its benefactor. The same year, too, the Cambridge graduates concluded to express their esteem for their own university by changing

pointed his Newtown friends by taking down the frame of his unfinished dwelling and setting it up in Boston. Lieutenant-Governor Dudley's house was completed, meanwhile, and his family installed therein; and he and the rest frigidly let Winthrop return to Boston without offering to accompany him. This affair, as was natural, caused a coolness between Winthrop and Dudley, which was not removed for several years. The Governor's excuse for quitting Newtown was somewhat strengthened in his own mind by the fact that Chickatabut, the chief of the neighboring Indians, had promised to be friendly, so that the necessity of having a fortified settlement in the country, three miles west, was somewhat less urgent. The commercial prospects of Boston, too, had begun to look brighter than Newtown's. Making the best of their opportunities, the remaining settlers proved so thrifty, and courtly too, that they soon began to deserve the praise accorded them by an English writer some years afterward, who warmly described the place as "one of the neatest and best-compacted towns in New England, having many fair structures, with many handsome-contrived streets." "The inhabitants," added this complimentary tourist, "are most of them very rich." In 1632 a number of settlers from Braintree, England, came to Newtown. The quarrel between Winthrop and Dudley continuing, the ministers justified the Lieutenant-Governor by ordering Winthrop to get a clergyman for the town, failing in which he should pay Dudley £20. This sum Winthrop had to render, but the pacified Dudley was magnanimous in his triumph, and returned it with a polite note in which he courteously intimated that he would rather lose £100 than Winthrop's friendship. Their difficulties settled, the two magnates lived on friendly terms thereafter.

HARVARD MONUMENT.

the name of the village from Newtown to Cambridge. The scholarly fortunes of the town were also aided by the establishment in it of the first printing-office in America north of Mexico, which was set up in Cambridge in 1639, and the place soon began to be quite a centre of influence both in theology and religion. In 1640 Charlestown Ferry was given to the college, which held it for a hundred and fifty years; in 1650 an act of incorporation was granted the president and fellows; in 1652 the first inn was established, one Andrew Belcher being granted liberty " to sell beare and bread ;" in 1660 a bridge was built over Charles River, making the distance to Boston eight miles; and in 1732 a portion of the territory of Cambridge, on the northwest, was set off into a separate town, Newton—a process repeated in subsequent years. The rest of the civic history of Cambridge is dull. It became a city in 1846; and early in the present century its trivial commerce induced the government to make it a port of entry, whence Lechmere's Point, one of the settlements within the town limits, became Cambridgeport.

The history of Harvard College is so closely connected with the literary and architectural annals of Cambridge that it is not worth while to try to dissever them. The Rev. Mr. Harvard, as we have seen, died in 1638, his malady being consumption. Little is known about his personal history, and antiquarian research has not thrown much light upon it. He graduated at Emanuel College in 1631, and came to Charlestown only a year before his death. The graduates of the college built him a plain monument in Charlestown in 1828. His widow married Thomas Allen, her husband's successor in the Charlestown pastorate, in 1639, and the two returned to England some eleven years later. Before this time the college Harvard endowed had become the principal object of interest in Cambridge, and his bequest had led others to follow his example. Who managed the affairs of the college during the first four years of its existence is not known. In 1640, however, there arrived from England the Rev. Henry Dunster, whose qualifications for the office of president seem to have been so apparent that he was elected almost by acclamation. Dunster was poor, and he had not only to look after his own support, but also to beg for the college and for some of the more needy of his students. Thus he was the prototype of the little army of presidential mendicants who have succeeded him. His administration of affairs was a prosperous one, however, and in 1642 he sent forth his first class of nine members, one of whom became an Oxford D.D., one an Oxford fellow, and one a Leyden M.D. The most illustrious of the nine was George Downing, who became knight, baronet, and minister of Cromwell in Holland, where his success seems to have been great enough to have led to his retention in office by Charles II. A grandson of this Downing was the founder of the youngest of the schools in the English Cambridge, Downing College. Dunster ruled with an iron rod, the students being compelled to stand in hatless silence before their superiors and elders. They had also to talk Latin within the college walls, and, on occasion, to be publicly whipped at prayers. He was a prudent manager of the little chest of the college, and once lent some money just received from England to the General Court, getting something over nine per cent. interest for it. This sum was not repaid until 1713, when interest from 1685 was added to the principal. But all Dunster's thrift, energy, and scholarship did not save him. Long suspected of Baptist, or rather of anti-pedo-baptist, opinions, he at length avowed them, and the theological cudgels of the zealous Puritans rang so smartly about his ears that he was compelled to resign, and took up his abode in Scituate. His love for the college did not die out, and on his death his body was buried, at his request, in the graveyard in Cambridge just opposite the college grounds.

Dunster's successor, Charles Chauncy, was also a heretic, but at the other extreme of the pendulum's swing. Chauncy firmly believed in infant baptism, but held that

PRESIDENT QUINCY.

life, and toward the close of the seventeenth century the Indian college seems to have been used for the printing establishment, Eliot's Indian Bible having perhaps been there struck off. The list of succeeding presidents may be briefly mentioned. From 1672 all of them were graduates of Harvard. Leonard Hoar (1672–75) was very unpopular with the students, and resigning, passed his closing years in melancholy obscurity. His successor, the Rev. Urian

PRESIDENT SPARKS.

such baptism was invalid unless performed by immersion. Another of his ideas—illustrating a sort of High-Church Puritanism —was that the Lord's Supper ought only to be administered in the evening. If Dunster took away from the creed of the majority of the colonists, Chauncy added to it, and was consequently compelled to endure something of the persecution which surrounded his predecessor. He held his own, however, and died in office in 1672. During

Oakes, pastor of the church in Cambridge, was suspected of conspiring for Hoar's seat, but proved to be a useful president until his death, in 1681. John Rogers, Oakes's successor, was the first layman to fill the office. In June, 1685, the celebrated Increase Mather took the chair, but rather neglected the college. "Priest, politician, and president," Mather retained until his death the pastorate of the North Church, Boston, and was once in Europe on a political mission.

PRESIDENT EVERETT.

PRESIDENT WALKER.

his rule the London Society for the Propagation of the Gospel erected a wooden building for the instruction of Indian youth, which stood nearly on the present site of Grays Hall. Only one of the red men ever graduated, the individual who stands in solitary state in the triennial catalogue as "Caleb Cheeshahteaumuck, Indus." He became a Bachelor of Arts in 1665, and promptly died of consumption the next year. Many of the Indian students returned to savage

PRESIDENT FELTON.

The colony, after all, was nearer his heart than the college, and to it he gave his more profitable counsels and services. Before his death, however, Harvard received what was then its largest gift, £1000 from Lieutenant-Governor William Stoughton, of the province, a member of the class of 1650. All this time, and for many years after, the college was clerical in its management, and the principal source from which the pulpits of New England were filled. In 1696, out of 121 clergymen in the eleven neighboring counties, 104 were Harvard men. It was still poor, and on one occasion the corporation "voted that six leather chairs be forthwith provided for the use of the library, and six more before the Commencement, in case the treasury will allow of it." This body now determined, warned by Mather's course, to compel the presidents to live in Cambridge. But the Rev. Samuel Willard, their next choice, was minister of the Old South, Boston, and he evaded the new rule by assuming the title of vice-president simply.

Willard's successors were most of them men of industry and faithfulness. John Leverett (1708–24), preacher, lawyer, councilor, judge, politician, and scientist; Benjamin Wadsworth (1725–37), minister of the First Church, Boston; Edward Holyoke (1737–69), minister in Marblehead; Samuel Locke (1770–73), compelled to resign in consequence of immorality; Samuel Langdon (1774–80); Joseph Willard (1781–1804), minister in Beverly; and Samuel Webber (1806–10), mathematician and natural philosopher. In Leverett's time there was a fierce clerical fight over the seats in the corporation—a quarrel repeated in the present century. Wadsworth was annoyed by the attempt of the Episcopal ministers of King's Chapel, Boston, and Christ Church, Cambridge, to claim a place in the Board of Overseers as "teaching elders." Holyoke's

administration embraced the time of Whitefield's bitter attacks upon the New England seminaries, and Harvard in particular, for irreligion—attacks vigorously repelled by the Harvard professors, headed by Edward Wigglesworth, Hollis professor of divinity. In President Langdon's time the affairs of the college were greatly troubled by the Revolution. The buildings were occupied by the provincial troops in 1775–76, the few remaining students were transferred to Concord, and the library and apparatus carted to Concord and Andover. Then, too, John Hancock, treasurer from 1773 to 1777, proved himself a much better patriot than financier, and greatly annoyed the college authorities by carrying their bonds to Philadelphia, and refusing either to give an account or to resign. When the Revolution was over, the nominal property of the college was $100,100, its real property $25,787. About the only gain it received from the war was a few books from the General Court, which that body found among some confiscated Tory property, and gave away, perhaps as a sop to conscience for goods ill-gotten. The other presidents of Harvard have been John Thornton Kirkland (1810–28), who somewhat revived the literary spirit in Cambridge, Josiah Quincy (1829–45), Edward Everett (1846–49), Jared Sparks (1849–53), James Walker (1853–60), C. C. Felton (1860–62), and Thomas Hill (1862–68). President Kirkland was personally a great favorite with his students, and was a man of a good deal of dry wit. The

PRESIDENT ELIOT.

WADSWORTH HOUSE.

famous old tavern on Harvard Square, now the horse-car office, was in his day a great resort of students, whose favorite beverage was "flip," a palatable drink, made more grateful by being stirred with a red-hot poker. Once Kirkland repaired to this tavern and solemnly called for a mug of the beverage, which he drank in silence. Setting down the mug, he remarked to the publican, "I understand the students come here a good deal to drink flip." "Yes, Sir," was the frank reply. "Well," said Kirkland, "I should think they would," and walked away.

By an unexampled experience Presidents Quincy, Everett, Sparks, Walker, and Felton were alive at the same time, and these five heads of the college sit side by side in a portrait hung in the office of their successor, the present occupant of the presidential chair, Charles W. Eliot. President Eliot was inaugurated on May 19, 1869, and was the youngest to sit in Parson Turell's legacy, with the exception of President Locke. A Boston boy, the son of a former treasurer of Harvard, President Eliot graduated from the Boston Latin School in 1849, and from the college in 1853. Before his election he had been tutor and assistant professor in the college, and had also taught in the Institute of Technology in Boston. Probably the event in his pre-presidential life upon which his under-graduates look with most enthusiasm is the fact that he once sat (while a tutor) in a university boat.

The centre of Cambridge is Harvard Square, around which the college buildings cluster so closely that the student, as he takes some country friend into the "yard," finds it hard to divest his descriptions of the guide-book manner. This so-called square is a somnolent triangle, three miles from Boston, whose natural state of calm is vexed only by the bells of the horse-cars that trundle through it, or by the scream of their wheels as they round the curve. Once in a while, too, its dust is stirred by some mortuary procession of cattle on their way to the neighboring *abattoirs*. At the eastern end of the triangle, just where the street begins to widen, stands a generous old gambrel-roofed wooden building, now known as Wadsworth House, which was built in 1726 for the official residence of the presidents of the college. Wadsworth was the first to occupy it, the house having been completed the year after his inauguration. The elms which overtop its venerable roof were set out by President Willard sixty years after the last brick was laid on the chimneys, but they are quite successful in feigning to be coeval with the mansion itself. For a hundred and twenty years the dwelling was occupied by the successive presidents, Wadsworth, Holyoke, Locke, Langdon, Willard, Webber, Kirkland, Quincy, and Everett having dwelt in it. Presidents Sparks and Walker lived in their own houses, and Felton was the first to occupy the new president's house on Quincy Street, at the eastern end of the yard, a modest brick edifice erected a dozen years ago by Peter C. Brooks, of Boston. No building in Cambridge has sheltered so many people of eminence, probably, as Wadsworth House. Washington slept here several times before taking the Vassall House as his permanent

GENERAL VIEW OF THE UNIVERSITY BUILDINGS, CAMBRIDGE.

head-quarters in 1775; and here he was received when he visited Cambridge in 1789. When President Everett, its last occupant, held his final reception, he stood at one door of the generous drawing-room to receive the guests, while the equally court-ly Webster welcomed them at the other. In good preservation, the ancient edifice is now used as a dormitory, while the office of the college bursar is in a little brick addition, built in President Webber's time, and lately transferred from the western to the northern side.

Near by, but farther to the west, stands Dane Hall, a rather ugly brick building, built in 1832 for the law school, then just established. Judge Story's lectures attracted so many students that it had subsequently to be enlarged; and in 1870, when the foundations of Matthews Hall were laid, Dane was moved bodily to the southward and denuded of its unpleasing classic portico. Near by stood all the edifices of the First Congregational Church save the present one, a wooden Gothic building on the other side of the street, built the year after Dane Hall was completed. Matthews, mentioned above, was finished in 1872 at the cost of a Boston merchant, whose only condition in giving it was that half the revenues from its rooms should be devoted to the support of students in the college designing to enter the Episcopal ministry. It is built somewhat after the pattern of many of the Oxford colleges, in Elizabethan architecture. North of Matthews and at right angles to the street is Massachusetts Hall, the oldest of the existing buildings. Built in 1720, it originally contained "thirty-two rooms and sixty-four studies," which were occupied as dormitories until 1870, when the four stories were made into two, and the structure began to be used as a reading-room and a place for examinations. The same year a new railing was put upon the roof, which has so caught the spirit of the place that it looks as old as the pile it surmounts. The eastern gable used to contain the college clock, traces of the face of which may still be seen. Tradition accounts for the wooden patch where the clock used to be by averring that the devil, once summoned into Massachusetts Hall by the incantations of students, burst his way out through the attic bricks, and that the hole he made had subsequently to be patched up with wood.

Harvard Hall, just opposite, and also at right angles with the street, was built in 1766 to replace a predecessor of the same name and on the same site, destroyed in 1764. That year the General Court, scared by the small-pox in Boston, came out to Cambridge to sit, occupying this hall for its deliberations; and one cold winter's night, the students being of course absent, the building caught fire from the legislative stove, and burned to the ground, with the college library and apparatus. President Holyoke delicately hinted that since the hall had been destroyed in the service of the commonwealth, it would be proper for the commonwealth to rebuild it, which was done two years later. But much of the loss was irreparable. This fire not only endangered Massachusetts Hall, but also Hollis Hall, built the previous year, just north. Hollis is in excellent preservation, and is still used as a dormitory for students. In its ancient rooms many an eminent man has lived during his college days, of such occupants being Edward Everett, Ralph Waldo Emerson, Charles Francis Adams, J. G. Palfrey, Prescott, Sumner, Wendell Phillips, Thoreau, and Judge B. R. Curtis. Hollis Hall was struck by lightning in 1768. The shapely old building commemorates a generous family of Baptists in England—Thomas, John, Nathaniel, Timothy, Thomas a nephew, and Thomas his son, all benefactors of the college, which received from them gifts of books, apparatus, and money, and the foundation for professorships of mathematics and divinity. This last endowment caused a fierce theological controversy at the beginning of the present century. The third Thomas Hollis was a man of much eccentricity. He stamped his coat of arms—an owl—on the back of his books, expressing his disapproval of a volume by turning the bird upside down. Several of these condemned works are now contained in the college library. On his death Hollis was buried, by his direction, ten feet deep, in the centre of a field, which was then plowed and sowed with grain.

The next building north of Hollis in the old row is Stoughton Hall, built in 1805 to replace a building of the same name which stood behind Massachusetts and Harvard, and which, having become insecure, was torn down in 1780. This first Stoughton Hall was built in 1699. Stoughton, like Hollis, has had illustrious occupants, rooms within its walls having been occupied by Josiah Quincy, Caleb Cushing, Oliver Wendell Holmes, President Felton, W. H. Furness, E. R. Hoar, Edward E. Hale, and Charles T. Brooks. Everett and Sumner roomed here as well as in Hollis. Between the two halls stands Holden Chapel—a small but beautifully proportioned building, erected in 1744 by the widow and daughters of a London merchant, and originally used as a chapel. Afterward it became in turn a carpenter's shop and a chemical lecture-room, in which latter capacity it was used by Professor John White Webster, the murderer of Parkman.

These various buildings form the west side of the college quadrangle, the northern end of which is filled by Holworthy Hall, built in 1812 from the proceeds of a lottery

EVANGELINUS APOSTOLIDES SOPHOCLES.

losophers, probably, looked less Platonic or Socratic than this their modern expounder.

Turning the corner and passing down the eastern side of what ambitious collegians are already beginning to call the " quad," the first building is Thayer Hall, built in 1870 by Nathaniel Thayer, of Boston, to commemorate his father, old Dr. Thayer, and his brother, John Eliot Thayer. Mr. Thayer will be remembered as the generous patron of Agassiz, who made his Brazilian tour at Mr. Thayer's expense. Next is University Hall, built in 1814, of white Chelmsford granite, and bitterly criticised at the time of its erection. University has a bright and new appearance, and contains the offices of the president, college dean, etc. Weld Hall, just opposite Matthews, was built in 1872 by a Boston merchant in memory of his brother, and, like Matthews, is of English collegiate architecture. The southern end of the triangle is filled by Grays Hall, built in 1863—a modest brick building, which commemorates the gifts of three men of the name of Gray—Francis Calley, John Chip-

GORE HALL.

authorized by the State. Holworthy has always been a favorite dormitory and the head-quarters of the Senior Class—a precedence which the newer and more elegant buildings have not stolen from it. The Prince of Wales visited room No. 12 in 1860, and left there his autograph and portrait, a process repeated by the Grand Duke Alexis in 1871. In the westernmost room of the second story has lived for many years Evangelinus Apostolides Sophocles, University Professor of Greek. Himself a native of Greece, Sophocles came to the United States under the auspices of the American Board of Commissioners for Foreign Missions, studied for a time in Monson Academy and Amherst College, taught in Hartford, and ultimately settled at Harvard as tutor in Greek. He lives in the simplest manner, his room being furnished with Spartan severity; and the students tell many a story concerning his eccentricities and encyclopedic knowledge. A Harvard professor living in his old age within grim and unadorned bachelor walls, and with frugal economy sending his earnings home to Lycabettus or the banks of the Ilissus, is surely a noticeable person. The scholarly attainments of Professor Sophocles honor his adopted country, and his face, framed in hair and beard as venerable as Bryant's, reminds one of what might have been seen any day in the groves of the Academe. Half of the Greek phi-

LOUIS AGASSIZ.

man, and William. The other edifices within the college inclosure—which contains twenty-two acres—are, besides a row of houses on Quincy Street, mostly occupied by members of the faculty, Boylston Hall (1858), a jail-like structure, containing cabinets and chemical laboratories; Gore Hall (1842), the library; and Appleton Chapel (1858). Gore pretends to be a copy of King's College Chapel in the English Cambridge; but it can not be called a very successful rival of that celebrated building. With its tall and meaningless minarets, it not inaptly suggests to others as well as to James Russell Lowell the similitude of a North River steamboat. The building, in fact, is a somewhat melancholy failure. Its towers began to tumble down before they had been built half a dozen years; it contains no officers' rooms, not even one for the librarian; its books suffer from dampness, and its occupants from the stifling heat of a furnace. Appleton Chapel has been about as unlucky. Sixty or seventy thousand dollars were spent when it was built, in 1858, but its acoustic properties proved to be bad, and it was

generally ill heated in winter. A few years ago, however, it was restored throughout, two galleries and some stained-glass windows were put in, and now the students enjoy the unwonted privilege of *hearing* the Gospel within its walls.

The university buildings outside the college yard are College House, a long brick structure occupied as a dormitory in all save its lower story; Holyoke House, built by the corporation in 1871 as a hotel, but now occupied by students; Divinity Hall (1826), an eighth of a mile to the northeast, on a pleasant elm-shaded avenue, the seat of the Unitarian divinity school; the observatory, half a mile west; the herbarium, near by the observatory, in a large botanic garden; Lawrence Hall (1848), just opposite Holworthy, the location of the scientific department, founded by Abbott Lawrence; the medical and dental schools, in Boston; the gymnasium, small and shabby; and the Bussey Institution, an agricultural and horticultural school in West Roxbury. The observatory has been fully described in previous numbers of this Magazine.

Near Divinity Hall, and not far from Norton's Woods (called by the name of Andrews Norton, Unitarian theologian), stands the building of the Museum of Comparative Zoology, so dear to the heart of Agassiz, and densely stored with his priceless collections. As it stands, it is but a single wing of a projected building conceived on so vast a plan that it probably will never be completed. Agassiz dwelt in a house at the corner of Quincy Street and Cambridge Street, now occupied by his son Alexander. Few Cambridge students will soon forget his enthusiastic face and his pleasant voice as he used to expound some favorite theory in the lecture-room of the museum. Agassiz's personal appearance was very fine; he looked well and hearty, and his enthusiasm was contagious. Despite his long residence in Amer-

MUSEUM OF COMPARATIVE ZOOLOGY.

MEMORIAL HALL.

ica, his English pronunciation was quaintly imperfect: thus *laboratory*, a word he must necessarily have pronounced ten thousand times, always came from his lips lab*oratory*. He was a splendid drill-master for his students and assistants; and his renown was greatly enhanced by the skill with which he utilized their clumsier investigations.

Pretty much the only Harvard building we have thus far omitted to mention is the new Memorial Hall. The *alumni* of the college, when the civil war was over, at once felt a desire to commemorate those who had died in service. After some debate, the erection of a hall was decided on; the triangular plot of ground called the Delta, used by the students as a ball ground, was selected as the site, and the corner-stone was laid in 1870, Judge Hoar delivering the oration, and Phillips Brooks offering the prayer. The building, erected after the designs of two Boston architects, comprehends a large dining hall, a memorial hall with tablets, and an academic theatre for public exercises. The first two are now completed, and the dining hall, adorned with the university's portraits and busts, is used by about five hundred students, organized into a club, which is only indirectly controlled by the corporation. In the memorial hall proper, which is at right angles with the dining hall, is inscribed the name of every graduate or member of the college or professional schools who died in battle or from ailments contracted in the field. The architectural proportions of the building, which has cost over half a million dollars, are, on the whole, pleasing, despite some manifest defects, and its lofty tower is visible for many miles around. The dining hall is a room of im-

posing size, and the sight of a great body of students at commons has become so rare in this country of late years that visitors not infrequently enter the gallery overhead for the sake of watching Harvard eat, or, as the boys themselves express it, to "see the animals feed."

By the middle of the seventeenth century Cambridge had won the reputation of being a favorite abode of courtly as well as scholarly people, not all of whom, by any means, were connected with the college. A hundred years later, curiously enough, the majority of the houses in Old Cambridge were occupied by members of the Church of England, who had little doctrinal, social, or political sympathy with the college authorities, and who were regarded by them, in turn, with considerable suspicion as enemies of the Congregational Church polity, and possible possessors of the hard-won Puritan birthright. Once, as we have seen, an attempt to get seats in the Board of Overseers was made by the Episcopalians, which was repelled by the existing managers with a speed which betrayed their anxiety. Could these worthy men have foreseen that Harvard's increasing catholicity would accept a dormitory from an Episcopalian, and maintain therefrom twelve Episcopal scholarships, their concern would have known no bounds. The Church of England men, most of them persons of considerable wealth, satisfied their social conscience by giving, each of them, an annual entertainment to the president and instructors, while for the rest of the year they confined themselves to their own social clique. The faculty, on their part, considered that they were doing quite enough in the way of Christian charity when they

CHRIST CHURCH.

accepted these stately invitations every twelvemonth. "Church Row" was the name popularly applied to the homes of these polite citizens, loyal to their king and their Church, most of whom lived on Brattle Street. Their ecclesiastical home, Christ Church, was built in 1761, just opposite the common, its architect being Peter Harrison, who had designed King's Chapel, Boston, seven years before. Its organ was made in London by the renowned Snetzler, and during the Revolution some of its pipes were melted into bullets. Between Christ Church and the Unitarian church lies the old village cemetery, celebrated in the verse of Longfellow and Holmes, in which are buried Presidents Dunster, Chauncy, Leverett, Wadsworth, Holyoke, Willard, and Webber; Andrew Belcher, Cambridge's first inn-keeper; Stephen Day and Samuel Green, the first printers; Thomas Shepard, the first minister; and many another man of the elder day. The first rector of Christ Church was the Rev. East Apthorp, a native of Boston, who wanted, the Congregationalists thought, to be appointed Bishop of New England. Apthorp built a large and beautiful house on Main Street, just opposite the present Gore Hall, which is still called the Bishop's Palace. He was disappointed in his aspirations for the rochet, and was so sensitive to the coldness and the somewhat persecuting antagonism of his theological opponents that he resigned and moved to England in 1764. In his house General Burgoyne was imprisoned after his capture. Subsequently a new proprietor built a third story, for the accommodation, it is supposed, of his household slaves.

Christ Church presents its ancient and shapely front toward Cambridge Common, over which a chime of bells, placed in the tower in 1860, pleasantly rings every Sunday. The common contains some twenty acres, and will always be remembered as the place where the American troops mustered and encamped in 1775. Every morning there started from this now peaceful inclosure the guards for Lechmere's Point, Winter Hill, and the other posts, and here the roughly equipped and poorly drilled provincial troops prepared to lay siege to Boston, held by ten thousand experienced and well-prepared soldiers. At the western end stands the elm under which Washington on July 3, 1775, formally assumed his position as general-in-chief of the Continental army. This venerable tree is, it is thought, of an age far greater than a hundred years. It is surrounded by a simple iron fence, and a plain granite slab tersely records the fact that "Under this tree Washington first took command of the American army, July 3, 1775." Just behind stands the new granite edifice of the Shepard Congregational Church, the pulpit in whose chapel is partly made of wood from a branch of the elm necessarily removed. In the middle of the common, facing the college buildings, is a costly but very ugly monument erected to commemorate the men of Cambridge who fell in the rebellion.

North of the common stands a gambrel-roofed old house, near where the sign of the Red Lion Inn used to swing, which was the home of Abiel Holmes, the annalist of New England, and the birth-place of his more famous son, Oliver Wendell Holmes. To the readers of the doctor's books the house and its surroundings are not unfamiliar. About a hundred and fifty years old, it had among its proprietors before Dr. Abiel, Jabez Fox, tailor, of Boston, Jonathan Hastings, farmer, and Jonathan, his son, college steward. During the ownership of the latter the building was occupied by the Committee of Safety, who established themselves in it in 1775, and formed plans for the collection and management of the provincial forces. In one of the ground rooms Benedict Arnold received his commission as colonel; and here, probably, were the headquarters of General Ward. Washington dwelt in it for three days. It is now owned by the college, and occupied by William Everett, a son of Edward. When Dr. Holmes lived in it the house was in the heyday of its architectural glory, and although it proved a few years ago to be somewhat decayed, recent repairs have pretty much restored it to its old strength. Although the eminent author of the *Autocrat* has always lived in Boston, he has never lost patriotism for his birth-place, in which he seems to consider himself fortunate to have been born. The foundations of his literary reputation were laid here; for in 1829, the year of his gradu-

OLIVER WENDELL HOLMES.

ation, when he was but twenty years old, he sat in one of its attic rooms and scribbled in pencil his poem on the threatened destruction of the frigate *Constitution*, or "Old Ironsides:"

" And one who listened to the tale of shame,
  Whose heart still answered to that sacred name,
  Whose eye still followed o'er his country's tides
  Thy glorious flag, our brave Old Ironsides!
  From yon lone attic, on a summer's morn,
  Thus mocked the spoilers with his school-boy scorn."

HOLMES'S HOUSE.

HENRY WADSWORTH LONGFELLOW.

Brattle Street, which begins at the University Press and extends in a westerly direction, is one of the most venerable of American thoroughfares. The winding course of the street was caused by the necessary avoidance on the part of the Puritan road-makers of the worst parts of the marsh which used to cover this portion of the town. Nearest the university printing establishment is the Brattle House, formerly owned by Thomas Brattle, a Boston merchant, who founded the Brattle Street or "Manifesto" Church in that city. It was the head-quarters of General Mifflin, quartermaster of the colonial troops. In later times Margaret Fuller lived in it, and in her optimistic philosophy "accepted the universe." Judge Story's residence, in which dwelt, too, his son William, the sculptor and poet, is near by. Farther down the street, on the southern side, is one of the most venerable mansions in the country, certainly built during the reign of Queen Anne. Before 1720 it was the home of the Belcher family, one of whom, Jonathan, was Lieutenant-Governor of Massachusetts Bay from 1730 to 1741, and then Governor of New Jersey until his death, in 1757. Its present owner retains, at the age of ninety-one, his physical vigor and his literary tastes, and spends much of his time in his large and choice library. Nearly opposite this ancient mansion, which stands in generous grounds, are the three new buildings of the Episcopal Theological School, established in 1867 by Benjamin T. Reed, of Boston. The pretty St. John's Chapel, pertaining to the school, was built by Robert M. Mason, of the same city, in memory of several members of his family, of whom his father, Jeremiah, of the New Hampshire bar, was the most distinguished.

Few private houses in the United States are so well known as the residence of Henry Wadsworth Longfellow, so often has it been described by affectionate antiquarians and enthusiastic pilgrims. It is not only the

LONGFELLOW'S RESIDENCE.

LONGFELLOW IN HIS STUDY.

home of our most celebrated poet, it also surpasses in historic interest any building in New England, with the sole exception of Faneuil Hall. Its age, as compared with that of other Cambridge houses, is not great. It was built in 1759 by Colonel John Vassall, a firm loyalist, who fled to England in 1775, his property in Cambridge and Boston having been confiscated. Its next occupant was Colonel John Glover, a bold little Marblehead soldier, who quartered some of his troops in the spacious structure. When Washington rode into Cambridge on Sunday, June 2, 1775, he was greatly pleased with the appearance of the house, and having had it cleaned, he established himself therein during the same month. Martha Washington arrived at the house in December, and Washington remained in it until April of the following year. The southeast room on the first floor Washington took for his study, in which the councils of war were all held during the stay of the commander-in-chief in Cambridge. He slept just overhead, always retiring at nine o'clock. The

spacious room behind the study, which Mr. Longfellow now uses for his library, was occupied by Washington's military family, as a rule a pretty large one. A general's "military family," in English parlance, comprised his whole staff. Washington was not averse to a certain amount of official splendor, and was luckily rich enough to carry out his whim in the matter of making his assistants a part of his ordinary household. Trumbull, the artist, complained rather sarcastically that he, for one, could not keep his head up in the magnificent society of the house. "I now found myself," he averred, "in the family of one of the most distinguished men of the age, surrounded at his table by the principal officers of the army, and in constant intercourse with them. It was further my duty to receive company and do the honors of the house to many of the first people of the country." But Washington was thrifty and frugal personally; and his generous maintenance at his own cost of a sort of court was of great service to the colonial cause.

JAMES RUSSELL LOWELL.

The owners of the house after the Revolution were Nathaniel Tracy (whom Washington visited for an hour in 1789), Thomas Russell, and Dr. Andrew Craigie. Talleyrand and Lafayette slept in it, and in 1833 Jared Sparks commenced to keep house within its historic rooms. Everett, and Worcester the lexicographer, also occupied it for a time, and Mr. Longfellow took up his abode in it in 1837. At first he merely rented a room, establishing himself in Washington's southeast bed-chamber. Here he wrote "Hyperion" and "Voices of the Night." In the dwelling, in one room and another, almost all his books, save the two which date from his Bowdoin professorship, have been produced. Longfellow had not long been an occupant of the house before he bought it. Its timbers are perfectly sound. The lawn in front is neatly kept; and across the street there stretches a green meadow as far as the banks of the Charles, bought by the poet to preserve his view. Mr. Longfellow himself, as he draws near seventy, is a fine picture of beautiful manhood. It has been remarked by his friends that his health has much improved since he delivered his poem, "Morituri Salutamus," at the fiftieth anniversary of his graduation. And all Cambridge, down to coal-heavers and hod-carriers, reveres him for his benignity, and remembers him not only as a poet, but as a kind and gentle man.

The Lechmere House, on the same Brattle Street, used to bear a certain resemblance to Mr. Longfellow's. It was built in 1760, or thereabouts, by Richard Lechmere, who sold it to Jonathan Sewall. Both of them were royalists. Baron and Baroness Riedesel had their quarters here as prisoners, and one of them wrote an autograph on a window-pane, which the baron's biographer claims as his, but which is generally supposed to be that of the baroness. West of this Lechmere mansion, lately repaired and raised a story, stands what is probably the oldest house in Cambridge, a building generally supposed to date from the days of Charles II. Its foundations are cemented, like those of the Belcher House, with clay mixed with pulverized oyster shells, since mortar was unknown at the time of its erection.

Quitting this shady and venerable thoroughfare, one sees between Brattle and Mount Auburn streets what is, on the whole, about the most attractive of all the residences of American authors—Elmwood, the home of James Russell Lowell. Save the porter's lodge, an entire square is occupied by the wide grounds surrounding the old house, which is of wood, nearly square, and three stories high. It was built about 1760 by Thomas Oliver, the last Lieutenant-Governor of the province. Four thousand patriots mobbed the house in 1774, and demanded Oliver's resignation; and he, fearing for the safety of his family, handed them back a paper signed thus: "My house at Cambridge being surrounded by four thousand people, in compliance with their demands I sign my name, Thomas Oliver." He went to England in 1776, and died there in 1815. Elbridge Gerry succeeded him as occupant some years later, and in 1817 the Rev. Charles Lowell, father of the poet, bought it of Mrs. Gerry, the Vice-President's widow. Mr. Lowell was pastor of the West Church, Boston, a Unitarian organization, which in these days, under Dr. Bartol, has become a headquarters of the Free Religious wing of that denomination. Mr. Lowell, however, was hardly so radical in his views, and never permitted himself to be called a Unitarian. He preached in the old edifice for the great space of fifty years. James Russell Lowell was born in the house on Washington's birthday, 1819, only two years after his father occupied it, and he has had the somewhat rare good fortune, for this country, of living all his life in his birth-place. He graduated at Harvard in 1838, in the class with Nathan Hale, W. W. Story, Dr. Rufus Ellis, of Boston, Dr. E. A. Washburn, of New York, and Professor Eustis, of the Lawrence Scientific School. R. H. Dana, Jun., and Henry D. Thoreau were in the class before him, and Edward E. Hale in the succeeding one.

Few remember that Oliver Wendell Holmes began life as a law student, and not many more care to know that Lowell did the same thing, and was actually admitted to the bar and opened an office in Boston. Whether his legal duties were arduous or not, he soon relinquished them, and four or five years after his graduation entered the field of periodical literature as editor, with Robert Carter, at present also a resident of Cambridge, of *The Pioneer*, a very æsthetic magazine, for which Poe and Hawthorne wrote, and which went to the tomb after the publication of three numbers. In this magazine William W. Story, then a Boston lawyer, made his first essays in art in the shape of some outlines in the Flaxman manner. Lowell's early volumes were almost all published at Cambridge. Mr. John Owen, who first issued them, and also Longfellow's "Voices of the Night," "Ballads," "Poems on Slavery," and "The Belfry of Bruges," is still alive, and

ELMWOOD.

as he walks around Cambridge, with long white hair and venerable beard, is one of the most noticeable of its citizens. One of Mr. Lowell's first books was dedicated to William Page, the artist, in language of the most extravagant sentimentalism. Those were the days of sentimental friendships; but Page, Lowell, and Mr. Charles F. Briggs, who then formed a triad of kindred minds, still retain their mutual esteem. In 1853 died Mr. Lowell's wife, Maria White, of Watertown, herself a poet; and the next year Longfellow commemorated the event by publishing in Mr. Briggs's magazine "The Two Angels," one of his best poems. From his Elmwood windows Mr. Lowell can look across the flats stretching toward Boston, four miles away, while on the other side lies Mount Auburn. The grounds are not adorned with any modern landscape gardening, but stand in simple beauty, while the tall trees to the westward are almost sombre when the nightbreeze blows through them. The old yellow house is a poet's home, and thither bards, as well as birds, seem naturally to fly. When the owner was in Europe lately for a couple of years he gave his keys, for occupancy of the house, to Mr. Thomas Bailey Aldrich, whose dainty verse was written meanwhile to the crooning of the Elmwood chimneys mentioned somewhere by the elder poet. Mr. Lowell himself is now in the full vigor of middle life. His hair and beard are tinged with auburn and streaked with gray; but he is a muscular bard, in perfect health, and of uniform courtesy and good nature. In his personal appearance, as in the management of his affairs, there is nothing of the traditional heedlessness of the poet. The

poetical nature, he thinks, is akin to order, and in his own case certainly the opinion is true.

Many of the old houses in Cambridge have been torn down or moved away, and not a few have been turned over to Celtic occupants. Of the former the most celebrated is the Inman House, in Cambridgeport, Putnam's head-quarters, now standing on a strange street, and so transformed as to be scarcely recognizable. But of dwellings built in the present century which have already acquired some little interest there are not a few. Thus, Dr. A. P. Peabody, preacher to the university, and well known as an orthodox Unitarian theologian, occupies the large house on the corner of Quincy and Harvard streets, within the college inclosure. It was once used as an observatory, the late George P. Bond having thus occupied it while professor in the college. Dr. Peabody's predecessor in his official chair, Dr. Huntington, now Bishop of Central New York, also preceded him as occupant of this house. Without great age, it presents a stately and dignified appearance well befitting the home of a professor of Christian morals. The town, too, seems to-day quite as attractive as of yore to men of letters, several of its present residents being of our younger authors, not graduates of Harvard, but drawn hither by their literary tastes, and readily domesticated in the old haunts. The most eminent of these newer settlers is William D. Howells. Mr. Howells is an Ohio man, who never went to college, but acquired his education at the compositor's case and the country editor's desk. President Lincoln sent him to Venice, where the duties of a somewhat unimportant consu-

WILLIAM D. HOWELLS.

late left him ample opportunity for study and thought amidst specially attractive and romantic surroundings. He likes, we imagine, his poetry better than his prose, but the public chooses to rank him as one of our best masters of style, and most delicately witty tellers of tales. A man of medium height, of a temperament so happy as almost to seem jovial, he lives in his own house on Concord Avenue, under widespreading trees, and not far from the Washington Elm and the historic common. Toward the town Mr. Howells has proved a most dutiful adopted son, his *Suburban Sketches* having celebrated anew, in agreeable prose, many of her old and new features.

Cambridge contains some cabinet organ, glass, and other factories; but, curiously enough, the only industries by which it is known to the outside world are its printing establishments. The first press in the colonies was set up here in 1639, and the University Press of to-day claims to be the direct successor of Stephen Day's office. The late Charles Folsom made an attempt to organize an establishment which should be after the pattern of the University Press at Cambridge, England, and the Clarendon Press at Oxford, but he failed; and the present University Press is such only in name, not even printing all the college catalogues. There are two other printing houses, the Riverside Press, occupying handsome brick buildings on the banks of the Charles, and John Wilson and Sons', domiciled in an old wooden structure on Dunster Street. The late Mr. Wilson, a Scotchman, was an author as well as a printer, having written a couple of books on punctuation and several treatises in defense of the religious faith he professed.

We have thus traced the records of an old New England town from its foundation in struggle and poverty to its calm and modest prosperity of to-day. In a country none too rich in historic landmarks it has something to remind one of a creditable past. Perhaps Sir Charles Dilke was not unduly enthusiastic when he wrote of it: "Our English universities have not about them the classic repose, the air of study, which belong to Cambridge, Massachusetts......Even the English Cambridge has a breathing street or two, and a weekly market-day; while Cambridge in New England is one great academic grove, buried in a philosophic calm which our universities can not rival as long as men resort to them for other purposes than work."

A VOICE IN THE DESERT.

THE west was gorgeous with the sunset splendor—
 The gathered flowers of Light's resplendent crown;
Bloom after bloom did Paradise surrender,
 As if the Gardens of the Blest came down.

The east was piled with clouds of storm and thunder—
 Huge mountains seamed with bolts of hurtling fire—
Now swept by gales that tore their cliffs asunder,
 And then in weird convulsions heaving higher.

O'er the sun's couch the roses still kept blowing,
 And royal lilies, starred with purple eyes;
And banks of golden daffodils kept growing,
 Soft ridge on ridge, along the glowing skies.

But down the gorges of the storm's sierras
 The rain and hail in roaring cascades fell;
The lightning, playing like a dance of Furies,
 Pictured the nameless scenery of hell.

On the vast plains where I beheld the vision,
 On one side beauty, on the other dread—
Between the Tempest and the scene Elysian—
 An antelope unfrighted bowed its head.

Beside a stunted shrub, alone, unfriended,
 It waited 'midst the awful desert place,
As if at home and tenderly defended,
 Eve's radiance and the storm-glare on its face.

I saw the dying of the western splendor,
 I saw the darkness of the tempest fall,
And heard a mystic voice, in accents tender,
 Out of the brooding Terror to me call:

"O wanderer o'er Life's deserts and its mountains,
 In storm and sunshine, with uncertain feet,
Pining for joy of the immortal fountains,
 And clinging still to all of earth that's sweet,

"One heart is in the thunder and the roses,
 One hand the honey and the gall distills:
He who upon the INFINITE reposes
 His place in Heaven's grand order meetly fills.

"Whate'er his path, however sad its seeming,
 The glory or the darkness overhead,
Upon it Love's unchanging smile is beaming,
 And to the perfect GOOD his steps are led."

5

COLUMBIA COLLEGE

WHEN "God save the King" had given place to "Hail Columbia," and the clouds of war were cleared away, the thoughtful people of the new nation saw that they must build on deep and wide foundations of education. The several colleges existing at the opening of the Revolution — Harvard (founded 1638), William and Mary (1693), Yale (1701), Princeton (1746), the University of Pennsylvania (1748), King's (1754), Brown (1764), Dartmouth (1769), Rutgers (1770) —had suffered more or less from the war, and King's not least among them. Her men had done good service in the patriot cause. "There were early found Jay and Livingston, Morris and Benson, Van Cortlandt and Rutgers, and Troup and Hamilton." The college building had been seized for a barracks, and afterward used as a hospital, and worthy Mr. Lispenard meanwhile loaned a house for the use of Mr. Moore, President *ad interim*, until Tory President Cooper should return. The class of '76 was graduated with six men, and two students were matriculated in 1777, but except for an occasional meeting of the governors, the college seems to have slept a sleep very like death during the turmoil of the war.

In 1784 came a vigorous awakening. In response to an earnest recommendation of Governor Clinton, the Assembly passed an act granting new privileges to King's College, and providing for the establishment of a university.

The scheme which it embodied was a grand one. The "Colledge of the Province of New York," as revived, was to be called Columbia College, and was to be "the Mother of an University" whose influence should be felt throughout the State. In fact, it was at first proposed to name the institution the State College. Accordingly, eight State and city officials, and twenty-four persons, two from each county, were incorporated "by the Name and Stile of the Regents of the University of the State of New York," and were made the governing body of the revived college, as well as supervisors of the schools and colleges which they were expected to found in different parts of the State. The clergy of each religious denomination in the State were authorized to designate a regent from their own body, and the president and a second representative of each school connected with this university system were also to be regents. The regents might hold "Estates to the annual Amount of forty thousand Bushels of Wheat"— to which strait of financial nomenclature the new nation was driven by the confusion of the colonial currency—but might not levy a fine above "the Value of one Bushel of Wheat," nor expel or "resticate" a student without fair hearing. The regents lost no time. Three days after the passage of the act they met at the house of Mr. John Simmons, in the city of New York, and the next day elected Governor Clinton, Chancellor, Hon. Pierre Van Cortlandt, Vice-Chancellor, Brockholst Livingston, Esq., Treasurer, and Robert Harpur, Esq., Secretary to the university. Mr. Livingston, who served the college faithfully for forty years, was, curiously enough, a son of the William Livingston who had so bitterly opposed King's College thirty years before, and Mr. Harpur had been a professor therein seventeen years back. Thus began, a hundred years ago, the first of those repeated attempts to make Columbia a metropolitan university, whose history we shall trace to their successful realization in our own day.

France was then the sister country to our new nation, and the regents promptly expressed their patriotic sentiments at this first meeting by appointing the Rev. J. P. Tetard as Professor of French. The classics were obliged to wait a few days, when Mr. William Cochran was appointed master of the proposed grammar school and college teacher of Latin and Greek. On the 17th of May the first student presented himself in the person of the Governor's nephew, De Witt Clinton—a name afterward illustrious in the Empire State —and being duly examined in the august presence of the Chancellor, the Vice-Chancellor, the Secretary, the Mayor of New York, and Professor Tetard, he was admitted, at the age of fifteen, to the Junior class. His memory is held in great reverence by his *alma mater*, and the chair in which he died, presented by his son, stands, with the chair of Benjamin Franklin, among her especial treasures.

The regents not only examined, through a committee of their body, all candidates for admission, but they drove ahead in the most approved modern fashion. The income of the college was reported at but £1000, yet by December our fearless regents had organized "the four faculties of Arts, Divinity, Medicine, and Law, making the first to comprise seven professorships; the second to consist of such as might be established by the different religious societies within the State, pursuant to the act instituting the university; the third to be composed of seven professors; and the last of three; besides which there were to be nine extra professors, a president, a secretary, and a librarian." The staff of the college during the period of the regency, which lasted until separate trustees were provided by the act of 1787, really consisted of Acting President Moore, Professors Tetard, Cochran (Greek and Latin), Kunze (Oriental Languages), Gross (German and Geography), Bard (Natural Philosophy and Astronomy), Moyes (Natural History and Chemistry), and Tutor Kemp (Mathematics), besides Professors Bard, Kissam, McKnight, Crosby, and Romaine in the School of Medicine. No president was appointed, for lack of funds—though Colonel Clarkson had been sent to France and the Netherlands to procure donations — and the professors took turns in filling the executive chair.

"The Plan of Education," as drawn by the regents, shows what was the real literary standing of our colleges at the close of the war of Independence. Candidates were required to be able only to construe Cæsar, Cicero against Catiline, four books of Virgil, and the Gospels in Greek, "to turn English into grammatical Latin," and "to understand the four first [*sic*] Rules of Arithmetic, with the Rule of Three." The curriculum was essentially classical: for the Freshmen, twice a day, Livy and more of Cicero, Xenophon, Lucian, and Demosthenes, with written Latin exercises daily, and written translations into English once a week; for the Sophomores, once a day, Tacitus, Sallust, Virgil again, more Demosthenes, Homer, Euripides, and Sophocles, and they were "to continue to make Latin every day"; for the Juniors, these or other authors, at the choice of the professor, with Latin compositions; for the Seniors, Longinus, Quintilian, etc., "in their chambers."

In mathematics the student learned vulgar and decimal fractions, extracting the roots, and algebra in his Freshman year, and soared in the Sophomore to Euclid, trigonometry, and conic sections; the Freshman's tasks were completed with English grammar, and "the art of reading and speaking English with propriety and elegance"; the Sophomore's with geography. The Juniors were to be taught logic and natural philosophy; the Seniors, ethics, universal grammar, and criticism.

But a hundred years ago the plan of making Columbia "the Mother of an University," which is now being realized, was premature; and the scheme proved too grand. The original act and others succeeding were codified in 1787, as is witnessed by a copy of the charter and statutes printed "at the Bible, in Pearl Street, M,DCC,XCVI," now among the treasures of the college library. The Regents of the University, as they are still curiously called, became what they now are, a useful supervisory body, to visit, inspect, and report upon the colleges, academies, and schools established within the State; and a separate body of trustees was established "in perpetual succession" for the government of the college. This act, passed April 13, 1787, is said to have been drawn by Alexander Hamilton.

In May, 1787, the trustees found a worthy first president for Columbia in the person of the son of the worthy first president of King's, and elected to that office William Samuel Johnson, LL.D., one of the most distinguished citizens of the young nation. He was then sixty years old. He had en-

WILLIAM SAMUEL JOHNSON.

tered Yale at thirteen, and was the "scholar of the house" who won the Berkeley bounty in the graduating class of 1744. His father said of his two boys: "It was a great damage that they entered so young, and that when they were there they had so little to do, their classmates being so far behind them." After graduating at Yale. the future president attended law lectures at Harvard, and was in 1747 made a Master of Arts by that university, having to pay, as he wrote to his father with great sorrow, £10 for a proper wig and £8 for his degree. In 1766, having already been a member of the Connecticut Assembly, he was honored by his State with the appointment of special commissioner to England to secure the claim to a large tract of land. During his five years' residence abroad he made many friends amongst noted men, and sought out his namesake, the great Dr. Johnson, "as odd a mortal," he wrote to his father, "as you ever saw. You would not, at first sight, suspect he had ever read or thought in his life, or was much above the degree of an idiot. But, *nulla fronti fides*, when he opens himself after a little acquaintance, you are abundantly repaid for these first unfavorable appearances." A family tradition says that when he introduced himself as an American, the gruff old doctor retorted: "The Americans! What do they know, and what do they read?" "They read, sir, *The Rambler*," was the polite

Johnson set sail from Gravesend August 3, 1771, and reached Stratford October 1. His State thanked him "for his constant endeavors to promote the general cause of American liberty," made him a judge, and sent him to the Colonial Congress which met in New York, September 5, 1774, but his appointment as arbitrator on the Van Rensselaer estate at Albany caused him to resign this honor in favor of Silas Deane. In the war of Independence he did good work at home, sending a substitute to the front, and in the constructive period that followed he was one of our ablest statesmen. He represented Connecticut in Congress from 1784 to 1787, and in the Constitutional Convention of the latter year, and he was named first on the committee, with Hamilton, Morris, Madison, and King as his associates, appointed "to revise the style of and arrange the articles agreed to by the House." He was elected President of Columbia College, May 21,

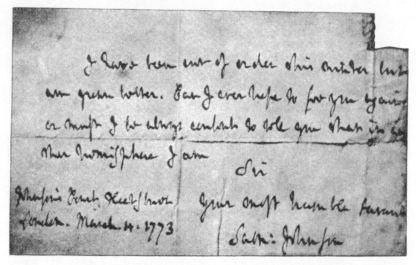

PART OF LETTER OF DR. SAMUEL JOHNSON TO PRESIDENT JOHNSON.

and apt reply, which so won the doctor that before his namesake left London he presented him with "an elegantly bound copy of his large folio dictionary, and an engraving of himself from a painting by Sir Joshua Reynolds, which he considered his best likeness." The two became lifelong correspondents, and some of the letters are still preserved at the Stratford homestead.

At last, successful in his mission, Mr.

1787, and held that office conjointly with that of Senator from Connecticut until after the removal of Congress to Philadelphia in 1793. The bill for reorganizing the judiciary was drawn by him and his colleague, Oliver Ellsworth.

Columbia has good reason to be proud of its patriot first president, and he proved himself as vigorous for the college as for the country. But in 1799, returning through a snow-storm from the meeting

JOHN RANDOLPH.

held in Trinity vestry to lament the death of General Washington, he fell ill; and July 16, 1800, he resigned his post and retired to Stratford. But he lived to marry a second wife that same year, and to pass his ninety-second birthday in 1819.

At the time of Dr. Johnson's accession there were thirty-nine students in the college, nearly half of whom were in the Freshman class. Five of them lodged and boarded in the college, and five more had rooms and studied there. Among those who entered in 1788 were John Randolph of Roanoke, then a pretty and attractive lad, and his brother Theodoric; but the latter left in the Sophomore and the former in the Junior year. The income of the college was about £1330. The faculties of Arts and of Medicine consisted of three professors each; there were no faculties of Law and Divinity, and the only extra professor was a German who served without salary. In 1792, however, the Medical Society of the State urged the trustees to establish the Medical School on a broader basis, and accordingly seven medical professors were appointed, with Dr. Samuel Bard as their dean. A grant was obtained from the Legislature of £7900, and £750 annually for five years, new professors were appointed, an addition was made to the library, and the foundations laid for two new buildings at right angles to the old. But again the authorities seemed to have gone ahead too fast, and when the five years had passed and the grant was not renewed, they were obliged to consolidate the professorships, and, instead of completing the buildings, to sell the materials they had on hand.

BENJAMIN MOORE.

On Dr. Johnson's retirement the senior professor filled his place at the Commencement. Rev. Dr. Wharton, of Philadelphia, was elected to fill the vacancy in May of 1801, but resigned early in December, and it was not till the last day of the year that, in accordance with an understanding that professional duties should be detached from the presidency, Right Rev. Benjamin Moore, Bishop of New York, an alumnus who had been President Cooper's whilom successor six-and-twenty years before, was again made president. The professors were intrusted with the daily charge of affairs, and the college prospered, receiving a fresh grant of lands from the regents in 1802, and completing the hall and recitation-rooms on the north end of the new foundation.

The Medical College enjoyed at this time the vigorous services of Dr. David Hosack as Professor of Botany and Materia Medica. The good doctor, though he got together an excellent library of books, wisely insisted that his students ought to be taught from the living plants, and after several almost successful attempts to induce the State Legislature to provide for a botanical garden, he himself in 1801 "pur-

chased of the corporation of the city of New York twenty acres of ground, situated on the middle road, between Bloomingdale and Kingsbridge, and distant from the city about three miles and a half." By the autumn of 1806 he was able to publish a catalogue of about two thousand species, and in 1810 he succeeded in obtaining from the Legislature an agreement of purchase by the State. Various experts appraised the land at about $2500 per acre, and for the ground and improvements, aside from plants worth above $12,500, for which no charge was made, the doctor received $74,268 75. This tract, then called Elgin, is the property between Forty-seventh and Fifty-first streets and between Fifth and Sixth avenues, no longer "near the fourth mile-stone," but in the very centre of the city. In 1814, to replace certain property ceded to Vermont at the settlement of the boundary, the State gave this land to the college, with the proviso that the buildings should be removed thither within twelve years; but five years later it rescinded this condition, besides granting to the college $10,000 in cash, and the ground-rents of a portion of this property are now one of the chief sources of revenue of the college.

In 1810 the college made a great stride forward. A committee of the trustees, headed by Rufus King, had reported during the previous year in favor of bettering the literary standing of the college. The requisites of admission were accordingly raised with the opening of the college year 1810–11, and a more advanced course of studies was adopted. The Legislature had granted in the spring of 1810 a new charter, one of its provisions permitting the trustees to lease property for sixty-three instead of for twenty-one years, and the trustees, who at this time reported 135 students, expressed their intention "to lay a broader and stronger basis for sound and thorough education than (as they believe) has hitherto been known in these States."

The committee presented a strong and able report, which was for some years printed with the college statistics, and is still of value. It laid down as "the primary principle of all sound education, *the evolution of faculty and the formation of habit*"—a definition curiously in line with the scientific nomenclature as well as the best scientific thought of to-day. It disclaimed any intention "to try that most fruitless and mischievous experiment, the added rhetoric and algebra to the Sophomore; gave the Juniors spherical trigonometry and conic sections from the Freshman studies, ethics from those of the Seniors, and history and chronology;

JOHN McVICKAR.

experiment of educating either the naturally stupid or the incurably idle." The changes in the course of study from the "plan of education" of 1784 added two books of Xenophon and two of Homer, and decimal and vulgar fractions, to the entrance requirements, advanced the classical course so as to leave the Senior studies to the discretion of the provost, transferred Euclid and part of geography from the Sophomore to the Freshman year, and and in the Senior year provided for fluxions, natural philosophy, and astronomy; criticism and universal grammar; history and chronology; intellectual philosophy, logic, and the "law of nature and nations."

To make way for a more concentrated and vigorous administration, Bishop Moore resigned in 1811. Dr. Mason, an energetic leader in the college affairs, was the general choice for the headship of the college;

but the president must by the charter be an Episcopalian, and the doctor was "the champion of the Presbyterians." The office of provost was therefore created for him, and the honorary position was given to Rev. Dr. William Harris—"worthy, paternal Dr. Harris"—"a man," said Professor McVickar at his death, "of a tender heart, great firmness, and deep piety." In 1816, Dr. Mason having resigned the provostship, that office was abolished, and President Harris reigned *de facto* as well as *de jure*, till his death in 1829. During Dr. Mason's administration the medical school had been given up (1813) in favor of a new institution established by the regents under the title of the College of Physicians and Surgeons, which returned to the fold in 1860.

In 1817 the trustees began the long-contemplated improvements in the college building. Two wings, each fifty feet square, were added to the main building, providing residence for four professors, and room for a chapel and library was found in the old building. "How grand," wrote Dr. Haight, in later reminiscences of his Freshman days of this time—"how grand everything about the college seemed!—the stately sycamores on the green, venerable from age, overshadowing the edifice, the old building, the great staircase, the chapel with its strange hanging gallery, the dais at the east end, and the white-haired president in his robes, and the professors on his either hand."

Among the professors of Columbia in these years were many men of strength and note. Dr. Robert Adrain—"Old Bobbie," the students called him—was one of these, serving the college from 1813 to 1825 as Professor of Mathematics. He was "an Irish gentleman, of large size, broad, beaming face, and silvery voice"—a genial soul, and a great lover of chess. Once having heard of an old salt who had "checkmated" pretty well around the world, he put on his old clothes, invaded the sailor's boarding-house *incog.*, and, on beating the old fellow, was amply rewarded with the spontaneous praise, "You must be the devil or Dr. Adrain!" Chancellor Kent, who had been a professor from 1793 to 1798, was re-appointed in 1823 to the chair of Law, and delivered the famous lectures that became the chief commentary on the Constitution.

The college was very proud of the fact that Professors McVickar, Moore, Anthon, Renwick, and Anderson, who for some years constituted the entire faculty, were all alumni. Professor Anderson, who succeeded Dr. Adrain, and served till 1843, is spoken of as a man whose character approached as near to perfection as is permitted to poor humanity. He was strong, able, modest, so versatile in his knowledge of languages that his students were afraid to wager what language he did not know. One day he was noticed listening to a strange conversation on the street; it proved to be Bohemian, which he had quietly added to his stock of tongues. His mathematical ability was still more noteworthy. Mr. A. S. Hewitt tells that he once went with the professor to make some observations at the Observatory at West Point, when it was found that they had left behind some necessary and elaborate formulas. It was ten o'clock at night, and their only chance for the observations was early the next day. "Never mind," said the professor; "go to bed, and I'll see what I can do." By morning he had reconstructed all the formulas from the material furnished by his marvellous memory, and the observations were successfully made. His classical attainments commanded the exacting respect of Dr. Anthon, and he had found time also to train himself in out-of-door work, so that he had several times walked fifty miles in a day.

Dr. Charles Anthon was another of the giants of those days. His father, born in Germany, came to the New World as a British officer during the French war, and was Surgeon-General at Detroit. His mother was the daughter of a French officer. The father was a practicing physician in New York during and after the Revolution, and in 1796 he was made a trustee of Columbia College. The son, born in 1797, entered Columbia at fourteen, and so far surpassed his classmates that he took the gold medal twice, and was accordingly "excluded from competition," as are the pictures of the great artists in the Paris Salon. On graduation he studied law in the office of his elder brother, but though admitted to the bar, it was his appointment in 1820, at the age of twenty-three, to the adjunct professorship of Greek and Latin that determined his life-work. Thenceforward for forty-seven years, till he died in harness in 1867, he devoted an iron frame, an obstinate and unflagging industry, an extraordinary knowledge,

CHARLES ANTHON.

and a patient habit of accumulation, to the instruction of his students and the editing of books. His Horace is believed to be the "first attempt at a critical edition of an ancient author in this country," and his series of text-books, dictionaries, and manuals of antiquities, amounting to forty volumes, covered almost the whole field of the educational classics. The students of to-day scarcely know how much they are indebted to him for making easy and delightful paths which previous writers had blocked with difficulties on the principle that "struggling makes strong." His works, republished in England, made him almost as well known there as here. The *Athenæum* said: "Dr. Anthon has done more for sound classical school literature than any half-dozen Englishmen." Wedded only to his work, he knew no respite and no other cares. His working day was from four in the morning till ten at night. With his students he showed a curious mixture of harshness and friendliness, so that some—probably the lazy ones—recall him as a monstrous tyrant, and others as the embodiment of kindness. One of his chief services to the college was the training of his coadjutor and successor, Professor Henry Drisler, who began his college service in 1843, and is now the honored senior of the faculty.

Professor McVickar graduated at the head of his class in 1804, at the age of seventeen, and at thirty was made full professor. As Professor of Political Economy, which subject was introduced, at his desire, as a Senior study, about 1817, he is said to have given the first course of lectures on this subject delivered in any American college, and in 1825 he published what is said to have been the first work on political economy from an American pen. His *Hints on Banking*, published in 1827, unfolded the principle of free banking under a general statute which is at the foundation of our national-bank system. "Quiet perseverance" was his secret of success. He preached as well as taught, and he had some very clear ideas about churches. "Decorate construction, never construct decoration," said he, strikingly ; and he was a great advocate of free seats: "No proprietorship in the house of God." He also served the college forty-seven years, until he was made an *emeritus* professor in 1864, four years before his death. The roll of Columbia is, in fact, so full of honor-men that it is impossible to continue the roster.

On Dr. Harris's death, in 1829, Hon. William A. Duer, LL.D., "a respectable layman who deservedly stands high in the confidence of the community," became the fifth president of Columbia, and at once the venerable college was called upon to show its prowess. The proposal in 1830 to establish the University of the City of New York roused the trustees—who demurred to two institutions within the city while Columbia lacked $2000 per year of its expenditure—to lay fresh claim to a university *status* by the establishment, in addition to the "full course" for matriculated students, of a "scientific and literary course," open to such persons as might be pleased to attend. For the full course the requisites for admission had in the intervening years been raised by adding algebra. The mathematical subjects were strengthened in the Freshman year. The Sophomores now studied analytical

geometry, descriptive geometry and linear drawing, mensuration, surveying, and navigation ; they had a well-balanced course in physics, including "the *relations* of heat, electricity, magnetism, and light"; their English compositions were to be criticised by the professor in the presence of the class, and they were each to make a weekly analysis of their work in history. The Juniors had reached practical astronomy with the use of instruments, chemistry applied to the arts, and mineralogy and geology, and enjoyed lectures on English and modern literature, "with references to authorities." And the Senior class had undertaken the calculus, mechanics, architecture, and engineering, the history of philosophy, the evidences, and political economy, besides attending lectures from Professor Kent on the constitutional jurisprudence of the United States and on international law. All this marked an advance corresponding to that of knowledge and of the country. The "scientific and literary course" was planned to cover three years, and, as gradually developed, aimed to be "a complete system of instruction for young men designed for civil or military engineers, architects, superintendents of manufactories of all kinds, or for mercantile or nautical pursuits." The applicant was required to have a knowledge of French, and some mathematical and geographical information; he then entered upon a course of studies selected from the regular curriculum, with the French language in place of the classics, and the addition of chemical manipulation, assaying, book-keeping, perspective drawing, and the use of water-colors, and technical drawing "according to the intended profession of the student."

The new scheme introduced many other changes ; nearly a score of public lectureships were provided for, whose incumbents should fix and receive the fees for their lectures; various societies, the religious denominations, and all schools sending at least four students, and any person paying $1000, were to have free scholarships; and any religious denomination or person paying $20,000 endowment might found a professorship and nominate the professor. In the classes students were to be seated, as before, according to their grade of merit, but now a gold medal, awarded to the best student of each class, was to give him individual precedence in the first grade. Two gold medals put the student on an honor list "beyond competition," as a sort of student *emeritus*. Here was, in fact, the germ of a real university, as well as of the scientific school rian as well as professor for some years, became his successor in 1842. He was "a refined scholar," and highly cultivated gentleman of the old school, living a

HENRY DRISLER.

afterward started as the School of Mines; but the scheme came to an untimely end in 1843, when some of the studies were adopted into the regular course, and German added.

On the resignation of President Duer, "the high-toned gentleman," Professor N. F. Moore, LL.D., who had been libra- bachelor's life in the world of books, "of a pleasant petulance and an engaging earnestness," a model of good-breeding. He is described by Dr. Haight as "tall, spare, lithe, with a firm, intellectual face, bearing the marks of years of hard study and close application." He resigned in 1849, and was succeeded by Hon. Charles

King, LL.D., a representative of one of the historic families of New York, and another gentleman and scholar of the good old days, who served the college for fifteen years, till the inauguration of President Barnard in 1864. In 1857 there was established a "post-graduate course," in which Professor Arnold Guyot lectured on physical geography, and Professor George P. Marsh on the English language; but this continued only a year. Nevertheless, the foundations of a university were again laid, and this time more permanently, by the establishment of the School of Law in 1858, with Professor Theodore W. Dwight as warden, by the re-adoption of the Medical College in 1860, and by the modest beginning of the School of Mines in 1863–5, under the vigorous inspiration and efforts of Professor Thomas Egleston, Jun.

For nearly a hundred years the college had found its home in that fine "limehouse" with the cupola which the trustees had proudly completed in 1760. There had been extensions and additions, and the college was proud of its site, its grounds, and that umbrageous and delightful College Place into which old Chapel Street had been transformed; but now commerce was crowding it. The Botanic Gardens were the destined site, and when in 1851 a resolution was passed to "lay out building lots, with space for a church and college," the plot west of Fifth Avenue between Forty-ninth and Fiftieth streets was left at its original level for the college buildings, for which Upjohn was preparing a design. Pending their erection, that portion of the Trinity gift on which the college actually stood was sold, and a temporary investment of the proceeds was made in the old Deaf-and-dumb Asylum and its grounds, between Madison and Fourth avenues and Forty-ninth and Fiftieth streets. The college moved into this temporary home in 1857, and appears to have made this site its permanent one. The east dormitory became the chapel and library, the west one homes for the professors. In 1862 a President's House was completed on the grounds. The war put a stop to the new plans, and now the college is anchored. The old Asylum, with its columned portico, still exists, and is known to irreverent undergrads as the *maison de punk,* but it will soon give way to the new buildings which are to replace it. This site is estimated to be worth over $400,000.

Columbia, under the administrations of Presidents Moore and King, preserved her easy equanimity even into the stirring times of the war, though she was sending many a brave boy to the field, as she had done a century before. But with the inauguration of President F. A. P. Barnard, in 1864, a new era began. He was then a veteran educator, having been graduated at Yale in 1828, and he had been Chancellor of the University of Mississippi until the war drove all Northern sympathizers out of the South, and sent him to Washington. Years before he had been connected with the Deaf-and-dumb Asylum, little thinking that he would be called back to the old halls with this great future opening before them. His inaugural address showed a far look ahead. He was deeply impressed with the university idea, and with the educational needs of the metropolis, and his faith has been justified by works. At his coming, there were but one hundred and fifty students in the college proper, the School of Mines was in an inchoate state, the schools of Law and of Medicine were connected with the School of Arts by the merest thread of association. To-day, a thousand students, under-graduate, graduate, and professional, throng the college grounds, and, with the exception of the Medical College (which has five hundred students in its building on Twenty-third Street, and whose connection with the university consists chiefly in the signing of its diplomas by the President), all the schools are part of a compact and centrally governed university, to which a splendid future is assured.

The trustees had foreseen the need of more room, and each member of the faculty had been requested to furnish an estimate of what the future would demand in his special department. A building was erected for the School of Mines in 1865, but only as a temporary expedient; and in 1871 the trustees appointed a Committee on Site, who examined various locations, and presented three plots to the board for their choice. But in 1873 the pressure for room became insistent, and against the judgment of the president, who entered a written protest on the minutes, the die was cast by the erection of a solid and permanent building for the School of Mines on the old grounds. Columbia has found her permanent home, and her architect has had to meet the difficult problem of housing a great and grow-

FREDERICK A. P. BARNARD.

ing university within the contracted limits of a city block.

The difficulty has been very well met by planning a double quadrangle, both "quads" being open on the south side. Throughout, the architect, Mr. C. C. Haight, has had the good sense to plan from within outward, instead of cramping interior accommodations to provide for architectural effects, and the result of "decorating construction and not constructing decoration" has been as happy as it is honestly reached. The general style of the new buildings is the English collegiate—of whose early examples at the English universities Mr. Haight has been a careful student—worked out in red brick and Potsdam sandstone. Hamilton Hall, which occupies the western or Madison Avenue frontage, is the home of the School of Arts, or college proper, and contains the president's, faculty, and trustees' rooms. In planning it, each professor was given opportunity to state his needs, and the windows, and consequently the entire façade, were worked accordingly. A graceful and slender bastion tower at the upper corner and a hanging bay give variety of effect to this front, and make it, although there are no doorways to provide striking features, an architectural adornment of Madison Avenue. The Fourth Avenue frontage is occupied by the new building of the School of Mines, with fine halls for the geological, chemical, and other collections, and for the drawing-room; and the present site of the President's House will give place for the organic laboratory provided for in the munificent Phœnix bequest, and for large lecture-rooms for the scientific professors. The Fiftieth Street side is now occupied by the older School of Mines building, and by the original asylum edifice, with the chapel and old library adjoining. The site of the asylum will afford room for the graduate schools of Political Science, etc., and the chapel will be replaced either by a new chapel and a college hall, to hold a thousand hearers, or by additional stack-rooms for the library. The Law School below, and the library above, with the observatory in the top of the adjoining tower, occupy the very striking building dividing one quadrangle from the other, which is one of the chief architectural features of this notable group of buildings. It has been completed during the past year at a cost of about $200,000. The interior of this building is finished in brick, and it is altogether a most honest and noble piece of work. The present library building is separated from the old college by a space of only a few inches, which the boys have christened the Pass of Thermopylæ. Under the east quadrangle is the engine-room, connected with the library and the School of Mines by under-ground passages, and the high chimney forms a noteworthy architectural feature of the new School of Mines building.

The most important interior feature of the new building is the noble library hall, a room of grand proportions, with a triple-arch roof supported by iron truss-work, so that the floor space—113 by 75 feet—is unbroken by divisions. A gallery makes the circuit of it, and the walls, within reaching distance of the floor and of the gallery, are lined with that best of decorations, books. The Phœnix collection, of above 7000 valuable and rare books, occupies the entire south gallery. The general arrangement is by subjects, and every frequenter of the library has unquestioned access to the 25,000 volumes here shelved as a reference library. The floor is dotted with tables, to which the reader may freely take as many books as he requires, and as the dusk comes on, a tap of the bell from the librarian's room to the engineer puts at his disposal a movable electric light, which he may turn on or off at will. All the tables have individual lights, and the shades for these burners and for those about the room were so arranged, in consultation with Dr. C. R. Agnew, who is one of the trustees, that all the light falls on the books or tables, and no ray glares into the reader's eye. The assistant librarians have their desks on the main floor, and are ready to put their knowledge of their special subjects at the service of the reader. It is pleasant to note that the conveniences of this library are to be extended not only to the 1600 members of the university and its alumni, but to such other scholars as may rightly seek its privileges; so that what the Astor and Lenox libraries have not given to New-Yorkers, Columbia will

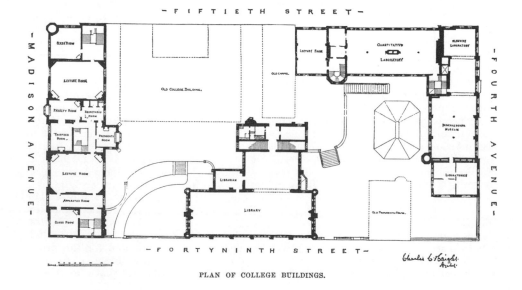

PLAN OF COLLEGE BUILDINGS.

give—a working library open every day in the year except Sundays and Good-Friday, and from eight, morning, till ten, night. modern library co-operation, of which the new librarian, Mr. Melvil Dewey, has been a leading apostle. The modern librarian

A BIT OF OLD AND NEW.

Such facilities as these are made possible only by the adoption of the improved library methods and fittings resulting from the aims, above all, to have his books used, to give them the greatest accessibility at the least possible inconvenience to the reader, albeit to the dire disturbance of the old-fashioned book-keeper, who fears his precious books will be hurt by using. In respect of facility of use, the Columbia College library promises to be the most notable in the country. The libraries of the several schools are now brought together under one administration, and the law librarian, the science librarian, and other specialists are staff officers of the university librarian. They, in turn, have the help of a staff of bright Wellesley girls, of the class of 1883, who are trained as cataloguers and library assistants. The staff hours are so arranged that no one need work more than seven hours. Catalogueing goes on without closing any part of the library; it will require three years to complete the work.

The system of registry, which makes free use possible, is centred in a desk at the very entrance, in the transept of the great hall. This desk is in easy communication, by means of sliding-boxes, with the stack-rooms, in which the body of the collection not needed for reference is packed with such economy of space that a low room, 61 by 22 feet, houses 40,000 volumes. These are, indeed, catacombs of books, with lettered avenues and numbered streets but twenty-six inches wide, so that a book can be had instantly when called for from the card directory below. Each book has pasted inside its cover a pocket, into which slips a book-card; each reader is represented also by a card arranged according to his initials in a case at the registry desk. The book's number is entered on the reader's card; the reader signs his initials on the book's card, which, while the book is out, is kept in a second case at the registry desk, arranged by subjects. Thus any book "out" can be instantly traced, and the receipt for it produced. When a reader wishes to return a book, he has only to hand it in at the registry desk; and if he is in a super-American hurry, he need not wait even the instant required to make sure that the attendant, by stamping the date of return on the book card, has cancelled his receipt. There is no field in which modern organization has achieved a greater triumph than in this single example of library administration.

The library itself has been of slow growth, that of King's College, which should have been its nucleus, having apparently been dispersed during the Revolution, by the seizure of the college buildings for military purposes. In 1806 six hundred volumes from it came to light in a room in St. Paul's Chapel. Several donations and purchases had increased the collection in 1862 to 16,000 volumes, valued at $34,000. In 1882 the munificent bequest of Stephen Whitney Phœnix brought to the college his superb collection. The united libraries in 1883 numbered 50,000 volumes, and the accessions this year add about 12,000 more. In the upper stack-room is housed the fine Torrey herbarium, covering 60,000 specimens, and valued at over $25,000. Above the wing of the library building is the tower and paper dome of the astronomical observatory, with the Rutherfurd telescope and transit instrument.

After many false starts, Columbia College has at last physically and intellectually begun to build thoroughly the foundation of a true metropolitan university. Her system now includes "a School of Arts, a School of Mines, a School of Law, a School of Political Science, and a School of Medicine, employing a president and one hundred and twenty professors, instructors, and assistants"—almost as many as her students in old days—and numbering over fifteen hundred students. To this the trustees have voted to add a School of Library Economy, for the training of librarians, of which the librarian will be the chief professor.

The progress made in the School of Arts since "the plan of education" first cited is interestingly shown by an examination of the present course. The classical course is bettered in the selection of authors, but the chief change has naturally been in rounding out education with the new studies. For entrance, the would-be Freshman must construe more of Cæsar, Cicero, and Virgil than a hundred years ago, and something of Xenophon and Homer in place of the Greek Gospels; he must be versed in English, Latin, and Greek grammar, prosody and composition, writing an English paper off-hand in the examination-room; he must know the elements of ancient and modern geography, of ancient history, of arithmetic, algebra, and geometry. In the Freshman class, the classic authors are Horace and Cicero, Homer and Herodotus; in the Sophomore, Horace (Satires) and Livy, Euripides and Xenophon (*Memorabilia*). In both, the student must elect one modern language, having choice of German, French, Italian, and

THE LIBRARY.

Spanish. The Freshman completes algebra and geometry, with conic sections; the Sophomore reaches trigonometry, mensuration, and surveying, and has a course in general chemistry. The Freshman studies English grammar and analysis, and the history of English literature, with special attention to the prose of Addison and Thackeray; the Sophomore, historical grammar and the poetry of Shakespeare. Rhetoric is a study of both years, and the Sophomore adds German and French history. The elective system was introduced in 1869, and now Junior and Senior studies are chiefly elective, with the exception of, for the Junior year, English, with Anglo-Saxon grammar and the special study of Bacon, Milton, and Spenser, English history, and political economy; for the Senior class, Anglo-Saxon literature and Chaucer, and the constitutional history of the United States. The Junior elective studies include Juvenal and Cicero, a drama of Sophocles, and a dialogue of Plato; analytical geometry and mechanics; heat and electricity; botany, logic, psychology, and a modern language. The Senior elective studies include Terence and Cicero's epistles, archaic Latin and the Latin inscriptions, Æschylus and Demosthenes (On the Crown), comparative philology, differential and integral calculus, astronomy (practical as well as theoretical), and the higher physics, chemistry, botany, geology and lithology, psychology and the history of philosophy, the constitutional history of England and Europe, and political economy. The choice of elective studies is coupled only with the provisions that there must be altogether not less than fifteen hours of college work per week, and that students shall not change their elective studies without permission from the faculty.

STAIRWAY LEADING TO LIBRARY.

After six years of development a competent authority declared that "among all the most famous schools in the world there is not one so well supplied with apparatus, and not one where all the departments are carried on with the same equal care."

The interesting and admirable feature of summer work includes classes in practical mining, started in 1877, in which the men go with pick and drill into the mines alongside the working miners; in mechanical engineering, in which they visit the great foundries and machine-shops of New York city, making working drawings, handling tools, and listening to work-shop lectures from their instructors, in which the workmen, during their noonings, show equal interest; and in geodesy, in which valuable field work is done on the New York State Survey. The membership of the school now includes nearly three hundred students, and it has a capable faculty, of which Professor C. F. Chandler is dean.

The School of Mines is a partial title for what is really a very broad school of science, with six specific courses in mining engineering, civil engineering, metallurgy, geology and paleontology, analytical and applied chemistry, and architecture. For the first of the four years all students pursue a common course, which is a general training in the elements of science and in French, German, and drawing. Thereafter each must select his specialty, and hold to it. The school arose from small beginnings, for Mr. Thomas Egleston, its projector, in his first proposals of 1863, promised that the college should not be asked to support it. A room was provided in the basement of the old college building as a laboratory, to accommodate but twelve students. Twenty-five, however, applied for admission, and during the session of 1864–5 the number reached forty-eight.

The School of Medicine—the College of Physicians and Surgeons on Twenty-third Street, having over five hundred students, with Dr. Alonzo Clark as president—has but a nominal connection with the university; but the School of Law, under the management of its distinguished warden, Professor Theodore W. Dwight, with its home on Lafayette Place, is now housed with the other schools, and is entirely under the government of the college authorities. Its success has been so great that two sets of lectures are required from Professor Dwight, one in the morning and one in the afternoon. Two moot - courts are held each week, for which printed slips containing the case to be discussed are given out to the students in advance, and in which questions of law are argued by six or eight students, and a decision is given by the professor acting as judge;

and these are supplemented by debating clubs, in which students discuss more fully the same cases. The course occupies two years, and above four hundred students are in attendance.

The School of Political Science, the youngest child of the group, which was an outgrowth of the School of Law, has become, under the headship of Professor John W. Burgess, a distinguished member of the university family. It was established in 1880, "to prepare young men for the duties of public life." It requires for admission the qualifications necessary for the Junior class in college, and it awards the degree of Ph.D., after a prescribed three years' course in physical and political geography, the history of philosophy, the history of the literature of the political sciences, the constitutional history of Europe, England, and the United States, Roman jurisprudence, the comparative constitutional law of European states, the United States, and the several States of the Union, the history of diplomacy, administrative law, political economy, statistical and social science. Provision is made for special students in any of these departments. The school has already attracted an attendance of forty students, and it shows growth.

Columbia decided in 1883 to extend its examinations so as to grant certificates of proficiency to such women as prepared themselves elsewhere to pass them. The university idea was further advanced by the establishment in 1871 of two fellowships, in literature and science, which secured to members of the graduating class $500 per year for three years, to enable them to continue their studies at the college or elsewhere, under the direction of the president.

The future should see Columbia, under wise management, one of the great universities of the world. Her "physical basis of life" is a magnificent endowment of real estate valued at over $5,000,000. The progress of the last ten years points to the possibility of a university in this great commercial city which, like the great city universities of the Renaissance, shall attract thousands of students by the facilities for study which only a great centre of civilized activity can supply. With the resources of great libraries, of music, and of art, at her disposal, with the other great educational institutions of the city acknowledging her university character as giving a centre and head to a general educational system, with a true spirit of scholarship which permits no jealousy but always inspires union to a common end, Columbia University ought to be in the next century a source of intellectual and moral strength whose influence shall be felt, through New York, by the whole of America.

FRANKLIN'S CHAIR.

DE WITT CLINTON'S CHAIR.

6

THE FOUNDER OF HARVARD
UNIVERSITY

BY LYNDON ORR

THE ALMOST UNKNOWN ENGLISHMAN WHOSE NAME HAS BECOME
A LANDMARK OF AMERICAN HISTORY AND AMERICAN LIFE

TO the west of the beautiful Memorial Hall, in Cambridge, Massachusetts, stands a statue of John Harvard, who gave his name to the oldest of American universities. The inquiring visitor, who thinks, perhaps, that he is gazing upon a likeness of that gentle-minded scholar, soon learns that such is not the case, and that the statue is purely an ideal one from the hand of Daniel C. French. In modeling it, the artist had not even so much as an old-time print or a bit of personal description to guide his hand. For, curiously enough, although John Harvard's name is known all over the world, the man himself is almost as mythical a personage as Agamemnon, or Homer, or William Tell. Mr. Henry Shelley has lately written a volume about him which extends to more than three hundred pages, and a most ingenious book it is; yet if we deduct from it mere surmise and conjecture, the unquestioned facts could have been compressed within the limits of a single page.

Not very long ago a reward of five hundred dollars was offered for any new information about John Harvard. English records were ransacked. Local traditions were earnestly sought for. Everything was done to wrest from the past a shred or two of knowledge. Yet John Harvard still remains a figure shrouded in the sort of mystery which after the lapse of centuries envelops lives that were in their very nature uneventful.

The meager information that we possess comprises, at least, some points of interest. In the first place, we know that last year was the three hundredth anniversary of John Harvard's birth. His father was one Robert Harvard, a butcher, of Southwark—now a central borough of London, but then a riverside suburb. Robert Harvard apparently died when his son was a little child. The mother married twice after her husband's death, and made good matches, so that she became well-to-do, and sent her son to Emmanuel College in the University of Cambridge, where he remained for eight years, taking his bachelor's degree in 1631 and becoming a master of arts in 1635.

Emmanuel College was a place of quiet learning and decorous living. Archbishop Laud once called it scornfully "a nursery of Puritanism." It is not surprising, therefore, that in the eight years of his residence at Emmanuel, John Harvard turned away from the Church of England and became a nonconforming minister. It was natural, also, that having married Ann Sadler, the daughter of a clergyman, he should, with many of his companions, have emigrated to New England, where in 1637 he became assistant pastor of the First Church at Charlestown, in the colony of Massachusetts Bay.

The young minister knew that his health was already undermined, and he seems to have looked forward to the early death which came to him in the following year. In making his will he desired to do a lasting service to the colony of which he had been made a freeman. Two years before, the General Court of Massachusetts had chartered a college at what

THE FOUNDER OF HARVARD UNIVERSITY

was then called New Towne, and had voted for its establishment the sum of four hundred pounds. John Harvard in his will left to this college an equal sum, and the sum of four hundred pounds was esteemed a munificent gift; so the nascent college was named Harvard College, and the hamlet of New Towne was

STATUE OF JOHN HARVARD, BY DANIEL CHESTER FRENCH, IN THE GROUNDS OF HARVARD UNIVERSITY—THE FIGURE IS PURELY AN IDEAL ONE, AS THERE IS NO AUTHENTIC PORTRAIT OR DESCRIPTION OF JOHN HARVARD

and also his whole library, which contained two hundred and sixty volumes.

At that time, in the American colonies, a library of two hundred and sixty volumes was a noble collection of books, called Cambridge, in honor of the English university where John Harvard had been trained. And this is all that is really known of the man who founded so great a university, and to whose memory during the past year so many impressive tributes have been offered.

Some years ago a skilful and patient investigator, Henry Fitz Gilbert Waters, discovered that Harvard's mother, Katherine Rogers, spent her early years in Shakespeare's town of Stratford-on-Avon. Fortunately—almost by a miracle —the house itself, like Shakespeare's early home, had not been leveled to the ground. It stands upon the High Street, opposite the Corn Exchange, and in its time was a fine old Elizabethan house. The interior was originally decorated with beautiful wood carvings, over which some unappreciative vandal had later spread a coat of plaster. Not long ago it was in a state of increasing dilapidation, when Miss Marie Corelli set herself the task of restoring it and preserving it as a memorial to John Harvard. Mr. Nelson Morris, of Chicago, gave Miss Corelli *carte blanche* to purchase the building and restore it to its early dignity.

The work was done with loving care. The paint and plaster were removed, and the fine old oaken panelings and carvings were once more brought to light. The exterior was artistic-ally treated in the Elizabethan manner. Thus the house in which Katherine Rogers married Robert Harvard now looks as it looked in 1596, and it will remain among the most interesting show-places of the quaint old town of Stratford. It will no longer, as heretofore, be the office of an auctioneer, but will recall the name and the generosity of him who laid the firm foundations of a great university in another hemisphere.

Just as the home of Harvard's mother has been restored and made a permanent memorial, so in Southwark, where his father lived, and where he himself was born, there has been created another Mecca for Harvard men. In the cathedral church of St. Saviour's, close to the south end of London Bridge, there is a baptismal register where one may read the record of John Harvard's baptism on the 29th of November, 1607. Out of the north aisle of the choir opens the chapel of St. John the Divine, one of the oldest parts of this beautiful medieval building—older, indeed, than the church itself, since beneath its Norman walls there is a foundation ascribed to Saxon times.

THE HARVARD MONUMENT ON BURIAL HILL, CHARLESTOWN, MASSACHUSETTS—JOHN HARVARD WAS INTERRED IN THIS OLD CEMETERY, THOUGH THE EXACT SITE OF HIS GRAVE IS UNKNOWN

HARVARD HOUSE, STRATFORD-ON-AVON, RECENTLY RESTORED AS A MONUMENT TO JOHN HARVARD—THIS WAS THE HOME OF HIS MOTHER, KATHERINE ROGERS
From a photograph by McNeille, London

St. Saviour's is an edifice of immense historic interest; and, curiously enough, its associations are full of literary memories, and especially of memories which associate it with the stage. It is an odd coincidence that John Harvard's mother should have spent her maidenhood in Shakespeare's town, and that John Harvard and his brothers should have been baptized in the church where Shakespeare's brother Edmund was laid to rest. Philip Massinger and John Fletcher, the dramatists, are also buried here; while the parish records note the death of Richard Burbage, who first created the part of *Hamlet* under the eye of Shakespeare himself. Chaucer's fellow-poet, John Gower, also rests here; and there is a memorial window commemorating Edward Alleyn—an actor of

Shakespeare's time, and a churchwarden of St. Saviour's—who founded Dulwich College, and of whom Francis Bacon said: " I like well that Alleyn playeth the last act of his life so well."

Some time ago a number of wealthy Harvard graduates resolved to restore the chapel of St. John, and provided the money needed to strengthen the crumbling walls and check the ravages of time. A beautiful painted window, from the hand of John La Farge, was set

vard Memorial Chapel, in the presence of the American ambassador, Mr. Whitelaw Reid, the mayor and corporation of Southwark, and a very distinguished company of Americans and Englishmen. Mr. Reid officially delivered the restored chapel to the bishop on behalf of Harvard University. In his brief address he declared that the American institutions of learning, such as Harvard, Yale, Dartmouth, King's College (Columbia), and William and Mary, which Englishmen

THE CHAPEL OF ST. JOHN THE DIVINE, IN ST. SAVIOUR'S CATHEDRAL, SOUTHWARK,
RECENTLY RESTORED AS A MONUMENT TO JOHN HARVARD, WHO WAS
BAPTIZED IN THIS HISTORIC LONDON CHURCH

From a photograph by Underwood & Underwood, New York

there; and a panel of glass, at the left of the altar, is flanked on the left by the arms of Harvard University and on the right by the arms of Emmanuel College.

Last July, the chapel was rededicated by the Bishop of Southwark as the Har-

had founded long ago, were to-day among the strongest ties that bind Great Britain and the United States together; since they indicate not only a common origin and a common faith, but also the same aspirations and the same ideals.

7

The True History of the Founding of the University of California

BY SAMUEL L. LUPTON

FACTS of history sometimes grow dim in the past, the memories of men fail, and when the living witnesses pass away it is not always an easy task to rescue the truth from oblivion. The University of California has now been in existence for the period of time usually allotted as the duration of one generation, and the men who brought it into existence have nearly all passed away. It seems to me the true history of its foundation should be recorded, while there are yet some living witnesses.

On July 2, 1862, Congress passed an act under which this State became entitled to 150,000 acres of public land for maintaining an agricultural and mechanical arts college.

When the legislature met in December, 1865, the State was but fifteen years old. At this session William Holden, a lawyer from Ukiah, represented Mendocino County as an Assemblyman. Notwithstanding the burdens of the people of the State had been great and taxation heavy, Mr. Holden was in favor of accepting the grant of the Government and establishing and providing support for a State College, and he proposed, in making the effort to carry out this purpose, to have the institution located, if possible, in his part of the State.

We therefore find on page 135 of the Journal of the Assembly at that session, under the head of introduction of bills, this entry, "By Mr. Holden, for an act to establish an Agricultural and Mechanical Arts College in Sonoma County. Read first and second times, referred to a select committee of five, and the usual number of copies ordered printed."

On page 138 of the same journal, we find, "The speaker announced the following special committee on agricultural college, Messrs. Holden, Hunt of Santa Clara, Reed, Smith of Eldorado, and Meredith."

The Reed here mentioned was Charles F. Reed, assemblyman from Yolo County, and who was at the time the president of the State Agricultural Society, and the Hunt, assemblyman from Santa Clara County, was A. B. Hunt, a lawyer, and now registrar of the United States Land Office in San Francisco.

On page 271 of the same journal, a clerk was allowed the committee, on motion of Mr. Holden, for one week.

The special committee appointed on Mr. Holden's Bill was in favor of the purpose of the bill, but not in favor of fixing the location in Sonoma County, and favored the changing of the title and purpose of the bill to "An Act to Establish an Agricultural, Mining and Mechanical Arts College." The committee therefore adopted a substitute to the original bill so as to put the three leading industries of the State upon an equal footing.

Accordingly on page 372 of the same journal, we find this entry, "Mr. Holden made the following report, 'Mr. Speaker: The special committee to whom was referred Assembly bill No. 49, an act to establish an agricultural and mechanical arts college in Sonoma County, have had the same under consideration and report it back to the Assembly with a substitute therefor, and recommend the adoption of the substitute.

Holden, for committee.'

"On motion of Mr. Holden the usual number of copies of the substitute above

Bridge and walk made by students in 1896.

reported was ordered printed."

This substitute was passed by the legislature and became a law March 31, 1866.

On page 702, same journal, we find, Mr. Holden introduced, "An act to provide for the selection of the lands donated to the State of California by the Act of Congress, approved July 2, 1862, for the endowment of colleges for the benefit of agriculture and the mechanic arts, and all lands that may be granted to the State for like purposes," which act became a law April 2, 1866.

On page 770, same journal, we find Mr. Holden offered a joint resolution for the meeting of the Senate and Assembly in joint convention for the purpose of electing five directors for the new college, which joint resolution was adopted.

The joint convention was held, and Messrs. Joseph B. Meader, Henry Phillips, Felix Tracy, William Holden and C. F. Ryland were elected directors, (see Assembly journal pages 803, 806, 809), to act in conjunction with the three ex-officio members, who were the Governor of the State, F. F. Low; the president of the State Agricultural Society, Charles F. Reed; and the president of the Mechanics' Institute of San Francisco, who was at the time, I believe, A. S. Hallidie, the inventor of the cable street-car system.

Thus the organization for the establishment of a State College was put in motion, and William Holden was all through the proceedings leading up thereto the moving active agent thereof.

When the State once resolved and undertook to establish a State college, "a high seminary of learning, in which the graduates of the common schools can commence, pursue and finish a course of study, etc.," its character and usefulness in the future was necessarily but a matter of evolution and development. The title by which this institution was named was the one used in the act of Congress making the grant of land with the department of mining added. The word college was used therefore instead of university, although the latter was used in article IX of the first State constitution, wherein it was provided that all grants of land made by the general government, or others, in the past, the present or in the future, should be carefully protected, and the fund accruing from the rents or sale of such lands, or from any other source, shall be a permanent fund for the support of a university, (that is when the fund got to be large enough to establish a university), "for the promotion of literature, the arts and sciences."

In the memorial of the State Constitutional Convention to Congress asking for the admission of the State, on motion of William M. Gwinn, who was afterwards for twelve years United States Senator from this State, and the most influential representative the State has ever had at the National Capital, a grant was asked of public lands for the founding of a university. There were, however, at that time not people enough west of the Rocky Mountains to support a university.

The word university was not used as advisedly in those days as now. It was then often used to mean simply a higher class of college. Practically universities did not exist in the United States in those days. Even Harvard and Yale were then commonly known as colleges instead of universities by name. The so-called universities at that time in the United States were generally such only in name, and were institutions of comparatively minor educational importance and standing.

When this Agricultural College bill had become a law, the directors met, organized and elected Governor Low President of the Board. They then selected a site for the State College, which was located about a mile north of the present site of the university.

Prior to this time there had been several colleges established in the State. In 1851, the Methodists had established a college at Santa Clara and which is now known as the University of the Pacific. Very early in the fifties the Catholics had also established a college at Santa Clara, now known as Santa Clara College. These colleges have graduated many students.

Another college known as the College of California principally under Presbyterian and Congregational influences, had been established about 1860, and it was located in Oakland. This college was the outgrowth of a classical school or seminary established by Doctor Durant. It had no president but the Rev. Dr. Willey, the vice-president, acted as such. Having the advantage of location, being near the leading commercial city, San Francisco, and the then center of the State and convenient to its controlling influences, a strong effort was made by its several professors to bring to its support the men of education and the possessors of wealth. A list was made of all the known graduates of colleges of the United States residing in the vicinity of the bay. Invitations were sent to them to attend the commencement exercises of the college, and their aid and interest sought in all available directions. The institution, however, was sorely pressed for means, and placed its hope for future development and strength upon the support of the influences above mentioned which it sought to draw around it. It had, however, obtained title to 160 acres of land where the university now stands, and which had at the instance of Frederick Billings been named Berkeley. This college was in existence for five or six years and graduated about twenty students during that time.

The passage of the bill to establish the State Agricultural College, and its proposed location near Oakland, was to this college of California as the handwriting on the wall. Its friends knew that the influences on which it must depend for prosperity and support would gather around the State institution, and that their college could not for want of support exist with the State College in its immediate neighborhood.

The proposal to establish this new agricultural and mining college met with such universal support and encouragement from the men of education in the State and the tax-payers that its future was assured. Those having charge of the College of California saw this. They could not absorb or unite the new colleges with theirs, for the act of the legislature expressly prohibited its being united or connected with any other institution of learning in the State, and also from in any manner whatever being connected with or controlled by any sectarian denomination, while the College of California was at least a semi-Presbyterian and Congregational institution.

Such being the state of affairs with the College of California, those who controlled its affairs concluded that they might as well join in with the friends and supporters of the new college and help it along for the general benefit of the State. They therefore consulted with the friends and directors of the new State institution in regard to its future. As they had resolved to quit business and disincorporate, they agreed to turn over to the directors of the State College the 160 acres of land where the State University now stands, so that the location selected by the directors of the State College could be relinquished. This proposition was accepted. They also asked that the law be so extended that distinct provision should therein be made for a classical department for the new institution, as well as the departments for instruction in agriculture, mining and the mechanical arts, and for future extensions or affiliated colleges.

These suggestions all coincided with the views of the directors and friends of the new institution, and all agreed that the title of the new institution was cumbersome and inconvenient for use. It was therefore fully agreed by all concerned that the title of "University of California" should be adopted. It was also deemed wise to change the method of selecting directors and their number. These matters being fully agreed upon the trustees of the college of California stipulated to turn over to the State institution whatever assets it might be possessed of.

A bill by consent of all parties having interest therein was drawn embodying these proposals and agreements, and was introduced into the legislature at its next session by John W. Dwinelle, a prominent member of the San Francisco bar, and a graduate of Hamilton College, and who was at the time a resident of Oakland, and a member of the Assembly from Alameda County. Of course this bill being intended to supersede the old law, as it did, was carefully drawn, though since many times added to and amended, and was designed to cure what crudities or imperfections existed in the original law. It was the result of two years' experience and reflection of the directors and friends of the new State college. It became a law March 23, 1868. When it passed the legislature, William Holden, who had been in the mean time elected Lieutenant-Governor of the State, and acted as president of the State Senate, advocated the passage of the bill. It substituted the more mature and perfected new law for the old one, and repealed the old one. If, however, the Holden bill had not been a law, the new bill introduced by Mr. Dwinelle and which became the substituted law, would never have had an existence.

I think these facts show that William Holden was the father of the University of California.

I was not uninformed about college matters in this State at that time, for a fellow college student, my senior in age and in classes, became in the early fifties one of the Professors of the University of the Pacific at Santa Clara, and remained with that institution for a number of years; while a college classmate of mine was the instructor in mathematics in the college of California at the time the agricultural bill became a law. In Rev. Dr. Willey's history of the College of California will be found a list of the known college graduates residing in t is vicinity at this time and whose interest and influences were sought in behalf of the welfare of that college. My name appears in that list.

When the Holden bill was passed establishing the agricultural and mining college, and the Dwinelle bill was passed as an amendment or substitute therefor, I was at both sessions a member of the Assembly from San Francisco, being at that time elected by the city at large. I voted for and actively interested myself in the passage of both laws. I felt so much interest in the matter that, when the Holden bill was passed, I wrote an article calling public attention to the law, and urging encouragement and support to the new institution. It was published as an editorial in the Evening Examiner, October 23, 1866.

The writing of this present article has been incited by the fact that the only formal history of the University of California published that I know of, and which seems to have the endorsement of that institution, intimates strongly that the reason the university was not founded earlier was because the people of the State were ignorant, and had to be educated up to the point of realizing the necessity and advantages of such an institution. It even intimates that the legislature was occupied in passing bills for the establishment of prisons and that the one that passed the Holden bill, was too ignorant to know enough to pass a bill establishing a State university at once. The exact language being, "Thus, in their blindness, did the legislators of 1866, seek to defeat the predestined organization of the university," thus attacking the real founders of that institution. As inducing causes to the establishment of the university, it recites vain acts of individuals of more or less erratic character, but whose efforts were devoid of effect or influence. It also gives great credit to persons who delivered speeches on occasions such as college commencements, in which the establishment of a university in the future was predicted, just as a fourth of July orator would predict the advancement, growth and glory of our republic in the future, drawing vividly on his imagination, regardless of fact or conditions, and had about as much influence in one case as in the other. The first thirty or forty pages of that history I believe to be untruthful in theory and fact. It assumes facts and gives cr dit where such does not belong, and withholds or suppresses credit from those to whom it belongs in connection with the foundation of the State College or university, and its intimations in some instances are wholly without just foundation. I believe it is due to the people of the State and to the character of the university that that part of the history should be rewritten.

The extraordinary circumstances under which California became a part of the United States, and was rapidly settled and became a State of the Union and has grown into a great commonwealth, passed so rapidly into history and under such uncommon and exceptional circumstances that it seems often difficult for the generation of to-day to comprehend fully the changes that have occurred, the growth that has been ma 'e, or the circumstances under which events took place or the trials and difficulties encountered by the early residents, not to say pioneers.

When the United States forces took possession of California in 1846, there were in this great State, which is seven hundred miles long and from two to three hundred miles wide, only about 5000 white inhabitants, with perhaps ten thousand so-called domesticated Indians, the wild Indians being unestimated. These few people were scattered over the surface of this great State. Yerba Buena, of which the great commercial city of San Francisco is the successor, had at the time about 300 inhabitants, while cities like Sacramento, Stockton, and Oakland had none or only a nominal existence.

In 1850, when California was admitted as one of the States of the Union, its entire population was 92,597.

The character of this population and that of a few years after that date and its burdens, seem nowadays not generally understood.

The civilized world was electrified by the stories of the discovery of gold in 1848, and when the truth concerning the existence of gold became generally known intelligent, enterprising men of every State in the Union and every civilized and semi-civilized country in the world, began to wend their way to this State. It was as if the unfixed, unanchored possessors of energy and intelligence in the world bent their way to California. They came by steamers or sailing vessels around Cape Horn, or from south of the equator, across the Isthmus of Panama, or from the distant Orient, while others sought to reach the same destination by traveling thousands of miles across the uninhabited, trackless and unknown plains and deserts, and over the Rocky and Sierra Nevada Mountains, in those days thought to be a trip to be undertaken only by the most hardy and venturesome, while fierce Indians and dangerous wild beasts were likely to be encountered at any hour of night or day.

Some of these people came with their families, others came to repair or make their fortunes and then return therewith to their homes. Many came and many after a short stay returned, some with fortunes, others without. But others, attracted by the climate and business opportunities, and who saw a great future for the State and city, remained here to make their future homes.

The enterprise which these people displayed was extraordinary, the endurance heroic, with hope ever undismayed, one failure resulting usually but in another effort. Intelligence of the highest order dominated these people. All through the Placer mines, and in every branch

of business were found educated and experienced merchants, lawyers, doctors, and all kinds of professional or semi-professional and educated men. While the mechanics and common laborers were of the highest intelligence and energy of their class. The trip across the plains or a long distance by sea to reach this State required large sums of money for an outfit and for cost of passage, and the people generally who in those days could command such sums were people of energy, enterprise, and character.

Of course there were some others. There are in all communities. But there never has been a day in the history of the State of California that the large majority of the people of our city and State was not peaceable, orderly, and law-abiding, and of the better class of citizens. The other elements that came to the surface like the froth of the sea were, when deemed necessary, severely dealt with, and human life and property in the early fifties and later on was, generally speaking, as safe throughout this

A glimpse of the University campus.

Among the Berkeley oaks.

city and State as it is to-day. Considering the fact that many thousands of people from all parts of the Union, and in fact from all parts of the world, were suddenly thrown together in quest of gold and fortunes, the record is astonishingly creditable. The world's history had never recorded like circumstances.

No ordinary men laid the foundations of this city and State. Many of them had held high positions in their former homes, and many in after years became distinguished or wealthy men in all the States of the Union, as well as here in our own midst. Many officers of the army and navy became citizens, and when the Civil War broke out this State contributed from among its then or former residents such men as Halleck, Sherman, Hooker, Geary, Grant, McPherson, Baker, Stone, Fremont, Hancock, Naglee, Dent, Sheridan, Ord, Lippitt, and others, and to the navy Farragut, and to the Confederate side Albert Sidney Johnson. All of these men had relations with the people and their affairs, and had influence in the community. Many educated, energetic and ambitious young men who had just started in life, or who had just completed their college course, were here and gave their best energies and efforts to the building up of these communities.

At the time the Civil War had commenced, it has often been said and among the older residents thoroughly believed, that no city of the same size as San Francisco could have in all respects produced a people, in proportion to population, the superior of those to be found then in our city. The Civil War, however, and the discovery of the Bonanza and Constock mines and the completion of the overland railroad produced great changes in our population.

From 1856, for ten or twelve years after the Act consolidating the City and County of San Francisco went into operation, this city had no superior as to government in the world. The public officers were thoroughly honest, thoroughly capable, intelligent in the performance of all their duties, and gentlemanly to all who had personal or business intercourse with them.

The extent of the burdens these people had to bear in building up a great State from the very foundation, as from the naked earth, is not always remembered.

These 92,597 people, constituting the population of the State at the time of its admission into the Union, and their successors, were compelled to build a State house and State prisons, insane asylums, County Court houses and jails, hospitals, wagon, and stage roads and bridges, trails across the mountains, school houses and churches, and even the houses to live in and to do business in. Gas and water works had to be established, all taking capital to do so, while all building material had to be brought from a distance.

They had to contribute to the building of telegraphs, stage lines and railroads, and establish all the industries of the State, and their efforts met with discouragement or were unsuccessful. In many instances, as in mining, new methods had to be devised and put into operation. Coal was brought around Cape Horn. Hundreds of miles of streets had to be graded, sewered, curbed, paved and sidewalked in the cities and towns, which themselves had to be created and the ground to be graded and made orderly.

Agriculture was comparatively unknown, orchards and vineyards had to be planted as an experiment as to soil and climate, tons of clippings for the latter being brought from Europe. Land was held in large tracts. In many instances the most desirable parts were held under Spanish or Mexican grants, and was used only as grazing places for cattle and horses, with a few sheep.

State, city, town, and county governments had to be established. At the beginning the State was under military rule. Irrigation was unknown. Ditches had to be made to carry water to the mines, mills had to be erected, and tunnels run to the mines. The flour consumed had to be brought from Chili or some far distant port. In 1852 San Francisco was destroyed by fire, and a like fate at various times befell many of the interior towns, while Sacramento, in consequence of floods, was compelled twice to raise the grade of her streets ten feet. In the winter of 1861-2 many parts of the State were flooded, doing great damage, especially in the Sacramento and San Joaquin valleys, and the Legislature was compelled to adjourn to San Francisco, while in 1863 a great drought caused many thousands of cattle to die for want of pasturage and water.

In 1861 the Civil War broke out, and the State was compelled to meet the additional burden of fitting out five or six regiments of soldiers and maintaining them during the war, yet neither the State nor the city had any public debt.

Millionaires were unknown in those days, the bonanza mines on the Comstock had not yet yielded their millions. Many men became poor holding on to land and paying taxes, while hoping it would improve in value, and the result of many extensive and expensive enterprises were still undetermined. California was the young mother of the States and territories west of the Rocky Mountains. She was the first admitted into the Union. It was her capital, energy, and people that discovered and first developed the resources and industries of those States and territories.

Under such circumstances, here partly set forth, the burden was considered to be too great and taxes too heavy to undertake to establish a college at State expense, until the National government lent its aid by grants of land. The man who attacks the intelligence of energy of the early settlers of this State but manifests his ignorance of facts, and attempts to pervert truth. The exercise of intelligent energy in this State in those days was so universal as to e looked upon as a matter of course.

When the university was finally set going, the brothers John and Joseph Le Conte were called from South Carolina, and were made professors, the former of them being elected President. Professors Durant and Kellogg, both former professors of the College of California, were also made professors. This latter fact and its attendant associations may in some degree account for the excessively partial statements made in the published history of the University as to the participation of these latter gentlemen in its origin, notwithstanding the fact that the passage of the bill for the establishment of a State college was without their procurement or wish.

In conclusion I would say: All honor to William Holden, the country lawyer, the father of the University of California.

8

Stanford University—the Real and the Ideal

BY CECIL MORTIMER MARRACK

GREAT colleges go in pairs. Less than twelve years ago a throng of people gathered at Palo Alto for the exercises at the opening of Leland Stanford Junior University. In less than twelve years the brightest pages in the educational history of California have been written, and she has given to the world another illustration of the value of intellectual emulation. Oxford and Cambridge, Harvard and Yale, Stanford and the University of California— all have responded to the quickening impulse of a noble competition.

President Jordan once remarked, "When the university was opened it was the opinion in the east that there was as much room for a new university in California as for an asylum for broken down sea captains in Switzerland." The first entrance examinations at Stanford seemed to bear out this disheartening opinion. Three candidates were present —two men and a woman. It spoke well for the educational standards of the new institution that the two men were turned down. Today the two great universities of California stand in the first rank and their halls are overflowing with enthusiastic young men and women. Every state in the Union has its representation at Berkeley and Palo Alto, and the influence of these two great centers of intellectual activity is unbounded. The sec-

DONAGGHO, PHOTO, PALO ALTO

STANFORD UNIVERSITY, PALO ALTO, CALIFORNIA, LOOKING EASTERLY TOWARD SAN FRANCISCO BAY FROM THE HILLS ABOVE THE LAKE

SECTION OF DESIGN OF ST. GAUDENS, CARVED IN STONE UPON THE
AS A DECORATIVE FRIEZE, PORTRAYING

ondary schools of the state have felt and responded to it, so that today it is said: "There is more education to the square inch in California than in any other part of the United States."

President David Starr Jordan of Stanford University must always be dear to Californians as the man who is most of all typical of the spirit of western education. Rugged and direct, with a touch firm and unwavering, and yet fine enough, his true work was just what he has made it—that of a pathfinder for things higher. His life has been strenuous and he must surely have fallen by the way if he had breathed anything of the spirit of the effete centers of the old learning. As it is, his steps have been unfaltering, and even when he has been the center of storms he has met them with the unswerving poise of our granite boulders. It is he who has interpreted into educational possibilities the unparalleled munificence and devotion of the Stanfords, and at all times it is he who has kept before the students of the uni-

DONAGGHO, PHOTO, PALO ALTO

ENTRANCE TO MAIN DRIVE, STANFORD UNIVERSITY, MEMORIAL ARCH AND CHURCH IN THE
DISTANCE

STANFORD MEMORIAL ARCH, THE DESIGN RUNNING ABOUT THE ARCH
"THE PROGRESS OF CIVILIZATION IN AMERICA"

versity their indebtedness to the founders. Much of his success as president has been due to the unique relations that have existed between the students and himself. President Jordan possesses none of that aloofness which is too often regarded as the necessary accompaniment of "culture." His students admire and respect him—more than that, they love him. Their feeling of camaraderie is natural, for the humblest freshman is sure of recognition and a polite tip of

MEMORIAL ARCH, STANFORD UNIVERSITY, SHOWING FRIEZE BY AUGUSTUS ST. GAUDENS

SECTION OF DESIGN OF ST. GAUDENS, CARVED IN STONE UPON THE
AS A DECORATIVE FRIEZE, PORTRAYING

the slouch hat when he passes the "Prex." on the quad.

Dr. Jordan's scientific specialty is ichthyology and his work in that field, while it has covered a wide area, has been of the highest order. In 1896 he assumed charge of the Government commission for the fur seal investigations. As a result of political conditions the work of that commission was of international importance. He has directed a great number of scientific expeditions for the Government in all parts of the world, and has been a most prolific contributor to the literature of science.

To Europeans the most wonderful feature of our civilization is the generosity of American philanthropists in the cause of education. They cannot appreciate the spirit behind the gifts of a Rockefeller, a Carnegie or a Stanford. And yet the influence of any institution must be measured to some extent at least by its material equipment, and that university is indeed fortunate which can press forward to the fulfilment of its ideals with-

DONAGGHO, PHOTO, PALO ALTO

LOOKING FROM AN ARCHWAY INTO THE QUAD, SHOWING ARTISTIC ADAPTATION OF MISSION
ARCHITECTURE

STANFORD MEMORIAL ARCH, THE DESIGN RUNNING ABOUT THE ARCH
"THE PROGRESS OF CIVILIZATION IN AMERICA"

out being hampered financially. The endowment of Stanford University is greater than that of any other two institutions of learning in America—amounting to over $30,000,000. It consists mainly of interest-bearing securities, and a landed endowment of over 100,000 acres. The Vina estate in Tehama county and the Gridley estate in Butte county are the largest tracts. In the erection of the university buildings it has never been necessary to touch the principal of this vast endowment. The interest has met all requirements.

The location of the university is ideal. The Santa Clara valley is, in climate and natural beauty, one of the most attractive portions of California. It is protected from the fogs and winds of the coast, and yet is close enough to the sea to escape the summer heat of the interior. Over thirty thousand acres are included in the university estate, which stretches up into the foothills of the Santa Cruz

DONAGGHO, PHOTO, PALO ALTO

MEMORIAL CHURCH, STANFORD UNIVERSITY, A MARVEL OF ARCHITECTURAL BEAUTY.   SHEPLEY,
RUTAN & COOLEDGE, CLINTON DAY AND E. C. HODGES, ARCHITECTS, AND
JOHN D. M'GILLVRAY, CONTRACTOR

mountains. To the east, Lick Observatory crowning Mount Hamilton, the highest peak of the Monte Diablo range, stands out in the sunshine. To the southwest, between the valley and the ocean, the heavily-wooded mountains rise to the height of four thousand feet.

If old Father Junipero Serra could be put down in the Stanford "quad" he would doubtless rub his eyes in bewilderment and then breathe the complacent sigh of one whose fondest dreams are realized. In all that he saw—in ivy-clad arches and red-tiled roofs, in rough, brown stone, and in the slender cross glittering against the sky two hundred feet in air—the good padre would recognize his cherished mission architecture in its fairest form.

In the long drive up the avenue of

LOOKING TOWARD THE CHANCEL, MEMORIAL CHURCH, STANFORD UNIVERSITY

palms, from the university entrance to the quadrangle, the arch, massive and majestic, gives a fitting presage of the glory that it guards. Towering like the triumphal arches of imperial Rome, the beauty of its detail saves it from becoming too formidable. The sculptured frieze represents a noble conception of the American sculptor, Augustus St. Gaudens. Right around the arch pass majestic figures, vividly presenting the "Progress of Civilization in America." The central figure, tall and fair, represents, "Civilization," the beginning and the end of the processional scene. Columbus, taking his mission from "Providence," tears the veil from "America" and makes way for the long line of Spanish crusaders and the Franciscan friars and Pilgrim Fathers, who, under the guidance of "Liberty" and "Religion" open up the glories of the new world.

LOOKING WESTWARD TOWARD THE ORGAN GALLERY AND ROSE WINDOW, MEMORIAL CHURCH, STANFORD UNIVERSITY

Above the frieze is a corbelled arch course terminating in a parapet wall four feet above the roof. A circular iron stairway leads up to the roof from which there is a superb view of the surrounding country.

Right across the quadrangle is the Memorial Church. The original rudimentary architectural design of Shepley, Rutan and Cooledge, who drew the plans for the inner quad, has been developed and ennobled by Clinton Day of San Francisco. Although surrounded by the majestic buildings of the outer quadrangle, the church fulfils the original architectural conception by its dominating pre-eminence. From every point on the campus it is the spire with its glittering cross which first meets the view, just as the notes of the great organ roll out, and the sweet chimes of the tower bells ring across the tiled roofs and greet the ear. The architecture is a modification of the Moorish and Romanesque and the ground plan is in the form of a cross with rounded ends. It is almost two hundred feet long through vestibule, nave and apse, and over one hundred and fifty feet wide through the transept. The buff sandstone has lent itself readily to the most elaborate effects. Flying buttresses and ornate columns help to beautify the exterior of the most costly church in California.

IN THE QUAD AFTER THE RAIN

The beauty of the interior defies description. The soft light floats down from the windows in the great dome aloft. The rich glass in the arms of the transept flashes out blood red and royal purple against the neutral tints of the natural stone and the yellow-brown of the wood work. In the choir gallery at the rear the massive silver pipes of the great organ tower up on each side of the little console—the instrument has nearly three thousand pipes and forty-six stops.

Much of all this the awe-stricken visitor observes with the half-felt expectancy of something yet to come, for he has caught a glimpse of gold and color from the altar in the apse, where all the glory centers. For months Venetian workmen labored to reproduce, in the most costly mosaics, the richest treasures of mediæval art. Regardless of expense and with a precision now-a-days so rare, Signor Del la Toffola Angelo and his assistants have wrought for an effect worthy of their art. The whole frame of the altar, one hundred and forty feet from floor to ceiling, is rich with color and gleaming with gold. To right and left of the central group representing the Last Supper, are long panels—the "Gloria die Angeli." Michael Angelo's "Prophets," heroic marble figures of the Apostles, and the smiling faces of innumerable cherubim carved in the soft sandstone, help to complete a scene almost bewildering in richness and variety of detail. The ceiling, which springs from the crown of the great arches, is also finished in a mosaic of angels with trumpets. It narrows to a small open circle which shows the frescoed ceiling of the true dome high above the floor. Over the organ gallery is a great rosette window with the Christ child as a center picture, and the large windows of the nave and transept all illustrate the life of Christ.

The Assembly Hall and the Library are adjoining buildings of the outer quadrangle. The former has a seating capacity of seventeen hundred and, with its stage and dressing rooms, possesses all the conveniences of a modern theater. Not far away from the main quadrangle stands the recently completed chemistry building, now only awaiting its laboratory equipment to make it one of the finest in America. Close at hand the workmen are setting in place the last

VAUGHAN & KEITH, PHOTO   PRESIDENT DAVID STARR JORDAN

stones in the building to be used by the history department.

To the students who witness this daily growth of the college buildings there comes the most delightful sense of proprietorship. The development of character and the adding of stone to stone seem to be naturally harmonious processes. And this feeling of contented participation in the growth of the university is quite typical of the "Stanford spirit." It is the natural accompaniment of the college life which centers on the univer-

sity campus. Within the last few years the fraternities have all moved out from Palo Alto to the campus and their propinquity has induced a marked neighborliness and good fellowship. The new houses are all handsome and substantial.

But Encina Hall—the men's dormitory—remains what it was intended to be, the real center of college spirit. It is a superb structure—four stories high, and built of the same rough brown stone as the quadrangle. Electric lights, hot and cold water, steam heat, numerous

99

DONAGGHO, PHOTO, PALO ALTO
MUSEUM RECEPTION HALL, STANFORD UNIVERSITY

bathrooms—everything ministers to the physical comfort of the three hundred students who occupy the rooms. The large clubroom with its billiard and pool tables, is used as a trophy room and, because of its associations, is rapidly becoming a center of historic interest. The class dances are all held there, and every Friday the men have an informal "stag" on the polished floor.

When the visitor has been through the university buildings and taken in its wealth of equipment, it is difficult for him to realize that this is but the beginning. It needs the evidence of his senses to convince him that ground is being broken for the new buildings which are to complete the group. The full greatness of Stanford University lies in the future.

California is destined to become the center of the world's influence. Long years ago, Von Humboldt, the scientist of statesmanship, foresaw the coming glory of the Pacific slope, and predicted the advancement of Anglo-Saxon civilization from the "right hand of the continent." Already the fulfilment of his vision has come to pass, and the eyes of the world are directed from our shores out across the Pacific to the lands of the slumbering east. From California and from the Pacific coast must radiate the life to graft the principles of liberty upon the ruins of the dying empires of the Orient. Upon western men and upon western women has fallen the privilege of advancing the fulfilment of their Nation's destiny. That privilege is a great one, and will bring with it problems demanding for their solution all the faculties of minds well trained. Our universities have risen to meet the needs of the new century. These have been but years of preparation. Even yet the giants are girding themselves for their task. Stanford is just emerging from the "stone age." On every side are signs of untiring activity. And yet the creak of derricks and the shouts of workmen never seem to disturb the quiet-eyed girls and stalwart college men seeking knowledge at Leland Stanford Junior University —the tribute of devoted parents to the memory of an only son.

Stanford Red

*One of the songs of the students of Leland Stanford Junior University, Palo Alto, California;
written by Charles K. Field, '95 (Carolus Ager); air, "Gipsy John," by Frederick Clay*

The jolly stars are burning!
　Then lay your work away,
With song and story spurning
　The drudgery of day;
The cheer is on the table set,
　The smoke is overhead,
Tomorrow brings him no regret
　Who drinks to Stanford red!

CHORUS

Then all together, lustily,
　Your glasses fill again;
A health to you, a health to me,
　A health to Stanford men,
So everybody, lustily,
　We'll be a long time dead;
A health to you, a health to me,
　A health to Stanford red!

The soldier marches singing,
　The song may be his last;
The sailor's voice goes ringing
　Above the icy blast;
But free from care for life and limb
　Our hearty songs are sped—
No war nor water threatens him
　Who sings the Stanford red!

The world outside is sleeping,
　Small heed of it have we;
One vagrant thought still keeping,
　One tender memory;

For more than all the songs and wine
　My love desires instead
The little heart that lies on mine
　And beats for Stanford red!

The day was almost ended,
　The sun was dropping low;
In blue and golden blended
　We watched the daylight go;
But soon a change prophetic came,
　The gaudy colors fled,
A glory filled the west with flame
　And all was Stanford red!

FOR THE FOOTBALL TEAM

The Team is lining up, boys,
　Our banner burns in air,
We'll pledge in one more cup, boys,
　The men that keep her there,
And cheer them onward to the test
　By Stanford spirit led;
He dares to fight his level best
　Who fights for Stanford red!

FOR ALUMNI

The campus lies behind us,
　Some miles and years away,
And sundry things remind us
　The distance grows each day;
But though some memories grow dim
　When years count up toward ten;
The golden age returns to him
　Who drinks with Stanford men!

STANFORD UNIVERSITY MUSEUM, CONTAINING MANY RARE COLLECTIONS

9

THE FUTURE OF THE UNIVERSITY OF CALIFORNIA

By Benjamin Ide Wheeler

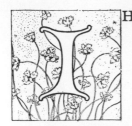

I HAVE been ten days in California and nine days in the president's office of its University, and every day has added to my admiration of the institution and enhanced the wonder I feel before its inner power and its unmeasured opportunity. I accepted the presidency without knowing the half. It stands by the gates of that sea upon which the twentieth century is to see the supreme conflict between the two great world-halves. It is set to be the intellectual representative of the front rank of occidentalism, the rank that will lead the charge or bear the shock. In the Old-World struggle between East and West, the Ægean was the arena and occidentalism militant faced east, orientalism west ; in the new struggle occidentalism faces west, orientalism east. The arena is the Pacific. The old struggle made Constantinople the seat of cosmopolitanism ; San Francisco is appointed by the fates of geography to be the cosmopolis of the next era. All this one could know and foresee without setting foot in the land of sunshine ; but until one has felt the life and power there is pent up in the University of California one does not know how far California has advanced toward preparation for her task. For years the University has gone on in quiet development. Foundations have been laid strong and sure. Devoted lives have built themselves solidly into its walls. Less effort has been spent on tower and minaret to catch the eye of the far world than on the substantial construction of wall and buttress. Square and plummet have been faithfully used. Every day as one studies the structure one marks the traces of wise forethought and consecrated patience. Many have been the hands of faithful builders, but the wise prudence of President Kellogg has built with a soundness which commands, as I am daily coming to appreciate it more and more, my sincerest admiration. He has brought the forces of the inner university into unity and coöperation and laid this solid foundation upon which the university of the future will build. It is the only sure foundation upon which any university life can build.

The possibilities of work opening before the University and the obligations of service to the State and the nation exceed in their far-reaching importance those which are involved in the mission of any other American university. Its relation to the schools of the State through the accrediting system indicates a peculiar responsibility, and one which must be exercised, in order to be effective, in a spirit of the largest wisdom

C. M. Davis Eng. Co.

Photo. by O. V. Lange.

THE UNIVERSITY OF CALIFORNIA AND THE GOLDEN GATE.

Looking west from the Berkeley Hills.

103

and of fullest sympathy with the work and mission of the secondary schools. The College of Commerce just founded represents a field of activity in which the State can be benefited most directly and in most timely fashion. If properly developed, it will provide men suited to the opening need of a nation that is suddenly awakening to find itself an exporting rather than an importing country, and that is soon to be before the world a creditor nation instead of a debtor. This school will collect, collate, and teach information regarding the conditions and demands of international commerce, the state of markets, the methods of trade. It will provide the commercial missionaries, trade agents, and consuls of the next generation.

The existing departments must be fostered and developed. Among them are included some that rank already with the best in the country. New departments cannot be established to the detriment or hindrance of what already exists. The department of agriculture is already highly efficient and under superb leadership. California will justly demand that nothing be spared in the development of this work. Especially in relation to the culture of fruit-trees (pomology) and horticulture, provision for extension of the work must be provided. A department of forestry ought to be established at the first opportunity. What does California need more for its naked hills and its thirsty brook-beds? What does the whole Western slope of the continent need more for its desert stretches? Ultimately this must be a problem for the national government to deal with, but California must lead and point the way.

A harbor that produced the "Oregon" deserves to have by its side a school of naval and marine engineering. Some large-minded citizen of California will yet arise to see this opportunity and provide for its satisfaction. We cannot look to the State for everything; we must not. Private wealth can find no surer way for large public usefulness than in such endowments at the University of California. It will be a healthy state of things when every Californian who writes his will remembers to insert a clause making the University his beneficiary either for small or great—a thousand dollars for a scholarship or a special book-fund, ten thousand dollars for a lectureship, seventy-five thousand for a professorship, two hundred thousand for a department.

The new plan for buildings, which Mrs. Hearst's far-seeing wisdom and generosity have provided, offers every variety of opportunity for the consecration of wealth to noble public use. By no device known to man can wealth be established in such abiding form and monument as when delivered to the keeping of a great university whose life spans the generations; by no device is it assured a nobler use. Among all the manifold

C. M. Davis Eng. Co.

SOME OF THE PRESENT BUILDINGS.

Photo. by O. V. Lange.

needs of the University none ranks above the need for a great library. The isolation of the Pacific Coast from the centers where thus far the world's history has made the great deposits of the world's accumulated experience and lore makes peculiar and emphatic demand that here be established a New World's great Alexandrine Museum. The present library is utterly inadequate to the uses of the University. If we are to attract and hold here the ablest scholars, we must give them tools and material to work with. First there must be a fire-proof library building capable of indefinite extension for the storage of classified treasures of books. Without this we cannot ask men to give funds for the purchase of books. Then we want book-funds. A university-class or an individual can give to the University for the purchase of books either on a specified subject or without specification a fund small or great. The income of this will be expended each year in perpetuity, and the donor's book-plate will appear as recognition in the books thus purchased. Reckoning the average cost of a book at two dollars, a gift of $1000 will put twenty-five books into the library each year while time and order last. This is an illustration of what university endowments mean. The needs and openings I have mentioned are only samples.

The appeal which this University today makes to the loyalty and generosity of its State, is such an one as no opportunity for the uplifting of man and society has ever made since the light began to shine abroad.

10

THE PAST AND PRESENT OF THE UNIVERSITY OF CALIFORNIA

By Elmer Ellsworth Brown

THIS University has, in fact, had three origins. The first is the grant of lands from the national government—the seminary grant of two townships in 1853, and the still more important allotment of 150,000 acres under the Morrill act of 1862.

The second origin is found in the old College of California, incorporated in 1855 and formally opened in 1860. This was an old-line, undenominational, Christian college. It was founded and carried on with that whole-hearted devotion to higher education, in the face of overwhelming discouragements, which has made the history of American colleges heroic. Its career was crowned with an act of institutional self-sacrifice, such as has rarely been seen. A bill had been passed by the State legislature in 1866, devoting the Federal land grants to the support of a narrow polytechnic school. The trustees of the College proposed in 1867 to turn over to the State the valuable lands which they had secured at Berkeley, opposite the Golden Gate, together with all other assets of the College remaining after its debts were paid, provided the State would build upon the proffered site a University of California, to include permanently both classical and technical colleges. They agreed that when this should have been done, the College would disincorporate.

The third origin of the University is found in the organic act by which it was finally established. This act was prepared by one of the trustees of the College of California. It was passed by the legislature in March, 1868, and was approved by the governor on the twenty-third of that month. After some slight modifications, it was put beyond the reach of more legislative amendment by being re-affirmed in its entirety in the new State Constitution of 1879.

The charter established the University distinctly as an in-

C. M. Davis Eng. Co.   LOOKING WEST FROM THE UNIVERSITY.   Photo by O. V. Lange.
Mt. Tamalpais in the distance.

stitution of the State, and made it possible for this institution to become one of the chief centers of civic interest and pride. It provided a system of administration which tended to prevent the University from becoming in any narrow sense a representative of the State government : which made it instead a real educational representative of the State as a whole. Full control was intrusted to a Board of Regents, twenty-three in number. The chief State officials are *ex-officio* members of this board, as are also the presidents of the State Agricultural Society and of the Mechanics' Institute. The remaining sixteen members are appointed by the governor, with the concurrence of the State Senate. Their terms are sixteen years in length, and two are appointed every second year. These provisions are of the greatest practical importance ; they bind the University firmly to the governmental system of the State, but at the same time guard it against abrupt change with each

C. M. Davis Eng. Co. GOLD MILL, COLLEGE OF MINING. Photo. by O. V. Lange.

C. M. Davis Eng. Co.   E. Benard, Archt.
GENERAL GROUND PLAN.

change of the party in power. The arrangement is favorable to real freedom and responsibility.

The endeavor is made continually to avoid anything like isolation from the vital interests of the State. This appears, for example, in the effort on the part of the College of Agriculture to keep in close touch with the farmers and orchardists of the State, through publications, correspondence, and farmers' institutes; in the courses of university extension lectures and other public addresses which are given by University men in all parts of the State; in the close connection maintained between the University and other portions of the State educational system; in the inspection and accrediting of high schools, and in the preparation of teachers for such schools. In the inspection of high schools, the University is not seeking primarily to secure students for itself, but rather to build up strong schools.

The University as now constituted consists of Colleges of Letters, Social Sciences, Natural Sciences, Agriculture, Mechanics, Mining, Civil Engineering, Chemistry, and Commerce, located at Berkeley; the Lick Astronomical Department at Mt. Hamilton; and the professional colleges in San Francisco,

C. M. Davis Eng. Co.   Photo. by O. V. Lange

MACHINE SHOP, COLLEGE OF MECHANICS.

namely, the Mark Hopkins Institute of Art, the Hastings College of Law, the Medical Department, the Post-graduate Medi-

C. M. Davis Eng Co.   ROOM IN PHYSICAL LABORATORY.   Photo. by O. V. Lange.

cal Department, the Colleges of Dentistry and Pharmacy, and the Veterinary Department.

One of the earlier legislative schemes for the University, introduced in 1858, proposed to unite under a Board of Regents "all the colleges then established and thereafter to be established in the State, with whatever faculties they might have, and wheresoever situated"—a plan probably suggested by the University of the State of New York. The charter finally adopted for the University was not so comprehensive. Yet it made liberal terms for the affiliation of suitable educational institutions. Under these provisions the schools of art and the professions in San Francisco have entered into the affiliated relation, as appears above. A few years ago the Regents, because of their reputation for sound management, were made trustees of a fund for the establishment of a trade school. The Wilmerding School has been established in San Francisco under their direction, in accordance with the terms of this bequest.

The State has provided, in San Francisco, a new building costing $250,000, in which the several professional schools are to be brought together. Ample and attractive quarters are thus provided for all of the affiliated colleges, excepting the Institute of Art, which is housed in the fine residence built and occupied for a time by the late Mark Hopkins. These professional schools are making notable advance in their equipment, their instruction, and their requirements for admission and graduation. The Medical Department enforces an entrance requirement equivalent to that in the colleges of general culture, and a full four-years' course for graduation.

The Lick Observatory at Mt. Hamilton is an integral part of the University and sustains a very close relationship with the Department of Astronomy at Berkeley. In addition to the superior equipment provided for this Observatory by the bequest of James Lick, including the great 36-inch equatorial, numerous gifts of valuable pieces of apparatus have been received from time to time. Chief among these is the three-foot reflecting telescope presented by Edward Crossley, Esq., of Halifax, England.

On the noble site provided for the colleges at Berkeley, there have been erected from time to time such buildings as were imperatively needed. There are now thirteen of these, some of them substantially built of brick, but the most of them temporary wooden structures. Yet unsightly and inadequate as the present buildings may be, they house collections and equipment of great value. The University library contains not far from 80,000 volumes, selected with great care. Students have direct access to the shelves, and the actual daily use which is made of the books is astonishing.

In the library buildings there are the beginnings of a collection of paintings, including some works of considerable value. The general museum is especially rich in collections of California minerals, fossils, birds, and shells, and of ethnological specimens. Many valuable additions have recently been made to the zoölogical collections. The Agricultural Department has extensive collections of seeds, beetles, and specimens of soils. The several engineering departments have valuable collections of machine and other models. The botanical collections include, in the phænogamic herbarium, about twenty-five thousand sheets of mounted specimens, and in the cryptogamic herbarium over four thousand sheets, besides important collections of native woods and cones. There are valuable collections of mathematical models, of coins and medals, of photographs illustrative of classical archæology. These things may be found described in detail in various University publications. But this brief reference to some of the more valuable collections may serve to show that promising beginnings have been made.

It would require an extended notice, too, to give any adequate account of the various University laboratories; but the general remark should be made that, owing to the great care exercised in the making of purchases and in the keeping up of repairs, there is a surprisingly low percentage of waste observable in them, and a correspondingly high degree of practical usefulness is secured. The physical, chemical, botanical, zoological, mineralogical, and various agricultural laboratories are well equipped for both under-graduate work and advanced research. The students' observatory at Berkeley leads up to and supplements the work of the Lick Observatory at Mt. Hamilton. It is equipped with seismographs and instruments for meteorological observations. All of the technical colleges are well supplied with laboratory facilities. Special mention should be made of the extensive provision which has been made for experiment and demonstration in mining, mechanical and electrical engineering. The new psychological laboratory is admirably housed and equipped, and proves a very valuable addition. There are botanical gardens and a well stocked conservatory on the grounds at Berkeley. Here, too, is the central agricultural experiment station, which is supplemented by four sub-stations, two forestry stations, and a viticultural station, in various parts of the State.

The courses in the several colleges of general culture lead to different degrees—A. B. in the College of Letters, B. L. in that of Social Sciences, B. S. in that of Natural Sciences. The course leading to any one of these degrees consists of 125 semester units of instruction, of which 65 units are prescribed —including various options—30 units are group-elective, and

C. M. Davis Eng. Co.

E. Benard, Architect.

THE PHEBE HEARST PLANS FOR THE UNIVERSITY.
General Perspective of Grand Reception Hall.

C. M. Davis Eng. Co. ROCK DRILLING, COLLEGE OF MINING. Photo. by O. V Lange.

30 units are free-elective. The group system is now firmly established. It assures the student the command of a fairly large range of closely related knowledge, and also makes possible a considerable advance into the higher methods of the subject elected.

The great expansion of graduate work in the past few years has been accompanied with a stiffening of the requirements for higher degrees. For the degree of Ph. D. in particular, the requirements are severe and are strictly enforced. The Engineers' degrees in the technical colleges rest upon requirements substantially equivalent to those for the degree of Ph. B.

The value of the property belonging to the University on the first of July, 1899, was estimated at a little over $4,426,-000, and the several endowment funds at the same time amounted to something more than $2,843,000; a total—"plant" and endowment—of over seven and one-quarter millions. These figures include the property and endowment of the affiliated colleges and of the Wilmerding school. The total income for the year ending June 30, 1899, was, in the general fund $364,940.45 ; and in special funds, $127,715.86 —a total of $492,656.31. This includes the sum of $220,-090.64 raised by the permanent tax of two cents on each one hundred dollars of assessed valuation in the State; and the sum of $26,564.56 the income for the year from the Wilmerding fund. It does not include the income of the affiliated colleges.

A highly significant point in the history of the University was the unanimous passage by the legislature, in 1897, of a bill doubling the permanent tax for the University, which had up to that time been only one cent on the hundred dollars.

This institution has been conspicuous among the State universities of the country for the number and value of the gifts which it has received from private individuals. Prominent among these should be mentioned the bequest of $700,-000 left by James Lick for the establishment of the Lick Observatory ; the gift of $75,000 from Mr. D. O. Mills, for the endowment of the Mills professorship of intellectual and moral philosophy and civil polity ; the bequest of Michael Reese, $50,000 for a library fund ; the gift of a tract of land by Hon. Edward Tompkins for the endowment of a chair of Oriental languages and literatures ; the gift of a fine estate and dividend-bearing stocks to the value of three-quarters of a million dollars from Miss Cora Jane Flood ; and numerous scholarships, provided by Mr. Levi Strauss, Mrs. Phebe Hearst, and others. This list is far from being exhaustive. The extremely liberal provision made by Mrs. Hearst for the recent architectural competition, and her promise to erect valuable buildings as soon as plans shall have been finally adopted by the Regents, are matters of such general interest and information at this time as to call for no extended mention here.

The athletic interests of the University serve as its first introduction to many who afterward come to know and care for others of its varied activities. *Clean sport* is the ideal to which these athletes have held with great fidelity. The athletic team which went out from Berkeley in 1895 to make a tour of the leading Eastern colleges, set a high standard for both gentlemanly behavior and the winning of events ; and these things have come to have a fixed place in the University traditions. The military side of University life is maintained on a high plane under officers assigned to this duty by the general government. Our young collegians were prompt to respond to the call for troops in 1898. They rendered intelligent and courageous service. And three of them gave their lives to the cause.

The student body at Berkeley in the year 1898–99 numbered 1716, of whom 953 were men and 763 women. 194 of these were graduate students. Including the number at Mt. Hamilton and in the professional colleges in San Francisco, the total University enrollment for the year was 2438, of whom 908 were women. Within the first few weeks of the current academic year, the registration of students at Berkeley has surpassed that for the whole of the year preceding, which makes it altogether likely that the total enrollment at Berkeley for the year will reach at least 1900.

Connected with the University in all of its departments are 118 officers of administration, and 365 officers of instruction and research ; 149 of the latter number being employed in the colleges at Berkeley. In the attempt to give some hint of the general spirit and purpose which makes the University of California itself and not another, it must not be forgotten that the men who have taught here during the generation that the University has been in existence have more than all things else determined the character of the institution. Among these, a goodly number marked by high scholarship, great moral force, and world wide reputation, have given to the University standards and traditions which must be reckoned among the choicest of its endowments.

Berkeley, Cal.

THE UNIVERSITY THAT REACHES ANYBODY, ANYTIME, ANYHOW

Sending a State to College

WHAT THE UNIVERSITY OF WISCONSIN IS DOING FOR ITS PEOPLE

By Lincoln Steffens

Author of "The Shame of the Cities," etc.

ILLUSTRATED WITH PORTRAITS AND PHOTOGRAPHS

I T is related of a professor at the University of Wisconsin that one day when he was coming through the grounds, carrying under one arm a copy of Geiger's "Humanismus" and under the other a cheese purchased at the College of Agriculture, he stopped a couple of his colleagues to ask, with humorous nods at his burdens, if he "didn't illustrate pretty well that this was a university." He didn't; but another man did. This other man may be described as the Milwaukee drummer for the university at Madison. He led me out to one of the great machine shops of Milwaukee, where, in a room and "in time" set aside by the firm for "the school," he showed me a class of mechanics taking and paying for the regular correspondence course in "shop mathematics" under the direction of the faculty of the state university.

Cheeses and Prize Pigs

The learned professor with his Latin book and his college-bred cheese only illustrated pretty well the realization at Madison of the old ideal of a university: "a place where anybody may learn anything." And a more striking illustration would be a farmer's family of which I heard. The son was on one of the 'varsity teams, the daughter was in the College of Letters and Science, and the mother and father came to Madison in the winter, the one to attend the "Housekeepers' Conference" in the College of Agriculture, the other the Farmers' Course: ten days in which the professors come into the ring with their horses, cows, pigs, pumpkins and apparatus to show and, as one of them put it, "rub in" to the ever-increasing hundreds of "old farmers" who come there, the results of the year's scientific experimentation in grain and cattle breeding and feeding, etc., and in the chemistry of dairying—of which the professor's cheese was a mere commercial by-product.

Madison is indeed a place where anybody who can go there, may learn anything. And between five and six thousand people do go there; all sorts of people, young and old, rich and poor, men and women from everywhere; and among them they do learn almost everything. Which sounds universal. But it isn't, of course. The population of Wisconsin alone is two and a quarter millions. The great majority cannot go to Madison, ever, even for ten days. They all contribute to the support of this state university; they all need, and many of them want to learn something—as the fortunes made by the private correspondence schools prove. The University of Wisconsin is reaching for these people. It has organized a public correspondence school and the Milwaukee class in shop mathematics is but one of many such "schools" by means of which the university is mailing instruction out to the homes, farms and shops of the people who cannot go to Madison.

Breaking thus the bounds of Madison, the university is breaking also the bounds of that old definition of a university and setting up a new ideal for education. The University of Wisconsin is offering to teach anybody—anything—anywhere.

Harvard Degree for Madison

President Eliot of Harvard has characterized the University of Wisconsin as "the leading state university." This glowing title was conferred formally after deliberate study. State universities have been growing rapidly of late, particularly in the West, and the older, private institutions of the East have felt the effect. Western students have been staying West. Eastern educators have been asking why and some of them have gone West themselves to find the answer. President Eliot is one of these. He lingered at Madison. He showed his interest plainly. He saw the new things being done there. He heard about the very latest experiments, the Farmers' Course and the Correspondence School, and he shook his head dubiously at first over these. He inquired critically into them; he asked jealous questions about the old things: the scholarship, pure science, the morale of the classical courses at Madison. Were the departures sound? Was the old suffering from the new? And President Eliot must have been pretty well satisfied, for at the next commencement, June 24, 1908, Harvard conferred a title upon the University of Wisconsin, in these indirect but unmistakable terms:

"Doctor of Laws: Charles Richard Van Hise, pre-Cambrian and metamorphic geologist; professor successively of metallurgy, mineralogy and geology; president of the *leading state university*, the University of Wisconsin."

Now the achievement of this title is recent and Madison's hold upon it may be brief. Ann Arbor (Michigan) used to be first and some educators think that Illinois soon will be, with Cornell, California, Michigan, Minnesota and Missouri close up in the van. But I am not reporting a race. On the contrary, the point is that the University of Wisconsin is only the leader in a movement general among the state universities; a great movement which promises well for this Republic and for civilization; an educational counterpart of that still greater democratic movement visible all around the earth. Government everywhere is being democratized and the beginnings are here of the democratization of industry. The democratization of knowledge is in sight at the University of the People of the State of Wisconsin.

Whether the democratization of the university is a result or the cause of the democratization of the state of Wisconsin is a local question which Senator La Follette and President Van Hise answer. The leader of the democratic political movement, Mr. La Follette, says that the university started him. As governor, he helped to have his classmate, Van Hise, made president of the university, but President Van Hise, who has studied the history of the educational movement, goes back to Oxford and Cambridge, the British parents of the American college, and, in his recent addresses outlines the American development as a great natural evolution, moving largely and in two ways: expansion and extension,—the expansion of the scope of the studies and the extension of the numbers and kinds of students taught.

Aristocratic in spirit, the English schools were exclusive both as to studies and as to students. "And," says Dr. Van Hise, "the original American college was essentially a counterpart of the English . . . well into the nineteenth century." Greek, Latin, belles-lettres—the liberal arts were the means used to cultivate young gentlemen. "For a long time in the East, science was regarded as an intruder and when finally grudgingly given a place in some of the more important institutions it was made an appendix to the college, and, in a number of cases, a new name was attached, illustrated by the Lawrence and Sheffield Scientific Schools" at Harvard and Yale.

Eastern Origin of Western Colleges

The West led in the expansion of the curriculum. As the older Eastern colleges followed the British, so the Western state universities followed the Eastern model, and, at Madison for example, the "liberal arts" are

PRESIDENT CHARLES RICHARD VAN HISE, WHO CANNOT
SEE WHY HIS UNIVERSITY SHOULD NOT REACH ALL
THE PEOPLE OF WISCONSIN STATE ALL THE TIME

still the heart of the university. But there was a difference from the very start. Partly because the West was more utilitarian and democratic, partly because the state, not private persons, endowed the Western universities, they let science in on the ground floor, and progress was so rapid and general that Dr. Van Hise can say that "no one doubts now the right of pure science to full admission to the list of subjects which may be pursued for a liberal education."

"Pure science" means to learning about what "art for art's sake" means to æsthetics, and Dr. Van Hise fights hard for it. He has to. The utilitarianism of the West has its narrowness, too, and "practical" regents want teachers to teach; they don't want them to be pottering around making experiments the ultimate use of which cannot be foreseen—in a state university. President Van Hise insists upon the value of research, whether we can or cannot see the application of the possible discovery,—especially in a state university. "The German statesman regards it as a matter of course," he says, "that the production of scholars and investigators at the university is a necessity to the nation. To them, he believes, is largely due the position Germany has taken during the last half century." The fight for "pure science" is the fight for the truth, for the blind pursuit of knowledge no matter where it may lead, and for the training of experts who will work in this abstract spirit regardless of consequences.

Johns Hopkins University, privately endowed, led in "this upward movement, which was more quickly felt in the East than in the

West." But even in the West teachers, who studied, too, and did original work, increased in number till now the (typical) University of Wisconsin has a strong group of such men and maintains a graduate school which is turning out many more.

"But the Western people were not content with the expansion of pure knowledge," says President Van Hise. "They demanded schools of applied knowledge." That is to say, they wanted knowledge to be sought and taught in its relation to life and the needs of men. Consequently colleges, not only of law and medicine, but of engineering and agriculture, were established at the Western state universities almost from the beginning; and courses in business or commerce and many other "practical lines" have been added. The field of knowledge is not covered; not in any of these institutions, not in all of them put together, but they are young yet and, at least, this much is true: the disposition of these Western faculties, and especially of that at Madison, now is to learn and to teach anything that anybody knows or wishes to know.

University Extension

So much then for expansion, the broadening of the college into the university which makes and sells the Latin professor's cheese. As to university extension, that is a general story, too. Everybody knows how great has been the increase in the number and the proportion of students who go to college; how women have been admitted to higher and in some state

universities to co-education. And all "old grads" will recall the importation from England along in the eighties of the idea of extending university opportunities to the people who cannot go to college. That was a fad. "Culture," not education, was the purpose; lectures, not work, the means; and the burden of the courses was what people ought to know, instead of what they wanted to learn. This exotic plant died out everywhere, except at Chicago, where it approached right lines; and it is said to be dying there.

Meanwhile the real thing was coming up spontaneously (and simultaneously) at the state universities. Postmaster Keyes at Madison, the former political boss of Wisconsin, tells how naturally university extension was begun there. He says that the university, founded in 1854, had struggled along, growing always, but very slowly under the heavy weight of rural prejudice against higher education at the public cost. There was an agricultural college, but the farmers despised it and it was hard even for the boss regent, who acted as university lobbyist, to get appropriations out of the legislature.

"I made up my mind," Mr. Keyes says, "that we had to get those farmers' sons to Madison even if they came with the dung on their boots."

This was just about the time when "university extension" arrived from abroad, but Mr. Keyes doesn't remember that. He does recall, however—and so do other Wisconsin men—a certain private meeting at the house of the late United States Senator William F. Vilas in Madison. Regent Keyes was there, and Dean Henry of the Agricultural College, besides Regent Vilas. Dean Henry was animated by his very living interest in farmers and farming; Keyes, by the practical intent to loosen up rural legislators through their constituents; Senator Vilas had visions, as he has shown in his will, which left to the university, principally for research, three millions of property under terms that will make the gift some $30,000,000 by the time it is available. They canvassed the situation, and this is the way it looked to them:

The farmers, like many business men and the practical world generally, thought they "knew it all"; they regarded science as theory and higher education as a waste of time. The problem was to convert the farmers, and the Agricultural College presented itself naturally as the means. But that college had "no students." The few farmers' sons who entered it each year rarely stayed, and the reason was that the first two years were academic; the work was arranged to lay a foundation of general culture. When the boy went home after the first term, and his father asked him contemptuously what he had learned about farming, he had to confess, "Nothing; we haven't got to that yet." And so it was after the second term, and the third, and the fourth. The last two years were agricultural, but by that time the disgusted farmer had kept his boy at home.

The obvious remedy suggested was to cut off the first two years, but that wouldn't do. The Long Course was good, so they left it, modified by putting some practical work upon the freshman class. They simply added the Short Course, which leads to no degree, but was adapted to the needs of the farmer. Dean Henry knew those needs; he had studied farming all over the state and he knew that with a couple of classes, he could begin in Wisconsin a revolution in the ignorant methods of practical farming. He drew up his course in feeds and feeding, breeding, soils, laboratory practice in plant life, dairying, crops, elementary agricultural chemistry, and farm bookkeeping. This is the first year's course; and the second is only higher, "with seventy hours' practice in stock judging" and managing, drainage, veterinary science, "with demonstrations," "one hundred and twelve hours at work-bench

MADE BY A FARMER STUDENT

in forge," seventy hours of grain-breeding, with laboratory practice, bacteriology, etc., etc.

Appealing to workers, Dean Henry advertised his course to open, not with the academic year but later in the fall, when the crops were all in; and it was to close early in the spring before ploughing began. Nor did "the great dean" stop there; he went forth to drum up his trade. In later years, he hired regular drummers; they bear more dignified titles, but drummers they are, and the first of them was Dean Henry himself who, using his personal influence and knowledge, brought into his first Short Course in agriculture (1885–'86) nineteen students.

"Short Horns" the other students called these farmers' sons and hired hands and, whether they came, as Boss Keyes hoped, with "dung on their boots," they got it on them at Madison. "Students should provide themselves with overalls and jackets," is one of the warnings given in the bulletin of the course. Another is that, "Students are required to

assist in the practical feeding and management of cattle, horses, sheep and swine of the university herds." In other words, these young men were put to work in the paddocks, barns, pens and laboratories of the university and, having had the manual training of their trade, were taught the science of it while at work.

There were lectures, too. In animal husbandry, for example, they heard all about the origin, history and characteristics of the breeds of live stock adapted to the state, but the lecture rooms were equipped with skeletons, apparatus and lantern slides and, when the ideal type of milch cow was understood, the class went into a great classroom shed and there, with the university herd before them, were called upon to "recite." And the recitation consisted of judging by points with a score-card, each student acting as judge while the rest judged him. So with the horse and the diseases of the horse, which the students treat under the veterinarian; and so with sheep and hogs, which the students help to treat and breed.

Farmers and Citizens, Too

The Wisconsin tradition of state service was not forgotten. Though the Short Course was designed to make intelligent farmers, the chance to make intelligent citizens was seized upon early. Ransom A. Moore, dubbed "the Daddy of the Short Horns," attended to that. This remarkable man was the superintendent of a country school district when Dean Henry found and retained him to drum up students, manage them and advertise the course. Moore knew how. In closer touch even than the Dean with the needs, tastes and faults of the farmers, Moore brought students to Madison; he herded them there, showing the resources and opportunities of the university, with its libraries, apparatus, colleges and sports; he gave tips to the professors about keeping their science close to the ground and to the boys on specializing. But it was his business also to see that the Short Horns had a good time, and it was as fun that he taught citizenship. One of the sports of Wisconsin is debating. Moore knew his boys "loved" it and he organized the game, directing the subjects to government and politics, and arranging with the professors of economics, history and sociology for references. The Short Horns read good books by way of preparation for debates.

Educators of the old school may smile at this, the culture side of the Short Course, but let us judge the course as a whole and by its results. It was a success in every way. It grew in number; the young farmers liked it and said so.

"TO HAVE A WISCONSIN HORSE AS FAMOUS AS
WISCONSIN WHEAT AND WISCONSIN DEMOCRACY"

"I have increased the production of my herd about seventy-five pounds of butter per head as a result of the Short Course," writes one. Another says: "I learned how to care for live stock. We have increased our number 25 per cent., the quality 60 per cent. and the production of our herd at least 50 per cent." A "hired hand" wrote that "it doubled my earning capacity"; another that it "tripled" his. And a young farmer testified: "Not only did I become acquainted with the newest and best agricultural practice, but the lines and methods of study were so clearly pointed out that every plant and animal became an object for investigation; and progress naturally followed."

There are hundreds of such letters on file at the college and since the writers talked as they wrote and, better still, *showed* what they had learned, other boys came. From 19 in 1885, the entrances increased to 90 in 1895, in 1905 to 322, and in 1907 to 393.

City and Country Life

Moreover, it did not hurt, it established the long course in agriculture. That took time. The Short Course was enough for a while, but, as its annual crops of young men "made good," the respect and demand for scientific knowl-

edge increased. The entrances in the Long Course ran along from 2 in 1885, to 1, 5 or 6 for the next ten years; in 1898 they jumped to 10; in 1900 to 24; in 1905 to 143, and in 1908 to more than 200.

And this live interest in the life of the farm kept home farmers' sons who meant to move to the cities. One wrote typically: "I intended to leave the farm, but since the course I have established a fine flock of Shropshire sheep which I have shown successfully at several fairs, and I am now building up a herd."

Won over themselves, the young farmers won over the old farmers. "Since I left the short course I am raising better calves, and feeding our cows a balanced ration with such good results that I got father interested and he is going to buy a pure-bred Guernsey bull this fall, and also have ventilators in our barn."

"Father" appears in many of these letters, and those "ventilators in our barn" are the signal of Dean Henry's victory over bad farming methods. And there is triumph in them for the Boss-Regent-Lobbyist. Mr. Keyes soon was able to get money for the university out of the legislature, lots of money, a regular tax and all on account of the "dung on the Short Horns' boots." But "Daddy" Moore and Regent Vilas had their victories, too. The farmers of Wisconsin became intelligent voters

"LEARNING SCIENCE WITH BOTH HANDS": SHORT COURSE STUDENTS JUDGING CATTLE AND SWINE OF THE UNIVERSITY'S HERDS

as well as intelligent farmers; La Follette's reform which overthrew Boss Keyes and his successors was a state, not a municipal movement, and the country put it through against the cities. As for Senator Vilas, he saw the Short Horns teach the professors such specific needs of the farms that the scientists went to work upon actual problems. That is to say, they began researches along practical lines, that produced results which forced on the revolution in agriculture and farm life in Wisconsin.

"Daddy" Moore illustrates this point. The drummer and drum major became a teacher and, learning while he taught, he took certain scientific discoveries in grains and, applying them to Wisconsin conditions, brought about the complete solution of several local problems. First, he learned how to treat oat smut in Wisconsin, and through his Short Horns and his personal propaganda, got the farmers to try it. Five millions a year were saved in this way. Then he took up grain-breeding and, studying Wisconsin soils and mapping off the state in sections, developed breeds of corn, oats, wheat, etc., adapted to each section. Raising seed of pure stock and the greatest potency, he organized the Short Horns into an association of seed-breeders and sellers. The university grew its high-bred seed, sold it exclusively to its own students, who planted and propagated it;

showed on their own farms the results and then sold their crops as seed. The monopoly was profitable to them but, since they were inspired with the ideal of improved agriculture, they broke their own monopolies one by one by spreading the good seed with the good doctrine. Whole sections of Wisconsin went into the production of uniform grains, which became famous and increased the output and the profits from fifty to one hundred per cent.

President Van Hise estimates that this work alone has paid the state several times over for its university, and Professor Moore's reckoning proves it. The average increase per acre of corn alone was from 27.4 to 41 bushels; or, in gross, 15,000,000 bushels a year, worth at least $6,000,000. But the total profit directly traceable to university reforms amounts to more than $20,000,000 a year.

The best individual example of the reciprocal benefits of the democratization of the College of Agriculture, is that of Stephen Moulton Babcock, the famous chemist. Professor Babcock was, and still is, at work upon an analysis of the force of gravitation, but when the Short Course in Agriculture had succeeded and a Short Course in Dairying was established, a practical problem arose which was turned over to him. Wisconsin is peculiarly adapted to dairying, and a dairying people—Scandinavians—had come there. In some places the farmers had established cooperative dairy plants. There was trouble. Some farmers turned in poor, others watered milk, and the honest men were the sufferers. What was needed was a measure of butter fat in milk. Chemists could separate the fat from the milk, but their processes were laborious and complicated. A practical separator was required. Professor Babcock went to work and in a few years invented one,—simple, sure, cheap and he gave it to the farmers. It was worth millions to them; it "made" a great industry. Thereafter a dishonest farmer could pump as much water as he liked into his milk; it made no difference since, with the Babcock Test, the dairies bought not milk and not water, but butter fat. Dairying thrived in Wisconsin and, as it grew, a new problem arose. The farmers needed a casein test to measure that other element in milk from which cheese is made. Professor Hart took up that problem and he has just solved it; soon the dairies and cheese factories will buy butter fat and casein, the farmers getting back their milk, "skimmed" —for the hogs; to whose rescue the faculty are moving fast.

Good Spreads Like Evil

Having standardized milk, the demand arose next to standardize the cow that gave the milk. The farmers themselves found that some cows which gave much milk, gave very little butter fat. The Madison faculty knew why, of course, but the professors moved scientifically and practically. They soon had the farmers astir. It seems that the cunning practice of the "cute" farmer was to raise cattle which, when used up as milchers, could be sold for beef. They gave milk, but the professors, applying the Babcock Test, showed that the "dual-purpose" cow gave little butter fat. They advocated beef cattle for beef and milch cows for milk, butter and cheese; and they named the breeds. There was an awful howl from certain breeders; "reform was hurting business" again; but the university was strong and the truth did the rest. The farmers demanded high-bred cows; the university bought and bred some splendid bulls and its students and friends imported others. The reformers made such profits that all the herds of Wisconsin have been pretty nearly cleared of bad stock. And they are being cleaned up too. The university is "hurting business" in diseased cattle now. And Professor Alexander, the university veterinarian, is after the horse, both with the facts and with the law.

For it must be remembered that what the university professors did to the grains, pigs and pumpkins of Wisconsin, the university students were doing to the legislature and the government. They have a political fat test for politicians in that state and the "dual-purpose" legislator is passing away. It was a reformed legislature that helped Professor Alexander slide through a sort of a "pure-food law" for stallions; it set up a standard, and pure-bred animals "may" (soon to read "shall") have a university label. The others are going into Illinois. Wisconsin is to have "the Wisconsin horse" to take rank with Wisconsin wheat, Wisconsin corn, Wisconsin cheese, butter and milk, and—Wisconsin democracy.

Extending University Extension

The by-products of the extension of the university opportunities to farmers are infinite and we cannot follow them here. The extension of the extension is our theme, and that leads far enough. Agricultural Colleges and United States Experiment Stations, cooperating or combined, produce constantly new findings, which they have long been reporting to the farmers. Couched in the slang of science these bulletins are often unreadable, even to farmers. The problem was to get the knowledge in them to the man with the hoe. Wisconsin found that the professors, brought down to earth and plain English by the Short Horns, could make themselves understood if they were brought face to face with the students. So it was decided that the scientists must meet and "show" the farmers; they must follow their bulletins into the field with demonstrations. Seed trains were run through some of the Western states; trains of cars which were moving lecture-rooms with exhibits that looked like a county fair. And Wisconsin and other faculties seized opportunities to take a field of potatoes or an orchard and, by spraying one half for the potato bug or the fruit pest, leave the other uncured, to illustrate the difference. But it was manifestly impossible for each professor to go to each farmer and tell him all he knew. Some wholesale system of education must be devised.

Professor Moore's association of Short Horns, each member of which is a center for seeds, ideas and demonstration, was one basis for such a system; and a map hanging in the office of Dean Russell (Dean Henry's successor), which indicates the number of Agricultural College men in each county, shows the state pretty well covered. The state and county fairs were another means, and the University of Wisconsin is the principal exhibitor at every one of them. And not only the principal, but the most interesting. Dean Russell has been known to take a fine-looking cow out of a show herd and, before the shocked owner and the instructed neighbors, have it cut open to let the crowd see the frightful ravages of tuberculosis. And there are lectures and demonstrations and advertising. I saw members of the Madison faculty "bark" for a crowd at the state fair in Milwaukee, and then demonstrate the Hart Casein Test, with a good word for

illustrated by the experience of the Babcock Fat-Separator. Described and commended in bulletins, the dairymen reported that it "didn't work." The Madison faculty, alarmed, despatched to the dairy districts a flock of demonstrators who found that the apparatus had not been half tried. The farmers and the dairymen, suspicious and impatient, dropped the "new-fangled thing" at the first hitch and the demonstrators had to demonstrate; plead; pull; and peddle their "goods" to have them ac-

"OLD" FARMERS COME TO MADISON IN THE DEAD OF WINTER
TO GET THE RESULTS OF THE YEAR'S EXPERIMENTATION

the university and its readiness to "teach you anything you want to learn."

This is university extension; this is the democratization of knowledge, but these methods didn't reach all the farmers. So the Farmers' Institute was established. A sort of Four Corners organization, the institute is spreading all over the West and Middle West. A town, village, crossroads—any natural center for the farmer—is picked out and the men of the neighborhood are organized into an institute. There, at certain set times, professors, educated farmers and other experts give lectures for from two to five days (with illustrations and demonstrations); then visit the fields and answer questions. They learn and report the special needs of each neighborhood and the central organization selects experts with a view to those needs. But the general news of science and the progress of agriculture are reported at all the institutes.

The use of such methods to reach farmers is

cepted. They prevailed, but they learned vividly the need of the man behind the bulletin.

The problem, you see, is one of adult education. Boys are quick to learn anything; their fathers are slow, and yet they can be made willing, as the next step taken in Wisconsin shows almost pathetically. In 1903, a Farmers' Course was started at Madison. It was suggested by the Short Course and modeled upon it, but the "old farmers," not their sons, were the students sought. The time chosen was two weeks in the dead of winter, when no work was doing on the farm, and the instruction was to be all "practical," all with demonstrations, all to the point. In the first year 175 farmers came; in the second, 227; in the third, 410; in the fourth, 601; last year there were 701; and the stadium building for this year's course is designed for 2,000! And President Van Hise, who is planning all his new buildings and plants for a "10,000-

THE INVENTION OF THE BABCOCK MILK TEST RETURNS TO THE STATE
ANNUALLY THE COST OF THE UNIVERSITY FOR THE SAME PERIOD

student university," says that this stadium is too small, and he gives his reason.

"I was coming through the grounds one winter day during the first year of the Farmers' Course," he related, "and I met a farmer. His face was aglow and he wanted to express himself. Mistaking me for a farmer, he stopped me. 'Great stuff we're getting here, ain't it?' he said. And when I drew him out he declared he was coming back next year, 'to bring all his neighbors with him.' And he did, and they do. Men, more and more grown men," the president added thoughtfully, "are going to demand what we educators have been giving only to boys and girls: an education. And," he went on, "women want what we are giving their sons, daughters, husbands."

He cited, as proof, the Housekeepers' Conference. This university course is a by-product of the Farmers' Course and it illustrates beautifully the spirit of Wisconsin. When the old farmers came to Madison in 1903–4, their first year at college, some of them brought their wives. The women were seen about the town, grounds and buildings, and somebody said to the president: "Let's do something for them too." True to his instinct, President Van Hise got up something that the farmers' wives know something about: cooking, housekeeping, sanitation and decoration. Such a course was arranged and in the next year, was given. Like the Farmers' Course, the Housekeepers' Conference is an established feature of the university now.

With 3,500 Short Horns in the state, all acting as radii, with the county and state fairs going every year, with some 200 Farmers' Institutes established and supported by the state, and the Farmers' Course preparing for 2,000, you would think that Wisconsin was covered. But no, President Van Hise, Dean Russell and all the other conspirators for good, are still plotting to "get at all farmers and to keep on educating them all the time." The latest scheme is to catch them young, as children. The university is offering high-bred seed to country school children to raise for competition at the county fairs, and there were 800 entrances in Dane County alone this year. Little gardens are encouraged both at home and at the school, and such a demand has been created among the children for instruction in agriculture that the teachers are demanding in their turn instruction to enable them to hold their places.

To Reach All Men

"Now you can see," said President Van Hise, after reviewing this agricultural extension, "how natural it was to look farther. Why couldn't we do for artisans and manufacturers, teachers and preachers and—all men and all women and children, all that we were doing for the farmers and their wives and their children?"

There, then, is the true birth of the pure idea of universal university extension. No thought in that of money for the university; no philan-

LEARNING TO TAKE A STEAM ENGINE TO PIECES,
PUT IT TOGETHER AGAIN AND MAKE IT RUN

thropic fad-notion about culture for the masses; nothing but the instinct for democracy and needed service. President Van Hise says that after the idea came up, the only hesitation he had was to find a way to go about the business. Looking around for a method, he noticed the private correspondence schools. They seemed to be thriving. He sent Dr. Charles McCarthy, a former foot-ball coach and an Irish enthusiast, to see what these were doing, and how. McCarthy came back full of the idea. These schools had thousands of pupils; they taught almost anything that was wanted by mail; and some of them were getting rich. And yet, they did nothing that a university couldn't do better.

President Van Hise drew up his scheme, modeled upon the private correspondence schools. Assuming that these institutions knew what was wanted, the first courses outlined were copies of theirs both in subjects and in method. Having a great faculty to draw upon, he had more and better teachers, but if the university lacked instructors for courses demanded by the patrons of the correspondence schools, Dr. Van Hise proposed to hire them. And as a matter of fact, a second, special "correspondence corps" is growing up in the university faculty.

When he presented his scheme to the regents, they hesitated; who wouldn't? But Mr. Van Hise pointed to the schools of law and medicine. They were all private institutions once. When they had proved the demand, the states had taken them over and the patronage

of the private correspondence schools in Wisconsin proved the existence in the state of a demand for education which the state university had overlooked. The regents decided to try it; they voted $2,500 to make a test. In three months they appropriated $7,500 more. The Correspondence School of the University of Wisconsin showed results, i.e., students.

Conserving Our Human Resources

Started thus in 1906, the University Extension Division is too new to be pronounced a success. It had 1,200 students in September, 1908: laborers, apprentices and skilled mechanics; salesmen, clerks, drummers and merchants; teachers, club-women, lawyers, clergymen, physicians and officials. Of these, 330 were doing (by mail) "regular university grade work," which may lead to a degree; but the largest group, 660, was taking "special vocational studies," like shop mathematics, 266; electrical and mechanical engineering, 163; "highway construction" (farmers learning to make roads, culverts and bridges), 139; business administration, 70; drawing, 75; and higher mathematics, 90. Thirteen were studying ancient, 80 modern languages; 25 natural sciences; 32 political science. The number and the variety of the subjects and students taught, proving the demand, promise success, for President Van Hise has adopted the policy of the School of Agriculture; he is meeting the demand and—pushing his business.

"We would like to have the university reach all the people of the state," he says and, a quiet, cautious man, he presents his scientific dreams in a very deliberate way. "There is no reason, that I can see, why our resources for knowledge, training and experiment, should not be thrown open to everyone. We are beginning to think about the conservation of the natural resources of the country; why not conserve also the human resources? This can be done by giving everybody an equal opportunity to discover and develop his highest efficiency, and it would save to the state all special talent. We want no mute, inglorious Miltons to be buried in the graveyards of Wisconsin." And the president tells a story:

"Out in the little town of Cottage Grove," he says, "there is a boy named Mellish. He lives with his mother, sister and an aged grandfather on a forty-acre farm, from which their support must come. That boy is so deeply interested in astronomy that he made himself a telescope, and after his day's work in the field, when his chores are done at night, he searches the sky with his telescope. Last year (1907) he discovered two of the seven or eight comets that were found by all the astronomers of the world. That boy must continue to work the farm. He cannot go to school. His only way is through university extension and he is taking our correspondence course in mathematics."

The point is that the university went out and found that boy, and it is looking for other such boys and men and women. I quote the story from a speech of the president to the merchants and manufacturers of Milwaukee, to whom he was appealing for support. For, having planned his extension, and announced it, the president went forth, like Dean Henry of old, to promote it. Individuals applied for instruction; a few here and there, but the retail business wasn't enough. Education by wholesale is the president's ideal and, following the Agricultural College again, he looked around for natural groupings of people, which might be used as centers. Shops, labor unions, debating and other societies, brotherhoods, women's and farmers' clubs—these existed and the president went after them. In his address to the Milwaukee business men, he was begging leave to send his drummers into their shops and factories to organize classes.

"Yes, I was drumming myself," he said, taking up seriously a jest I made. "And why not?" he added. "Private business, run for profit, drums up its trade; why shouldn't public business? Breweries plant saloons at seductive corners where the people pass; why

shouldn't the university seize every crossroads?"

So Charles Richard Van Hise, LL.D., etc., leader of the leading university, led in the promotion of the education business. He put Dr. Louis E. Reber, a university man, in charge at Madison, but for the field work, he hired professional canvassers. He won away from his competitors, the private correspondence schools, their experienced agents. These came willingly, bringing their methods and students with them.

The Teacher Behind the Lesson

"Looking for no profit, you can speak with assurance," said one of them to me. "Sure of your goods, you can get a hearing, and since it is a state institution, neither Capital nor Labor is suspicious."

"And they brought home to me one other advantage," the president said. "They reported that students who started courses often struck difficulties they could not be carried over by mail. They dropped out. We could beat our competitors and, best of all, save the student by doing what the College of Agriculture did: send the instructor after his mailed instruction. The private schools can't afford to do this. We personally conduct the student over the hard places where he gets stuck."

There is still another advantage, which this extension system has, not over the correspondence school, but over all other kinds of education. A member of the Milwaukee class in shop mathematics expressed it very well. He said he had gone to school, as a boy, and had taken mathematics along with the other studies, but he had had no interest in the subject then.

"And now," I said, "you are paying for the chance to bone away hard at it."

"Yes," he answered, "but in school I didn't see what mathematics were for; didn't know I could use them. Here, in the shop, I see the need of mathematics. The examples we take up are shop problems; right out of this shop; the things we work on at the bench. So, you see, we know what it's all about and, of course, *we want to learn.*"

There's a big principle in that. It's the force that makes the agricultural colleges go with such life and it's the force lacking in schools and colleges. As I told that young mechanic: after my college course, when I had gone to work and become interested in the problems of life and my shop, I felt as he did: that I'd like to go to college again. And how often one hears college graduates wish they could go back and *learn* what they had *taken* in

B. H. MEYER
PROFESSOR OF POLIT-
ICAL ECONOMY AND RAIL-
ROAD COMMISSIONER

DR. CHARLES McCARTHY
LOBBYIST-IN-CHIEF TO
THE LEGISLATURE
AND LECTURER

PROF. RANSOM A. MOORE
THE UNIVERSITY "DRUM-
MER" AND "DADDY" OF
THE SHORT HORNS

SOME OF THE FACULTY HOLD PUBLIC OFFICES AS WELL

their college course. Some day they will. Work and study must be dovetailed somehow. Work, developing manual or professional skill and a living curiosity, gives point, meaning and interest to study, and these fortunate extension students, farmers and mechanics, have all these incentives. "They don't loaf and cut lectures," said one of the instructors. "We don't have to drive it into them; they drag it out of us."

"But what about the discipline and the culture of what you call abstract study?" said an Eastern educator, who objected to what he called "your utilitarian—ah, ah, university education."

In the first place, extension students are not getting a substitute for training and culture; they are getting something, where otherwise they would get nothing. In the second place, they are getting culture and training; there is intellectual discipline and development in vocational as well as in abstract study. In the third place, the University of Wisconsin is conspiring to give the people of that state not only what they want, but what they need and what most men, including many cultivated scholars, lack: enlightenment; science in its relation to conduct and life. Madison is using the conscious demand for "utilitarian" instruction, to develop the unconscious demand that exists in the American people to-day for light. Here is the scheme:

In the mind of President Van Hise and his great faculty, you will find that all these farmers' centers—Short Horns, "Old Farmers' Classes," fairs, institutes—are looked upon as machinery to be used to spread knowledge, not only of agricultural facts, but other facts, too, and ideas, and desires. And so with the shops, labor unions and clubs. Used now for teaching the science of the trades, they are regarded as so many centers for spreading all science to all men all the time. This means culture and the beginnings, humble, but natural and promising, have been made.

It will be remembered that "Daddy" Moore encouraged debating by the Short Horns and directed the "sport" into public questions. He and his Short Horns and the farmers and their institutes have carried on this game, till now assistance for debaters is a regular, big part of the business of the university. The Extension Division has taken it up systematically. Rollo L. Lyman, Assistant Professor of Rhetoric and Oratory, is in charge and his bulletins suggest clubs by telling, in the simplest language, how to organize them, all about procedure and parliamentary rules, and they furnish a model constitution and by-laws. Issued frequently, these bulletins offer topics for discussion and debate: "Resolved, that a system of Postal Savings Banks should be established in the United States"; and "Resolved, that the Parcels Post, advocated by Postmaster General George von L. Meyer, should be established." There's no hint that the pen is mightier than the sword. No, this "utilitarian" university keeps in touch with live political questions and during the last presidential campaign, one October bulletin gave references on both sides of the "Guaranty of Bank Deposits"; and ever-recurring suggestions are: "The Initiative and Referendum,"

vented. . . . In all lines of investigation . . . the investigator should be absolutely *free to follow the indications of truth wherever they may lead.* Whatever may be the limitations which trammel inquiry elsewhere we believe the great State University of Wisconsin should ever encourage that continual and fear-

A MILWAUKEE CORRESPONDENCE CLASS TAKING SHOP
MATHEMATICS FROM THE UNIVERSITY OF WISCONSIN

"Proportional Representation," "The Election of United States Senators by Popular Vote."

Academic Freedom

This is all very indirect and superficial, of course, but a faculty has to be careful, even in Wisconsin. Academic freedom is a settled tradition and a matter of record at Madison. In 1894, when Professor Ely was tried (and vindicated) under charges of "Socialism," the Board of Regents made the following remarkable declaration of policy:

"We cannot for a moment believe that knowledge has reached its final goal, or that the present constitution of society is perfect. We must therefore welcome from our teachers such discussions as shall suggest the means and prepare the way by which knowledge may be extended, present evils removed and others pre-

less sifting and winnowing by which alone the truth can be found."

Members of the Wisconsin faculty who have served in other universities, all agree that there was no such liberty anywhere as they enjoy. And yet, at this very time, the regents were investigating the "Socialistic" doctrines and methods of the professors. The conclusion I drew from talks with both sides, both the Tory regents and the "radical" instructors, was that while there are no "Socialists" on the faculty, there are several men who are more radical than they dare to teach. They do "the best they can"; they "suggest" the truth, but, as one of them put it, "we have to smear it a little."

No matter about that, however. The University of Wisconsin is rapidly gaining such a place in public confidence that it will soon be able to accomplish what it consciously plans to do: distribute scientific knowledge and the clear truth in plain terms to all the people for their self-cultivation and daily use. The Extension Division, finding some and forming more groups, for the purpose of teaching workers the theory of their trades, is offering also "popular and untechnical" courses in astronomy, botany, biology—all the sciences; in history, philosophy and in some of the arts. (President Van Hise wants to teach all the arts: music, painting, sculpture.) The advertisements of courses are so alluring that you can't read them without thinking of taking some. Professors Ely, Scott, Commons, Ross, Hess and others offer political economy "peculiarly adjusted to the needs of all who have or wish to cultivate a live and intelligent interest in present-day problems." Ely offers "the elements of Political Economy" and "Socialism"; Commons, "The Labor Movement: the growth of unions, their policies and methods, the conditions of employment, the trend of wages and public activity in behalf of workers, with the Socialistic criticism of the present economic system"; Dr. Hess, "Transportation," dealing "not with technical details, but the relation of the railroad to (shippers and) other branches of our industrial life"; Scott, "Money and Banking" and "Practical Banking"; and Ross, the author of "Sin and Society," offers "Social Psychology" and "General Sociology": "the key to many perplexing problems in government, education, religion, morals and social policy. . . . Society is regarded as happening, not as having happened. The forces at work in America to-day differ in relative strength but not in kind from those that shaped historic society. The aim is to qualify the student to play an intelligent part as citizen by showing which forces are to be restrained, which guided, which stimulated." And Professor Ross, who, turned out of Leland Stanford Jr. University, has learned to smile internally, says his courses are "needful to those who, as editors, teachers, clergymen or public men, aspire to influence the course of public discussion."

A Servant in the House

Very few students are taking these courses as yet. Highway construction and seed-breeding lead now. But those who call the University of Wisconsin "utilitarian," miss its essence. It is useful, but so was Jacob and he served seven years for Rachel. Jacob got Leah; and though he married and, so far as we know, was a good husband to Leah, it was Rachel he was after and he went on patiently serving seven years more for her; and he got her. It may be seven years before the classes in shop mathematics will be brought into Commons's course

in "The Labor Movement," and it may be seven more before they will go in for Ross's "Sin and Society," but the University of Wisconsin, serving Leah now, is dead set after Rachel. It will furnish the farmer with seed, but not without reminding him also that it is state seed; and that the same shop has economics to sell, and history, and—other seeds good to plant in the mind of a citizen. And citizens are beginning to ask for such seed. A Boston paper exclaimed that this university had been asked by some voters for references and an expert judgment upon a partisan political issue right in the heat of a campaign, and that the faculty had furnished the matter requested! There was no complaint because it is the custom in Wisconsin to apply to the university for anything right, from a bull to the material for a speech. Just before I was out there, a stove manufacturer had had the use of the laboratory and of the professor of chemistry, to carry through an invention which seemed about to fail.

Professors in Public Office

What the brain is to a man's hands, feet and eyes, this university is to the people of the state: the instinctive recourse for information, light and guidance. And the state itself, responding to the general feeling of confidence, draws constantly upon the faculty. The legislature summons professors not only to hearings, but to working membership on committees; and governors and heads of departments, not only consult, they appoint them to office. There are forty-one professors in public office; some of these do two or more services; President Van Hise, as geologist and head of the university, performs five distinct functions under the government, city and state; and counting all the regular and no honorary services rendered by all the professors, the total is sixty-six.

Some of these services are crucial. Professor Meyer, for example, is on the Railroad Commission and, since he and other professors were called in by La Follette to draw the Wisconsin bill to regulate rates, the law is comprehensive. The Wisconsin Commission can regulate; it can regulate the rates and the financing of railroads; and not only railroads, but practically all the public service corporations in the state, including those in cities; and not only that, it "shall" and it is laboring now to put a value upon all those businesses and their plants. And even the railroad men admit, grudgingly, that this commission is doing this delicate work well "so far."

But the most remarkable example of state service by the university, is the bureau of legislation. Dr. Charles McCarthy, the Irish football coach who investigated the correspondence schools for President Van Hise, established, with diplomatic skill and native political sense, an office in which he gets bills drawn right. His theory is that legislation is expert work, and that laws enacted break down in the courts partly because they are badly drawn by inexpert men. Now La Follette's "radical" legislation all stood up in court, and one reason was that he had it written by professors and other men who knew. With his university backing him, McCarthy proposed that all legislators should have all their bills drawn by him and his staff of voluntary and other experts and, following Madison methods, he not only offered to do this work; he went forth and "blarneyed" elected legislators into accepting his offer. And why not? He explained that he would take the rough draft of an intention, any intention, and, looking up all previous legislation along the same line anywhere in the world, would follow it through the courts and, with the help of professors and attorneys, draw and deliver, in confidence, a bill which, containing all experience, correcting all discovered defects and meeting all court and other objections, would probably sustain the test of debate, judicial scrutiny and actual practice. Also, McCarthy would furnish arguments to beat said law.

President Van Hise keeps in the faculty the professors who take public office; he insists upon it; they are better teachers, he says. And anybody can see that they must be. When I asked a question of a Madison professor, his answer was more often a fact from "the little town of Caribeau" than an academic reason from a book. These teachers come into the classrooms of Madison, like the Short Horns, with "dung on their boots," the dung of the farm, of commerce and of politics. Think of Dr. Charles McCarthy, lobbyist-in-chief to the legislature, as a "lecturer on political science" and of Railroad Commissioner Balthasar Henry Meyer as he is: Professor of Political Economy, lecturing, and so reaching also the boys and girls. And meanwhile he and McCarthy are teaching men, busy people who don't know they are being taught. McCarthy has heart-to-heart talks with legislators and leaders and he furnishes the latest references for speeches and debates all over Wisconsin. And Meyer and his Railroad Board, called upon constantly to arrange differences between shippers and the railroads, and between towns and public service corporations, apply university methods. First they send out young experts, usually university-bred, to get the cold facts; then they might decide; but they don't. They go down there with blackboards and lantern slides and, calling a mass meeting, explain the whole thing; explain it, too, in its relation to other business, to the state and to the life and progress of the human species; and having explained this, and settled a row, they leave behind them not merely peace, but light; not merely the right of a wrong, but a sense of the use, of a university and of the state.

One way of stating what is going on all about us today, is to say that communities—cities and counties, states and nations, are becoming conscious. Like man himself, human society is rising out of the instructive into an intelligent state of being. A common sense is developing of the relations of individuals and institutions to one another and to the whole. This means mind; a public mind distinct from the minds of any or even of all the individuals in the community. And this public mind, conscious of a common purpose, is co-ordinating all the resources, efforts and powers of states and their people to the service of the welfare of all. Some European countries, notably Denmark and Belgium, are approaching complete co-operation. Wisconsin is a leading example of the drift in America. President Van Hise has entered his university into an agreement with Beloit and the other lesser colleges of the state, dividing their functions and merging their uses. His great university library is but one of the public libraries which are co-operating to such an extent that you can send to any one of them for any book; it will be drawn for you from the library that has it. It is merger and custom everywhere in Wisconsin; and what is the result? Most of us think of the state and a university as great institutions, above, beyond and separate from us and our daily lives. In Wisconsin the university is as close to the intelligent farmer as his pig-pen or his tool-house; the university laboratories are part of the alert manufacturer's plant; to the worker, the university is drawing nearer than the school around the corner and is as much his as his union is his or his favorite saloon. Creeping into the minds of the children with pure seed, into the debates of youth with pure facts, into the opinions of voters with impersonal, expert knowledge, the state university is coming to be a part of the citizen's own mind, just as the state is becoming a part of his will. And that's what this whole story means: the University of Wisconsin is a highly conscious lobe of the common community's mind of the state of the people of Wisconsin.

WOODROW WILSON

The New President of Princeton University

BY JESSE LYNCH WILLIAMS

SOME undergraduates in the first class Professor Wilson addressed at Princeton tried to single out the thing which made him a successful professor. Common law, surely, does not sound attractive; yet not only was his the largest class on record, but he compelled attention from every part of the room. He did not seem to play for popularity; he had earnestness and dignity, this erect young man of the long, lean face and vigorous forefinger. Some said he was a good teacher because a brilliant scholar (he was only twenty-nine when " Congressional Government" appeared; and at thirty-three he published " The State," which Mr. Brice admired, and we were using as a text-book); others maintained it was due to the fact that he was distinctly a good fellow. A few declared it due to the literary charm he put into his lectures as well as in his essays. But the next year a student, who has since made it his occupation to put feelings we all have into phrases we all want, said, " That fellow seems to be a man."

That was Booth Tarkington, more than a decade ago. To-day quite as contradictory reasons are given in predicting Woodrow Wilson's success as president. He has affirmed his belief that true education cannot be divorced from true religion, and the preachers have applauded. Also he has declared—not with the conciliatory bleat of a recluse, but in the assured tone of a man of the world, that the windows of the class room must be open to " the air of affairs," and practical men of the world have nodded their practical heads, and urged his name for the United States Senate. Again, he is a young man known to be in touch with the advanced theories of modern education, he has had experience in teaching all kinds of pupils, from girls at Bryn Mawr to law students in New York, and so it has been assumed that he will fall in line with other young progressive presidents, and overturn traditions. But, on the other hand, he believes in the old system of classical training, is constantly harking back to the past, spells honor with a " u," writes English with the elegance of style of the days when there were " gentile " people. He has even dared to squint at science!

None of these views is altogether wrong, but most of them miss, as the undergraduates did, the point that makes them all correct. Not as an academic personage, with sworn allegiance to this or that theory, but as a man among men, will President Woodrow Wilson undertake his task, realizing always that the students he is to lead " are to be citizens and the world's servants, and the college . . . must make men of them."

Take notice, you who deem yourselves practical men, that in his way of thinking the world of affairs from which the university " must not hold itself aloof," is not merely the world of Cuban reciprocity and Wall Street mergers. " The world of affairs is so old, no man can know it who knows only that little segment of it which we call the present." There may be seen his reason for harking back to the past, though a modern man. See how practically he regards it: " We should have scant capital to trade on were we to throw away the wisdom we have inherited and seek our fortune with the slender stuff we have ourselves accumulated." Here, then, is his confession of faith: " I believe that the catholic study of the world's literature as a record of spirit is the right preparation for leadership in the world's affairs, if you undertake it like a man, and not like a pedant."

A scholar himself, and a man of letters, he believes that scholarship is worthy of pursuit only when it quickens knowledge into wisdom; that the pursuit of learning for the sake of learning is like buying books merely to display on one's shelves. Neither thing makes a better man or citizen. With science he has no quarrel; on the contrary, he says, " we have not given science itself too big a place in our education," but have made " a perilous mistake in giving it too great preponderance in method in every other study." And religion can never be separated from education, because, " conceive it but literally enough, it is the true salt wherewith to keep both duty and learning sweet against the taint of time and change." For whatever else it is, the college should be a school of duty if " the business of the world is not individual success, but its own betterment."

PRESIDENT ELIOT
From a medallion by W. H. White, of Boston
Copyright, 1903, by W. H. White

The Personality of President Eliot

By Mark Sullivan

AT each Harvard Commencement, when President Eliot calls before him the men who are to receive honorary degrees, it is his custom to sum up in a dozen terse words the character and achievements which have entitled each recipient to this distinction. His happy facility in compressing a heroic achievement or a scholarly career into one compact, pregnant phrase entitles these characterizations to a distinct place in literature. The ringing strength, the severe simplicity, of his phrases go fittingly with his singularly beautiful, bell-like voice—a voice so striking that foreign visitors writing about America have repeatedly mentioned it. With the noble background of tradition—the Harvard Commencement is the oldest ceremony in America—these exercises have a solemn, impressive dignity. If, in this jubilee year of his life, one were called upon to condense into so brief a space some such characterization of President Eliot himself, one might haltingly attempt it by saying: "Charles William Eliot, fearless, serene, and wise, worthy descendant of the Founders of Massachusetts, lawful heir to their character and ideals, conscientious standard-bearer of their ancient cause—a Puritan of the twentieth century."

And this would be no mere ceremonial compliment. Take St. Gaudens's statue of the Pilgrim Father, remove the bell-crowned hat, the doublet, and the spreading cloak, and replace them with modern attire; take from the countenance that somber gloom which expressed the Puritans' attitude of suspicion toward pleasure, and replace it with the expression of a sane and healthy capacity for the joy of living; temper those rugged, austere features with sensibility to grace and beauty: in the result you will have a facial resemblance, startlingly vivid, to the present President of Harvard—a resemblance which will explain in a degree the incomparably impressive beauty and dignity of his countenance.

President Eliot's physical kinship with

the Puritans, coupled with his direct descent from them, must appeal to every imagination: ethically and intellectually, no one ever attributed to the Puritan a public or a private virtue which is not found again and again in the life of President Eliot. Each stands for the same spirit of individual liberty coupled with devotion to public service. Each is characterized by the same firm confidence in his own convictions as right, and by the same intense, although perfectly calm-tempered, desire to impress those convictions on the rest of the world. Both are the heirs of that militant moral courage which led Luther to proclaim his convictions in the very sanctuary of the opposition—President Eliot's most radical utterances on labor unions have been made in labor union halls, to labor union audiences. Nothing is more suggestive of the Puritan than President Eliot's scorn of the middle course, his taking up of the lance in fields far remote from his chosen path of education, his virile, uncompromising partisanship on questions of politics, of religion, of labor and capital, concerning which public prejudice is sensitive to the quick. Both President Eliot and the Puritan might well repeat, at pretty frequent intervals, the prayer of the Scotch clergyman: "Be pleased, O Lord, to guide us aright; for Thou knowest that, whether right or wrong, we be very determined."

And it is no small part of the analogy that President Eliot is at the head of that college which is the animating heart of the whole body of tradition that the Puritans bequeathed. Not only through its ideals, but actually, physically, Harvard College is as close as is possible in nature to its Puritan founders. The six men who form the governing body of Harvard are each of them the descendants of at least seven generations of natives of Massachusetts, an unbroken line of heredity, a New England dynasty, running straight to the beginnings of Puritan history.

But in just one respect this analogy between President Eliot and the Puritans is apt to cause misconception. We are all prone to think of the Puritan character as like the poet's description

of the coast they came to—"stern and rockbound." And this omits to consider a side of President Eliot which the world sometimes seems to assume is inconsistent with his usual public aspect. The present writer had rather not be the one to call attention to President Eliot's likeness to the Puritan, if the effect be to suggest in Harvard's venerable head any lack of the gentlest and sweetest humanity. It is but one of many misunderstandings that a portion of the public should think of President Eliot as intellectually cold and hard. It is not the manner of New Englanders to speak much of these things; but those who are close to Harvard's President know well the qualities to which their traditional reserve allows them to bear testimony only by a sort of shamefaced intimation. "It was not," says one of his classmates, "till years after graduation that Eliot's classmates came to know his courage in adversity and affliction, his tenderness of heart, and the sympathy which he always gives to others when they are in trouble." In almost the same words President Hadley, of Yale, with rare tact, knowing how many would mention distinguished public service and intellectual primacy, added to his recent letter of congratulation his appreciation of these same softer and more gracious qualities. In the address which was signed by ten thousand alumni and presented to him on his seventieth birthday, it was stated that "your outward reserve has concealed a heart more tender than you have trusted yourself to reveal."

It is safe to assume that, as a reserved man, President Eliot prizes these acknowledgments more, perhaps, than an outspoken one. In one of his informal addresses he told of hearing a student say, whom he passed in the college yard one night, "I wonder what 'Charley's' doing out so late." It was easy to infer from the manner of his telling that he took a naïve pleasure in the humorously affectionate familiarity which the student assumed. On the occasion of his birthday celebration, when he was visibly touched by the clamorous, thrilling ovation of his undergraduates, he said that "in the first twenty years of my service

PRESIDENT ELIOT

From a hitherto unpublished portrait designed by John A. Lowell & Co., Boston, who will publish the original in
November in the form of a steel engraving.   Copyright, 1904

here I was generally conscious of speaking to men who, to say the least, did not agree with me." Think of twenty years breathing constantly an atmosphere charged with suspicion, looking into eyes hard with opposition! Surely one may now drop a little reserve in order to atone for an experience which few men would have the courage to endure.

" But," he went on to say, " for the last fifteen years the atmosphere has seemed to grow gradually different, and now, yesterday and to-day, I have been overwhelmed with expressions of confidence and affection. Yesterday, at a family gathering, a lady handed to me a note which she said a lady in Boston had asked her to deliver. I opened it and

PRESIDENT ELIOT'S HOME

there was not a word in it—not one—only a leaf, but that leaf was laurel." Quite apart from the speaker's manner, which plainly told how deeply touched he was, this was not the speech of a cold man.

In Cambridge scores of stories circulate which illustrate his almost impulsive generosity. It is well known that on one occasion a student, sick with contagious disease and shunned by those about him, was taken into the President's own house. A raw sub-freshman from a country village in Connecticut, on the evening of his first day in Cambridge, found himself in need of a Latin grammar to prepare for the next day's examination. Quite without friends at the University, he told his need to the first man he met, and was bidden to the stranger's house. There a long search unearthed a Latin grammar, but it proved to be of too old an edition to serve the present need. By this time the stranger's perplexity and anxiety to get the book exceeded the student's own, and, after some thought, he sent the young man off with a note to a friend in a neighboring street who might be likely to have the right edition. It was weeks before the student learned that the chance stranger who had given an hour of his time and an even more precious measure of his sympathy to a lonely and troubled student was the President of the University. In a university that numbers over four thousand, the opportunity for personal touch between student and President is small; but there are scores of stories of the enlistment of the President's personal interest in some student's behalf. There was a young man who desired to study botany, but had failed to satisfy some technical preliminary requirement. The committee which stood between the student and his wish have a vivid recollection of the warmth of manner and the emphatic gesture of the President as he declared, " If that young man wants to study botany, he shall study it."

President Eliot's writings abound with with the appreciation of domestic happiness, and exhortations to young men to cultivate it as one of the chief ends of life. For one who wishes to know President Eliot's gentler side, for one who will give a few hours' time for the priceless privilege of an intimate glimpse into the home life of the most cultivated class in America, there is a memorial volume prepared by President Eliot shortly after the death of his son, and inscribed " For the dear son, who died in his bright prime, from the father." It is such a book as a mother, rather than a father, might have prepared. It is conceived in the spirit which preserves playthings as souvenirs of a dead child. There are reproductions of the rude sketches and drawings made by the lad, lists of the books he read, accounts of the games he played when he and his mates called themselves the "Lances of Lancaster" and the "Knights of the Wood," and out-adventured Scott's heroes in the peaceful parks of Cambridge. The boy was of a sensitive, imaginative temperament, and ran the gamuts of suffering that such souls endure. President Eliot describes himself as "sanguine, confident, content with present action." Such temperaments as the father's are not always sure to understand the less hopeful ones, but the tender sympathy and protecting care which breathe through every page of the book are the final proof of the exquisite sweetness of the father's soul. The book describes the lad as having "days of mingled exaltation and dejection. A flood of thought and feeling, such as he had never experienced before, swept over him. His head was full of memories and dreams, of fearful hopes, dreads, and pains." And there is this passage, full of the most sympathetic insight into the less buoyant soul : "Charles suffered a good deal at times from that mental and moral struggle, that questioning of self and the world, which all thoughtful and reserved boys who have a good deal in them have to pass through. They become aware that they are thinking and responsible beings, and find themselves forced to consider questions of conscience, faith, and love, and the meaning of life and death. Sudden floods of emotion overwhelm them, and seasons of uncontrollable doubt, misgiving, and sadness distress them. The struggle is apt to be a lonely one. Nobody will or can answer their deeper questions. 'I have trodden the wine-press alone.' "

To the brightening of these fits of gloom, to inspiring hope and faith and courage in the diffident boy, the father devoted himself. The father's love that compiled this book is a trait apt to be lost sight of in the contemplation of the rigid administrator and the fearless, opposition-challenging propagandist, who utters a novel and disagreeable truth with the same nonchalant assurance as a proposition in geometry.

Charles William Eliot entered Harvard in 1849, at the age of fifteen. In these present days, when young men are Freshmen at nineteen and twenty, one may fall into the error of inferring precocity from this early entrance. But those were the days of extremely youthful Bachelors of Arts. Edward Everett Hale graduated at seventeen, Lowell at nineteen. Eliot was of the usual age. Far indeed from any early exhibition of his talents, the record is that he passed his college years in the quiet paths of faithful and steadfast devotion to daily tasks, utterly unnoticed by his fellows. The class of '53 numbered ninety men. Most of them are now dead, and in the great majority of their obituaries the first fact mentioned is that they were classmates of Harvard's great President. And yet the truth is that they had little or no knowledge of him during those four years when they were acquiring the wholly accidental right to shine in the reflected glory of his later fame. Eliot is said to have had but three intimates, while the majority of his classmates were practically unacquainted with him. "He was shy and retiring," says his classmate Hill. "From the beginning of our Freshman year I sat near him for an hour or two every day in one of those small sections into which every class was divided, but it was months before I made his acquaintance, and I never, in undergraduate days, knew him well. Few of his classmates did."

Eliot's aloofness was an inherited reserve, an integral part of his New England birthright, characteristic of every born New Englander, and especially of that well-born, well-bred class which Holmes has called "the Brahmin caste" of New England. If this sensitive reserve has, then as now, cost him the intimate and sympathetic understanding of his fellows, it repaid him with the compensation of ample time for quiet thought and uninterrupted devotion to study. "His ambition," says the same classmate, "was for scholarship in college and in after life." During this Freshman year he stood third, in the Sophomore second; in the Junior year he rose to first, but fell back to second when his work was interrupted by trouble with his eyes. And he stood just as high in the distasteful tasks of the prescribed studies as in the congenial courses that he elected.

With this record of scholarship and with his studious temperament, an appointment as a teacher in the college appealed to his taste, and was easy to secure. For ten years he taught mathematics and chemistry. His achievements took the simple form of thorough and effective teaching. He instituted but one reform—written examinations as a substitute for a peculiarly lax and unequal system of oral tests. In 1863 he resigned to spend two years in study abroad. On his return he became a teacher at the Massachusetts Institute of Technology, and there remained until called to the presidency of Harvard.

One inquires why, among the scores of men eligible to the Harvard presidency, the mantle fell on this one. His especial qualifications were three—marked efficiency as a teacher during fourteen years of experience; noteworthy ability as an administrator—a kind of ability which his predecessors had lacked, and which was recognized as of increasing importance in the rapidly growing university; finally, Mr. Eliot had published in the " Atlantic Monthly " for 1869 two papers entitled " The New Education—Its Organization." These had attracted universal, thoughtful attention because they approached the problem of how to educate American citizens, with a completeness in the grasp of fundamental principles and with a length of vision that have not been equaled before or since in any discussion of the problem of education in America.

Just here is the apt place for adequate tribute to the men who placed a young and untried man in the president's chair, who had the insight to realize his possibilities and the faith and courage to put them to the test in spite of opposition. In the light we now have, it is not too much to honor President Eliot's sponsors as prophets. He did not come to his office as a next step in a steady line of promotion, nor by any universal acquiescence in his selection as the right man for the right place. His choice was a shocking defiance of tradition and routine. The burden of this defiance was borne by two men, who performed, with no small pains, the task of bringing the man and the opportunity together, and thus made his usefulness possible. We see President Eliot's career as history; they saw it as prophecy. Their names were Lowell and Crowninshield. As members of the Corporation of Harvard College they had observed young Eliot's work as a teacher. But the story goes that their especial realization of his executive ability came about through contact with him while he was attending to some difficult business matters in connection with his father's estate. These two men were directors of a cotton-mill at Lowell. In 1865 the superintendency of the mill became vacant. They showed their faith in young Eliot's executive capacity by offering it to him. The office yielded a salary of $5,000 a year and the use of a house—fully twice the income then yielded by any educational position in America. Nevertheless, Eliot stuck to his chosen line, and by doing so doubtless emphasized in the minds of his sponsors his fitness for the more exalted office in which they later placed him. It was some four years later that the presidency of Harvard fell vacant. To suggest Eliot for the place required, in Mr. Lowell and Mr. Crowninshield, with their high sense of responsibility to the institution in their charge, a very exalted faith in their choice, and a moral courage not readily realized to-day. Harvard and New England were communities where tradition was not lightly to be defied; and it was the almost universal tradition, not only for Harvard, but for every American college, that the President must be not only a man of mature years, but also, generally, a clergyman. The suggestion of Eliot's name was the signal for stern opposition. He was opposed because of his youth. Among the six members of the Corporation whose business it was to choose a president, only one was under sixty; Eliot was thirty-five. The elderly faculty looked with resentment on the suggestion of setting over them one whom they regarded as a mere youth. He was opposed because he was not a clergyman; his chief competitor was of the cloth. This phase of the opposition was intensified by the fact that in his " New Education " he had attacked with merciless severity, among other shams and mischievous traditions of American education, the notion that a college president should be a superannuated clergyman. Why, he asked, should a man whose experience consists of having written a sermon a week for some years be considered any more capable of sudden translation to the highest position in the teaching profession than to the highest position in the legal profession? He is as well prepared for one as for the other; and Dr. Eliot opposed the choice of him for the one with as much indignant warmth as law-

kind of intellectual detachment from personal feeling and prejudice, which, because it is so rare, men have found it difficult to comprehend; and it has been the cause of much misunderstanding even among those close to him. While the struggle was on, he publicly complimented one of the alumni on his ability as a leader of the opposition. One needs to know Dr. Eliot well to understand that this compliment was perfectly candid and frank, with no trace of irony. During the same period he wrote in a letter to a friend, "As far as I have heard the objections to me, I quite agree

PRESIDENT ELIOT'S STUDY

yers would oppose the choice of him for a judge. Moreover, this aggressive young chemist's predilection for science was well understood, and the friends of the traditional education feared.

For all these and for many minor reasons, the advocacy of Dr. Eliot for the presidency was resented and opposed. The representatives of the alumni, who had a veto power, once did formally refuse to ratify him, but some months later were persuaded to yield. In connection with the fight over his choice there are two incidents which reflect a mental trait in Dr. Eliot which appears again and again in his career. It is a

with them. As Theodore told Edward Hale, 'I quite agree with your general views, only you don't know Eliot.'" This singular intellectual detachment from passion appears in two stories which illustrate the spirit in which the faculties met the new President, and the spirit in which the new President met them. Dr. Eliot had a grave conviction that the business of a president is to preside; true, his easy-going, elderly predecessors, of the superannuated clergyman type, had largely abdicated this function; and the law and medical faculties were accustomed to going their own way. But at the first meeting of the law school faculty following his election the new President appeared in the chair. " Well, I declare," said one of the professors (ex-Governor Washburn), " the President of Harvard College in the Law School! This is a new sight."

That particular incident is rather colorless ; it merely illustrates how the new President took a vigorous grasp of all the executive business that belonged to him. The other anecdote is both more spicy and more characteristic. Dr. Oliver Wendell Holmes told it in a letter to his friend Motley, the historian. The letter first described how curious it was to see " a young man like Eliot, with an organizing brain, a firm will, a grave, calm, dignified presence, taking the ribbons of our classical coach-and-six, feeling the horses' mouths, putting a check on this one's capers and touching that one with a lash, turning up everywhere in every faculty (I belong to three), on every public occasion, and taking it all as naturally as if he had been born president." Then he tells the story :

" 'How is it, I should like to ask,' said one of our number the other evening, 'that this Faculty has gone on for eighty years managing its own affairs, and doing it well—how is it that we have been going on so well in the same orderly path for eighty years, and now, within three or four months, it is proposed to change all our modes of carrying on the school ; it seems very extraordinary, and I should like to know how it happens ?'

" ' I can answer Dr. ——'s question very easily,' said the bland, grave young man ; ' there is a new President.' "

It will be difficult to persuade those who read the story and do not know the man that there was not a touch of rather offensive youthful smartness in this reply of the young President to the petulant old professor. And yet the fact is, this answer merely expressed a sort of intellectual detachment characteristic of the man. The reason for the change which the old professor so volubly protested against, the exact answer to his question, was that there was a new President ; and Dr. Eliot said so in the fewest and simplest words. There was no snapping acerbity meant. It was a simple fact simply stated, and no feeling went with it. The same spirit of intellectual detachment, of severely excluding all feeling from the conduct of the executive business of the University, is illustrated in the story of a teacher who was called by Dr. Eliot from another university to teach at Harvard, and who approached the President with expressions of gratitude whose warmth was more conspicuous than their good taste. Said the President, with characteristic simplicity, " I did what was best for the University." Here, again, a terse statement of fact in the fewest words seems to convey feeling. But none who know will believe that the President meant a rebuke, that he thought either more or less highly of the grateful teacher after the event. Of a similar tenor was his remark to a Harvard professor who had been, in the faculty meetings, a conspicuous opponent of his policies, and who had an invitation to go to another university. " I suppose," said the President, " you understand fully that your opposition to my policies will not in the slightest degree affect your promotion here." The men with whom he had to deal were long in learning this complete intellectual detachment from prejudice, this thoroughgoing respect for men who stuck to their own opinions in opposition to his. " For the first twenty-five years," writes Dr. Hyde, " President Eliot was misunderstood, misrepresented, maligned, hated, with and without cause." But when the lesson of his fairness was learned, and when, with that lesson, came the conviction that here was a man of extraordinary far vision, President Eliot was rewarded with a loyalty among those about him such as is received only by men of the most exalted character. One of the best-known members of the Harvard faculty once gave the writer a glimpse of the sort of enthusiastic faith which is held by those who know President Eliot best. The professor who tells the story, with another member of the faculty, was walking home one night from a faculty meeting in which some incident had illuminated for them the soundness of the President's judgment and the length of his vision ; and they both agreed that if Dr. Eliot should ask them to resign they would go to him gratefully and thank him for having pointed out a way in which they could serve the University. It was, for these two mature men, like the exalted faith which imaginative small boys sometimes have in the omniscience of a teacher.

The new President began his reign with a twofold conception of his functions. He was, first, the executive head of a large and complicated establishment, with a plant valued at some millions of dollars, and a considerable force of employees. On this side he has looked upon the University as a superintendent might look upon his factory. Indeed, he seems to have this analogy consciously in mind. In one of his annual reports he figures out the economic loss involved in letting a plant valued at several million dollars lie idle during the long vacation of three months. On this side his efficiency is incomparable. He is constantly appearing, often in the very early morning, on trips of inspection of the University buildings. A broken lock on a door is not too small a detail to escape him, and an attendant in the library has been personally reminded that an electric light in the stacks should not be permitted to continue to burn when nobody was using it. To be able to do things with his own hands is a hobby with him. The tenants of a house of which President Eliot had charge complained that the furnace was out of order. The next day, within a few hours after he had dined with a foreign ambassador, Dr. Eliot appeared, descended into the basement, and shortly returned with the announcement that the furnace would now be found to work properly. In his executive capacity he is as hard a worker as his splendid physique, his natural taste for detail, his equable temperament, and his great endurance will permit. He has remarked, although in a spirit of satisfaction rather than complaint, that his work averages twelve hours a day ; and that but for the summers at Mt. Desert he would "hardly have more time for reflection and real living than an operative in a cotton-mill." But he has always nourished his physique with exercise. His erect, dignified body astride a big-boned horse is a common

sight to students hurrying to breakfast. While he was a student and an instructor, he rowed regularly, once appearing in a public contest. For twenty years he spent his summers with his family partly in tents on an island off the Maine coast, and partly aboard a forty-foot sailing yacht along the New England coast.

With the other side of President Eliot's functions, with his service to the University and to the community, as a reformer, the world is familiar. He has not been a teacher in the formal sense—he has practically never appeared in a class-room since he took office. But, before he became President, he had wrought out certain original, independent theories of education. Clearing the ground of all tradition and custom, approaching the question as if there was no system of education already in existence, he considered the problem, What sort of education does America need and how shall it be got ? "The American university," he said, "will not be a copy of foreign institutions, but the slow and natural outgrowth of American social and political habit." In this unbiased spirit he approached the subject of education in America, and his conclusions made the fashion-followers in education rise up in protest. He ripped from Latin all its trappings of tradition and held the shrinking skeleton up in the pitiless light to ask exactly what purpose it serves in education. As Dr. Hyde expresses it, he went "up and down the whole length of our educational line, condemning every defect, exposing every sham, rebuking every form of incompetence and inefficiency as treason to the truth, an injury to the commonwealth, a crime against the individual."

But he was not an iconoclast merely. The "New Education" was conspicuous not so much for what it destroyed as for the robust vigor of what it constructed. The "New Education" was published in 1869, and the inaugural address of the same year outlines an entire system of education, from kindergarten to professional school, adapted to the needs of America. In these two productions will be found the germ of all the reforms which President Eliot has brought about in Harvard and America during the past thirty-five years—with how much patience there is not space here to tell.

It is a pleasant fancy to think how future generations of Harvard will look back to the administration of Eliot. By what flower of speech, by what equivalent of the trite "Golden Age," will they designate it? In length alone it is unprecedented. His thirty six years are equal to ten years more than the combined terms of the five presidents who immediately preceded him. Only one other college president, the famous Mark Hopkins, of Williams, ever served so long. Dr. Eliot's term has spanned the growth of Harvard from 1,059 students to 4,328, from 58 instructors to 550, from two millions of dollars in resources to sixteen. But, as President Eliot has said himself, " numbers do not contitute a university, and no money can make it before its time." Measured in a different way, it is enough to quote the tribute of another New England college president: " No one can begin to measure the gain to civilization and human happiness his services have wrought."

THE ACADEMIC CAREER OF
EX-PRESIDENT WOOLSEY

By George P. Fisher

THE WOOLSEY MEDAL.—OBVERSE.

THE completion, by Dr. Theodore Dwight Woolsey, of an academic service of fifty years in official relations to Yale College, where he has been successively Professor, President, and Member of the Corporation, was chosen by the professors in the various departments of that institution as a suitable occasion for manifesting to him their reverence and esteem by the gift of a gold medal. The medal—a beautiful product of art—is the work of Chaplain, of Paris. On one side is a spirited and correct likeness of Dr. Woolsey; on the reverse side stands the inscription:

> " PRÆCEPTORI SVO
> PRÆCEPTORES YALENSES
> MDCCCXXXI
> MDCCCLXXXI."

Not all of the permanent " preceptors " or teachers now at Yale have ever been formally enrolled among his pupils, or have passed through the college either during his connection with it as an instructor or since his resignation. But there is not one who does not honor him as a " preceptor "—as an intellectual guide and example. Those of their number who have long been associated with him, whether graduates of Yale College or not, are profoundly aware of the debt which they owe to him. They prize, in a degree not easily estimated, the influences, both moral and scholastic, which have gone forth upon

them during many years of intercourse with him. This unanimous appreciation of Dr. Woolsey's worth and usefulness was expressed in the felicitous address at the offering of the medal, which was read in an assembly of the professors by Professor Thomas A. Thacher, the one of them who had been longest an officer of the college, he having entered it as a pupil on the day when Dr. Woolsey was installed in the office of Professor of Greek. Professor Thacher was naturally restrained by the presence of Dr. Woolsey from the utterance of any direct or prolonged eulogy; but in adverting, as he did, in well-chosen phraseology, to the truthfulness, courage, and disinterestedness of the venerable President, which he had evinced through so extended a course of academic labor, the obviously suppressed emotion of the speaker indicated how much was held back which would gladly have found utterance, and made his reserved allusions to the virtues of his friend more expressive than any profuse encomium. The reply of Dr. Woolsey was one of characteristic simplicity. Having referred to the utter surprise with which he had received, a few days before, from Professors Newton and Packard, the information that he was to be the recipient of this honor, he spoke of the pleasure it gave him to have a

THE WOOLSEY MEDAL.—REVERSE.

testimony of the approval of those with whom he had acted and who knew him best. He then reverted to circumstances relating to his early connection with the college. He was a theological student at Princeton when he was elected (in 1823) to the place of tutor in Yale, where he had been graduated in 1820. His wish was to be a minister, but he had scruples of conscience about his fitness for that profession, and the call of the college came as an audible voice of Providence, pointing out to him another path of work. The striking contrast between the Yale College of half a century ago and the Yale College of to-day was made a topic of brief remark; and the informal address of the ex-President closed with an expression of confidence in the good prospects of the college for the future, and of cordial wishes for the success of the body of professors who were gathered around him—happy to listen once more to his familiar voice.

Avoiding whatever might be thought by such as have little knowledge of Dr. Woolsey to savor of adulation, something may without impropriety be said respecting his academic career and his public services. Happily his published writings will serve as indices both of the character of his studies and of the measure and variety of his attainments. Reference to these will help to give a somewhat more impersonal quality to the observations which follow. The reader will understand that the aim is not to paint a portrait. No attempt will be made to delineate in full the characteristics either of the man, or of his work in the capacity of a teacher and author.

The drift of President Woolsey's studies and pursuits, one may think, was in some degree foreshadowed by the character of his ancestry and by his earliest associations. In childhood he had the opportunity of seeing at the table of his father, who was a prominent merchant in the city of New York, leading men of the Hamiltonian Federal school of politics. Conservative political sentiment and a practical ability for the handling of economic questions, which abstruse investigations in philology and history did not weaken, were natural to one thus born and bred. On his maternal side the lineal descendant of Jonathan Edwards, he would be likely to partake of the religious earnestness which has come down, with some notable exceptions, in this famous New England family. In his early days he listened to the animated conversation of President Dwight, his mother's brother, and to some of his eloquent and pathetic sermons; for President Dwight did not die until several months after Dr. Woolsey had entered college. So his early studies can be seen to have had an intimate bearing on the labors which he was destined afterward to perform for the country and the Church. The period which he spent at the theological school at Princeton, and the period which he passed in the law office of Charles Chauncey, in Philadelphia, may possibly have seemed to him time lost, when he found himself a Greek professor at Yale. To a superficial student these early occupations might in truth have proved fruitless. There can be no doubt that to Dr. Woolsey they were, even though not protracted according to his original purpose, periods of thorough work. They did their part in turning his reflections and researches into the channels of which the outcome is seen in the treatise on International Law, and in the important service done by him as a preacher in the college pulpit and as a translator of sacred scripture. To trace more carefully the process by which seemingly discordant threads in this instance converged to form the web of a consistent and beneficent life might be interesting; but it is impossible here to pursue the topic.

When Dr. Woolsey became tutor he was twenty-two years of age. It happened to be an era when a disorderly, mutinous spirit prevailed among the students at Yale—a period which Dr. Day, who was then president, used to designate as the "reign of terror." In his address, at the reception of the medal, Dr. Woolsey, alluding to Professor Thacher's ascription to him of uncommon courage, modestly disowned any title to this virtue, but remarked still that his experience as a tutor was the "making of him." The pluck, however, which developed itself out of the necessity of facing bands of unruly youth would never have come out if it had not been a latent natural quality. No doubt it was a tonic for a retiring young scholar to be placed in circumstances where the exercise of manly intrepidity was imperatively called for. Certain it is that unflinching courage, united, as we might expect it to be, with transparent sincerity, essentially contributed to the ascendancy which Dr. Woolsey maintained over professors and students while he held the presidency of the institution. Whether by nature, or as the result of self-training, he had no lack of the quality vulgarly termed "grit." He was never afraid of the students. He stood in no dread of a perverse public opinion. He despised mobs and the tyranny of numbers. The righteous indignation which wrong-doing excited in his soul, no matter who might be confederated in the performance of it, lifted him above cowardly considerations of expediency.

Theodore D. Woolsey

ENGRAVED BY COLE, AFTER A DRAWING BY ABBOTT THAYER OF THE BUST BY AUGUSTUS ST. GAUDENS.

The "Schuljahre" are followed by "Wanderjahre." But the years of travel, or rather of residence abroad (1827–1830), were mainly employed by Dr. Woolsey in study in German universities. He devoted himself chiefly to the Greek language and literature. But concentration upon a chosen branch in his case did not mean indifference to kindred studies in art, history, and general literature. Few students who have attained to distinction in certain special branches have been more catholic in their studies. Few have been more avaricious of knowledge in fields beyond the limit of their own private domain. Politics and religion, with which are inseparably involved the vital interests of mankind, could never cease to be directly or indirectly themes of thought and investigation. Professor Woolsey—he assumed the professorship of Greek in 1830—was a philologist, with a native bent for the study of languages, and with attainments, especially in Greek, which at that time were not excelled, if they were equaled, in America. His editions of four of the classic Greek tragedies, and of the Gorgias of Plato, brought before the teachers and the students of our colleges the best results of German linguistic scholarship. The notes exhibited a grammatical accuracy, combined with a critical acumen, to which American students were little accustomed. These publications did much to create a new epoch in the study of Greek on this side of the ocean. At the same time it was not in the nature of Dr. Woolsey to treat, in the spirit of a Dryasdust, the masterpieces of human genius merely as illustrative of Greek syntax and prosody; he himself felt, and he helped his readers and pupils to feel, their power. The contents of the writings of Æschylus, Sophocles, and Plato, profoundly interested his mind for the truth and beauty which belong to them, and as presenting types of thought and phases of sentiment which it is in the highest degree instructive to compare with those of Christian ages. In the Gorgias, Dr. Woolsey sympathized with that disdain of rhetorical show and sophistical adroitness which is the key-note of this wonderful dialogue. In reading his prefaces and annotations, one feels himself in contact with a scholar who is much more than a painstaking editor; with a scholar whose heart throbs in sympathy with the Socratic abhorrence of false dealing and of intellectual frivolity, and is quick to catch glimpses of that eternal truth which Christian revelation has brought more fully to light. The effect of a long study of antiquity, and of communing with the masterly productions of the Attic poets and philosophers, on a mind capable of appreciating them on every side, while yet keenly alive to the problems of immediate interest to society, it is not difficult to understand. The effect is *culture* in the broadest meaning of the term.

On the resignation of Dr. Day, in 1846, Dr. Woolsey reluctantly complied with the desire of his colleagues, and the request of the corporation, and accepted the presidency of the college. He now retired from the chair of Greek, and placed in it a scholar whom he had selected and trained for the post,—James Hadley, whose death, in 1872, just as he had reached the maturity of his powers, deprived the college and the world of a man of rare gifts and of accurate and varied learning. Dr. Woolsey himself, on becoming President, took up the branches of Modern History and International Law, to which the wants of the institution, not less than his personal predilection, attracted him. His comprehensive studies had made him no stranger to these sciences, to the further exploration of which he brought not only the advantage of a familiarity with the principal modern languages, but also the inestimable aid afforded by a thorough acquaintance, acquired by the labor of a score of years, with the history, literature, and polity of the ancient nations. The first notable fruit of his labors in this department that was given to the public was his "Introduction to the Study of International Law." The unpretending form in which this work was put forth did not prevent the legal profession, as well as historical students, from at once discerning the solid learning at the basis of it, as well as the soundness and sagacity of the comments which were interspersed in the course of the exposition. This work spread his reputation as a publicist. The successive editions which have been called for since its first publication, testify to the esteem in which it is held by competent judges in this country. Its use at Oxford is one proof of the appreciation of it abroad. In this book the author does not content himself with a bare recital of the actual state of public law, or a description of international jurisprudence as a fact; he points out the relation of agreement or antagonism in which the law of nations, as recognized and acted upon, stands to the immutable principles of justice, and suggests modifications which ought to be made in existing usages. But here extreme views are avoided. For example, while Dr. Woolsey attaches great value to arbitration as a method of adjusting differences among nations and of preventing war, he does not go so far as to hold that it is a remedy applicable to all cases, or to deny that grievances may exist which the offended party ought not to consent, and will never be disposed to consent, to refer to an umpire.

Indicative of the general line of Dr. Woolsey's studies are the two smaller works, that on " Divorce and Divorce Legislation," and the book on " Communism and Socialism." These bear closely on evils and dangers of the times. The treatment in each case is largely historical, but the historical review only paves the way for the more intelligent consideration of practical and present duties and problems. The laxness of the legislation and of the administration of the law respecting divorce in recent times, in a number of our States, has been such that the little treatise of President Woolsey was quite timely; and an effect of it in at least one of the States, Connecticut, has been to produce an alteration, in the right direction, of the statutes relating to the subject. The collected essays on Communism and Socialism explain the different phases which the portentous movement suggested by these terms has assumed. Following this retrospect is a statement of reasons why Socialism will not be able to overthrow the present form of society. This is succeeded by a discussion of the future prospects of Socialism. In these treatises, as in his other writings, the author never indulges in declamation. There is nowhere the least effort at fine writing. The truth is plainly and dispassionately set forth, with no eloquence save that which is inseparable from earnest conviction, and with no outlay of ornament save that which is unsought. There is a force of language, at times a startling force; but it is the spontaneous outcome of intense feeling. Illustrations from nature, as well as from literary sources, are not wanting; but they are such as suggest themselves at the moment to a full mind, enriched by reading and alive to the analogies of the outer world.

The elaborate treatise of Dr. Woolsey on " Political Science, or the State Theoretically and Practically Considered," was published after his retirement from the presidency. The survey of political theories and political constitutions which it contains is marked by an amplitude of learning such as it is doubtful whether any other American writer could bring to the illustration of the subject. Through the entire work, which comprises twelve hundred large octavo pages, we find an amount of vigorous thought which is fitly matched to this masterly historical review. The length of the work is owing solely to the variety and richness of the topics; for there is no waste of words. As in all of the author's writings, there is a compact body of thought which requires the close attention of the reader. The whole discussion in the volumes referred to is pervaded by a strong sense of justice and an intolerance of all violation of natural rights, together with a spirit of conservatism as regards political institutions. The distinction between natural rights and political privileges, or the exercise of political power, is sharply drawn. Hence, the doctrine of universal suffrage is combated, and shown to have no good foundation in sound political theory. The limitations as to age, sex, etc., which are always made in defining the qualifications of voters, are a decisive proof that political expediency, and not natural right, is the implied criterion in alloting political power among the members of a community. The author considers religious establishments to be excluded by no just theory of the function of the State, and holds that they are to be condemned only when, on account of a division of opinion in religion, or for kindred reasons, they are inexpedient. The work of which we are speaking has been received with honor by professed students of the science of politics, both in America and England. But as yet it has not commanded the attention of our public men to an extent corresponding to its just claims. It can hardly be doubted that its extraordinary value will be more and more recognized. Politicians who aspire to rise above the commonplaces of political knowledge will find it a mine of thought and information. A member of Congress could not better qualify himself for his post than by reading carefully, before he enters on the function of a legislator, this noble discussion, which is elevated above the level of partisan contests, and lifts the student into the pure atmosphere of a wise political philosophy.

The method pursued by Dr. Woolsey, in the writings which have been referred to above, is that which has been adopted by German scholars, but has been slow in establishing itself among American scholars, or even in England. It is marked by the connecting of a thorough historical and critical survey of the field into which the author takes his reader, with the opinions which he himself propounds, and the arguments by which he supports them. The late Dr. Lieber remarked this German thoroughness of President Woolsey. It is the only method which gives a scientific character, the only method, at least, which is likely to secure a scientific progress to the philosophical and political branches. The new laborer begins where his predecessors left off. Instead of ignoring their work, or, perhaps, doing over again what has been accomplished before, he moves onward from a point previously gained.

On his accession to the Presidency, Dr. Woolsey was ordained as a Congregational minister. During his administration he conducted morning worship in the chapel. " He prays as if he were used to it," was the blunt comment of a student not over-attentive to religious exercises. The most thoughtless persons could not fail to be impressed at times by the earnest and edifying character of these services. When the office of College Preacher was vacant, and occasionally while it was filled, he preached on the Lord's Day. His printed volume of discourses, entitled " The Religion of the Present and of the Future," includes a portion of the sermons delivered from time to time in the chapel pulpit. They are packed with thought—not thought wrought into scholastic forms or cast in the mold of any theological sect, but such thought as a highly educated mind, long wonted to reflection on religious themes, and imbued with a profound sense of the verities of the Gospel, might naturally produce. To say that a deep spirit of reverence and a vivid consciousness of the evil of sin and of the transcendent importance of faithfulness to religious obligations breathes in every paragraph of these sermons, at once so evangelical and so catholic, is simply to express what every one who heard them or has read them must feel. Two additional discourses on " Serving our Generation " and " God's Guidance in Youth," given just as he withdrew from the presidency, bring out in an indirect but touching manner the thoughts which were evidently suggested to him at the moment of retiring from the active work of life.

In managing the affairs of the college, President Woolsey adhered to certain maxims which had long been observed at Yale, and on which, in his address when he handed his office over to his successor, he insisted as of primary importance in the government of such an institution. One was that no person ought to be chosen into a Faculty without the assent of the body of which he is to be a member. In other words, the Professors ought to have the privilege either of nomination or of veto, with regard to the admission of new members of their corps. When this right exists, whether by explicit law or by custom, the Faculty are likely to be a united body. They will have a satisfaction in one another which will enable them to coöperate cordially and efficiently in promoting the good of the college. When, by the fiat of a board of trustees, Professors are thrust into a Faculty who are distasteful to their colleagues, mischief is almost sure to arise. Moreover, generally speaking, the Faculty are altogether more competent than anybody else, or any collection of persons, to judge of the fitness of candidates for the chairs of instruction. Of course there must be a guard against nepotism and other sorts of favoritism; but the fact that the nominations by the Faculty are made with the foresight that they must have the approval of the corporation is commonly a sufficient protection against this danger. Another principle to which President Woolsey gave his sanction was that the internal administration of the college should be left mainly in the hands of the Faculty. They make it their business to take care of the college, and men generally understand their own business better than people who are busied with other occupations. The Faculty are on the ground; they know the students personally; they are supposed to be, and, if they are fit for their places, they are, conversant with the science of education, and with their own departments in particular. The trustees take care of the funds, and, we may add, ought to be interested in their increase. They are supervisors whose concurrence is necessary in every important change. But incalculable harm has been done in many American colleges by the meddlesome temper and dictatorial disposition of overseers who take on themselves work which they are incompetent to do, interfere with Professors in their appropriate business, or treat them as hired laborers whom they can appoint, dismiss, and direct with an arbitrary freedom. Not unfrequently they commit the blunders which persons who, because they are clothed with authority, feel bound to do something, they know not exactly what, are very liable to fall into. A better system has thus far prevailed at Yale College.

The relation of the President (who at Yale is a member of the Corporation) to the Faculty is another point of much importance in the practical working of a college. President Woolsey considered that parliamentary government is the right method. He presided in the Faculty, and his opinion necessarily, both from his station and his personal qualities, carried great weight. He had by the laws of the college the reserved right to interpose a veto on the action of the Faculty. This right he very seldom, if ever, exercised. On one or two occasions the intimation that he might feel bound to deny his concurrence to measures caused them to be dropped. One of these instances may, without impropriety, be mentioned. It was proposed that the honors of the college should be awarded on a basis compounded of scholarship and correct behavior. No one set a higher value on moral qualities in a student than the President. This measure, however, he told the Faculty, would have the effect to lower the standards of scholarship, and rather than have this done he would prefer to plant cannon before the buildings and blow them down. The mutual respect and harmonious action of the President and the Faculty of the Academical Department, or the college proper—the Faculty with which he was actively connected—conduced greatly to the prosperity and peace of the institution. Where there is a body of self-respecting Professors, there will not be a silent submission to the "one-man power," which the ancients, with whatever equity that power might be exercised, called "tyranny." Unless favored by circumstances, such as internal divisions in the Faculty which paralyze their action, a President who would play the part of an autocrat invites on himself a fate analogous to that of the "blessed martyr" of the House of Stuart, who was bent on ruling England without a parliament.

In relation to students, President Woolsey never favored petty interference with their doings, nor was he disposed to raise an issue and provoke a collision which good sense and forbearance could avert. But he believed in authority. It belonged to the Faculty and not to their classes, to govern. He never looked on the undergraduates as entitled to prescribe rules for the management of studies or of discipline. At a moment of popular excitement in college, one of the undergraduates waited on him, probably not without some fear and trembling, as the bearer of "Resolutions" from a students' meeting, but was struck with astonishment, if not dismay, when the President, not lifting his hand to receive the solemn document, said to him: "The Faculty do not receive resolutions; they receive petitions, but not resolutions,"—a reply which led to the speedy withdrawal of the alarmed deputy.

Mr. Donald G. Mitchell, in his "Reveries of a Bachelor," describes the professors of his college days as he saw them later, on revisiting the chapel at Yale. After speaking of President Day, he thus delineates his successor:

"A new man now filled his place in the President's seat; but he was one whom I had known, and been proud to know. His figure was bent and thin—the very figure that an old Flemish master would have chosen for a scholar. His eye had a kind of piercing luster, as if it had long been fixed on books; and his expression—when unrelieved by his affable smile—was that of hard midnight toil. With all his polish of mind, he was a gentleman at heart, and treated us always with a manly courtesy that is not forgotten."

There are two classes of college teachers. The one seems to be born for nothing else. They are pedagogues from center to circumference. Highly qualified they may be for their work, but it is plain that they could do nothing else. Their manners take their hue from their wonted and predestined occupation. The other class is made up of the smaller number, who were men before they were schoolmasters. They wear the impress of a larger contact with society and the world. It is evident that, even if they have not left a broader and more public arena, they would be at home elsewhere than in the recitation-room. A certain high-bred air and tone, it may be, indicates familiarity with an atmosphere more ample than that in which their daily work lies. The gentleman is not lost in the scholar. To this type, as Mr. Mitchell's brief delineation will suggest, President Woolsey belongs. From such a man the student, on leaving college, does not part. He does not look upon him as merely a companion adapted to his youthful needs. He recognizes him as a peer, a guide and example, through his whole career.

Of the special services rendered to Yale College by Dr. Woolsey while he was President; of the high ideal of scholarly and scientific excellence which he cherished, and moved all around him to cherish; of his unflagging punctuality in the performance of college work; of his self-sacrifice in taking on himself labors from which most men would consider that their position might properly exempt them; of his consuming abhorrence of false pretenses; of his contempt for all ostentation in learning, and of his intolerance of everything base in conduct; of the sense of religious responsibility which was obviously the ruling sentiment in his mind, and which he did so much to communicate to the corps of teachers associated with him, it is not for us here to speak. The thousands of young men who passed through Yale College during the administration of President Woolsey, and daily met him, in the senior year, in the class-room, had before their eyes, in this critical period of life, one to whom they all looked up. They are so many witnesses to the venerableness of righteous character. The superiority which inheres in those with whom duty, "stern daughter of the voice of God," is the controlling law, they could not avoid feeling. Who can measure the value of such impressions on the minds of youth?

If there is one lesson which it is desirable to stamp indelibly on students, it is that of the supreme worth of character. They are ready enough to admire power of every sort. They are roused to enthusiasm by intellectual ability, and in particular by intellectual brilliancy. Even moral excellence may fail to engage that respect which incites to imitation, when it is associated with only a moderate endowment of talents or a slender stock of knowledge. But when there is mental vigor and learning such as they cannot but admire, held in manifest subordination to the moral element, and leavened by a genuine spirit of justice and godliness, then are combined all the sources which tend to inspire young students with homage for the right. That which is most worthy in the soul is seen to be on the throne. The comparative worthlessness of mere dexterity of intellect, or of acquisitions of knowledge, by the side of moral rectitude, is vividly discerned.

The academic spirit it is not easy to describe in precise definitions. It is a spirit that finds itself at home in the serene atmosphere of study and contemplation. It is so far withdrawn from the turmoil of practical life that it can look upon it from an elevated point of view, and judge of it dispassionately. It is perpetually conscious that a great past lies behind, as well as a great future before, the present scene. The experiences of mankind, the analogies of history, are ever in mind as aids to the interpretation of passing phenomena. It looks below the surface of occurrences to the silent drift which the busy actors are apt to overlook. It is alien from the temper of partisans. It is self-contained and self-content. Yet the academic spirit may and should be in living sympathy with the struggles which are going forward on the public arena. It is not the spirit of a mere book-worm whom events that took place long ago excite, while with parallel events now occurring he is unconcerned. Rather, if an emergency occurs it is ready, as seen in the example of Milton or of Niebuhr, to close the volumes of which it is fond, and to mingle in the fray. The true academic spirit does not dwell in the air. It does not abide in a region aloof from the concerns of mankind in the day that now is. It brings its own contribution of light and help to the cause of human culture. Its aim is not the luxurious enjoyment of art and letters, but to do something, in its own way, for the well-being of the race. It is not too much to say, that of the academic spirit, in the best conception of it, Dr. Woolsey has been a living illustration.

The relinquishment of the Presidency of Yale did not mean a relaxation of industry on the part of Dr. Woolsey. Release from the routine of official duty gave him ampler opportunity for the prosecution of his studies. He took his seat in the corporation of the college, which still has the benefit of his counsels. He has given one course of lectures in the Divinity School, and more than one in the Law School.

His principal public labor has been in connection with the Board for the Revision of the New Testament, over which he has presided down to the completion of their work. For this task his learning and his critical acumen, not less than his relish for work of this kind, eminently fitted him. The substantial merits of the New Revision are discerned by competent readers now ; and whatever blemishes, real or fancied, may be detected in it, its excellence will probably be more generally recognized in time to come. It is safe to affirm that no member of the American committee contributed more to secure whatever is meritorious in the Revision than their chairman. Certainly no one devoted himself more conscientiously to the task that was laid upon him. No one was better equipped by previous studies, by familiarity with the original Scriptures of the New Testament, and by rigid fairness, for so responsible an undertaking.

When, in 1873, the Evangelical Alliance, composed of representatives of almost all of the Protestant bodies in this country and Europe, assembled in New York, Dr. Woolsey was selected to preside over its sessions. As he had never identified himself closely with ecclesiastical movements—although always earnestly interested in missions to the heathen—this appointment, to the propriety of which none demurred, may be regarded as a spontaneous tribute from the American Protestant Church to his eminence as a publicist, scholar, and divine.

Dr. Woolsey has afforded a signal example of the dignity, as well as the usefulness, of a purely academic career. His calling has been that of a teacher of youth. Without turning aside from that function or growing cold in his esteem for it, he has acted in other spheres, not obtrusively or of his own motion, but when his services were required or the public need imperatively invoked his aid. His opinion has been sought and given to the National Government on important points in controversy with foreign powers; but he has declined flattering offers of public office. It must be a gratification to this venerable man—a man who has never stepped out of his path to conciliate any person's favor— to receive, from his former colleagues and their associates, ten years after he has withdrawn from official labor in college, the spontaneous tribute of honor and affection of which the gold medal was the token. The gift might be taken as a symbol as well as a token—the symbol of a character of so genuine a quality, a character mingled with so little dross, that its like is seldom to be seen among men.

A Group of
AMERICAN
COLLEGE PRESIDENTS

BENJAMIN IDE WHEELER
PRESIDENT OF THE UNIVERSITY OF CALIFORNIA

CHARLES WILLIAM DABNEY
PRESIDENT OF THE UNIVERSITY OF TENNESSEE

Photograph by E. Chickering

HENRY SMITH PRITCHETT

PRESIDENT OF MASSACHUSETTS INSTITUTE OF TECHNOLOGY

WILLIAM DE WITT HYDE
PRESIDENT OF BOWDOIN COLLEGE

CHARLES FRANKLIN THWING
PRESIDENT OF WESTERN RESERVE UNIVERSITY

WILLIAM H. P. FAUNCE
PRESIDENT OF BROWN UNIVERSITY

  Photographed in Baltimore by Frances Benjamin Johnston

PRESIDENT DANIEL C. GILMAN,
Of the Johns Hopkins University.

CHARLES W. ELIOT, PRESIDENT OF HARVARD UNIVERSITY

DR. NICHOLAS MURRAY BUTLER

The new President of Columbia University, New York

 162

EDMUND J. JAMES
PRESIDENT OF NORTHWESTERN UNIVERSITY

Woodrow Wilson

WILLIAM RAINEY HARPER
From a photograph, copyright, 1903, by J. E. Purdy, Boston

DAVID STARR JORDAN

 166

DR. JOHN HUSTON FINLEY

WHO WAS RECENTLY INAUGURATED AS PRESIDENT OF THE COLLEGE OF THE CITY OF NEW YORK

≫ 167 ≪

PRESIDENT ARTHUR TWINING HADLEY OF YALE
UNIVERSITY.

SECOND

UNDERGRADUATE
EDUCATION
and the
EMERGENCE OF ACTIVISM

More than two hundred years ago, with the Enlightenment, man began effectively to proclaim the dignity of man, and the last one hundred years have seen the rapid expansion of universities to guarantee the continued teaching of that dignity. Not so many years ago, it seemed that the burgeoning knowledge of the social sciences, the humanities, technology, and the physical sciences would at long last bring about solutions to the few remaining problems which affect man's dignity, thereby freeing him once and for all to become more human and humane. As time passes and the rate of change increases, we see the promise of man's controlling his own destiny as something slippery and elusive.

With the rise of American universities and the coming of many adventurous and intense, impulsive and idealistic young people, it was hoped that the deteriorating process which has exploited and neglected man would be reversed. Higher education was seen as an institution to teach, inspire, and discipline; simultaneously, students were to inherit, grow, and lead. In short, the American university was established so that the fruits of science, the humanities, and technology would be turned exclusively to the service of man.

The following selection of writings clearly illustrates the undeviating dedication to undergraduate education and its complex tasks. With idealistic students having difficulty in defining the relationship between freedom, social commitment, and authority, between authority and authoritarianism, we see how similar the educational problems of the past resemble our own. Young people, then as now, came by their activism honestly by virtue of their age and national tradition. To many, anything less than all-out action represented a compromise. But, of course, then as now, there were very few simple or comprehensive answers. In article after article, undergraduates advocate new attitudes and values, reflecting their belief in the discovery of new ways of thinking and talking about man and their awareness of elements in traditional morality which no longer serve useful purposes. Surprisingly, the fundamental principles of contemporary student rebellions can be traced back to turn-of-the-century student concerns regarding the primacy of internal controls, individually relevant situations, and emphasis on human personalities rather than a priori standards. Confronted with tradition, undergraduates demonstrated and exemplified the values of education: they decided how they were going to channel their impatience, frustration, and activism into usable and relevant national debates.

Drawn by Harry Raleigh. Half-tone plate engraved by R. Varley

THE AMERICAN UNDERGRADUATE

BY CLAYTON SEDGWICK COOPER

FIRST PAPER: GENERAL CHARACTERISTICS

THE American college was recently defined by one of our public men as a "place where an extra clever boy may go and still amount to something."

This is indeed faint praise both for our institutions of higher learning and for our undergraduates; but judging from certain presentations of student life, we may infer that it represents a sentiment more or less common and wide-spread. Our institutions are criticized for their tendency toward practical and progressive education; for the views of their professors; for their success in securing gifts of wealth, which some people think ought to go in other directions; and for the lack of seriousness or the dissipation of the students themselves. Even with many persons who have not developed any definite or extreme opinions concerning American undergraduate life, the college is often viewed in the light in which Matthew Arnold said certain people regarded Oxford:

Beautiful city! so venerable, so lovely, so unravaged by the fierce intellectual life of our century, so serene! There are our young barbarians, all at play!

Indeed, to people of the outside world, the American undergraduate presents an enigma. He appears to be not exactly a

Drawn by Harry Raleigh

Half-tone plate engraved by H. C. Merrill

THE SERPENTINE DANCE AFTER A FOOT-BALL GAME

boy, certainly not a man, an interesting species, a kind of "Exhibit X," permitted because he is customary; as Carlyle might say, a creature "run by galvanism and possessed by the devil."

The mystifying part of this lies in the fact that the college man seems determined to keep up this illusion of his partial or total depravity. He reveals no unchastened eagerness to be thought good. Indeed, he usually "plays up" his desperate wickedness. He revels in his unmitigated lawlessness, he basks in the glory of fooling folks. As Owen Johnson describes Dink Stover, he seems to possess a "diabolical imagination." He chuckles exuberantly as he reads in the papers of his picturesque public appearances: of the janitor's cow hoisted into the chapel belfry; of the statue of the sedate founder of the college painted red on the campus; of the good townspeople selecting their gates from a pile of property erected on the college green; or as in graphic cartoons he sees himself returning from foot-ball victories, accompanied by a few hundred other young hooligans, marching wildly through the streets and cars to the martial strain,

There 'll be a hot time in the old town
 to-night!

In other words, the American student is partly responsible for the attitude of town toward gown. He endeavors in every possible way to conceal his real identity. He positively refuses to be accurately photographed or to reveal real seriousness about anything. He is the last person to be held up and examined as to his interior moral decorations. He would appear to take no thought for the morrow, but to be drifting along upon a glorious tide of indolence or exuberant play. He would make you believe that to him life is just a great frolic, a long, huge joke, an unconditioned holiday. The wild young heart of him enjoys the shock, the offense, the startled pang, which his restless escapades engender in the stunned and unsympathetic multitude.

This perversity of the American undergraduate is as fascinating to the student of his real character as it is baffling to a chance beholder, for the American collegian is not the most obvious thing in the world. He is not discovered by a super-

ficial glance, and surely not by the sweeping accusations of uninformed theoretical critics who have never lived on a college campus, but have gained their information in second-hand fashion from *questionnaires* or from newspaper-accounts of the youthful escapades of students.

We must find out what the undergraduate really means by his whimsicalities and picturesque attitudinizing. We must find out what he is thinking about, what he reads, what he admires. He seems to live in two distinct worlds, and his inner life is securely shut off from his outer life. If we would learn the college student, we must catch him off guard, away from the "fellows," with his intimate friend, in the chapter-house, or in his own quiet room, where he has no reputation for devilment to live up to. For college life is not epitomized in a story of athletic records or curriculum catalogues. The actual student is not read up in a Baedeker. His spirit is caught by hints and flashes; it is felt as an inspiration, a commingled and mystic intimacy of work and play, not fixed, but passing quickly through hours unsaddened by the cares and burdens of the world—

No fears to beat away—no strife to heal,
 The past unsighed for, and the future
 sure.

It is with such sympathetic imagination that the most profitable approach can be made to the American undergraduate. To see him as he really is, one needs to follow him into his laboratory or lecture-room, where he engages with genuine enthusiasm in those labors through which he expresses his temperament, his inmost ideals, his life's choice. Indeed, to one who knows that to sympathize is to learn, the soul windows of this inarticulate, immature, and intangible personality will sometimes be flung wide. On some long, vague walk at night beneath the stars, when the great deeps of his life's loyalties are suddenly broken up, one will discover the motive of the undergraduate, and below specious attempts at concealment, the self-absorbed, graceful, winsome spirit. Here one is held by the subtle charm of youth lost in a sense of its own significance, moving about in a mysterious paradise all his own, "full of dumb emotion, undefined longing, and with a deep sense of the romantic possibilities of life."

In this portrait one sees the real drift of American undergraduate life—the life that engaged last year in North American institutions of higher learning 349,566 young men, among whom were many of America's choicest sons. Thousands of American and Canadian fathers and mothers, some for reasons of culture, others for social prestige, still others for revenue only, are ambitious to keep these students in the college world. Many of these parents, whose hard-working lives have always spelled duty, choose each year to beat their way against rigid economy, penury, and bitter loss, that their sons may possess what they themselves never had, a college education. And when we have found, below all his boyish pranks, dissimulations, and masqueradings, the true undergraduate, we may also discern some of the pervasive influences which are to-day shaping life upon this Western Continent; for the undergraduate is a true glass to give back to the nation its own image.

HIS PASSION FOR REALITY

EARLY in this search for the predominant traits of the college man one is sure to find a passion for reality. "We stand for him because he is the real thing," is the answer which I received from a student at the University of Wisconsin when I asked the reason for the amazing popularity of a certain undergraduate.

The American college man worships at the shrine of reality. He likes elemental things. Titles, conventions, ceremonies, creeds—all these for him are forms of things merely. To him

> The rank is but the guinea's stamp,
> The man 's the gowd for a' that.

The strain of the real, like the red stripe in the official English cordage, runs through the student's entire existence. His sense of "squareness" is highly developed. To be sure, in the classroom he often tries to conceal the weakness of his defenses with extraordinary genius by "bluffing," but this attitude is as much for the sake of art as for dishonesty. The hypocrite is an unutterable abomination in his eyes. He would almost prefer outright criminality to pious affectation.

Sham heroics and mock sublimity are specially odious to him. The undergraduate is still sufficiently unsophisticated to believe that things should be what they seem to be: at least his entire inclination and desire is to see men and things as they are.

This passion for reality is revealed in the student's love of brevity and directness. He abhors vagueness and long-windedness. His speeches do not begin with description of natural scenery; he plunges at once into his subject.

A story is told at New Haven concerning a preacher who, shortly before he was to address the students in the chapel, asked the president of the university whether the time for his address would be limited. The president replied, "Oh, no; speak as long as you like, but there is a tradition here at Yale chapel that no souls are saved after twenty minutes."

The preacher who holds his sermon in an hour's grip rarely holds students. The college man is a keen discerner between rhetoric and ideas. No decisions are more prompt or more generally correct than his. He knows immediately what he likes. You catch him or you lose him quickly; he never dangles on the hook. The American student is peculiarly inclined to follow living lines. He is not afraid of life. While usually he is free from affectation, he is nevertheless impelled by the urgent enthusiasm of youth, and demands immediate fulfilment of his dreams. His life is not "pitched to some far-off note," but is based upon the everlasting now. He inhabits a miniature world, in which he helps to form a public opinion, which, though circumscribed, is impartial and sane. No justice is more equal than that meted out by undergraduates at those institutions where a student committee has charge of discipline and honor-systems. A child of reality and modernity, he is economical of his praise, trenchant and often remorseless in his criticisms and censures, for as yet he has not learned to be insincere and socially diplomatic. This penchant for reality emerges in the platform of a successful college athlete in a New England institution who, when he was elected to leadership in one of the college organizations, called together his men and gave them two stern rules:

First, stop apologizing! Second, do a lot of work, and don't talk much about it!

HIS NATURALNESS

THE undergraduate's worship of reality is also shown in his admiration of naturalness. The modern student has relegated into the background the stilted elocutionary and oratorical contests of forty years ago because those exercises were unnatural. The chair of elocution in an American college of to-day is a declining institution. Last year in one of our universities of one thousand students the course in oratory was regularly attended by three!

The instructor in rhetorical exercises in a college to-day usually sympathizes with the remarks of one Professor Washington Value, the French teacher of dancing at New Haven when that polite accomplishment was a part of college education. At one time when he was unusually ill-treated by his exuberant pupils, he exclaimed in a frenzy of Gallic fervor: "Gentlemen, if ze Lord vere to come down from heaven, and say, 'Mr. Washington Value, vill you be dancing mast' at Yale Collège, or vill you be étairnally damn'?' I would say to Him—' 'Sieur, eef eet ees all ze sem to you, I vill be étairnally damn'.' " The weekly lecture in oratory usually furnishes an excellent chance for relaxation and horseplay. A college man said to me recently: "I would n't cut that hour for anything. It is as good as a circus."

The student prefers the language of naturalness. He is keen for scientific and athletic exercises, in part at least because these are actual and direct approaches to reality. His college slang, while often superabundant and absurd, is for the sake of brevity, directness, and vivid expression. The perfect Elizabethan phrases of the accomplished rhetorician are listened to with enduring respect, but the stumbling and broken sentences of the college athlete in a student mass-meeting set a college audience wild with enthusiasm and applause.

Henry Drummond was perhaps the most truly popular speaker to students of the last generation. A chief reason for this popularity consisted in his perfect naturalness, his absolute freedom from pose and affectation. I listened to one of his first addresses in this country, when he spoke to Harvard students in Appleton Chapel in 1893. His general subject was "Evolution." The hall was packed with Harvard undergraduates. Collegians had come also from other New England institutions to see and to hear the man who had won the loving homage of the students of two continents. As he rose to speak, the audience sat in almost breathless stillness. Men were wondering what important scientific word would first fall from the lips of this renowned Glasgow professor. He stood for a moment with one hand in his pocket, then leaned upon the desk, and, with that fine, contagious smile which so often lighted his face, he looked about at the windows, and drawled out in his quaint Scotch, "Is n't it rather *hot* here?" The collegians broke into an applause that lasted for minutes, then stopped, began again, and fairly shook the chapel. It was applause for the natural man. By the telegraphy of humanness he had established his kinship with them. Thereafter he was like one of them; and probably no man has ever received more complete loyalty from American undergraduates.

HIS SENSE OF HUMOR

FURTHERMORE, the college man's love of reality is kept in balance by his humorous tendencies. His keen humor is part of him. It rises from him spontaneously on all occasions in a kind of genial effervescence. He seems to have an inherent antagonism to dolefulness and long-facedness. His life is always breaking into a laugh. He is looking for the breeziness, the delight, the wild joy of living. Every phenomenon moves him to a smiling mood. Recently I rode in a trolley-car with some collegians, and could not but notice how every object in the country-side, every vehicle, every group of men and women, would draw from them some humorous sally, while the other passengers looked on in good-natured, sophisticated amusement or contempt. The whole student mood is as light and warm and invigorating as summer sunshine. He lives in a period when

> 't is bliss to be alive.

Rarely does one find revengefulness or sullen hatred in the American undergraduate. When a man with these traits is discovered in college, it is usually a sign that he does not belong with collegians. His place is elsewhere, and he is usually shown the way thither by both professors and students. Heinrich Heine said he forgave his enemies, but not until they were dead.

The student forgives and usually forgets the next day. The sense of humor is a real influence toward this attitude of mind, for the student blots out his resentment by making either himself or his antagonist appear ridiculous.

He has acquired the fine art of laughing both at himself and with himself. A story is told of a cadet at a military school who committed some more or less trivial offense which reacted upon a number of his classmates to the extent that, because of it, several cadets were forced to perform disciplinary sentinel duty. It was decided that the young offender should be forthwith taken out on the campus, and ordered to kiss all the trees, posts, telegraph-poles, and, in fact, every free object on the parade-ground. The humorous spectacle presented was sufficient compensation to sweep quite out of the hearts of his classmates any possible ill feeling.

The faculty song, the refrain of which is

Where, oh, where is Professor ———?
Way down in the world below,

and is indulged in by many undergraduate students, usually covers all the sins and foibles of the instructors. One or two rounds of this song, with the distinguished faculty members as audience, is often found sufficient to clear the atmosphere of any unpleasantness existing between professors and students.

Not long ago, in an institution in the Middle West, this common tendency to wit and humor came out when a very precise professor lectured vigorously against athletics, showing their deleterious effect upon academic exercises. The following day the college paper gave on the front page, as though quoted from the professor's remarks, "Don't let your studies interfere with your education."

The student's humor is original and pointed. Not long ago I saw a very dignified youth solemnly measuring the walks around Boston Common with a codfish, keeping accurate account of the number of codfish lengths embraced in this ancient and honorable inclosure. His labors were made interesting by a gallery of collegians, who followed him with explosions of laughter and appropriate remarks.

Not long ago in a large university, during an exceedingly long and prosy sermon of the wearisome type which seems always to be coming to an end with the next paragraph, the students exhibited their impatience by leaning their heads over on their left hands. Just as it seemed sure that the near-sighted preacher was about to conclude, he took a long breath and said, "Let us now turn to the *other side* of the character of Saint Paul," whereupon, suiting the action to the word, every student in the chapel shifted his position so as to rest his head wearily upon the other hand.

RELIGION AND THE COLLEGE MAN

I HAVE often been asked by people who only see the student in such playful and humorous moods, "Is the American college man really religious?" The answer must be decidedly in the affirmative. The college boy—with the manner of young men somewhat ashamed of their emotions —does not want to talk much about his religion, but this does not prove that he does not possess the feeling or the foundation of religion. In fact, at present there is a deep current of seriousness and religious feeling running through the college life of America. The honored and influential students in undergraduate circles are taking a stand for the things most worth while in academic life.

The undergraduate's religious life is not usually of the traditional order; in fact it is more often unconventional, unceremonious, and expressed in terms and acts germane to student environment. College men do not, for example, crowd into the church prayer-meetings in the local college town. As some one has expressed it, "You cannot swing religion into college men, prayer-meeting-end-to." When the student applies to people such words as "holy," "saintly," or "pious," he is not intending to be complimentary. Furthermore, he does not frequent meetings "in derogation of strong drink." His songs, also, are not usually devotional hymns, and his conversation would seldom suggest that he was a promoter of benevolent enterprises.

Yet the undergraduate is truly religious. Some of the things which seem at first sight quite out of the realm of the religious are indications of this tendency quite as much as compulsory attendance upon chapel exercises. Dr. Henry van Dyke has said that the college man's songs and yells are his prayers. He is not the first one who has felt this in listening to Princeton seniors on the steps of Nassau Hall singing that thrilling hymn of loyalty, "Old Nassau."

I have stood for an entire evening with crowds of students about a piano as they sang with a depth of feeling more readily felt than described. As a rule there was little conversing except a suggestion of a popular song, a plantation melody, or some stirring hymn. One feels at such times, however, that the thoughts of the men are not as idle as their actions imply. As one student expressed it in a college fraternity recently, "When we sing like that, I always keep up a lot of thinking."

Moreover, if we consider the college community from a strictly conventional or religious point of view, the present-day undergraduates do not suffer either in comparison with college men of other days, or with other sections of modern life. The reports of the last year give sixty out of every one hundred undergraduates as members of churches. One in every seven men in the American colleges last season was in voluntary attendance upon the Bible classes in connection with the College Young Men's Christian Association.

The religious tendencies of the American undergraduates are also reflected in their participation in the modern missionary crusades both at home and abroad. Twenty-five years ago the entire gifts of North American institutions for the support of missions in foreign lands was less than $10,000. Last year the students and alumni of Yale University alone gave $15,000 for the support of the Yale Mission in China, while $131,000 represented the gifts of North American colleges to the mission cause in other countries. The missionary interests of students on this continent are furthermore revealed in the fact that 11,838 men were studying modern missions in weekly student mission study classes during the college season of 1909–10. At Washington and Lee University there were more college men studying missions in 1910 than were doing so in the whole United States and Canada sixteen years ago.

During the last ten years 4338 college graduates have gone to foreign lands from North America to give their lives in unselfish service to people less fortunate than themselves. Six hundred of these sailed in 1910 to fill positions in foreign mission ports in the Levant, India, China, Japan, Korea, Africa, Australia, and South America.

THE BACCHIC ELEMENT

FURTHERMORE, the standards of morals and conduct among the American undergraduates are perceptibly higher than they were fifty years ago. There is a very real tendency in the line of doing away with such celebrations as have been connected with drinking and immoralities. To be sure, one will always find students who are often worse for their bacchic associations, and one must always keep in mind that the college is on earth and not in heaven; but a comparison of student customs to-day with those of fifty years ago gives cause for encouragement. Even in the early part of the nineteenth century we find conditions that did not reflect high honor upon the sobriety of students; for example, in the year 1814 we find Washington Irving and James K. Paulding depicting the usual sights about college inns in the poem entitled "The Lay of the Scottish Fiddle." The following is an extract:

Around the table's verge was spread
Full many a wine-bewildered head
Of student learn'd, from Nassau Hall,
Who, broken from scholastic thrall,
Had set him down to drink outright
Through all the livelong merry night,
And sing as loud as he could bawl;
Such is the custom of Nassau Hall.
No Latin now or heathen Greek
The senior's double tongue can speak.
Juniors from famed Pierian fount
Had drank so deep they scarce could count
The candles on the reeling table.
While emulous freshmen, hardly able
To drink, their stomachs were so full,
Hiccuped, and took another pull,
Right glad to see their merry host,
Who never wine or wassail crost;
They willed him join the merry throng
And grace their revels with a song.

There has probably never been a time in our colleges when such scenes were less popular than they are to-day. Indeed, it is doubtful whether the American college man was ever more seriously interested in the moral, social, and religious uplift of his times. One of his cardinal ambitions is really to serve his generation worthily both in private and in public. In fact, we are inclined to believe that serviceableness is to-day the watchword of American college religion. This religion is not turned so much toward the individual as in former days. It is more socialized ethics. The undergraduate is keenly sensitive to the calls of modern society. Any one who is skeptical on this point may well examine the biographies in social, political, and religious contemporaneous history. In a recent editorial in one of our weeklies it was humorously stated that "Whenever you see an enthusiastic person running nowadays to commit arson in the temple of privilege, trace it back, and ten to one you will come against a college." President Taft and a majority of the members of his Cabinet are college-trained men. The reform movements, social, political, economic, and religious, not only in the West, but also in the Levant, India, and the Far East, are being led very largely by college graduates, who are not merely reactionaries in these national enterprises, but are in a very true sense "trumpets that sing to battle" in a time of constructive transformation and progress.

THE PLAY LIFE OF THE AMERICAN UNDERGRADUATE

UNDOUBTEDLY one of the reasons which helps to account for the lack of knowledge on the part of outsiders concerning the revival in college seriousness is found in the fact that the play life of American undergraduates has become a prominent factor in our educational institutions. Indeed, there is a general impression among certain college teachers and among outside spectators of college life that students have lost their heads in their devotion to intercollegiate athletics. And it is not strange that such opinions should exist.

A dignified father visits his son at college. He is introduced to "the fellows in the house," and at once is appalled by the awestruck way with which his boy narrates, in such technical terms as still further stagger the fond parent, the miracu-

lous methods and devices practised by a crack short-distance runner or a base-ball star or the famous tackle of the year. When in an impressive silence the father is allowed the unspeakable honor of being introduced to the captain of the foot-ball team, the autocrat of the undergraduate world, the real object of college education becomes increasingly a tangle in the father's mind. As a plain business man with droll humor expressed his feelings recently, after escaping from a dozen or more collegians who had been talking athletics to him, "I felt like a merchant marine without ammunition, being fired into by a pirate ship until I should surrender."

Whatever the undergraduate may be, it is certain that to-day he is no "absent-minded, spectacled, slatternly, owlish don." His interest in the present-day world, and especially the athletic world, is acute and general. Whether he lives on the "Gold Coast" at Harvard or in a college boarding-house in Montana, in his athletic loyalties he belongs to the same fraternity. To the average undergraduates, athletics seem often to have the sanctity of an institution. Artemus Ward said concerning the Civil War that he would willingly sacrifice all his wife's relatives for the sake of the cause. Some such feeling seems to dominate the American collegian.

CONCERNING ATHLETICS

BECAUSE of such athletic tendencies, the college student has been the recipient of the disapprobation of a certain type of onlookers in general, and of many college faculties in particular.

President Lowell of Harvard, in advocating competitive scholarship, in a Phi Beta Kappa address at Columbia University, said, "By free use of competition, athletics has beaten scholarship out of sight in the estimation of the community at large, and in the regard of the student bodies." Woodrow Wilson pays his respects to student athleticism by sententiously remarking, "So far as colleges go, the side-shows have swallowed up the circus, and we in the main tent do not know what is going on."

Professor Edwin E. Slosson, who spent somewhat over a year traveling among fourteen of the large universities, utters a jeremiad on college athletics. He found "that athletic contests do not promote friendly feeling and mutual respect between the colleges, but quite the contrary; that they attract an undesirable set of students; that they lower the standard of honor and honesty; that they corrupt faculties and officials; that they cultivate the mob mind; that they divert the attention of the students from their proper work; and pervert the ends of education." And all these cumulative calamities arrive, according to Professor Slosson, because of the grand stand, because people are *watching* foot-ball games and competitive athletics. The professor would have no objection to a few athletes playing football on the desert of Idaho or in the fastnesses of the Maine woods, provided no one was looking. "If there is nobody watching, they will not hurt themselves much and others not at all," he concedes.

> Meanwhile, regardless of their doom,
> The little victims play.

In fact, such argument appeals to the average collegian with about the same degree of weight as the remark of the Irishman who was chased by a mad bull. The Irishman ran until out of breath, with the bull directly behind him; then a sudden thought struck him, and he said to himself: "What a fool I am! I am running the same way this bull is running. I would be all right if I were only running the other way."

It will doubtless be conceded by fairminded persons generally that in many institutions of North America athletics are being over-emphasized, even as in some institutions practical and scientific education is emphasized at the expense of liberal training. It is difficult, however, to generalize concerning either of these subjects. Opinion and judgment vary almost as widely as does the point of view from which persons note college conditions. A recent college graduate from a State institution where mechanical education was always placed at the front said that if he were to return to college, he would take nothing that was practical. While a keen professor of one of the universities where athletics too largely usurped the time and attention of students, justifiably summed up the situation by saying:

The man who is trying to acquire intellectual experience is regarded as abnormal (a "greasy grind" is the elegant phrase, symptomatic at once of student vulgarity, ignorance, and stupidity), and intellectual eminence falls under suspicion as "bad form." The student body is too much obsessed of the "campus-celebrity" type,—a decent-enough fellow, as a rule, but, equally as a rule, a veritable Goth. That any group claiming the title *students* should thus minimize intellectual superiority indicates an extraordinary condition of topsyturvydom.

During the last twelve months, however, I have talked with several hundred persons, including college presidents, professors, alumni, and fathers and mothers in twenty-five States and provinces of North America in relation to this question. While occasionally a college professor as well as parent or a friend of a particular student has waxed eloquent in dispraise of athletics, by far the larger majority of these representative witnesses have said that in their particular region athletic exercises among students were not over-emphasized.

Yet it is evident that college athletics in America to-day are too generally limited to a few students who *perform* for the benefit of the rest. It is also apparent that certain riotous and bacchanalian exercises which attend base-ball and foot-ball victories have been very discouraging features to those who are interested in student morality. In another paper I shall treat at some length of these and other influences which are directly inimical to the making of such leadership as the nation has a right to demand of our educated men. At present, however, I wish to throw some light upon the student side of the athletic problem, a point of view too often overlooked by writers upon this subject.

In the first place, it needs to be appreciated that student athletics in some form or other has absorbed a considerable amount of attention of collegians in American institutions for over half a century. Fifty years ago, even, we find foot-ball a fast and furious conflict between classes. If we can judge by ancient records, these conflicts were often quite as bloody in those days as at present. An old graduate said recently that, compared with the titanic struggles of his day, modern football is only a wretched sort of parlor pastime. In those days the faculty took a hand in the battle, and a historical account of a New England college depicts in immortal verse the story of the way in which a divinity professor charged physically into the bloody savagery of the foot-ball struggle of the class of '58.

> Poor '58 had scarce got well
> From that sad punching in the bel—
> Of old Prof. Olmstead's umberell.

It will be impossible in this paper to take up the values of athletics as a deterrent to the dissolute wanderings and immoralities common in former times. Neither can one dwell upon the real apotheosis of good health and robust strength that regular physical training has brought to the youth of the country through the advent of college gymnasiums and indoor and outdoor athletic exercises. Much also might be said in favor of athletics, especially football, because of the fact that such exercises emphasize discipline, which, outside of West Point and Annapolis, is lamentably lacking in this country both in the school and in the family. While there is much need to engage a larger number of students in general athletic exercises, it is nevertheless true that even though a few boys play at foot-ball or base-ball, all of the students who look on imbibe the idea that it is only the man who trains hard who succeeds.

There is, too, a feeling among those who know intimately the real values of college play life, when wholesale denunciations are made of undergraduate athletics, that it is possible for one outside of college walls or even for one of the faculty to produce all the facts with accuracy, and yet to fail in catching the life of the undergraduate at play. Inextricably associated with college athletics is a composite and intangible thing known as "college spirit." It is something which defies analysis and exposition, which, when taken apart and classified, is not; yet it makes distinctive the life and atmosphere of every great seat of learning, and is closely linked not only with classrooms, but also with such events as occur on the great athletic grand stands, upon fields of physical contest in the sight of the college colors, where episodes and aims are mighty, and about which historical loyalties cling much as the old soldier's memories are entwined with the flag he has cheered and followed. While we are quoting from Phi Beta Kappa orators, let us quote from another, a contemporary of Longfellow, Horace Bushnell, whom Henry M. Alden has called, next to Emerson, the most original American thinker of his day. In his oration before the Phi Beta Kappa Society of Harvard sixty years ago, Dr. Bushnell said that all work was for an end, while play was an end in itself; that play was the highest exercise and chief end of man.

It is this exercise of play which somehow gets down into the very blood of the American undergraduate and becomes a permanently valuable influence in the making of the man and the citizen. It is difficult exactly to define the spirit of this play life, but one who has really entered into American college athletic events will understand it—the spirit of college tradition in songs and cheers sweeping across the vast, brilliant throng of vivacious and spellbound youth; the vision of that fluttering scene of color and gaiety in the June or October sunshine; the temporary freedom of a thousand exuberant undergraduates; pretty girls vying with their escorts in loyalty to the colors they wear; the old "grad," forgetting himself in the spirit of the game, springing from his seat and throwing his hat in the air in the ebullition of returning youth; the mercurial crowd as it demands fair play; the sudden inarticulate silences; the spontaneous outbursts; the disapprobation at mean or abject tricks,—or that unforgetable sensation that comes as one sees the vast zigzagging lines of hundreds of students, with hands holding one another's shoulders in the wild serpentine dance, finally throwing their caps over the goal in a great sweep of victory. One joins unconsciously with these happy spirits in this grotesque hilarity as they march about the stadium with their original and laughable pranks, in a blissful forgetfulness, for the moment at least, that there is any such thing in existence as cuneiform inscriptions and the mysteries of spherical trigonometry. Is there any son of an American college who has really entered into such life as this who does not look back lingeringly to his undergraduate days, grateful not only for the instruction and the teachers he knew, but also for those childish outbursts of pride and idealism when the deepest, poignant loyalties caught up his spirit in unforgetable scenes:

Ah! happy days! Once more who would
    not be a boy?

A friend of mine had a son who had been planning for a long time to go to Yale. Shortly before he was to enter college he went with his father to see a football game between Yale and Princeton. On this particular occasion Yale vanquished the orange and black in a decisive victory. After the game the Yale men were marching off with their mighty shouts of triumph. The Princeton students collected in the middle of the football-field, and before singing "Old Nassau," they cheered with even greater vigor than they had cheered at any time during the game, and this time not for Princeton, but for Yale. The sons of Eli came back from their celebration and stopped to listen and to applaud. As this mighty tiger yell was going up from hundreds of Princetonian throats, and as the Princeton men followed their cheers by singing the Yale "Boolah," the young man, who stood by his father, looked on in silence, indeed, with inexpressible admiration. Suddenly he turned to his father and said: "Father, I have changed my mind. I want to go to Princeton."

Such events are associated (in the minds of undergraduates) not only with the physical, but with the spiritual, with the ideal. The struggle on the athletic-field has meaning not simply to a few men who take part, but to every student on the sidelines, while the pulsating hundreds who sing and cheer their team to victory think only of the real effort of their college to produce successful achievement.

Standing beneath a tree near Soldiers' Field at Cambridge, with undergraduates by the hundred eager in their athletic sports on one side, and the ancient roofs of Harvard on the other, there is a simple marble shaft which bears the names of the men whom the field commemorates, while below these names are written Emerson's words, chosen for this purpose by Lowell:

Though love repine and reason chafe,
    There came a voice without reply—
'T is man's perdition to be safe,
    When for the truth he ought to die.

Not only upon the shields of our American universities do we find "veritas"; in spirit at least it is also clearly written across the face of the entire college life of our times. Gentlemanliness, open-mindedness, originality, honor, patriotism, truth —these are increasingly found in both the serious pursuits and the play life of our American undergraduates. The department in which these ideals are sought is not so important as the certainty that the student is forming such ideals of thoroughness and perfection. This search for truth and reality may bring to our undergraduates unrest or doubt or arduous toil. They may search for their answer in the lecture-room, on the parade-ground, in the hurlyburly of college comradeships, in the competitive life of college contests, or even in the hard, self-effacing labors of the student who works his way through college. While, indeed, it may seem to many that the highest wisdom and the finest culture still linger, one must believe that the main tendencies in the life of American undergraduates are toward the discovery of and devotion to the highest truth—the truth of nature and the truth of God.

17

THE AMERICAN UNDERGRADUATE

BY CLAYTON SEDGWICK COOPER

FIFTH PAPER: THE COLLEGE MAN AND THE WORLD

"HOW crooked can a modern business man be and still be straight?"

This question was propounded at a college dinner in New York by a young lawyer who, in behalf of the recent graduates of an Eastern university, had been asked to give utterance to some of the first impressions of a young alumnus upon his entrance into the life of the world. The question was not asked in a trifling manner, but it represented the query which inevitably arises in the mind of the graduate of ideals and high desires who to-day leaves his alma mater to plunge into the confused business and professional life of our times.

The question awakens the inquiry as to whether the colleges of America are to-day sending into the world trained leaders or subservient followers; whether graduates enter their special careers with a real message and mission, or whether, however optimistically they may begin their work, their high purposes are buried or not beneath the rush of practical and material affairs.

More than half a million students are to-day studying in our secondary schools and institutions of higher learning, with a money expense to the nation involving many million dollars. Tens of thousands of teachers and trained educators are devoting years of hard and faithful service in preparing these American youths for life. Are these students, after graduation, assuming real leadership? Are they contributing vision, judgment, and guidance in great national enterprises sufficiently definite and valuable to compensate the country for the sacrifices in time, money, and life that are made for the support and continuance of our educational institutions?

There seems to be a difference of opinion concerning this subject even in these times of vast educational enterprises. A business man of high repute wrote to me recently as follows:

I do not consider that our colleges are meeting the requirements of modern business life. From your own observation you must know that the most conspicuously successful people in business were conspicuously poor at the start, both financially and educationally. Grover Cleveland, who was not a college graduate, once said that the perpetuity of our institutions and the public welfare depended upon the simple *business-like* arrangement of the affairs of the Government.

This is the frequently expressed opinion of men of business and affairs, who present the successful careers of self-made men as an argument against collegiate education. This argument, however, fails to take into account that the same dogged persistence which has brought success to many of our present-day leaders in industrial and national life would have lost nothing in efficiency by college training.

Ask these masters of the business world who have risen by their individual force what they most regret in life. In nine cases out of ten the answer will be, "The lack of an opportunity for education." And they will usually add: "But my sons shall have an education. *They* shall not be handicapped as I have been." For the practical proof of the genuineness of this feeling, one has simply to read over the names in the catalogues of the great universities and colleges of America, where the names of the sons of virtually all the great business and professional men will be found.

While, therefore, we must take it for granted that Americans generally believe in a collegiate education, we may still question whether the colleges are really equipping for leadership the young men whom they are sending into our modern life. What, after all, do the colleges give? Out of one hundred graduates whom I asked what they had gained in college, twenty-one said, "Broader views of life," or perspective. Long ago John Ruskin said that the greatest thing any human being can do in the world is to see something, and then go and tell what he has seen in a plain way. To make the undergraduate see something beyond the commonplace is still the purpose of education. This enlarged vision is often the salvation of the individual student. It furnishes the impulse of a new affection. It attaches him to some great, uncongenial task. It gives him a mission great enough and hard enough to keep his feet beneath him. It saves him by steadying him.

THE ART OF RELAXATION

BUT no graduate is equipped for either mental or moral leadership until he has learned the art of relaxation. Both his health and his efficiency wait upon his ability to rest, to relax, to be composed in the midst of life's affairs. A real cause of American physical breakdown has been attributed by a famous physician "to those absurd feelings of hurry and having no time, to that breathlessness and tension, that anxiety of feature and that solicitude of results, that lack of inner harmony and ease, in short, by which with us the work is apt to be accompanied, and from which a European who would do the same work would, nine times out of ten, be free. It is your relaxed and easy worker, who is in no hurry, and quite thoughtless most of the while of consequence, who is your most efficient worker. Tension and anxiety, present and future all mixed up together in one mind at once, are the surest drags upon steady progress and hindrances to our success."

We find that one of the supreme purposes of education in ancient Greece was to prepare men to be capable of profiting by their hours of freedom from labor. In his writing upon education, Herbert Spencer gives special attention to the training that fits citizens for leisure hours.

The American college graduate is quite certain to receive early the impression that efficiency is synonymous with hustling; that modern life, in America at least, as G. Lowes Dickinson has said, finds its chief end in "acceleration." His danger is frequently in his inability to concentrate, to compose himself for real thoughtful leadership. Many a graduate takes years to get over that explosive energy of the sophomore, which spends itself without result. He takes display of energy for real force. His veins are filled with the hot blood of youth. He has not learned to wait. He is inclined to put more energy and nervous force into things than they demand. Like all youth, he is inclined to scatter his energy in all directions. He is therefore in danger sooner or later of breaking down physically or mentally, or both, and in spending the time which should be utilized in serviceableness in repairing the breakages of an uneconomic human machine. The average American graduate rarely needs Emerson's advice for a lazy boy, which was, "Set a dog on him, send him West, do something to him."

College training must give a man permanent idealism. Too often the graduate is inclined to fall into the line of march. He begins to worry and to lose his attractive gaiety and buoyancy. His habits of thought and study are soon

From an etching by Thomas Wood Stevens

THE LIBRARY AND THE THOMAS JEFFERSON STATUE, UNIVERSITY OF VIRGINIA

buried beneath the myriad details of business life or nervous pleasures. He becomes anxious about things that never happen. His anxiety about future happenings or results takes his mind from present efficiency. He becomes tense and tired and irritable. The attitude of composure and self-assurance which for a time he possessed in college is changed to a fearsome, troubled state, the end of which is the sanatorium or something even more baneful. I have sometimes thought that for a month at least I should like to see the office signs, "Do it now," "This is my busy day," "Step quickly," replaced by the old scriptural motto, "In quietness and confidence shall be your strength."

How shall our colleges assist American youth to secure the art of relaxation and to obtain the ability to relieve the tension of the workaday world by beneficial and delightful relief from business strain? Such gifts will often be the chief assets of a college man's training. Business men, and professional men, too, frequently reach middle life with no interest outside their specialties. When business is over, life is a blank. There are no eager voices of pleasant pursuits calling them away from the common round and routine tasks. It is too late to form habits. The rich rewards that education may give in leisure hours are lost, swallowed up by a thousand things that are merely on the way to the prizes that count. This is a terrific loss, and for this loss our colleges are in part at least at fault.

In certain institutions, however, we discover teachers who realize that a real part of their vocation consists in giving to at least a few students habits of real and permanent relaxation.

In a New England college recently I found a professor spending two afternoons a week in cross-country walks with students to whom he was teaching at an impressionable age habits that could be continued after college days. These walks occurred on Sunday and Thursday afternoons. With rigid persistence he had followed the plan of walking with his students for six or eight months, a sufficient time in which to form habits. He explained his object by saying that during his own college career he had engaged in certain forms of athletics which he was unable to pursue after graduation. While his college physical training had benefited him physically, he nevertheless found himself quite without habits of bodily relaxation. He was deprived of apparatus and the opportunity for many out-of-door games, but had found an immense value in walking. In passing on to these college boys this inclination for out-of-door relaxation, he was perhaps contributing his chief influence as a teacher.

Why should not habits of this kind be definitely organized and carried out by the physical department of our colleges? The opportunity to study trees, plants, and animals, and to become watchful for a hundred varying phases of nature, would furnish no small opportunity for projecting the influence of college into later life.

These tendencies toward relaxation take different forms according to individual tastes. One graduate of my acquaintance finds outlet for his nervous energy in a fish-hatchery. To be sure, he bores his friends by talking fish at every conceivable opportunity, and people frequently get the impression that his mind has a piscatorial rather than financial trend, as he loses no opportunity to dilate upon his latest adventure in trout; and yet his physician was doubtless right in saying that this man, the head of one of the largest financial institutions in America, owes his life as well as his success to this special form of relaxation.

A graduate of one of our large Western technical schools who is at the head of a big steel foundry has a private book-bindery, where with two or three of his friends the life of the world is lost evening after evening in the quiet and delightful air of books and book-making. The best treatises upon book-binding line the walls. Old and rare editions of the most famous masters are carefully sheltered in cases of glass. One end of the room is filled with his printing- and binding-machines. He showed me a beautifully bound volume which he himself had printed and bound. As he lovingly fingered the soft leather, reading to me his favorite passages from this masterpiece, I discerned in him a different man from the one I had often seen sitting in his grimy office discussing contracts for steel rails for China and bridge girders for South America. A deeper, finer man had been discovered in the hours of recreation. When asked how he happened to become interested in a matter so antipodal to his life-work, I found that the tendency started in college days, when he had been accustomed to browse among the books in the old college library under the faithful and regular guidance of a professor who once every week took his students to the library with the express purpose of inculcating a love for old and beautifully bound books.

The college, moreover, should start the graduate interest in philanthropic and serious enterprises which in themselves furnish suitable as well as pleasing relaxation to hundreds of American university men. Letters received from scores of recent

From an etching by Thomas Wood Stevens

THE ARCH BETWEEN THE DORMITORY QUADRANGLE AND THE TRIANGLE,
UNIVERSITY OF PENNSYLVANIA

graduates, many of whom are taking a large share in moral, social, and philanthropic endeavors, state that the beginnings of their interest dated with their experience in the Christian associations, settlement houses, boys' clubs, and charitable organizations of college days. One man of large philanthropic interest received his first view of a field of opportunity and privilege by hearing a lecturer on social betterment tell of finding a homeless boy hovering over the grating of a newspaper building on a winter night. The story touched a chord deep in the hearer, who

From an etching by Thomas Wood Stevens

OLD SOUTH MIDDLE, YALE UNIVERSITY

saw this vision of a world until then unknown to him—a world of suffering and hunger and cold; and when in later life it was made possible, he devoted his influence and his fortune to the erection of a home for friendless boys.

What is the college accomplishing toward the solution of that vital subject, the question of the immigrant? The possibilities of dealing with such far-reaching international problems is indicated by the influence of a college debate upon the subject, "What shall we do with the immigrant?" Through his reading and investigation of the subject, a certain student who engaged in this debate received his

From an etching by Katharine Merrill

THE MAIN HALL, UNIVERSITY OF WISCONSIN

first impetus toward what has proved to be one of the main contributions of his life to the nation by the establishment of Italian colonies that are probably as effective as any plans which are being suggested or utilized for the betterment of our foreign population.

MENTAL RESOURCEFULNESS

ACCORDING to President John G. Hibben of Princeton, graduates on the average earn only six dollars per week at the start. He justifies this low earning power by saying, "It is our endeavor to create a high potential of mental possibility rather than actual attainment."

We are inclined to consider efficiency only as expressed along social, economic, industrial, or mechanical lines. It is not strange in a period when financial standing bulks large in the minds of a comparatively new people that the recognition of the learned classes should be less noticeable than formerly. Yet reactive tendencies from strictly utilitarian education are evident. Individual and ideal aims of education are beginning to emerge above the commercial and mechanical aims. Already the salaries of college presidents and college teachers are increased, offering additional incentive for men of brains and scholarly achievement. Masters of industry who have been slaving for industrial and social progress are now becoming eager to push their accomplishments onward to mental and spiritual satisfactions. How otherwise can we explain such establishments as the Carnegie Foundation, the millions of Mr. Morgan for art, the vast sums contributed to religion and education in this and other lands? The ethical and social ideals of to-day are attaching thousands of our best youth to far-reaching endeavor. There is a new quest for that philosophy of life which, as Novalis stated it, could indeed bake no bread, but would give us God, freedom, and immortality. These are the signs of a new age of mental productivity—an age in which scholarship and learning will have a value for themselves; when people will appreciate that it is not merely the book one studies, but how he studies it that counts; that if we can produce a man of scholarly, thoughtful ability, we are sending into the world a person who will be proficient along any line in which he may engage.

In a Harvard address a few years ago, it was remarked by Mr. Owen Wister that America possessed only three men of unquestioned preëminence to whom students could turn for academic tuition in their respective lines. I believe it was Edmund Gosse who said that America had not produced a single poet deserving to rank with the unquestioned masters of English poetry. While these statements may be questioned, one realizes the general truth behind them when we contrast the marvelous and expensive architectural equipment of American universities with the paucity of great men and teachers.

The trend of the times, however, is slowly but certainly toward a new individualism. Attention is being focused more and more upon the values of life rather than upon the volume of life. The college graduate may not be able to deliver an oration in Hebrew in the morning and in Latin in the afternoon, but he is able to think through and around his problem, and this is mental resourcefulness, truly a chief aim of collegiate education and one of the first necessities for success. Emerson's prophecy may be realized in our day:

Perhaps the time has already come, when the sluggard intellect of this continent will look from under its iron lids and fill the postponed expectation of the world with something better than the exertion of mechanical skill. Our day of dependence, our long apprenticeship to the learning of other lands, draws to a close. The millions that around us are rushing into life cannot always be fed on the sere remains of frozen harvests. Who can doubt that poetry will revive and lead in a new age, as the star in the constellation Harp, which now flames in our zenith, astronomers announce shall one day be the pole star for a thousand years.

The challenge is to our undergraduates. And it will be accepted. The colleges will teach men to think, to be mentally alert and resourceful, and then the man will count in the leadership of modern life, in the sense intended by Dr. Simeon who, upon seeing a trained graduate approach, exclaimed, "There comes three hundred men."

In order to accomplish this, however, the college must make it a point to teach principles rather than dogmatic methods. Too often our systems of learning are too bookish. The boy is inclined to get the impression that there is only one way to do a thing, and that is the way he has learned from his professor or his text-book. A business man told me that he was recently obliged to dismiss one of his college graduates because the young man could not see or think of but one way to work out a mechanical proposition. His training had circumscribed him, cramped, limited, and enslaved him instead of freeing him. He was unable to move about easily in his sphere of chosen activity. He had gained a prejudice rather than a principle. He still lived in a classroom, though out in the world. His progress was waterlogged in academic conservatism.

From an etching by Helen B. Stevens

UNIVERSITY HALL, UNIVERSITY OF MICHIGAN

LIFE-WORK PROPAGANDA

It is, moreover, time for constructive action on the part of both college and alumni in the matter of directing students to their proper calling. While it is impossible for our colleges to make great men out of indifferent raw material, it is possible to assist undergraduates to discover their in-

herent bent or capacity. Until the student has made such a discovery, the elective system which is now general in our American institutions is something of a farce. The lazy student, undecided in his vocation, uses it as a barricade through which he wriggles and twists to his degree, or at best is tempted in a dozen various directions, selecting disconnected subjects, in no one of which he finds his chief aptitude. The elective system to such a student is an art-gallery without a key, a catalogue without the pictures. He does not know what he wishes to see.

This undergraduate ability or inclination is not easily grasped either by himself or by others. It requires study and discriminating sympathy, to extricate a main desire from many incidental likings. Frequently the desire itself must be virtually created. It is a common remark among American undergraduates, "I wish I *knew* what I was fitted for." The college is under deep obligation to serve the nation not merely by presenting a great number of excellent subjects, which, if properly selected, will land the young man in positions of leadership and usefulness; but it may and must go beyond this negative education, and assist the student actually to form his life purpose.

American institutions of learning are at present neglecting an opportunity *par excellence* for presenting different phases of life-work to undergraduates, especially emphasizing the relation of this life-work to the great branches of leadership and modern enterprise. There are hundreds of students being graduated from our institutions to-day who have not decided what they are to do in after life. Even if we assume that these men are prepared in an all-round way for life, it must be realized that they are severely handicapped by the necessity of trying different lines of work for years after graduation before fixing upon their permanent vocation. They not only miss the tremendous advantage of enthusiasm and impulse of the young, but they are also in danger of drifting rather than of moving forward with positive and aggressive activity.

A NEW COLLEGE OFFICER NEEDED

I SEE no possibility of bringing undergraduates to a decision of their proper life-work without the assistance of a new office in our educational institutions. A man is needed who can treat with students with real human interest, as well as with teaching intelligence. He should not be the college pastor, who is looked upon as a professional religionist, and therefore shunned by many students who need him most, but one definitely and actively responsible for the development of leadership. He should

be a close student of college affairs, sympathetic with students, human, high-minded, natural, and keenly alive to humor and social interests. In some institutions this man might hold the leadership in philanthropic, religious, and social-service interests. It might be his privilege to arrange lectures by leading men of the country who were filled with zeal for their callings. The man who could make possible the endowment of such a chair in a great university would be doing a great work for his country.

LEARNING AND INVESTIGATION

BUT while the American undergraduate may consistently look to the college to furnish him with ideals and with the methods of making these ideals effective, the world looks to the college for definite and advanced information. The college, with its accumulated stores of intellect, its apparatus, and its unusual means for observation, owes the world a debt that none but it can pay. And this is the gift which the college has given, and is still giving, to the world so quietly, so unobtrusively, that the world scarcely dreams of the source of its gain. Let one think of the myriad signs of modern progress by which society is being constantly carried forward. Behind the scenes you will find some quiet, hidden worker in a laboratory or library, an unpractical man perhaps, but one through whom a new realm of possibilities in science or industry or letters have been revealed.

What is the world's interest in these men—men who are so generally underpaid that much of their best work is made impossible by the necessary outside labors to support their families, who, beyond their own personal satisfaction, have as little recognition as perhaps any workers of modern society? When the world demands expert knowledge in industry, science, literature, and art, the college may well reply, "When are you going to show your gratitude for the self-sacrifice and far-reaching labors of thousands of devoted men whose work is both a challenge and an example to the world to-day?"

And this example of the man who learns to devote himself to one thing is not lost upon the undergraduate, to whom example is ever stronger than precept. Indeed, it is this tendency to learn how to do one thing well that is bringing the colleges into the attention of the modern world. The secret of genius is to be able to seize upon some concrete, near-at-hand piece of work, to see it with unobstructed and steady vision, and then, out of the rich treasure of knowing how to do one thing thoroughly, to draw by insight and expression the general principle.

For, after all, the contribution of the college to the world is often one which cannot be fully analyzed. It is not discovered in a thorough knowledge of a curriculum or in the statistics of athletics any more than a foreign country is discovered in a guide-book or in a hasty recital of its industries. There is no master word to express what a college career may mean or should mean to American youth who in years of high impression experience with a multitude of their fellows

Days that flew swiftly like the band
　That in the Grecian games had strife,
And passed from eager hand to hand
　The onward-dancing torch of life.

After we have said much concerning the life and the work of the American undergraduate, there is still a valuable thing which the college should impart to him, and through which he should become enabled to present with greater charm and with greater force the message which is in his soul. This valuable thing, at once both idealism and incentive, is the undergraduate's *individual* message to the world. It may be composed of knowledge, the ability to think, the faculty of relaxation, and the power to do faithfully and successfully some given task. These things, however, are all dependent upon the *spirit* of the actor, upon his vision, his determination, his ambitious and unflagging attempts. The true modern university contributes to the world a great-minded and a great-hearted man, to whom college life has been a soul's birth as well as a mind's awakening. It gives to its youth that peculiar but indispensable thing which burned in the heart of the young art-student who stood before the masterpiece and said, "I, too, am a painter."

THE END

THE UPPER CHAMBER

BY LIZETTE WOODWORTH REESE

OH, high and still!
　　As still
As drip of dew
In August, when no gusts do pass;
And marigolds, a score or two,
Pour their thick yellow down the grass
Under my neighbor's sill.

My neighbor 's gone. She went,
A little gray, a little bent,
A day or two ago.
Just now I saw her plain,
From the dull shop across the lane,
Homeward coming slow,
Her gay, plaid shawl
Upon her head,
Her apron filled with bundles small.
I had forgot that she was dead!

I hope that still place holds for her
Some common little thing,

Fit for remembering,
A bit of years that were;
A tall chair painted black,
With gilt rose on its back;
A dish or jug;
Or else a braided rug
Of red and blue,
The kind she used to make
On rainy days, when her old house did ache
With memories through and through.

For such a simple thing was she,
Close to the earth, as flower or tree,
A sweet and honest country wife,
Bound to a hard, belovèd life;
I hope that He,
Lord of that Chamber fair,
Some homeliness keeps for her there,
Some bit of long ago,—
A rug, a chair,—
Else will she miss it so.

18

UNDERGRADUATE LIFE AT HARVARD

By Edward S. Martin

WITH ILLUSTRATIONS BY W. H. HYDE AND HOWARD PYLE

IF anyone started out to write about the people of the city of New York and their customs and manner of life, he would hardly think it necessary to say that there were many different sorts of people there who were busy about many different sorts of things, and lived various lives under conditions of wide diversity. It is understood that in a big city these differences of people and aims and circumstances always exist, but it is not so well appreciated to what degree analogous diversities exist in a great college. We are all ready to think, for all that some of us know better, that a college-boy is just a college-boy, and that one college-boy is about like another, and that they all go to college for about the same purpose, and pursue it in about the same way. There is an approximation to truth in that supposition, but not a very close one. The extremes of humanity in a big town are, of course, vastly farther apart than any two lads in a Harvard class, but still the difference between Harvard undergraduates is so considerable that it must be appreciated if one is to form any just idea of the elasticity and comprehensiveness of the bond that includes them all. In the academic department of Harvard there are nowadays nearly eighteen hundred young men. Rather more than half of them come from places so near Cambridge, that they can spend their Sundays at home. Pretty nearly half come from Boston and the towns and cities immediately tributary to it. Six or seven hundred come from outside of New England, and of these about one hundred and fifty or seventy-five come from New York and its suburbs. New England, outside of eastern Massachusetts, sends the rest. These eighteen hundred young men possess eighteen hundred different outfits of personal idiosyncracies, and besides that are exponents of exceedingly various systems of raising. The lads who come from a long distance are apt, though by no means sure, to be sons of well-to-do parents, and inured from childhood to the comforts and in many cases to the luxuries of life. A great many of those who come from the Boston district are in a similar predicament, but a large proportion of those who live within easy reach of Cambridge are sons of people who have little money to spare, and who have to count carefully the cost of the education they give their children. In this great collection of young men there are lads who are used, when at home, to dine in a dress-coat, and very many others who never possessed a dress-coat and see no immediate prospect of requiring one ; there are lads with good manners and lads with no manners at all ; lads who have been taught to keep clean and lads whose ablutions are infrequent and perfunctory ; lads who are used to society and lads who are not ; lads who are eager after knowledge for learning's sake ; lads who covet it be-

The Johnson Gate (West). Erected in 1890.

cause knowledge is power ; lads whose parents are anxious that they should learn as much as possible because a smattering of knowledge is elegant.   And, of course, there are lads of strong character and weak lads ; lads whose minds have matured and lads who are still very young ; lads of good morals and lads with an inclination toward unwholesome experiment ; lads with an acute interest in athletics and physical prowess, and lads who are indifferent to muscle or speed ; lads for whom the serious business of life has already begun, and others for whom the material conveniences have been provided in advance and who seek mainly such a training and such experiences as may best enable them to profit by what they have got.   The usual length of time that a lad spends as an undergraduate in college is four years—not enough even under the most favorable conditions to make him over and turn him out a new man.   Accordingly, as lads differ widely when they enter Harvard, they also differ widely when they are graduated.   But they are perceptibly more alike than they were. They do not live together four years under conditions approximately similar without gathering some things in common.   A group of Harvard seniors look more like

individuals of the same breed than a group of Harvard Freshmen.   There is less difference in their manners, their dress, their talk, and they may even have come to hold a good many sentiments in common.   Big as she has grown to be, multifarious as her brood is, and in spite of the strong centrifugal tendencies that separate her children and send them each about his proper business, Harvard still stamps her own individuality upon them, in faint lines, it may be, but distinctly enough for practised eyes to detect.

There was an old Harvard and there is a new, and the line of separation is so recent that a graduate of less than twenty years standing can remember when it began to appear.   It came with the elective system, and has developed year by year as that system has developed, and as students' names have multiplied in the Harvard catalogue.   Twenty years ago there were still classes and class-feeling at Harvard.   Most of the studies of Freshman year and nearly half of the Sophomore studies were prescribed.   There were then about two hundred students in a class.   There were some lectures which a whole class attended in a body, but for general purposes of instruction each class was divided arbitrarily on

The Flower Rush on Class Day.

195

Vestibule, Memorial Hall, showing Memorial Tablets on the Right.

proportion of them by sight. Each class had its seats together, and was thus divided off conveniently for inspection according to its seniority. Most lads came to college with some ready-made friends, and those who came from the larger schools had a considerable squad of more or less intimate associates to start with. The members of these bands of school-mates were assigned to different divisions according to their names, and shared with one another the information they got about new men. Abbott, who had been at school with Smith and took his meals at the same club-table with him,

an alphabetical basis into divisions of thirty or forty men, who recited together. At that time all of a Freshman's class-room associations were with Freshmen. So were most of his other associations. He first got to know the members of his division by name from hearing their names called in the recitation-room. Presently, if he was of a reasonably social turn, he had scraped acquaintance with most of the men of his own division. To some lectures half the class, or even the whole class, went together. The roll-call at such lectures helped to identify the members of the class. At prayers, too, the Freshman saw his classmates all together, and usually his devotions did not absorb him so much but that every morning he looked a good many of his fellow-worshippers over. At prayers, too, every day he saw nearly all the undergraduates in college, and came to know a large

quickly formed the acquaintance of Adams, Arbuthnot, Allardice, Bates and Barstow, and imparted his views about those young gentlemen to Smith, who reciprocated by putting Abbott in possession of his impressions of Rathbone, Robinson, Sands, Sawyer and Thompson. Lawrence, at the same club-table, presently knew Knowles, all the Lowells, Lane, Mullins, Marvine, Notman, and Pope ; and Abbott and Smith learned very quickly what he thought of them. It seems to a retrospective graduate that in Harvard College in those days about three-fifths of the cursory talk of average undergraduates was about one another. It began when sub-Freshmen met to be examined for admission, and it continued until graduation. The amount of attention that men paid to one another and the time they devoted to estimating one another's intellectual, physical, social, and moral qualities, and discussing details of conduct was extraordinary. It cannot be said that every man in a class knew every other man, but the apparatus for bringing men of the same class together was efficient, and it did usually happen that by the end of Freshman year and estimates were in a constant state of revision and reconstruction. In those days the sentiment called class-feeling flourished. Men knew their classmates, and knew their class, though their acquaintance was by no means limited to it. After Freshman

Morning Prayers—Appleton Chapel.

nearly every man believed that he knew, or knew about, every man in his class whose acquaintance it seemed likely to be worth his while to make. Men were misjudged, misunderstood, overestimated and underestimated ; but acquaintance was very general and was constantly ripening, year, especially, they began to know the men in other classes, and often to form friendships with them. But they always felt a strong interest in their own class, bragged about it as a class, and believed it, if possible, to be the best class in college, or certainly better than the classes immediate-

The Delta Phi Club.

what best suits his taste, inclinations, and purposes. Most of the elective courses are open to students of several classes and to graduate students, and when a Freshman has sorted out the studies he purposes to pursue, he finds himself in the lecture or recitation room with an unclassified body of learners, most of them no doubt Freshmen like himself, but very likely with plenty of Sophomores too, and possibly with other upper-class men and graduate students. Compulsory prayers have passed out of existence, and he rarely or never sees his own class all together at one time. Indeed, there is not a lecture-room in Harvard College that will seat all the members of the present Freshmen class at once. He rarely even sees a group of men together in any class-room of whom he can be sure that all of them are his class-mates. Instead of reciting day after day throughout a college year with the same squad of youths, he recites with four or five different sets, each of which is composed of men who happen to have chosen the same course as he. It is possible, in the course of a year or two, under favorable conditions to learn to know a good deal about two hundred men, but to get the run of four or five hundred men under conditions that are not particularly favorable is, obviously enough, impracticable.

ly ahead of it and next behind it. They knew it could cheer louder than any other class, and so far as demonstrated facts allowed, they tried to believe that it had the best ball-nine and the fastest crew. A Harvard class in the centennial year of American independence was still a family, not very closely united, but still conscious and appreciative of a tie which was recognized as existent, even though it did not bind very tight.

Nowadays a Harvard class has come to be a much larger and looser aggregation of individuals, and the facilities for knitting it together have almost disappeared. Between four and five hundred men now enter college together. Only a single study, English, is prescribed to all of them. All the rest they select, each man choosing

But though the tie of class has been so stretched and honey-combed at Harvard that it does not serve the social purpose it once did, it must not be supposed that every Harvard man goes his own gait without definite ties of association with his fellows. The Harvard " Club Book " and the Harvard " Index " for last year record the ti-

UNDERGRADUATE LIFE IN 1679.

" We found there eight or ten young fellows sitting around, smoking tobacco, with the smoke of which the room was
so full, that you could hardly see."

tles, and in most cases the membership of some ninety organizations of students, some primarily social, some remotely so, but all of them serving in different degrees to bring men together. In this list are the half-dozen organizations which are devoted to the interests of the college press ; the score, or thereabouts, devoted to sports and athletics ; the five or six devoted to music ; the school clubs, as the Andover, Groton, St. Mark's, and St. Paul's clubs, where the tie is a common experience in a preparatory school ; the clubs of locality, as the Canadian, Southern, and Maine clubs ; the religious societies, half a dozen of them ; the clubs based on an interest in a particular study, as the English, Classical, and Natural History clubs ; the clubs where French and German are spoken; the political clubs ; the clubs in derogation of strong drink ; the debating clubs ; many other clubs devoted to other interests, and finally the half-score or so of clubs chiefly social, some large, some small, whereof whatever other excuse they find for being, the chief basis of membership is general affinity. In this latter group belong the Hasty Pudding and Pi Eta, the Porcellian and the A. D., the Institute of 1770 and its shadowy satellite,

Suit Worn by Barnabas Hedge, a Member of the Class of 1783, at the Graduating Exercises of the Class.

the "Dicky ;" the Alpha Delta Phi, the Delta Phi, the Zeta Psi, and the Theta Delta Chi, all of which have houses or rooms where the members meet and spend more or less of their time. These last four clubs are all of comparatively recent origin. So is the Delta Upsilon, which differs from them in having a larger membership, and, at last accounts, in allowing considerations of scholarship and literary proclivities to influence its choice of members. Like it in that respect are the O. K. and the Signet, societies of age and standing, but without club-rooms. Finally there is the Med. Fac., and such social apparatus as Harvard has these various organizations constitute. There are enough of them to cover a good deal of ground if their membership was widely enough distributed, but, as a matter of fact, the societies that are of the most use in promoting acquaintance and social relations affect only a small proportion of the undergraduates. A few men belong to more clubs than they have time to attend to, and a large majority of their fellows belong to none at all. What concerns the majority is possibly of the most importance, but as long as there is a social machine at Harvard it is as well to look it over and see how it works and what it does.

When Thomas Bulfinch, of Boston, enters Harvard with some four or five hundred other young men, he finds himself in possession of a good many ready-made social advantages. He has been fitted for college at a good private school in Boston, where the other lads of his year were boys whom he had known ever since they were all in knickerbockers. A dozen of them enter at the same time. They are sons of well-to-do people in Boston society, and are a reasonably good-looking, civilized squad of youths. They organize themselves into a club-table, and take their meals together at the best boarding-house they can find or afford. They not only know one another pretty well, but they all have more or less acquaintance with the upper classmen, and most of them have cousins or brothers or old family friends in college. So Thomas steps into a ready-made circle, and proceeds to take notice how he may profitably enlarge it. He has talked Harvard college pretty steadily with his pals for some years, and has a fairly accurate knowledge of the salient social facts about it. He is a fair student, and has a good preparation, and a tolerably well-trained mind; and if he was ambitious to be a high scholar he could probably be one, but college offers him so much besides high-scholarship that seems worth his while, that he is quite satisfied to be a fair scholar only, and to devote a considerable share of his attention to the experience of other sensations and the accomplishment of other ends. He has a good equipment of energy, both physical and intellectual, and is a lad of force, a good deal of it being still undeveloped. Besides the necessary book-learning which he got at school, he acquired exceptional proficiency in manipulating a base-ball. He enjoys playing base-ball and intends to play in college, and his pals know of his proficiency, and think and talk a good deal about it. Wherever Thomas goes, to his lectures and recitations, to Jarvis and the Soldiers' Field, to his meals and his room, to other fellows' rooms, to the billiard-room in Harvard Square most affected by Freshmen, and to punches, and in and out of Boston, he sees new faces and takes note of them. He has a room in a private dormitory where several of his club-table companions also live, and he gets to know by sight other men in that building. He and his pals presently form relations with other squads of youths from other schools who constitute other club-tables, and with whom they discuss issues of class politics. At the class-meeting Thomas's crowd run him for captain of the ball nine, but a bigger crowd from another school down him and get their man in. Still Thomas's name has been spoken in the meeting and he has made one or two more acquaintances there. It must not be supposed that he is or ever becomes while in college overready to make acquaintances. He is polite and civilly responsive, but is hardly more likely to speak to a man whom he does not know in the yard or in a Cambridge street-car than you would be to speak to a stranger on Broadway or in an elevated railroad train. He is especially strict with himself at first about scraping an acquaintance with a man, and especially an upperclass-man, whom he wants to know, for fear that any betrayal of unchas-

tened eagerness would be discerned and remembered to his social detriment. Being of a social turn, however, Thomas does make acquaintances, some by hook, and some by casual crook, but most of them by more formal processes of introduction. Some of his friends in the upper classes have him in their minds, and pay him the civility to call upon him. He has something to say to new acquaintances, and has been used to having views and expressing them, and his manners are good, and more than all he has in fair measure that balance of faculties that is called common sense; and so it happens that he usually leaves an agreeable impression behind him. He studies intelligently but not to such excess as to prejudice his interest in the social side of college life. When spring comes he plays base-ball on his class-nine, and such men in his class as care for athletics get to know him by sight. So do men in other classes whose interest in base-ball is acute. He doesn't necessarily become popular because he is a base-ball player, but he becomes conspicuous enough to promote the establishment of his identity and to make the men who direct the social destinies of the place

The Porcellian Club.

aware of his existence. The upshot of it is that Thomas, becoming conspicuous enough to be discerned, and being agreeable enough to be liked, and being satisfactory in most overt particulars, presently finds himself the possessor of a coveted distinction in being one of the ten Freshmen elected members of the Institute of 1770.

The precise relation of the D. K. E. society, vulgarly known as the "Dicky," to the Institute, is a secret which is shared pretty equally between the members of the society, and the newspapers of Boston. The newspapers explain annually that the "Dicky" is a society behind the Institute, and that the first two-thirds or so of the hundred men who are elected into the Institute become members of the "Dicky." The newspapers are quite confident that the first ten of the Institute are also the first ten of the "Dicky," and when members of first tens are seen shortly after their election doing all manner of fantastic things about Harvard Square, and even in Boston, the explanation is that these young men are "running for the Dicky." Judging from outward manifestations this "running" seems to be a process of probation wherein the candidate is handed over to tormentors whose will for the time being

"In Noyes's room the awful pot appeared."

Drawing by Washington Allston, class of 1800. Reproduced in the Souvenir of the Hasty Pudding Centennial.

Programme of a Pi Eta Entertainment.

Drawn by F. D. Millet.

takes the place in him of his own. When Thomas Bulfinch, after his name has been spelled out in the yard at night by the Sophomore members of the Institute, is seen leaving newspapers at Sophomores' doors in the early morning, wheeling baby-wagons along Massachusetts Avenue, and doing other such humble offices, no body who knows Harvard College will have any doubt that he will presently be a member of the "Dicky." From that time on it is plain sailing for him. There is no bushel over his candle. It has been put in a candle-stick, and set forth, and if it does not shine it will be because of a defect in luminosity, and not from any lack of fit position.

When Thomas returns to college in the beginning of his Sophomore year, he occupies a place of considerable social power, for it falls to him and his nine peers of the Institute to select the next ten of their class-mates who seem most suitable for membership of that society. With four or five hundred men to choose from, whom do they select? Naturally their choice is limited to the men they happen to know, and perhaps between them all they know half the class. Thomas's special interest in this process of selection is to look after the interest of those of his particular fa-

Strawberry Night at the Hasty Pudding Club.

miliars whom he likes the best. He sees to it that as many men as possible from his club-table get into the second ten. The beneficiaries of his influence, on being admitted, aid him as far as they can in getting a due number of their pals and his into the third ten, so that in due time the whole club-table is taken into the Institute, and a fair proportion—perhaps all—of them get in early enough to share in the advantages of the shadowy Dicky. And as it happens with Thomas's club-table, so it happens with other club-tables, made up of men from other schools. The club-tables do not have things all their own way in Sophomore year; neither do their members necessarily abuse the advantages of their position, but their position is advantageous, and they profit by it.

Early in Sophomore year, Thomas, continuing his triumphant social career, is invited to be a member of one of the small clubs made up mainly of Seniors and Juniors, which take in a few Sophomores. He joins, say, the Delta Phi. It affords him the conveniences of a pleasant club-house and the society of three or four members of his own class, ten or twelve Juniors, and a like number of Seniors. Very likely also it relieves him of the risk of suffering inconvenience from the enforcement of the no-license law which prevails in Cambridge, and that is a consideration, for it should be known that there is no public place in Cambridge where two sojourners may lawfully share a bottle of beer over their lunch. Thomas finds the society of the Delta Phi club-house agreeable and its privileges handy, and it is possible that he might spend too much of his time there if it did not happen that while his habits as a Delta Phi clubman are still in a formative state he learns that he is one of three or four gentlemen who have been chosen to represent the Sophomore class in the A. D. Club. Being already an active member of one club and two societies, two certainly, and all presumably, with club-rooms to maintain, Thomas blinks a little at the prospect of incurring liability for another set of club dues, especially as he has about as much present use for two clubs of the same general character as a cat traditionally has for two tails. Nevertheless, he bows gracefully to the system, and promptly joins the A. D., thereby securing another set of club-house privileges and further advantages of social intercourse with selected outfits of Seniors and Juniors.

Thomas has now been in college only a year and a half, but his social career is practically complete. The only club that

Hasty Pudding Club Poster, 1876.

Silver Medal Bearing the Seal of the Pi Eta Society.

is left in college to which he considers it an imperative necessity to be joined is the Hasty Pudding; and into that he will glide in due time to a certainty, and at no necessary cost of the slightest intermediate effort. If his aspirations are satisfied he will pay such attention as is necessary to his studies, and spend the greater part of his leisure in his clubs. He will find congenial society in them, and will probably make friendships which will be a pleasure to him in after life. He is well situated to have a certain kind of fun. He has the usufruct of one complete set of the social privileges of the Harvard system, unhampered by any reasonable possibilities of reverses, or any irksome responsibilities about anything but his personal comfort. He must study enough to keep up with his classes, or else he will be dropped, but even if that happens he will always enjoy some of the most agreeable privileges that can belong to a graduate. There will always be a couple of pleasant houses in Cambridge where he will be welcome and will receive polite attentions from agreeable young fellows, whether he comes out to a dinner, or to class day or commencement, or stops on his way in town after watching some game on the Soldiers' Field. It is not surprising that some men after achieving membership in the small clubs take little thought thereafter about the further extension of their experience of Harvard life. Into the clubs they go, and there they stay, content with ease and good company, as calmly and ingloriously as a billiard-ball in its pocket, their main use in the college microcosm being to afford observers awful examples of Harvard indifference.

The small clubs are not conducive to sustained effort in the public service on the part of their members, but, after all, their seductions are not necessarily irresistible.

inherited vigor to permit his powers to stagnate, he will still keep in the ring, for all that there are cushioned seats reserved for him in private boxes among the spectators. He will still, in spite of his embarrassment of social opportunity, pay decent attention to his work as a student, he will play baseball if his efficiency in that continues to be so exceptional as to make his services desired by the captain of the University nine;

One of the More Luxurious Rooms (Claverly Hall).

Young men of energy and ambition may find it amusing on occasions to sit on the edge of a table and throw dice for drinks, but they will not be content to settle down to that sort of thing as a steady occupation. For superior men who are too active to be pocketed, the clubs are pleasant without being unprofitable. It usually happens, in spite of the apparently haphazard system by which the small clubs are recruited, that a good many superior lads get into them, who continue to be forces in the college during all the remaining years of their course. It is the instinct of leaders to lead, and lead they will if for nothing more than for leadership's own sake. There are usually such leaders among the Harvard clubmen, but they are leaders because it is in them, and rather in spite of their being in the clubs than because of it. Supposing that Thomas is a young fellow of too much

when he gets into the Pudding he will act in theatricals perhaps, and he will try generally to keep his finger in such of the college pies as come within his reach. If he is recognized as a representative man of energy and influence he may be chosen into the Signet or O. K., even though he has no special turn for letters, and has evaded the importunities of the editors of the college papers. When his class graduates, he will very likely figure as one of its class-day marshals, and what is more important, he will carry away with him, along with some scholarship and friendships and associations of value, a considerable share of true education which will be useful to him in transacting the various business of life. Harvard will have been a generous mother to Thomas ; somewhat too indulgent no doubt, but still truly munificent.

If Thomas's luck had taken a slightly different turn he might have gone in the Zeta Psi and Porcellian clubs, and so into the Pudding; or he might have failed to reach either A. D. or Porcellian, but still have been a member of one of the younger clubs, and still a member of the Pudding; or he might have taken a different course at the start and brought up in the Pi Eta or Delta Upsilon clubs, in either of which he would have found plenty of companions. And again it might have happened to him, as it does actually happen to two-thirds of his classmates, to go through college without joining any club or society whatever, except such as are based on a common interest in some study, or some school, or locality, or in some form of religion. If this latter experience had been his there would have been nothing deplorable about his fate. In Harvard College proper twenty years ago there were less than eight hundred students. At the beginning of the present year there were 1,754. The social apparatus of the college has been devel-

oped and supplemented to some extent, but its enlargement has not begun to keep pace with this large increase of membership. There is the less need that it should have kept pace with it fully because the bulk of the increase is due, not to Harvard's reputation as a social centre, but to the opportunities she offers to students. Hundreds of men come to her every year for purely scholastic purposes, to learn what her professors teach, and with no more idea of such a course of social, athletic, and convivial experiences as our young man, Thomas, has gone through than of going to the moon. Some of these men are unsocial persons, who are satisfied to go their own gait on their own hook; others are unsocial because their work as students engrosses their energies; others because money is scarce with them as well as time. The command of a reasonable amount of money does not secure social success to its possessor at Harvard, or in any college, but it does give opportunities. A student whose means are very narrow, often has to supplement them by money-getting work, which occupies the hours that his studies leave him. If he takes a scholarship his rank must be high, and high rank involves hard work and devotion to one's task. He is not only more frugal but busier than his fellows whose allowances are bigger. He avoids even harmless dissipations, because he cannot afford them. Consequently, so far as he seeks society at all, it is the society of men of like aims and conditions with himself, as being more convenient for him, and more congenial too, as well as more feasible. A man does not have to be joined to a club or a society before he can converse with his fellow. The clubs have their uses, but probably the most satisfactory talk that goes on between undergraduates is not the talk of the clubs, but the seasoned communications born of intimacy and affinity

A Room in College House.

A Room in Holworthy.

which pass from man to man by gaslight in the college rooms. A man may be too poor or too busy in college to form a large acquaintance, but not to make friends and to get the good of friendship. That the richer and the poorer lads are not ordinarily thrown more together at Harvard may be a misfortune to both of them, but it is one that they both bear with equanimity. The man who has a scholarship and lives in College House has, usually, begun the serious work of his life. He hasn't begun altogether from choice, but partly from necessity, and his environment and its opportunities are presumably satisfactory to him. He didn't come to college to have fun, but to work. He finds all the work he can do, and as much chance for recreation as he can improve besides. As a student he is in the position which his brethren of the clubs will be in a year or two later when they enter the professional schools. There the more sensible of them will realize that their success in life depends on what they are able to do with their heads, and they will put away childish things and apply themselves for all they are worth.

Let no one be sorry for the poor student at Harvard. He is the right man in the right place. He may choose all knowledge to be his and the best the university has will be spent to aid him in making good his title to his property. He has everything to work for, everything to work with, and much fewer distractions than his more affluent fellow. He is the especial pride and pet of all the benefactors the college has ever had. All the prizes that are intrinsically valuable have been until this year for him and for no one else. He is not an exception for whom allowances are made and who suffers by contrast. He is, apparently, the rule, and his brethren are the exceptions—very numerous to be sure—and allowances are made somewhat grudgingly for them. It is not the poor student who suffers because the present social apparatus has been outgrown so much as the student who is not too busy to have social aspirations, or too poor to cultivate them, but whose reasonable inclinations are never quite satisfied because the fact of his presence in college does not transpire in the right quarter at the right time. It will be remembered that when Thomas Bulfinch got into the

An Editorial Council of "The Daily Crimson."

through college alone, but they split up into small groups. They form friendships and they find their satisfactions, but some of them make not more than a score of acquaintances all the time they are in college. It is the presence of such men in considerable number at Harvard that makes it evident that the present societies are very imperfectly representative. Twenty years ago when the Hasty Pudding and Pi Eta clubs had elected as many men from a class as they could, they were reasonably sure that they had taken in nearly all the men in that class not otherwise provided for, whose idiosyncrasies seemed adapted to the requirements of their membership. These clubs took in in those days about three-fifths of a class; now, they and Delta Upsilon between them take in hardly one-third. The evil result of this difference is that a good many men who would

Institute and presumably into the Dicky also, he bestirred himself to get all the best fellows—that is, the fellows most congenial to him—into those societies. So did the other club-table representatives, who got in with him. By the time the club tables were sufficiently represented, and the fellows who happened to know one another were duly provided for, the Sophomore societies were full. Of course, in a college, where no man knows more than a third of his classmates, and where the class as a social unit has passed away, it is perfectly possible for social gems of a highly desirable ray to be entirely overlooked. This seems to happen pretty often, Lads go to college from small schools, unallied with any strong company, and without social connections of any sort, and miss associations which would be both pleasant and profitable to them, not from personal unfitness, or from individual defect, but because their qualities are not discovered in time. Such men do not go

The Weld Boat-house.

Practice at Tackling.

Soldiers' Field, showing the Memorial Stone.

like to be in the Pudding or some other of the organized clubs and societies, and who are qualified for membership of them, don't get in ; the good result of it is that failure to get into the societies and clubs no longer necessarily implies a serious disparagement of a man's social qualities. When two-thirds of all the men in college are left out of all the purely social clubs and societies it makes it easy not to be in any of them. The bigger the crowd is that the clubs exclude the more salubrious and cheerful it is for the excluded. It is pleasant oftentimes to be in the coop, but the position outside of the slats has its advan-

tages. It is a condition of great freedom which a really sturdy chick may appreciate.

It is doubtless due to the failure of Harvard's older clubs and societies to provide for the wants of the growing family that so strong a movement has lately developed to start a large new club which shall admit not less than a thousand members, and which shall practically be open to any member of the college who desires to join it and who is able to pay its very moderate fees and dues. Such a club, it is believed, would afford a common meeting-ground for all the members of the university who care to rub against one an-

An Anxious Parent Sees the Dean.

other, and would meet a want which is felt to be rather urgent in Cambridge of a public place where the ordinary incidents of civilized life in the way of food, drink (possibly), newspapers, shelter, and companionship could be experienced. Dr. Birkbeck Hill, in his recent book about Harvard, laments the lack there of anything corresponding to the common rooms of Oxford. " I wish," he writes, "some generous and worthy benefactor would rise ; some hospitable man who knows how much a pleasant meal removes awe and gives us "suppler souls," who would provide Harvard with a hall for the professors, assistant professors, tutors, and instructors, a noble kitchen, a good cellar, a stock of old wine, and a half dozen Common Rooms. Perhaps, large though the staff is, one Common Room would suffice at first till the art of using it had been acquired. . . . Let Harvard once get two or three Common Rooms built, and hospitable customs will begin to form." This lack which Dr. Hill deplores, a university club of the right sort might contribute very materially to supply. If it did no more than serve the purposes of the Princeton Inn, at Princeton, it would be helpful, for at present there is no pub-

lic place in Cambridge where a graduate can get a comfortable dinner and find shelter for the night. Boston is so near that old Cambridge has never developed a good hotel. If college men have a dinner to give or visiting strangers to entertain, they do it at a Boston hotel. Unless an undergraduate belongs to some undergraduate club, he cannot buy a bottle of beer without sending to Boston. Beer is said to affect the livers of some persons unfavorably, and it is undoubtedly liable at times to be consumed in excessive quantities by individuals, especially in youth ; but whether the waste of time and energy that would result in having beer and other potable fluids procurable in Cambridge, is a more serious evil than the waste of time and money and the dearth of certain social opportunities which is incident to the practice of keeping all the Cambridge beer in Boston, is a nice question.

A great undergraduate social club in Cambridge might possibly help to ameliorate the embarrassment to which Harvard is subject just now, because of the difficulty of providing suitable food at moderate cost for her growing children. Students who can pay well for their board do well enough at their private boarding-houses, but those whose expenditures are more limited suffer much inconvenience. Memorial Hall takes care of at least a third more men than it has room for, and five or six hundred men who would like to share the competition for meals which takes place there cannot be admitted even to that privilege, but keep their names on the waiting list until a vacancy occurs. The Foxcroft Club, where life can be sustained at smaller cost than at Memorial Hall, is also overcrowded, but hopes, not confidently as yet, to be presently enlarged. Such a university club as is proposed certainly would not undertake to provide cheap board to undergraduates, but even if it only afforded an occasional change of diet to those of its members who boarded at Memorial or Foxcroft, it might make their condition more agreeable.

Because the organized social apparatus of a great college is tangible and in sight there is always danger of having it engross too much of the observer's attention. It is a relief to turn from the whole scheme of clubs and societies, and the hopes and jealousies of their members, and would-be and wouldn't-be members, to those elements of Harvard life which are outside and independent of all of them. Every Harvard graduate, whatever pleasure he may or may not have had in clubs, must look back with satisfaction to experiences to which they contributed nothing. Honest study is like any other form of virtue in being its own reward. There is a satisfaction in it that of course many youths fail to appreciate or cultivate in any-

thing like the degree that it deserves, but the majority of Harvard men nowadays do appreciate it. They are interested in their daily work, and in the enlargement of their intellectual horizon which follows the attention they pay to it. And then, a college room is a delightful place. Its occupant for the time being is its master. He can do as he will in it; lock his door and be not at home; admit all comers; sit alone and read or study, or sit with his congenial friend and talk out whatever he may have the good fortune to have in his mind. One Harvard graduate certainly, who found many pleasures of very varied sorts in college, remembers very few with such a sense of solid comfort duly taken as certain talks had in college rooms with good men though young, about letters and life and people, the immediate environment, and the greater world on the brink of which all college men stand. Music has charms, superlative charms, in college too. In this same graduate's memory there are few musical associations more consoling than the memory of what he heard, half asleep in a chair before a fire, while a good mu-

Interior showing the Mantel of the Hasty Pudding Club.

sician, who was his classmate, sat at his piano in the corner. Some of the calmest and most peaceful memories of college are the best. The more boisterous pleasures we smile to recall, and wonder as we remember them at the vigor and the folly of youth. But about those quieter streaks of happiness there was no folly and they involved no remorse.

A Harvard professor tells with satisfaction a story that illustrates the number of different interests that may prosper simultaneously at Harvard nowadays without at all interfering with one another. One night a year or two ago, Mr. David A. Wells gave a lecture in a large room in Sever Hall, on some subject connected with political economy. On the same evening a mass-meeting of students was called in Massachusetts Hall, to determine what action should be taken at a critical juncture in intercollegiate athletics. The professor started rather late to hear Mr. Wells, and as he went he lamented to himself that the mass-meeting would draw so great a crowd that the lecturer might have to talk to empty seats. When he got to Sever, he found the lecture-room so full that he had to stand up. He got tired of standing after awhile and went away, and as he came through the yard it occurred to him to look in at the rooms of the Classical Club. There he found twenty-three men sitting around and discoursing upon such matters as the members of a classical club discuss when they meet. The mass-meeting was thoroughly attended too, and the professor went home very much impressed with the idea that Harvard had come to be big enough to take thought about several things at once.

An example of the comprehensiveness of the interests of Harvard students appears in the "Student Volunteer Work," in which a considerable number of undergraduates engage. It might be called an elective course in sociology, for that very nearly describes it, except that the work done does not count toward the A.B. degree. The work has an organized committee and a salaried Director who knows about the organized charity work of Cambridge and Boston, and who is qualified by special knowledge and long experience to steer young men who wish to learn to help their fellows, into the courses in which

experience has found that altruism can best work. Under the supervision of this director, students visit charitable institutions and learn how they are conducted ; they also serve the Associated Charities as visitors to the poor, provide entertainments for hospitals and asylums, manage boys' clubs and lending libraries, and serve their brethren in other ways. Another field of philanthropic labor is the Prospect Union in Cambridgeport, an enterprise of the university extension pattern, where working people who want to know, go to evening classes and learn. The classes, almost without exception, are taught by Harvard undergraduates who give one evening a week to the work. The other main attraction of the Union is its weekly lectures, most of which are given by members of the Harvard Faculty. It is stated that since the Union began in 1891, every member of the Faculty from the President clear around to the President again, has lectured there several times.

One dark night, just about twenty years ago, before Harvard had experienced the fundamental changes which have made her what she is just now, some young gentlemen, whose identity was never established, painted in large greasy black letters on the front of University Hall the words : "The University is going to Hell." There have always been persons, some of them sons of Harvard, some not, who have been in sincere accord with this sentiment. Doubtless there always will be such. Dr. Cotton Mather was of that mind and very discontented with his *alma mater*, when he wrote in 1717 to Elihu Yale, suggesting that if Governor Yale should make an important gift to the struggling college about to be moved from Saybrook to New Haven, he might very reasonably give his name to it. George Whitfield was of the same persuasion, in 1740, when he wrote that the light of the New England universities " has become darkness—darkness that may be felt ; " that " bad books have become fashionable amongst them ; " and "Tillotson and Clarke are read instead of Shepard and Stoddard." Some people may be of that mind even now, and think, perhaps, that Harvard has outgrown her backbone and is ready to tumble apart by her own weight. Others grieve over the dissolute tendencies of some of her scholars, and sigh for the olden time

The Tennis Courts.

when discipline was strict and manners godly and simple. There is more or less to mend at Harvard as in other places, but there seems good ground for the opinion that she never was so useful or flourishing as now, and that the standard of morals, manners, and erudition among her students was never so high. One gets the impression from reading some of the old laws of Harvard that in her early days her students devoted four-fifths of their time to pious works, and that butter rarely melted in their mouths. But laws are one thing, and the observance of them is quite another. Wherever one gets an eye-witness view of Harvard undergraduates, whether one or two centuries, or more or less, ago, they always appear to be young men. One of the earliest impartial observations of Harvard was made in 1679–80 by two Frieslanders, who made a tour in the American colonies, their record of which has been found and translated. They started at six in the morning to go from Boston to Cambridge, and made the trip in two hours in spite of having lost their way. They said : " We reached Cambridge about eight o'clock. It is not a large village, and the houses stand very much apart. The college-building is the most conspicuous among them. We went to

it, expecting to see something curious, as it is the only college or would-be academy of the Protestants in all America, but we found ourselves mistaken. In approaching the house, we neither heard nor saw anything mentionable ; but, going to the other side of the building, we heard noise enough in an upper room to lead my comrade to suppose they were engaged in disputation. We entered, and went upstairs, when a person met us and requested us to walk in, which we did. We found there eight or ten young fellows sitting around, smoking tobacco, with the smoke of which the room was so full, that you could hardly see ; and the whole house smelt so strong of it, that when I was going upstairs, I said, this is certainly a tavern. We excused ourselves, that we could speak English only a little, but understood Dutch or French, which they did not. However, we spoke as well as we could. We inquired how many professors there were ; and they replied not one, that there was no money to support one. We asked how many students there were. They said at first, thirty, and then came down to twenty; I afterwards understood there were probably not ten. They could hardly speak a word of Latin, so that my comrade could not converse with them. They took us to the library where there was nothing particular. We looked over it a little. They presented us with a glass of wine. This is all we ascertained there. The minister of the place goes there morning and evening to make prayer, and has charge over them. The students have tutors or masters. Our visit was soon over, and we left them to go and look at the land about there."

It is proper to say that these visitors happened upon Harvard at an unlucky time, when she had no president, and her affairs were at a particularly low ebb. Nearly fifty years later " grave excesses, immoralities and disorders " so afflicted the college, that the record of some of them is set down in President Quincy's sedate "History." One special trial at this time was the tendency of the people of eastern Massachusetts to crowd to Cambridge to spend Commencement week, and have all the fun they could. For a time the overseers combated this tendency by all possible restrictions and prohibitions, but the colonists fairly beat them, and Commencement continued for a century afterward to be a high Massachusetts holiday, earnestly kept, and not without a considerable admixture of revelry.

All through the eighteenth century and down to 1849, when commons were discontinued and the college ceased to try to feed its scholars, there was a succession of difficulties about food. The commons fare, it seems, was always pretty bad, and the students were dissatisfied with it. Dr. A. P. Peabody, of the Class of 1826, tells, in his "Reminiscences," how it was in his day. "The food," he says, "though not deficient in quantity, was so mean in quality, so poorly cooked and so coarsely served, as to disgust those who had been accustomed to the decencies of the table, and to encourage a mutinous spirit, rude manners, and ungentlemanly habits ; so that the dining-halls were seats of boisterous misrule, and nurseries of rebellion." From 1849 to 1865 there were no commons, and all students boarded where they might. In 1865 the Thayer Club was started for the benefit of men who wanted to board cheaply. It merged into Memorial Hall when that was opened. Now, as has been said, the college has outgrown her dining-halls, and needs more of them. Private enterprise and capital successfully supplement the efforts of the college to lodge its students, but it has not proved able to supply them with cheap board of attractive quality at a satisfactory price.

Where so many men are working on independent lines, with so much to keep them apart and so little, comparatively, to draw them together, one may reasonably wonder whether such a thing as a common Harvard spirit any longer exists. It does exist, so men say who abide by the university, and who ought to know. They see it and feel it. It does not penetrate all individuals in the same degree, but it is reckoned with and observed as a definite force. The men best qualified to judge of it insist that it makes for veracity, for a high sense of honor, and for good manners. Indifference has sometimes been charged against Harvard, and perhaps not without some basis ; but not indifference to truth. That is her quest in science and in philosophy, and the basis of her law in matters of conduct. *Veritas* was not written on the Harvard shield for nothing. The Harvard spirit may need to be awakened, and nourished, and kept alive, but it is worth keeping alive, for truth is its most pervasive element. " It is one merit of Harvard College," says Judge Oliver Wendell Holmes, " that it has never quite sunk to believing that its only function was to carry a body of specialists through the first stage of their preparation." No ; it has never come to that. There is more to its work, and it seems impossible that any person with even a moderate share of imagination could spend a week in Cambridge without becoming aware of it. If there is one Harvard prospect which is fitter than another to deepen this perception into a conviction, it is the sight of that simple marble shaft which stands under a tree near the entrance of the Soldiers' Field. It bears the names of the men whom the Field commemorates—names written before on tablets in Memorial Hall—and below them runs Emerson's quatrain, chosen for this use by Lowell :

Though love repine and reason chafe,
  There came a voice without reply—
" 'Tis man's perdition to be safe,
When for the truth he ought to die."

The lines read calmly enough on a page of a book, with other quatrains crowding them, but on that stone in that field—with a hundred youths, earnest in their sports on one side, and on the other the roofs and gables of Harvard, and beyond the tower of Memorial Hall—they seem the message of a perpetual voice, resonant, clear, sweet, blending with all other sounds, and yet always audible, always inspiring, always imperative and irresistible.

Wood-carving on Holden Chapel.

MEMORY

By Charles C. Nott, Jr.

UPON a night long after I had died
I rose and passed the portals of Her heart.
Therein no wreck nor ruin I espied,
But fair and quiet its dim-lit chambers lay
And a sweet silence breathed in every part.
And I, who once had dwelt there, stood and sighed
And thought, "While I have slept in the cold clay,
How soon the stains of grief were washed away,
That soon some tenant new might here abide."
And as I thought, one quietly entered in,
And in his hand, the key to every door.
I bowed my head and turned away and said :
"Pardon me if I return here from the dead ;
I dwelt here once, though I dwell here no more."
But he the keys did place my hands within,
And said, "Whate'er thy steward's is, is thine ;
My name is Memory, and this place is mine."

19

HARVARD COLLEGE IN THE SEVENTIES *

By Robert Grant

HE years 1870–1880 mark the beginnings of the reforms in the methods of government and instruction by means of which Harvard has become a University instead of a college. They were essentially a period of breaking ground, not merely in the college-yard, but all over the country. We were reconstructing the South, and the granger agitations of the West were being modified into law at Washington. In 1869 the last spike of the Union Pacific Railroad was driven, and in 1871 the Chicago fire infused a fiercer energy into an already active-minded community. The panic of 1873, following an era of wild inflation, did not prevent a display of the nation's resources in the exposition of 1876. In short, the decade which I am considering was essentially one of experiment and development consequent upon enlarged material conditions and possibilities.

I was examined for Harvard in June, 1869 ; was graduated in '73 ; took the course for the then new degree of Doctor of Philosophy from '73 to '76, and was a student at the law school from the autumn of '76 until I became a Bachelor of Laws in '79. Consequently I had some opportunity to observe the customs of University life then in vogue.

When I was examined for Harvard the college topographically was the old

college. Holmes House and the railroad station next it, the old Commons, were still standing. Neither Thayer, Weld, nor Matthews was in existence. There was no Hemenway gymnasium ; only the small, circular one ; there was no Memorial Hall ; and Gray's was a comparatively new building. Holworthy was regarded as the lady patroness of the dormitories. The suites there, consisting of a parlor and two bed-rooms and a coal closet, were much in demand, and even as late as 1876 we find " The Song of the Blood "—

Some like upon the winding Charles
　　To ply the bending oar,
Nor care they, though their backs are
　　burned,
　　　　And every muscle sore.
But as for me, it suits me not :
　　I'll ever be content
To loaf in front of Holworthy,
　　And toss the shining cent.

Some like to grind the livelong day,
　　And think it is immense,
To study for their Annuals,
　　And take in large per cents.
But, as for me, ah ! give me a rest,
　　And let me, free from care,
Sit on the steps of Holworthy,
　　And take the evening air.

The rooms in Massachusetts were still occupied and were rather favorite quarters ; but presently the building was altered and devoted to examination-rooms and other purposes. Though rooms were often picturesque, the family resources were rarely if ever taxed to provide new furniture for the precious Freshman. It was a Boston axiom then that nothing need match in a college room, but fond mothers exerted themselves nobly to make their sons comfortable, and everything in the way of red curtains, discarded bric-a-brac and sporting prints which the attic contained was appropriated to the collegian's use. And then, perhaps, as one of my friends told me happened in his case, the mother would buy a new

* The substance of this article was delivered as a lecture in Sanders Theatre, Cambridge, April 10, 1896, by request of the Harvard Memorial Society. It was the third in a course of three lectures treating of Harvard in three successive decades. The first of these, "Harvard in the Fifties," was delivered by President Eliot, and the second, "Harvard in the Sixties," by Mr. Moorfield Storey. My mode of treatment aimed to omit reference to what had been already included by my predecessors in the course ; consequently this paper was written mainly from the point of view of the average student of my own day, which was necessarily a limited one. It is a narrative of manners and customs, and does not pretend to describe the mental processes of those in authority at the time or to depict the results of scholarship. I insert this caveat merely for the benefit of any literal-minded readers who have never been to college and who might be disposed to ask where the study came in.

drawing-room carpet or new chairs for herself with the money which she had not been obliged to spend on the son's outfit. How much more sensible this than to set a youngster up with brand new, spick and span furniture, carpets and hangings.

My room was a cosey den of ancient but fairly gorgeous green rep upholstery, and was in Holworthy. I was a "Tutor's freshman," which meant then practically nothing in the way of servitude. I think I delivered a note once for my tutor, but am not certain. Number 9 was in the middle entry, ground floor, and after a few days my possessions were increased by a huge stone which came crashing through the window, just missing my chum and myself, who were conscientiously at work beside a student-lamp. This missile, which was the size of a small cantaloupe, was described to us as a transmittendum. That is, it went with the room, and had been handed down in some such forcible way from one Freshman class to another. Other men had less rude objects as transmittenda. A Worcester's Dictionary sometimes went with the room, and occasionally an ostrich egg or a manuscript hidden away in the wall and inscribed with the names of previous occupants.

Our entrance examinations began on Thursday and continued through Friday and a part of Saturday morning. Saturday afternoon we learned our fate. My class numbered 154. Students were received on probation, as it was termed, and were not matriculated as members in full standing until the end of the first half year. Our entrance examinations were in Greek composition, Greek grammar, history and geography, English into Latin, Latin grammar, plane geometry, arithmetic, and algebra. Besides these written examinations we had to translate orally Latin and Greek.

I belonged to one of the last few classes—'73—which was hazed or took part in hazing. President Eliot was inaugurated in October, 1869, and I was tossed in a blanket that same autumn in the gymnasium, one of the last Freshmen who underwent the ordeal. It was a new experience and not altogether agreeable. Hazing, so far as I knew it personally, was rather mortifying to one's self-esteem than painful. I think I had to recite "Mary had a Little Lamb" in my nightgown with a pitcher in my hand to a group of appreciative Sophomores who were smoking to a man as hard as they could. A few of my classmates had pails of cold water poured over them in bed, but I was little and perhaps that saved me. Smoking out a Freshman with tobacco smoke was a favorite device, and we were all liable to be called on at any time to treat to cigars either at our rooms or at Hubbard's, the apothecary. A Freshman, instead of being a gentleman and a scholar as at present, was regarded as the scum of the earth, without property rights. The following letter was sent by a Sophomore of my class to a Freshman. The '74 man had it printed and circulated.

DEAR SIR: I speak for the Sophomore class when I say that you need have no fear of further roughing if you are willing to follow the example of your classmates and the custom of the college in the matter of treating and are willing to promise to give up the use of a cane for the remainder of the term. If you choose to come with me to Hubbard's and get six cigars, I will give them to members of the class and see that your algebra is returned. I am disinterested in saying this, as I do not smoke. You had better consider this proposition, as the class are much provoked at your obstinacy, and will not be very careful in what they say or do otherwise. If you will call at 6 Gray's at any time within two or three days I will represent the class.

Yours, etc.

This was signed with the real name of the writer, and he added, in large letters, "*Sic Semper Stultibus*," a lapse in Latin which was the occasion of some merriment, and wounded our class pride.

"Bloody Monday"—the first Monday of the college year and long a terror to Freshmen—was practically obliterated from the calendar in the autumn of 1870. On that evening the Freshmen were expected to meet the Sophomores in the gymnasium for a "rush," and subsequent tossing. I remember that both classes were assembled, and that just as we Sophs were beginning operations a Professor appeared on the scene and, in the language of authority, commanded us to disperse. By way of comment on this occurrence the *Harvard Advocate* in its next issue declared: "Professor Eliot will receive, for his courageous interposition, the hearty thanks of all lovers of good order; while the Sophomores we suppose, are, after all, not so much aggrieved at the loss of what used to be a prized heirloom of their year. It may have been a very exhilarating thing, when the classes were small, to 'toss' a few dozen Freshmen. But, now, to toss the number of Freshmen which is necessary to secure any 'moral' effect upon a class of two hundred, the tossing requiring a huge canvas blanket to be forcibly elevated a few hundred times, is a physical labor which few of the Sophomores, who have on previous occasions sunk back, faint or exhausted from their work, would care to repeat. Nor has the effect upon the Freshmen been of late quite what the tossers desired. After two or three Freshmen have gone up and come down, receiving no severer hurt than a quickening of the breathing, caused by passing rapidly through the rarefied air in the upper strata, the exercise loses its terrors. Freshmen have been known to volunteer for a second ascent." Hazing received its final quietus in 1873, when the classes of '75 and '76, who were then Sophomores and Freshmen, entered into a compact with the faculty that there should be no more war if certain members of the Sophomore class, who had been caught in the act and had been suspended, were allowed to come back. Since then the Freshman has been allowed to live comparatively unmolested.

In my Freshman year Thayer Hall was begun, the first in the series of dormitories since erected by the generosity of friends of the college. Mr. Nathaniel Thayer was not a graduate, but his interest in Harvard had already been indicated in other ways, notably by his liberal contribution to the Thayer Club, the parent of the modern Commons, which, when I entered, was in the little building once a railroad station west of the Scientific School. It was then under the control of the students, but presently the authorities offered to co-operate, and little by little the enterprise prospered until it was duly installed in Memorial Hall in the autumn of '74. While I was an undergraduate Matthews and Weld were begun and completed.

In my time only a comparatively small number of students attended Commons. The thinness of the diet provided was a favorite theme for satirists in the college paper. Those who could afford it and many who could not went to club tables at boarding-houses. We paid eight dollars a week whether we spent our Sundays at home or not. The food was fairly good to middling bad, according to the capabilities of the landlady. I should judge that the fare provided at Commons to-day is superior to what we got for eight dollars.

As regards the cost of living, I spent just $1,000 a year during the first two years and a little more the last two. I should say that $1,300 would cover the cost of my senior year, without including my share of my spread. I sent my bills for tuition, rent, board and clothes, all my bills in fact, to my father, and was allowed $15 per month pocket money. I lived comfortably on this, bought a few books, and was a member of the "Dicky" and the A. D. Club. There were a number of men in my class who spent more, but I doubt if anyone much exceeded $2,000 a year. Scarcely anyone kept a horse, and very few of the students went to evening parties in Boston. For a Freshman or Sophomore to go was an unusual thing. On the other hand there was considerable simple social gayety in Cambridge. Assemblies were held in Lyceum Hall, under the management of the students, and small parties were given by the parents of the Cambridge young ladies. The piping query, "Going to wear a dress suit to-night?" called up from the yard to a man in his room, was a familiar sound in my day and shows that we were still simple souls.

We opened the day by going to prayers. In my Freshman year from the beginning of the first term until the Thanksgiving recess, and from March 1st until the end of the year, morning prayers began at a quarter before seven. After the Thanksgiving recess until the first of March at a quarter before eight. The first bell rang some time in the night, but the second bell five minutes before the exercises opened. In that five minutes many endeavored to dress and reach the chapel in time. An ulster and top boots were a favorite garb, and during the last few languishing notes of the bell some noble sprinting was done. When prayers began at a quarter before seven, recitations were at eight. Compulsory morning prayers and the rank list were the two leading grievances of the students. Changes in regard to the former and the abolition of the latter were among the first reforms introduced by President Eliot. Under the rank-list system marks of censure were combined with marks for scholarship, and a student's rank, as held out to the world, was gravely affected by deductions for cutting prayers and recitations, whispering in lectures and smoking in the yard. The elective system of studies made this combination of lesson and conduct marks still more distasteful, and in the famous regulations of the Faculty for 1871 they were separated. We were allowed by these regulations sixty excused absences from prayers instead of twenty in the course of the year. But penalties for evil conduct remained in all their awfulness. The list of them enumerated in the inverse order of their importance included marks of censure, parental admonition, private admonition, public admonition, special probation, suspension, dismission and expulsion. A public admonition was accompanied with a letter from the Dean to the father of the student. Special probation indicated that a student was in serious danger of separation from college, and on this occasion the letter was still more impressive. The office of Dean was established in the winter of 1870. Hitherto the President had been obliged to devote his personal attention to the minor details of college government. From this time the Dean was the official with whom the students came in personal contact when the faculty wished to communicate with them. The late Professor Gurney, ac-

cording to tradition, did so much to promote friendly relations between the authorities and the students and to encourage the undergraduates to govern themselves, that I am probably wrong in my belief that he took a "slant" against me from the first. Until I began to look over my scrap-book recently, I had cherished the impression that I was an amiable and well-behaved young man in my college days, and that I was misunderstood by the faculty in general and the Dean in particular. I still think I am right, but I feel bound in justice to submit a few documents on his side before I destroy them forever.

Letter to my Father.

HARVARD COLLEGE, June, 1870.

DEAR SIR: I am sorry to be obliged to inform you that at the last meeting of the Faculty it was voted that your son "be publicly admonished and be put upon special probation" for participating in disorders in the recitation-room of Mr. ——, Tutor in —— to the Freshmen.

Mr. —— has been greatly tried by the conduct of the Class, being an amiable person and a new instructor, and would have done more wisely, I have no doubt, to have provided earlier and vigorous measures against an evil which is fatal to the instruction and discipline of the College.

The indifferent manner in which your son receives warnings, and a certain mischievousness of disposition, which means no serious harm, I dare say, lead me to suggest to you the importance of impressing strongly upon him at the beginning of next year to be upon his guard against the temptation to pranks which is so strong at the beginning of the Sophomore year. I think I am doing him a kindness if I put any fresh difficulty in the way of heedlessness on his part.

Very truly yours,
E. W. GURNEY, *Dean of the Faculty.*

That was the beginning of the trouble. Then, alas! came the following little strips of printed matter, received from time to time through the post:

February 22, 1871.

A deduction of 32 is marked against Grant, Soph., on the weekly return of February 4th, for inattention and disorder at Italian exercise.
J. W. HARRIS, *Sec.*

JUNE 5, 1871.

Grant, Soph., is directed to come to the Dean's office on Monday.
J. W. HARRIS, *Sec.*

May 6, 1871.

Grant, Soph., is directed to come to the Dean's office on Monday.

J. W. HARRIS, *Sec.*

April 29, 1871, ditto; June 12, 1871, ditto, save that I was to come on Tuesday. To pile up the agony, on June 13, 1871, as a sequel to the last interview, my father received the following:

DEAR SIR: At the last meeting of the Faculty it was voted that your son, Robert, be publicly admonished for twenty-two unexcused absences from prayers.

Very truly yours,

E. W. GURNEY, *Dean of the Faculty.*

I think there is much to be said on the side of the Dean, but my own belief is that what he considered indifference on my part was really shyness. His impressions regarding me were unfortunately strengthened early in my Sophomore year by the blowing up of Stoughton, an episode which caused much excitement at the time. One evening late in the autumn of '70 the Yard was startled by a loud explosion which proceeded from the north entry of Stoughton. The ground floor room nearest Holworthy had been blown up by combustibles placed in the cellar. Its inmates were Freshmen, and among the occupants at the moment was my brother who was a Freshman of '74, and who tumbled out of the window in great haste. Those who tried to escape by the door could not, for the flooring had started. One man is said to have struck the ceiling, but in spite of the noise and smoke no one was hurt. I was at that time living in 5 Holworthy, in the entry next to Stoughton, just over Professor Sophocles, and was peacefully reading. I rushed down to see what the matter was, and so did everybody else in the yard. Conjecture as to who did it selected the Med. Fac. as the probable culprit; but no one was caught at the time. In about a fortnight my chum and I, and some dozen other members of my class, were sent for to see the Dean on the eve of the Christmas recess. I think that President Eliot addressed us in person. I remember that we were given to understand that the authorities had a clew, and were informed that if the matter were not confessed before the end of the recess the guilty parties would be prosecuted in the criminal court as well as expelled. We went home to think it over, and I, for one, felt aggrieved, for I was innocent as a lamb of the offence, and moreover was entirely ignorant as to who committed it. There were no confessions known to me made after the recess, and so far as I am aware the faculty never discovered who blew up Stoughton. I have heard it positively denied by those who claimed to know that the Med. Fac. had anything to do with it. I was not a member of the Med. Fac., so I am unable to testify on that point. The whole matter remained shrouded in mystery while I was in college, and my impression is that the father of one of my classmates was so indignant that his son was suspected that he sent his other sons to Yale.

With the beginning of the second term the Freshmen were privileged to wear tall hats and carry canes. They always celebrated their emancipation on the first Saturday of the new term by going in force to the theatre in all the splendor of their new possessions, and they were apt to show themselves on Beacon Street, Boston, on the following Sunday. In regard to dress on week-days I recall that among all the students a little round gray soft hat was very popular. The times were rather hard from '70 to '80, and many men went in for old clothes. Short pea-jackets were in common use. Some of the arbiters of college fashion chose to wear silk hats with them, when they wished to appear swell, thereby producing a somewhat mongrel effect. English clothes, or indeed a suit of new clothes, was so much an event that I recollect on the occasion when a member of the Class of '74 imported a suit of lively checks, his friends hung it outside the window of one of the buildings on exhibition. The Yard at that time, as very likely now, was often a lively centre for amiable indolence. Besides tossing cents at a mark in front of Holworthy, and dropping hot coppers out of the windows for the Cambridge urchins to pick up, I recall the slogan of "Heads out!" which brought every one to his window and from his books many times a week. No woman could cross the yard without hearing it, and events of much less import evoked it. Frequently we had the pleasure of listening to the Glee Club, which was then a flourishing body whose repertoire included "Seeing Nellie Home," and "Dearest maiden dance ever with me; can'st thou refuse me? can'st thou but choose me?" yet pandered to less noble emotions in "Shoo Fly," and the then popular

> Ha-ha-ha, you and me,
> Little brown jug how I love thee!

Among the college characters and celebrities of the years from 1870–80 were Jones, the bell-ringer; Billy, the postman, and Horace, the expressman, who helped to pack the baskets of soiled clothes which the Boston men sent weekly to town, and also "Daniel Pratt," the great American traveller and president of four kingdoms, a frequent visitor among the students with his ideas stated in his own modest language as "worth billions of dollars to all nations."

> Oh, where is the man so lean and fat
> Who has not heard of Daniel Pratt,
> Who gathers his wings and flies away
> To parts of earth where the light of day
> Shines but a little or not at all
> In the course of the awful waterfall?
> I ask you, friends, what muddy minds
> Have never conceived, unfurled to the winds
> That glorious banner that springs like a cat
> Into the air for Daniel Pratt.
> There never was nor ever will be
> Such a mighty man to stand like thee,
> I say, most magnificent Daniel Pratt,
> Above the throne where Plato sat!

So he sung and the students applauded the poor old man to the echo. In my time, too, there was a Johnny Cocoanut who met us as we came from recitations with cocoanut-cakes just before the noon meal, and a boy who played tunes on his teeth in Harvard Square by sucking in his breath. I recall, too, a malodorous goody who made herself famous by calling at the chamber-door of one of her charges, when he slept too late in the morning, "Git up, yer lazy divil, git up."

From the beginning of the academic year until November 1st, and from March 1st until the end of the year recitations began at eight and continued until one, and the dinner hour was one. From November 1st to March 1st they began an hour later and the dinner hour was at two. There were afternoon recitations from three to six. My class was the first to experience the benefits of the elective system under the new administration. In the college year 1871–72, the Seniors were required to take Physics, one lecture a week for a half year, Themes, and twelve hours of electives; the Juniors, Philosophy, two hours a week through the year, Physics, two hours a week for a half-year, and one lecture a week through the year, Political Economy, and the Constitution of the United States together, two hours a week for a half year, Rhetoric, two hours a week for a half year (in all six hours a week), Themes and nine hours of electives; the Sophomores, German, two hours a week through the year, Rhetoric, two hours a week through the year, Physics, two hours a week for a half year, History, two hours a week for a half year, Chemistry, three hours a week for a half year (in all seven hours a week), Themes, Elocution, and eight hours of electives. All the studies of the Freshmen were required. The courses in electives included the classics, philosophy, history, natural history, and music. From year to year during the seventies new courses were introduced, and these were amplified until aspiration culminated for a time in the Chinese professor. The details of changes are a matter of record, and I have no space for them here. The entrance examinations were made to cover a broader field, and experimental progress was the watch-word of the time with the authorities. In a tone of contemplative criticism the *Harvard Advocate* remarked that the only conservative body connected with the university was the students. However unscientific, from an educational standpoint, the matter and manner of the instruction then given may seem as compared with that of to-day, we were fortunate in our instructors. Many of the men whose pre-eminent scholarship has gained for the university repute on both sides of the water were then in their prime. Of course the classes from '71 to '80 were, so to speak, subjects of experiment, for old methods were in process of being exchanged for new. But we had the benefit of the ability and knowledge of Professors Child, Lane, Norton, Goodwin, Gurney, Cook, Bôcher, Shaler, Dunbar, Trowbridge, Henry Adams, J. M. Pierce, A. S. Hill, and Palmer. If I have omitted any names which should be mentioned I beg their owners' pardon. I remember well how interested I was in the history courses of Professors Gurney and Adams, which were conducted after the then new method of lectures with outside work by the class. Dr. Peabody and Professor Torrey were still actively instructing and were much beloved. I used to wonder sometimes that men who applauded loudly at the mention of their names should put off preparation in their courses until the night before examination - day. Professor Lowell still had a few courses in Spanish and Italian. I remember going up to his house in June, 1876, to be examined in Dante. I was a candidate for the degree of Ph.D., being one of the earliest applicants for that degree. My course of study for three years had been in English, German, and Italian literature. As it happened I was very well up in the "Inferno" and the "Purgatorio," but I was a little weak on the "Paradiso," especially the later cantos. I took counsel with myself and made up my mind that I would not be caught napping in case treachery should be practised on me. Consequently the night before, I made myself thoroughly familiar with Canto 33, the last canto. In the presence of two men like Professor Lowell and Professor Child, who was to sit with him in judgment on me, I naturally felt a little nervous, but my opinion of my own talents rose considerably when Professor Lowell, in an off-hand manner, told me to begin at the last canto. Later you know he became a distinguished diplomat.

I do not think that it was the fashion in my time for instructors to interest themselves in the students individually to the extent they do now. I do not mean that if an undergraduate broke a leg and sought his professor or tutor for advice or sympathy he did not get it; but there was certainly less working together in the matter of studies, and consequently more formal intercourse. The recitation in most cases, at least where I was concerned, was the sole medium of contact, and the expression "Not prepared," on the one side, and "That is sufficient," on the other, uttered in varying keys calculated to produce repulsion, were too often the Alpha and Omega of acquaintance. What infinite gradations of meaning those expressions "Not prepared," and "That is sufficient," were susceptible of! Only Mephistopheles could hope to compete with some of the faculty of my time in the way their Shibboleth was uttered, and to the sensitive ear there was often an entire Wagner tragedy in the phrase "Not prepared," though to an inexperienced listener it might convey merely an impression of bravado. To be sure there were individual instances where instructors and students affiliated more closely, as for instance the delightful Field Lectures in Geology of Professor Shaler, of which I heard at the time, though I did not take his elective; but there was comparatively little of that spirit of mutual interest, and of co-operation in work which I believe distinguishes the university today. I remember the solemnity of the occasions when one was sent to the black-board to demonstrate a problem in trigonometry or physics concerning which one knew nothing. I can see again, as plainly as though it were yesterday, one of my classmates in this plight draw with the chalk simply a huge square and walk back to his seat with the dignity of profound hopelessness.

There was no Freshman Society in my day, and the only two Sophomore Societies were the Institute of 1770 and the Everett Athenæum. The Juniors had the Hasty Pudding Club, the Pi Eta, and the Signet. The O. K. was the literary Society. At it we read papers and consumed beer and little cakes cut in the form of O and K. There were the Glee Club and the Pierian Sodality, and two Religious Societies, the St. Paul's and the Christian Brethren. The only secret societies were the Δ. K. E., and the Med. Fac. The Alpha Delta Phi was merged in the A.D. Club, which was founded just after I entered college. There were several members of my class who were members both of the Porcellian and the A.D., but '73 was the last class in which men were allowed to belong to both. The A.D. had quarters on Brattle Street, just beyond Harvard Square, two rooms, in one of which we sat and played whist and the other a sort of pantry in which we kept the crackers and cheese. But we were very proud of our club and we had capital times there. I judge from what I hear that the Δ.K.E., or "Dicky," is substantially what it was in my time. The oath which I took on the night of the initiation not to divulge its secrets binds me now, but I can see no objection to referring to a pleasantry practised on me on the occasion which I remember more vividly than the other horrors. I was sitting blind-fold on a chair, believing that the worst was over, when two upper class men, whose voices I recognized, approached me and told me to open my mouth. I did so and one of them placed a large plug of tobacco between my teeth, and told me to masticate it until I was given leave to stop. I was an innocent boy ; I had never smoked or chewed in my life, and I shall always remember the experience of that burning mouthful to which I was obliged to hold fast until late in the evening.

Early in my college course a reading-room was started by the students in lower Massachusetts. I was one of the officers. We provided the magazines and leading newspapers, and it presently became a popular and successful institution. A Telegraph Club was also established in my time. The Pudding and the Pi Eta theatricals were then as now prominent factors in the social life. "Running" for the Pudding was then in its glory. The names "Lyon's" and "Kent's" will recall to men of my time many a game of billiards, and those who sought amusement in town must have vivid memories of the Parker House and of

Selwyn's theatre where the combination of Tennyson's "Dora" and the burlesque "Black-eyed Susan," in which Stuart Robson played Captain Crosstree and Kitty Blanchard appeared in tights, drew the same students, like a magnet, across the bridge again and again. I was immersed in studying law at the time the Soldene troupe carried by cyclone the class of '77, but I believe that the college authorities retain keen recollections of the occurrence. The troupe went from Boston to Cincinnati, and the first words which Emily Soldene is said to have uttered on alighting from the train were, "Is there a University here ?"

I was the witness also of the last "Mock Parts," a custom which deservedly was voted out of existence by the Class of '72. It had been the habit for many years to hold a sort of travesty on the Junior exhibition (which has also ceased to be), at which ceremonial one of the Junior class delivered from the window of Hollis Hall an address supplemented by satirical and bitter "roughs" and personalities on other members of the class sent in anonymously. I remember listening to the Mock Parts of the Class of '71, and being shocked by the cruel thrusts which usage permitted to be made at those who were unpopular. Others evidently sympathized with me, for the next class did away with the practice forever.

The only college newspaper when I entered was the *Advocate*, but the *Magenta* — afterwards the *Crimson* — presently became a rival, and later the *Harvard Lampoon*, which was edited at first by students, but from 1876–1879 by a board composed chiefly of recent graduates. After this it was again conducted by the undergraduates. The promising Frederic Wadsworth Loring, who was killed in the West by Indians shortly after graduation, was one of the editors of the *Advocate* from the Class of '70. At the annual dinner of the editors of the *Advocate* in May, 1876, Dr. Oliver Wendell Holmes read his poem, "How the Old Horse Won the Bet," when he told us :

> Moral for which this tale is told,
> A horse *can* trot for all he's old !

There were no class officials in my day except the captain of the ball nine and of the crew, who were chosen at the beginning of the year at a meeting in Holden Chapel. The class-day officers were the same as at present, and they were generally chosen without much friction, but the Class of '77 came to loggerheads on the subject in consequence of a strife between the society and non-society men. A committee of graduates was invited to intervene, but in the end '77 had no class officers and no Class day. It was called Corporation day instead, and Professor Lowell invited them to breakfast at Elmwood.

I have the impression that, apart from the small contingent who were active candidates for the crew, or nine, the older classmen when I entered college were lazy as regards exercise. It is my recollection that some of them spent much time in drifting from room to room and in coloring meerschaums, and that those who took themselves seriously did not know what to do when they had studied enough. Certainly, between the years 1870 and 1880, a marked change took place in the matter of athletics, so that by the end of the period in question it had become the habit of the large majority, instead of a small minority of the students, to take part daily in some form of outdoor exercise. The beginnings of this change occurred while I was an undergraduate. I happened to be one of the party who owned the first tennis set at Harvard. We set it up and played on it back of College House. I happened, too, to be one of the half-dozen men who revived football, which had been dormant at Cambridge for some years. It was in my Sophomore year, I think, that a party of us took a black rubber football, such as we had been accustomed to use at school, and went out and played. Our example attracted others, and presently we had a following of some twenty-five or thirty men. We played at first, I think, on the vacant lot at the side of the Scientific School, for it was claimed that, with baseball and cricket already in possession of Jarvis field, there was no room for us there. The faculty, however, would not let us stay; accordingly we removed our rubber ball to Cambridge Common, where we played energetically for a year or so, at the end of which we were turned off by vote of the Cambridge town authorities. By this time the game had become so well established that we were able to insist on our right to play on Jarvis field. The game played by us was one which had originated with the old Oneida club of Boston some ten or fifteen years previous, and it was generally in use at the schools and colleges of Massachusetts, New Hampshire, and Vermont. One of the salient features of the game was the rule that a player could run with the ball only when chased, and he must stop as soon as pursuit ceased. Dribbling was forbidden. The ball was kicked a great deal, and there was much running and dodging. There were eleven men on a team, and the members were considerably lighter men, as a rule, than those who play nowadays. In October, 1873, a convention of the colleges interested in football was held and an association formed, but Harvard declined to take part in it or to join, alleging that the game as played by the other colleges was so different from ours that a compromise was out of the question, and also claiming that our game was more "scientific," an assertion which excited Yale. The rules of the other colleges, though differing in details, were substantially the English Association rules adopted in 1863. It was found that the game played by McGill College, Montreal, usually styled the Rugby game, differed less from ours than did that of any other college, and an arrangement was made under which, in 1874, the McGill team visited Cambridge and played two games—one according to our rules and one according to theirs. The teams met on May 14th and 15th, two elevens on the first day and two tens on the second. My brother was captain of the Harvard team. Harvard easily won the game played according to our rules, and that played according to the McGill rules resulted in a draw. After it the *Advocate* remarked: "The Rugby is in somewhat better favor than the sleepy game played by our men." In October, '74, we sent a ten to Montreal, which proved victorious, and for several years a match with McGill was a regular event. In November, '75, the first football match ever played between Yale and Harvard took place at Hamilton Park, New Haven. Fifteen men played on each side, and the game was substantially the Rugby game. It was divided into three half hours, and Harvard won. Yale did not score, and her defeat was ascribed to the fact that the rules were new to her. In November, '76, a second match was played, this time between two elevens instead of fifteens, by request of Yale, and on this occasion the blue prevailed. I regret to state that the *Advocate* had the poor grace to declare that "Our men have returned with the feeling that they owe their first defeat, not to any superiority in their opponents' play, but to an offensive combination consisting of the Yale eleven, backed by, first, a culpable ignorance or misinterpretation of the rules; second, an equally culpable carelessness in the arrangements on the field; third, to an unruly and unrestrained partisan crowd." The refusal of Yale to play with more than eleven men and Harvard with less than fifteen, prevented a match in '77. Yale's argument, as voiced by the *Courant*, was: "We are the champions of last fall, having won with eleven men and the Rugby rules, and all teams who wish to contest the championship with us should challenge us to play with eleven men and the Rugby rules." In reply the *Advocate* said: "Harvard having beaten all her opponents, Yale included, with fifteen men in '75 and '76, was the champion in the fall of '76, and had therefore a right to keep to fifteen men. She had been playing all the fall of '76 with fifteen men, and wished to play Yale with that number; but Yale insisted on eleven men. Harvard made the concession." So there was no game that year. But in '78, after parley, Yale consented to play with fifteen men, and the match came off in Boston on the South End grounds. It was a fierce contest on a rain-soaked field, and was won by Yale by a single goal. This time the *Advocate* admitted that, though a disappointment, the game was fairly won.

In the autumn of '74 the first field meeting of the new Athletic Association, the precursor of a long line of similar contests, was held on Jarvis field. The sports included a hundred-yard dash, in which eleven sprinters participated; a running high jump; a one hundred-yard hurdle race; throwing a baseball; a two-mile run, with seven contestants; a half-mile run; a three-legged race; and a three-mile walk. To quote from the records of the day: "The weather was true Indian summer—a perfectly clear sky, with a bright sun and very gentle wind. It was evident that the Field Committee had made every needful preparation for the afternoon's performances. A quarter-mile track, quite smooth but rather soft, had been laid out, surrounded by a rope; while a stouter rope, stretched around the entire field, with the aid of six policemen, kept the populace at a proper distance. Directly opposite the spectators' seats a judges' stand was placed, while in the centre of the field were the hurdles and jumping-poles, with a hundred-yard track marked out between them." It was an important day in the history of athletic sports at Harvard.

In the matter of baseball, the seventies were years of much activity and success. A great many men played for exercise in my time, whether they were candidates for the team or not, and there was plenty of material from which to choose a winning nine. My particular class contributed the pitcher and catcher of the nine which won in '72 and again in '73 the series of games with Yale. In neither instance was a third game necessary. The later years of the seventies saw the Harvard nine, under the leadership of Captain Thayer, repeatedly victorious against the blue in fiercely contested games, the memory of which stirs the blood in the veins of their now more than forty-year-old contemporaries. The Harvard nine in these years played with professional as well as college teams, and made tours in various directions to meet doughty adversaries. No gambling or jockeying features were then conspicuous; no newspaper lives of the players exaggerated beyond all semblance to truth the importance of the undertaking. The nine were simple-minded, earnest young men who were fond of baseball for its own sake and determined to beat Yale. Why we won then and do not win now puzzles many brains wiser in athletic lore than mine. I suppose the reason is that then we played better ball than Yale and now Yale plays better ball than Harvard. Naturally the best players win.

As to boating, the seventies saw similar activity on the water, and though in the early part of the decade Harvard took the wash of some of the fresh-water colleges for a considerable period, '77, '78, and '79 were among the most brilliant in the history of Harvard athletics. In those years the eight-oared crew under Captain Bancroft won three successive victories against Yale. In '71, '72, '73, '74, '75, and '76, races were rowed at Ingleside, Springfield, or Saratoga, under the auspices of the National Rowing Association of American Colleges. As many as ten or twelve crews took part in these contests, and fouls and consequent bickerings were numerous. Harvard never came in first, but she thought herself first in '73 for about three minutes, only to find herself third. That was the day of the famous diagonal line. In 1875 the Harvard color, which since 1864 had masqueraded under the name of Magenta, owing to some difficulty or carelessness in getting the proper shade of handkerchief for the crews, was definitely established as crimson. These were active days on the Charles for miscellaneous oarsmen. Class and scratch crews abounded and sunk each other from time to time, and every one tried to row. At one period, in '75 I think, club crews, made up from different sections of the yard, and named after the dormitories, Holworthy, Weld, Holyoke, and Matthews, took the place of the class crews for a time. Sliding seats were first introduced in the seventies, and eight substituted for six oars in the University boat in 1876.

There was much sociability among the students in my day. There was considerable loafing in one another's rooms, and sitting round doing nothing. I dare say there is still. Until well on in the seventies the classes were still small enough for a man to know all his classmates by sight, and the majority of them pretty well. As I remember us, we were an energetic lot, and, despite the statement I have quoted as to our conservatism, were as ready as the authorities to try new ventures. Those who did not study hard went in for something else with enthusiasm. I was well fitted when I entered, and was able to keep about the middle of the class by skimming like a swallow over the surface of my work. I hope that is not possible now. My senior year I, like many others, turned over a new leaf and did a little better, so that when I graduated I was anxious to do better still, and accordingly took a course for the Doctor of Philosophy degree, living in Boston and coming out now and then to consult Professor Child, whose valuable, friendly counsel I have always remembered with gratitude. When I entered the law school in '76 I found it a veritable bee-hive. Everybody was ardently in earnest, and it was interesting to see what a change had come over many of the men who had not been conspicuous for hard work as undergraduates. The leaven of the new administration was working.

It is not easy to describe the more elusive features of college life in my day, the friendships formed, the walks and talks, the grapplings with the problems of existence in company or by one's self. These are matters which count, perhaps, for more than anything else in the experience of every student. I refer to them to indicate that, though we were boyish, we were, as a rule, right-minded and eager at heart to do well, and thoughtful withal when no proctor's vicinity catered to our taste for mischief. I am sure that when the corner-stone of Memorial Hall was laid in October, 1870, some of us envied the glory of those in whose memory it was done, and felt that we had been deprived by fate of an opportunity. We were by no means a morbid lot, however. Indeed, feeling that we had just missed the great chance, we may have been disposed, after the manner of those who missed the last car from Scollay Square, to take things as comfortably as we could under the circumstances. Some of us read a good deal, but our miscellaneous reading was rarely directed by suggestions or hints from our instructors. The college library was then a place for storing books instead of circulating them, as at present, and was comparatively little used by the students. The *Harvard Advocate*, in bidding farewell to my class, said: "No longer will they sport at pitch-penny in front of Holworthy, or pass ball in defiance of proctors all over the yard. But, seriously, few classes have ever graduated more beloved by their fellow-students or esteemed by the faculty than '73." This was a little stiff perhaps, but I cannot allow such a tribute to my class to lie buried in the files of more than twenty years ago.

As I look back on my college days it strikes me that we were boys. Honest, energetic, square-trotting, manly boys, but still boys. The fault was not wholly ours; the apparent aim of the authorities was to keep us so, and one of the most significant and valuable of the results of the policy adopted by President Eliot and his faculty is the trust which is now reposed in the honor of the students and the breaking down of the barriers between the instructors and the instructed. We were spied on and watched. Proctors dogged our footsteps at night and stalked between the tables on examination-day. What wonder that the Freshmen and Sophomores "ragged" signs from the lampposts and the shops out of deviltry, and that even Juniors wore top-boots lined with "cribs," in order to baffle the argus-eyed? It was anything to get the better of our tutors, and with them the presumption seemed to be that a student was not to be trusted. It is evident to me that the relations of the undergraduates of the present day to their instructors is very different, and that, as a consequence, the Harvard man of the nineties is more disposed to put away boyish things and take advantage of the opportunities offered him for culture.

We were energetic, honest, and manly boys, and we were simple in our habits. The material wave which swept over the nation, as a result of the great for-tunes accumulated, had scarcely begun to be felt. Society in New England at the time of the civil war stood for noble ideals and great purposes. That grand generation has passed away. Its great men are dead; many of its theories seem a little nebulous to us now. We have entered on a new phase of civilization, and new problems bred of democracy and unrest confront us. Yet I believe that work as earnest and more intelligent than the work of the past is being done in the world to-day, and that much of it is being done at Harvard. I do not think that the University should be held responsible for that which should be learned at the mother's knee and impressed on the growing boy by parental precept and example. If the student is extravagant and self-indulgent it is because his elders are. If the tone and aspirations of society and the homes of this country are at fault, young men will be sent to Harvard unable to appreciate the benefits which are offered to them. But when we come to compare the Harvard of to-day with the Harvard of the seventies, I cannot but feel that from the point of view of a liberal education the young man of to-day, if he will choose wisely, and make the most of his time, has a grand chance. His faculties are stimulated in a way in which mine never were. He is allured, not clubbed into the path of knowledge and wisdom. The methods of teaching are charged with sympathy, and the standards of mental excellence have been greatly raised. Competition is fiercer, and, to excel, the mental athlete needs the full energies of a healthy body and a well-trained mind. In the plethora of choice and the abundance of the interests of university life, some may go miserably astray in the twilight; but even in the sixties all did not hearken to the inspirations of the hour, and in the fifties the connection of some with the college was abruptly severed.

Daughters of Time, the hypocritic Days,
Muffled and dumb like barefoot dervishes,
And marching single in an endless file,
Bring diadems and fagots in their hands.
To each they offer gifts after his will,
Bread, kingdoms, stars, and sky that holds
    them all.
I, in my pleached garden, watched the pomp,

Forgot my morning wishes, hastily
Took a few herbs and apples, and the Day
Turned and departed silent. I, too late,
Under her solemn fillet saw the scorn."

Harvard University to-day offers young men a chance to train themselves for the work of life such as it never offered me and the men of my time. The students have a gymnasium for the mind and for the body which will send them out into the world fit to control events and do battle for our motto *Veritas*. But the University cannot evolve a noble life from a shallow soul. It says choose, and it is for each to declare whether he will have the sky or the herbs and apples. We who were undergraduates twenty years ago must needs envy the men of the nineties their greater privileges.

20

MILLS COLLEGE, CALIFORNIA

BY SYDNEY PELL MAKINSON

COMPASSED about by the busy life of the world, an isle amid the strenuousness of every-day life, stands the only chartered college for women in the United States, west of the Rocky Mountains. In order to extend the influence of the institution to the fullest extent, it has been made a Christian college, but not a sectarian institution. The devotee of any denomination is equally welcome. Students of various religious beliefs have been received from all points of the compass, and the true womanhood reared under the protection of the walls of Mills Seminary is to-day spreading the refining influence of its teaching in China, in farthest India, in Hawaii and the Islands of the Pacific.

Correct conduct does not mean that the young woman who attends a seminary is to be deprived of outdoor exercise or the usual pleasures that attend any lover of all that is beautiful in nature.

Mills Seminary has a college life that is all its own. There is a serious and lovable camaraderie between teachers and pupils that seldom obtains in institutions of a like character. In California, and in one of its most favored spots, where out-door sports are possible the year around, it could not be otherwise. Health and physical culture are made one of the features of the range of study at Mills.

Regular daily exercise in the fresh air or in the gymnasium gives that health and strength which make study a pleasure. After the concentration and effort of thorough mental application, there is the glory of the campus, where many healthful games and exercises are provided, under such rules that moderation is

never exceeded. The gift of climatic excellence places Mills beyond the competition of most of the schools of the world, for its location gives it all the advantages of the far-famed land of sunshine and gold. There is no spot on earth where there is a greater number of perfect days and glorious nights than at Seminary Park. Just as the winds blow, just as the tides roll, the days are poured forth in majestic beauty, the breezes laden with ozone and tempered with the refreshing breath of the sea.

Mills College develops all that is true in women, fits them to take the place of true wives and mothers, and in case of necessity, self-supporting and self-respecting teachers or professional women.

Its Alumni is composed of some of the most distinguished, and among these may be counted Miss Luella Carson, Dean of Women and Head of the English Department of the University of Oregon; Miss Mabel Gilman, who ranks as one of our most successful singers. Among the graduates of Mills are many successful artists: Miss Edith White, Mrs. Mathews, Miss A. Briggs, Miss Froelich, Miss Alice Tabor. The school has also given us the famous soprano, Madame Emma Nevada Palmer; Mrs. Fannie K. Carpenter, a lawyer of prominence in New York City; Mrs. Carpenter is associated with her husband in business, and occupies a prominent position in the Federated Clubs. Mrs. Dita Hopkins Kinney, Head of the Department of Women Nurses, U. S. A. Miss Jane Seymour Klink, Inspector of Employment Bureaus, appointed by the New York City Government. Mrs. Benjamin Peart, formerly Superin-

El Campanil.

tendent of Schools for Yolo County, California; Mrs. J. S. Merrill, Miss Paulsell, Mrs. Morse, and a host of other equally capable and well-known women.

The social life of Mills College is an educating influence of no small importance. The juniors give re-ceptions to the seniors or the sopho-more class to the entering fresh-men. I have been told that the young ladies are cavalierly attended by their partners, that there is as much empressement as in a social function in real life, and that it is incumbent on the dancing partner to attend her lady home with all the gallantry that is usually expected from the gentleman in the case.

I quote from a statement made by a gifted woman, once a Mills College girl:

"The favorite recreation hall at the college is 'The Gym, as the gymnasium is popularly called. Each Friday evening is set apart for recreation, and then the students learn 'there is a time to dance,' and do so to their heart's content. But, on special occasions, the old 'Gym' is

Main Building.

transformed. Private boxes appear at the sides as if by magic, orchestra chairs occupy a front place, and even to the doors the house is filled with a sympathetic audience. Sometimes it is a gay operetta written by the students, '99 having given a very pretty one. Again, it is a Greek play by the seniors, or a Latin one by the less ambitious sophomores. Woods, flowers and vines make it a forest of Arden, on occasions when the Mu Sigma Sigma, the college fraternity, entertains its guests; for the obliging old 'Gym' lends itself to many uses. Then there are individual teas and receptions, class-teas and afternoons at-home, thus giving a charming social life to the students, the conventionalities of which they observe with minutest care.

"On Washington's Birthday a visitor at Mills College would think "ye ancient colonial dames" had assembled to welcome him. Madam Randolph of Virginia, stiff and stately, assists Mrs. Washington in receiving the guests. Pretty Dolly Madison is yonder, talking with Elizabeth, the Quaker spouse of "the first great American," and others cluster round to listen to her vivacious wit.

"Admission Day, September 9th, is always kept; the year's work has begun, the athletic teams, or clubs, have been organized, and it is a good time for the inauguration of college hospitalities, a good time to say: "We are organized for our year's work and recreation; let us give a thought to the social life among us.'"

The past history of Mills College is a guarantee of its future success. It has never strayed from the ideals of its founders, and that fact alone should endear it to all. It occupies the unique position in the central point in this western world; it fronts the great Pacific, its islands and the lands of immeasurable possibility beyond. The college, the only woman's college west of the Rocky Mountains, was given to the State of California; its charter was granted by the same legislative act as Stanford's, it offers the same course as Bryn Mawr, Smith or Wellesley, and in the very near future, if the endowment movement is fully successful, it will be rated the greatest women's college in the United States.

Mills College was named after its founder, the Reverend Cyrus T. Mills, D. D., and after his wife, Susan L. Mills, and it is to-day a State institution, an institution that should be a source of pride to all of California's citizens.

There is no limit to the good Mills College may do, located as it is, with its unrivaled climate, its beautiful grounds and buildings, aided by the proper endowment, the statement I have made that it will in time rival the very best of all the institutions of the East for women is no exaggeration.

Mills College does well to appeal to the large-hearted men and women of the Pacific Coast for its endowment, and it is safe to say that such an appeal, wherever the merits of the institution are known, will not be made in vain. Mills College will soon be on as permanent and as broad a footing as Bryn Mawr, Smith, or any of the great women's colleges of the Eastern States.

It should be evident to any one, with only a cursory glance at the situation, that there is an enormous advantage in one commanding institution as against many scattering and inferior schools.

Any reference to Mills College should contain the excellent report of the "United States Health Bulletins," which I append in full:

"It seems almost beyond belief, in these days when health is concededly dependent upon proper sanitary and hygienic surroundings, that the head of a family could for a minute lose sight of these matters and send

Mills College

Basket Ball Team.

his dear ones to a place about which he knows nothing concerning the care taken to preserve the health of the residents, when reflection will assure him that the most sedulous care is necessary.

"The United States Health Bulle-

shocked at the unsanitary and disease-breeding conditions existing at some of the highest-priced and most fashionable schools.

"These investigations have been made without the instigation of the proprietors, and generally without

Mrs. Susan L. Mills.

tin has had occasion to examine into this subject quite extensively during the past few months and if some of the facts that have come to our notice during these investigations were generally known, we believe that prospective patrons would re

their knowledge, consequently they are absolutely unbiased and unprejudiced.

"Among the schools that met with the general approval of the experts investigating these matters for us, and which we have no hesitation in recommending to our readers, in the Mills College, Seminary Park, Cal.

"We know nothing about the course of study at this school, for it is of no interest to us, but if the same care is taken with the mental welfare of the pupil as is shown and plainly shown to be taken with the physical, we feel that it deserves the support of parents and the encouragement of the public."

The names of the Board of Trustees of Mills College are representative in the community:

Rev. Charles R. Brown, Oakland, President; Warren Olney, Oakland; George T. Hawley, San Francisco; A. J. Ralston, San Francisco; Mrs. C. T. Mills, Mills College; Professor George C. Edwards, Berkeley; Cyrus W. Carmany, Oakland; Louis Lisser, Litt. D., San Francisco; Charles Nelson, Seminary Park; Reverend Charles R. Brown, Oakland; Edward Coleman, San Francisco; George W. Scott, Alameda; Rev. Raymond C. Brooks, East Oakland; Mr. Frank M. Smith, Oakland; Mrs. Frank M. Smith, Oakland, Rev. Ernest E. Baker, D. D., Oakland; Warren Olney, Secretary; Mrs. C. T. Mills, Treasurer.

BASKETBALL IN THE SMITH COLLEGE GYMNASIUM.

LIFE AT A GIRLS' COLLEGE.

The Smith girls at work and at play —Their college buildings, their studies and amusements, their secret societies, their customs and traditions.

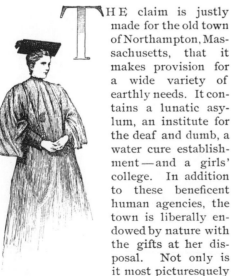

THE claim is justly made for the old town of Northampton, Massachusetts, that it makes provision for a wide variety of earthly needs. It contains a lunatic asylum, an institute for the deaf and dumb, a water cure establishment—and a girls' college. In addition to these beneficent human agencies, the town is liberally endowed by nature with the gifts at her disposal. Not only is it most picturesquely placed on elevated ground near the bank of the Connecticut River, but it affords a wide view of the Connecticut valley, so that for charms within and without it is a spot to be remembered.

The town, which Smith College has made notable, consists of one principal street stretching out interminably. The college is situated at one end of the village, on an eminence commanding a fine view of the surrounding country. The buildings are well constructed, though unpretentious in comparison to some of the larger American universities. But the whole place is wonderfully attractive and homelike. It has more the appearance of a group of well kept private dwellings than that of a seat of learning, a place for work and study. And they do study, the daughters of "Fair Smith," in a manner that would put the average college man to shame. Yet if any one supposes that these young women are a set of "grinds," that they all wear glasses and masculine collars, and go about continually talking women's rights

"PARADISE" IN SUMMER.

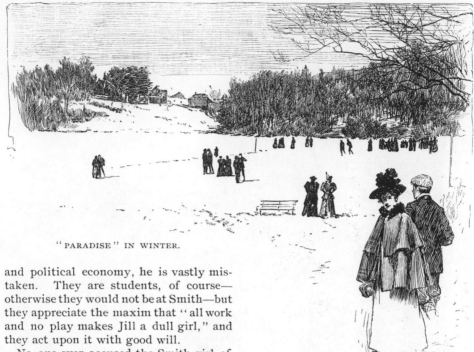

"PARADISE" IN WINTER.

and political economy, he is vastly mistaken. They are students, of course—otherwise they would not be at Smith—but they appreciate the maxim that "all work and no play makes Jill a dull girl," and they act upon it with good will.

No one ever accused the Smith girl of being dull. She blends work and fun in such happy proportions that to her life is always interesting. She is neither a bookworm nor an idler, but keen intellectual competition and wholesome physical activity combine to bring out all that is best in her. On any bright day the campus is an extremely interesting sight. From dawn till dark it is always full of life. The girls are continually flitting from one building to another, or meeting in groups on the smooth, well kept lawn.

> Here's a group of just eleven,
>   Talking o'er a hard exam. ;
> Here's a group of six or seven,
>   Eating ginger snaps and jam !

In pleasant weather the "Smithians"

THE MUSIC BUILDING.

THE COLLEGE HALL.

rarely wear any headgear ; or if they do, it is nothing but a " Tam-o'-Shanter." When the weather is cold, they slip over their shoulders a warm golf cape, which may be as easily slipped off again on entering a recitation room. The very sensible fashion prevails of wearing skirts that escape the ground by two or three inches, while many of the girls fairly live in their bicycle costumes.

Founded in 1871 by Sophia Smith, of Hatfield, Massachusetts, the college has long since outgrown the capacity of its own dormitories, but all about the grounds houses and cottages have sprung up which, during the college year, are devoted wholly to the use of the Smith girls. The campus houses are naturally more in demand than those outside, and there is always a long waiting list of applicants who are anxious to obtain rooms in them.

The outside houses are beyond the jurisdiction of the college authorities, and the girls living in them have greater freedom than those living in the college buildings, for here such rules as " lights

out at ten," " no breakfast if late," are more or less rigidly enforced.

A decided innovation in the dormitory life of Smith is the handsome building which has recently been erected outside the campus. It is a massive pile of masonry that conveys the impression of having wandered from its foundation in some large city. It has all the modern conveniences, from steam heat and electric lights to an elevator with a boy in buttons. These "improvements" are all very well in their way ; but when a girl surrounds herself with all the paraphernalia of hotel existence, she is apt to find that she is not quite in touch with that democratic spirit which is one of the greatest charms of the life at Smith. The cost of living in such a dormitory is, of course, greater than in the other houses, and so, naturally, the occupants are regarded more or less as a class by themselves—as girls of means. Such a distinction is, of course, made unconsciously, but it exists nevertheless, and results in the formation of "cliques"—always an unfortunate feature of undergraduate life.

A SMITH GIRL'S ROOM.

THE CHAPEL.

In the campus houses such cliques can have no existence. The daughter of the man who owns two or three railroads has no better surroundings and no more comforts than the ambitious girl who is working her way through college. Of the latter there are quite a number, and they exhibit much ingenuity in devising ways and means of self support. One girl is noted for the stylish shirt waists she makes, and her needle is kept busy in this direction. This same girl plays the piano for any dance that may be given. Another almost entirely supports herself with her camera, while a third is correspondent for several newspapers.

The curriculum at Smith is practically the same as that at any first class university, but the pastimes are vastly different. Basketball is the most popular game, and keen is the rivalry between the classes. The contests are held in the se-

THE OBSERVATORY.

ON THE CAMPUS.

THE PRESIDENT'S HOUSE.

clusion of the college gymnasium. Basketball is not unlike a mild form of football, and, while it avoids the danger of the latter, it is well calculated to arouse the enthusiasm of rival classes to the highest pitch. Boating and tennis are also favorite amusements in their season, and in winter there is skating, in which the Amherst students often join.

One of the first places shown to the visitor is "Paradise." This delightful spot — the name is applied, in a general way, to a pretty sheet of water and the charming, shady walks near by—is the favorite retreat of the Smith girls. On pleasant half holidays one may see many of them wending their way in its direction, laden with sofa pillows and

THE IVY PROCESSION.

"fudge"—a kind of home made candy, locally in great demand.

The principal secret societies at Smith are the Alpha and the Phi Kappa Psi, to either one of which a girl may be elected after her freshman year. In order to be eligible an undergraduate must possess decided talent for literature, or else be a general favorite.

Graduation time is marked by many time honored observances. The seniors wear white dresses for the last three days of the college year. One of these is known as "Ivy Day," and on it the departing class plants an ivy vine near College Hall. It is a pretty sight to see the "sweet girl graduates," all in white, marching two by two across the green campus.

Douglas Z. Doty.

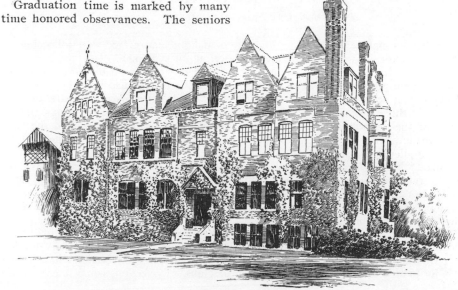

THE LILLY HALL OF SCIENCE.

22

STANDISH HALL, ONE OF THE FRESHMEN BUILDINGS IN WHICH HARVARD
IS TO TRY AN EXPERIMENT IN UNDERGRADUATE DEMOCRACY

From a perspective drawing by the architects, Shepley, Rutan & Coolidge.

THE STRUGGLE FOR COLLEGE DEMOCRACY

HARVARD UNDERTAKES TO SOLVE THE GREAT SOCIAL PROBLEM IN
AMERICAN UNIVERSITY LIFE BY A PLAN COMBINING FEATURES
OF THE OXFORD SYSTEM AND WOODROW WILSON'S FAMOUS
"QUAD," PRINCETON'S GRADUATE SCHOOL

BY JOHN CORBIN

Author of "An American at Oxford"

WHEN a man sends his son to the university, it is natural to suppose that the boy will mingle with other undergraduates man to man, and win friends and distinction according to the stuff that is in him. But a father who lately took counsel of the graduates of several institutions made a discovery which he found deeply disquieting. Everywhere it was recognized that in order to come into friendly relations with the leading men of his class a freshman had to make a set campaign of what the feminine world knows as social-climbing. "At Harvard," said this father, "they call it 'swiping,' at Yale 'heeling,' and at Princeton 'getting into a following.'

"Now, which do you think most likely to make a man of my son, following, or heeling, or swiping?"

The fact is that all our universities are rather sharply divided into the "ins" and the "outs"—the sheep who are not unwillingly shepherded in luxurious and exclusive clubs or fraternities, and the goats who lead an isolated and ineffectual existence in the solitary wilds without. As they have grown rapidly, the dividing-line has become more and more a matter of chance, and less a matter of desert. Where the fraternity system prevails, the line is often drawn in the freshman year, before the character and ability of the undergraduate has had time to develop. Where the social life centers in a system of clubs, the elections come later; yet the choice is scarcely more representative. If a boy is a member of a clique from one of the leading preparatory schools, or a distinguished athlete, the path is easy—so easy that often quite undeserving fellows rise to the crest of the wave. But, lacking such advantages, as many a good man does lack them, he finds himself in imminent danger of being submerged.

In the modern world no taboo is more powerful than that which rests upon American undergraduates who have failed to "make" a club or fraternity. They are hoi polloi, barbarians, outsiders—to mention only a few of the epithets. Every instinct of self-preservation impels a boy to get himself "run" for a fraternity, to follow, heel, or swipe; in short, to enter a conscious struggle against which every manly impulse revolts.

Two things equally grave result from this. An increasingly large proportion of undergraduates fail to get what they are capable of getting out of undergraduate life. Helpless and forlorn, they live in little cliques, remote from the moving interests, the priceless traditions, of the student body as a whole. And the universities in turn are failing to develop the full value of the material they have to work with; for if the right man fails to make a team, fraternity, or club, the institution as a whole loses precisely as he does.

Yet I for one do not accuse our universities of any snobbish intention or real exclusiveness of spirit. Everywhere the impulse and the ideal are right. Many poor men of character and ability yearly make their way into the inner circles at Yale and Princeton; and if Harvard is a shade less fortunate in this respect,—I do not say that it is,—it excels all other universities, I think, in what may be called the democracy of scholarship and intelligence. The universities in which the fraternity system prevails are the most obviously democratic in their dominant ideal; as, for example, the great state universities of the West.

The real need, as we are coming to see, is not of an ideal, but of a system—an organization which gives every undergraduate the opportunity of developing to the utmost his capacity for college life and college leadership. In a word, the disorder is functional, one of digestion and assimilation.

"The university," wrote a graduate of Harvard, toward the end of President Eliot's régime, "has very largely lost its power of social assimilation. A well-known professor, walking through the college yard, met a youth who seemed so forlorn and troubled that he was prompted to ask, 'Are you looking for anybody?' The young man answered, 'I don't know anybody this side of the Rocky Mountains.' Whether from shyness or from pride, many men hold Harvard degrees whose acquaintance at Cambridge is scarcely greater."

The anecdote was quoted from a university pamphlet written to convince the reader of the hospitality extended to newcomers; and the critic who took it so backhandedly was scolded at his alma mater for omitting to mention that the young man was a freshman, and, having thus been taken in hand, eventually found friends. In an address delivered at Yale, Dean Briggs listed this critic with the author of "Brown at Harvard," the leading actor in which, also a Harvard man, was rotten-egged by loyal undergraduates. Apparently the good dean thought that the offenders deserved alike to be in very bad odor amid the classic shades. So be it! It takes the breaking of eggs for the making of *Hamlets,* and a critic may similarly profit.

One fact, however, Dean Briggs failed to mention. The critic went on to urge that in order to insure a hospitable welcome to freshmen, and to restore "the power of social assimilation," it was only necessary to have a system of halls reproducing the residential features of the colleges of Oxford and Cambridge; and even while he was held up to the reprobation of a sister university, his idea was taking substantial form on the banks of the Charles in a system of freshman halls. "It has been remarked," said President Lowell, in explaining his innovation, "that the only advance in the art of the novel since Scott lies in the fact that we have learned to begin a story in the middle." The new halls are to plunge the freshman *in medias res.* Could any illustration be more suggestive of the dreary waste of the first half of an undergraduate's life in the conditions that have hitherto prevailed? Not that the figure walks on all fours. The literal fact is that these new halls are to begin the task of "social assimilation" at the beginning.

Other universities have been similarly criticized by their children. Yale is in chronic revolt against her societies, Princeton against her upper-class eating-clubs; and wherever the fraternity system prevails, it has its unrelenting foes. Nor is the remedy which Harvard is trying its own exclusive invention. President Wilson, when president of Princeton, attempted it in a somewhat different form. He failed to establish his "quads," and for reasons which, as I hope to show, were sufficient; but the idea lives on. Even as the Colonial halls for freshmen are building on the banks of the Charles, the Gothic tower of Dean West's graduate college is rising beautifully on the summit of the hill at Princeton.

At the University of Wisconsin, President Van Hise some years ago showed me architects' designs for a system of residential halls for which he was hoping to secure the necessary money; and he now writes: "Our plans have been presented to each session of the legislature and are pending before the present legislature. We have strong hopes that the appropriation will be made which will enable us to take the first steps in carrying out the plans." Apparently there is to be a single huge commons—a thing most undesirable socially, and of no considerable economic advantage. At Cornell, Andrew D. White cherished the hope of separate colleges from the start, and President Schurman has urged the plan in his reports during the last dozen years. There is now a good prospect that it will be realized and that each college will have its separate kitchen and dining hall.

There is no paradox in the fact that we are seeking a remedy in the English universities. Oxford and Cambridge have traditionally been, and still are in the main, the resort of the upper classes; but, thanks to their internal organization, they are in effect more democratic than any American university. This is the conclusion which, much to my surprise, was forced upon me by a rather wide experience as an Oxford undergraduate; and it was strongly confirmed by American Rhodes scholars whom I met during a recent sojourn by the Isis.

No freshman can live a single day in an English college without making several acquaintances, and at the end of his first week he can hardly escape having literally dozens. The porter who greets him at the gate expects him, and has a room already prepared to receive him. His first duty is to call on his tutor, who is destined to become a familiar and most helpful mentor. The tutor takes him to call on the master of the college, and introduces him not only to other freshmen, but to second-year men, whose duty it is to call on him, invite him to breakfast or luncheon, and in general supervise his entrance into the college life and activities. In our universities a freshman is regarded as an uncouth creature to be ridiculed, hazed, or at least ignored; in the English colleges he is a younger brother who is to be encouraged to develop his best capacities.

One difference of custom tells the whole story. With us rooms in the most favorably placed dormitories are the abode of upper classmen. The freshman lives as he can in an outer limbo of boarding-houses, or in college buildings justly despised. In Oxford the freshman is taken at once into the quadrangle, though upper classmen have to be turned out into the town to make room for him. In effect, the English system says: "For better or for worse you are one of us, and for four years we shall have to abide by your deeds. Come on! Let us make the best we can of you!"

At Harvard, if I may record an experience which is typical, I was plunged for two years into the gloom of a very tedious novel before I discovered, quite by accident, that I could run. Then the story began. At Oxford the master of my college, a philosopher of European reputation, walked circles around me at our first interview, and said that I ought to be able to row and play foot-ball. I suffered tortures by field and river before I was given over to the cinder track, and incidentally I made many good friends. I abhor public speaking, yet was drafted into the college debating society, and several times forced to expose a naked intellect. A man must be a goat by nature and preference if he is to escape the helpful friendliness of an English college.

It was in order to achieve some such organs of digestion and assimilation that

President Wilson proposed to divide Princeton into "quads." So far so good. Unfortunately, either from ignorance of the English universities or because of some formal and doctrinary theory of democracy, he added ideas alien alike to the English and the American university.

Each quad was to be mathematically democratic: so many rich men, so many poor men; so many men from north, south, east, and west; so many from the leading preparatory schools and so many who arrived friendless. Each quad was to be, so to speak, a cross-section of the undergraduate body as a whole. To any one familiar with the English colleges, this arrangement must seem somewhat cut and dried, as most cross-sections are. The life of any great university is rich and strong enough to give scope to various developments. In Balliol learning is tempered by sportsmanship; in New College sportsmanship is redeemed by learning. The dominant qualities are the same, yet the atmosphere of the two places, and of the men who are bred in it, is full of the variations that enhance character and make life interesting. Brasenose, Trinity, St. John's, Magdalen, Christ Church, have each its atmosphere, subtle and indefinable perhaps, but permanent and distinct. And so on through the list. Every college gives the stamp of Oxford, yet each adds an inestimable imprint of its own. Without knowing quite why, perhaps, Princeton revolted at the attempt to level it down.

The rock upon which the "quad system" split, however, was the upper-class eating-clubs. In the main they were, and still are, characteristic of the best elements of Princeton life. To me personally, and I have studied them at close range, they seem the most representative, the most truly democratic social system in any American university. It is the rule, and a rule which suffers comparatively few infractions, that their membership shall not be made up until the end of the second year, when the true character of all candidates has had time to develop.

Yet the fact remains that certain cliques are generally reputed to be in the following for Ivy, Cottage, Tiger Inn, and so forth; and not unnaturally there is strife to become identified with these cliques. And the members of the clubs wear distinctive hatbands, much prized, it appears, by the ins and deeply resented by the outs. In President Wilson's opinion, certainly, the clubs were the resort of exclusiveness, of snobbishness; and so they must go!

One difficulty was that many of them were heavily in debt for their buildings. Even the most doctrinary democracy cannot by fiat disestablish an issue of bonds. It was equally evident to the Princeton mind that, for all the abuses that seemed to center in them, the clubs were a most valuable asset to the university. They were the rallying-ground of those graduates who, on the whole, were the leading graduates, the ones who had the welfare of the alma mater most dearly at heart. To abolish them was to oust the Princeton spirit from its firmest vantage-ground. And it was to lessen the revenues of the university; for the returning graduate is the graduate who most easily loosens his heart-strings—and purse-strings.

To regard the clubs as opposed to the quad or college system, moreover, is, I believe, fundamentally to misconceive the situation. They are rather to be regarded as essential to its fullest and most helpful development.

Let us go back to Oxford. Each college is a microcosm in which the spirit of the place works powerfully, thoroughly; yet, after all, it is small, on an average numbering about two hundred. The little frogs are happy in their puddle; but how about the big frogs? The best thing in the world for a big frog in a small puddle is to try life in places where his advantage is less obvious. If an Oxford man is a good sportsman and a good fellow, he is elected to Vincent's; and there he meets the good sportsman and good fellows of the university as a whole. The debaters go to the Oxford Union; and to win one's way to the presidency of the Union is perhaps the greatest distinction of an Oxford career. There are half a dozen smaller debating clubs which foregather the most distinguished birds of a political feather from all the twenty colleges. There are purely social clubs, like Bullingdon, and there are the Gridiron Club for diners, the Musical Union, and the Dramatic Society. As soon as a man has won special distinction in any line, in short, he emerges from the little world of his college into a club, and is thrown among kindred spirits from the university as a whole.

In his university club a man takes part in activities which are wider and higher: he develops his own ability, and contributes his quota to the general life of the place. But, far from being cut off from his former mates, as he is in an American university club, he brings them an inestimable privilege. The major part of his life and activity is still in his college, and he carries back to it reports of what is being said and done in the world without its walls. The local life and the general life interpenetrate and fuse, so that the humblest man in college lives, actually or vicariously, in the general stream of Oxford tradition. Whereas the quad system means uniform, mechanical democracy, small in scope and without local distinction, the English combination of club life and college life means varied atmosphere and charm, with the largest possible outlook, and opportunity for vital leadership. In that vivid phrase of Oom Paul's, one hand washes the other.

The common run of men may feel regret at not taking active part in the affairs of the university; yet they have had a fair chance, and do not complain. The college still affords them a pleasant home and a life of very considerable scope. There is no taboo, no social stigma of being excluded. Not by the farthest stretch of the word could they be called outsiders, barbarians, hoi polloi. And the system works equally well in the case of the club man. To the end he is at home in college among brothers. Except when he is turned out to make room for incoming freshmen, he sleeps there, and takes most of his meals in his room and in the hall. He still plays on the college teams, rows in the college boat. And so he escapes the dangers of the club or fraternity man in an American university, whose life is largely limited to association with the favored few. There is no real exclusion on the one hand, no real exclusiveness on the other. The life is highly organized, highly specialized, highly efficient in giving scope to all grades and varieties of capability. If it is not more democratic, then there is something wrong with our conception of democracy.

In a recent political campaign it was asserted that at Princeton President Wilson routed the snobs and made the college democratic. To this a leading Princetonian retorted that Princeton was precisely as democratic as it had always been. He added, significantly, that it was still doing business at the old stand. These are harsh words on both sides.

The credit of first organizing undergraduate democracy, as it now seems, is to go to Harvard. In a way there is justice in this, for Harvard was the first prominently to advocate supplementing the club system with a system of residential halls—as long ago as 1894.

At that time a widely different plan was given preference, also of English origin. In the early nineteenth century Oxford was a victim of a quad system very closely similar to that which of late President Wilson advocated. The twenty colleges lived miniature, separate lives, with no common meeting-ground, no mechanism for developing special talents or for creating a highly organized university spirit. Then came the Oxford Union; and the university, which has always been more keenly political than any American institution, found a powerful unifying force in debate. Membership was open to all, and the library, periodical room, and auditorium of the Union—let us not forget the lawn, where afternoon tea was served in summer—proved a rallying-ground for all active spirits, political and social. It so happened, however, that the new spirit of unified Oxford did not stop with the Union. Other clubs were formed, as we have seen—clubs that took precedence from the fact that their aims were more definitive and interesting and their membership carefully selected. Long before the close of the century the unifying force of the Union had become a mere tradition. Except on the evening of a debate, those who foregathered there were a social fringe, with little unity and no real influence or power.

It was this Union, however, which Harvard chose to imitate, precisely as the framers of our national constitution took as model a form of the English constitution which had long been obsolete. For a time the spirit of democracy struggled mightily to make the Harvard Union the real heart and center of undergraduate life. To join it was represented as a patriotic duty. But from the first it was evident that there was no power in it to bring the club-man and the unassimilated into helpful intimacy and understanding. Of late years the number of members has relatively declined. The institution is a faint shadow of the decadent Oxford Union—a convenience for returning graduates and a pleasant resort for undergraduates who have no more direct and vital associations. Regarded as an instrument of democracy and efficiency, it has been only a dreary waste of time, of money, and of enthusiasm. And this the university itself now realizes.

The advocates of the residential hall, some of whom had predicted this outcome, bided their time. A group of patriotic graduates bought up a tract of land on the banks of the Charles, then a dismal slum, but now a beautifully gardened esplanade. To hold this tract, they went down into their pockets every year to the extent of twenty thousand dollars. Of almost any American university it may be safely said that, in spirit at least, it is as democratic as it has always been! Under President Eliot there was other use for such moneys as accrued to the university; but to President Lowell the residential hall was one of the most important of a group of reforms which are transforming and humanizing Harvard, and which are destined, as Harvard men believe, to mark a new era in American university organization.

Three halls, Standish, Smith, and Gore, will be ready for occupancy next September. Together they will probably house the entire freshman class, with the exception of students who live at home in Boston and its suburbs. Each hall is to be a distinct and separate community. Each will have a master and a staff of proctors to insure order and decorum. The proctors will be chosen as far as possible from among the instructors in courses frequented by freshmen, so as to assure acquaintance, and, indeed, familiarity and friendship between teacher and taught, proctor and proctorized. Learning and discipline will thus be immeasurably humanized.

Each community will have its separate common-room, kitchen, and dining-hall. The English plan of having no fixed seats at table will probably be followed. Thus groups coming from lecture-hall or athletic-field will sit down together, if they so choose; or a man may sit beside some one with whom he wishes to speak. Meal-time—the time when most people are readiest to develop social instincts—will bring a constant shifting of groups and of individuals. Universities which are planning to build a general commons will do well to study the workings of these separate dining halls. Harvard has tried the general commons—in its Memorial of unsavory memory.

Each hall will also have its separate athletic team in all major sports, and compete with other halls for the championship of the class. These teams will be a sort of complement to the regular freshman teams, affording sport and the discipline of athletic contests to men not capable of playing on the class teams, and developing material for them, precisely as class teams develop material for university teams.

Where residence is limited to the first year, a somewhat formal selection of the members of each hall should prove as helpful as it would be pernicious if applied to the college as a whole. "No definite rules have been made," I am told, "in regard to the distribution of the rooms; but undoubtedly care will be taken not to allow any one hall to become the camping-ground of any particular set of men. An endeavor will be made to have each community a cross-section of the class." Freshman classes nowadays number five or six hundred, and are composed of men of widely different interests and traditions. Everywhere it has proved impossible to develop generally a spirit of intimate comradeship. But by working in smaller units, composed of men of all sorts, the spirit of democracy can be made manifest from the start.

Fear has been expressed that the authorities will forbid men to leave the hall after nine o'clock, and will require those who dine out of hall to return before midnight. This is the rule in English colleges, sanctioned by century-old custom, and, indeed, by the general sentiment of the undergraduates, who recognize that it tends powerfully to keep the college homogeneous and give strength to its spirit and traditions. It is, however, contrary to all American custom, and President Lowell gives assurance that no such rules will be adopted.

These freshman halls are only a part of a very capacious and thoroughly thought-out plan. The men who have established them look forward to a time when it will be possible to erect a super-structure of halls in which the undergraduate may reside throughout the sophomore, junior, and senior years. Here, it is to be hoped, the mathematical scheme of division will be modified so as to develop communities each accentuating some desirable note of difference.

To allow a sophomore to choose his own upper-class hall without restriction would perhaps not be possible. Certain halls would inevitably grow too large, too rich, too social, too athletic. But the spirit which followed the forlorn hope of the Harvard Union may easily be so guided as to create in the upper-class halls an atmosphere of varied distinction which shall be in no wise unrepresentative or undemocratic.

In view of the expense involved, and of the fact that the dormitory accommodations are already sufficient, it is not thought wise at present to agitate the building of upper-class halls. Yet among undergraduates who fail to make the more congenial and homelike clubs there should be an increasing demand that the comfort and comradeship of the first year shall be continued. The development of the upper-class hall is only a question of time and money.

In the freshman halls, meanwhile, every member of the class will enter, from the day of his arrival, into familiar intercourse with a considerable part of the most prominent men of his year, and so will have a fair chance of election to the more coveted clubs. If he is not elected, he will still have a very wide acquaintance among those similarly situated. There will be at least one American institution where, in order to make the most of undergraduate life, it will not be necessary to follow, to heel, or to be run, or even to make a noise like a Rocky Mountain goat upon encountering a benevolent professor.

May it be timorously suggested that the sister-university might have a more profitable use for eggs no better than they should be than to bestow them upon exponents of this scheme of residence in groups? As a Harvard man of times past, I have a very deep respect for the Yale tradition. The senior societies made the undergraduate body heel to some purpose. But, as elsewhere, the social system gives signs of weakening in proportion as the university grows larger. Even the enthusiastic Stover despaired of creating any broad and permanent spirit of democracy under present conditions. But if the undergraduate body were divided into residential halls, each with its leading men in the senior societies, then, as it seems to me, democracy might become widely organized and permanent; and at the same time the societies would have a more powerful means than ever of manifesting the Yale spirit beneath the elm-tree shade.

Where the more usual type of fraternity prevails, the question is in one way more difficult, for residence in the chapter-house begins early in undergraduate life. Yet it should be possible to keep new-comers in the more democratic halls for at least the first year. In one way the problem is far easier. The fraternity universities have, for the most part, no dormitories, and for the most part they are, like Wisconsin, intending soon to build them. Thus no existing property will suffer if, instead of the old type of dormitory, they build a system of freshman halls and upper-class halls.

What Harvard has done for freshmen, Princeton has done for graduates, and most handsomely. Unfortunate as undergraduates have been, they have at worst lived among some hundreds of fellows who were entering upon a new and joyous experience, eager to make friends for the most part, and loyal to the class and to the university. They had many common interests even in study. The graduate is entering the world of serious professional labor. Whatever his desire for comradeship, he has little time to make friends or to enjoy them.

If he has migrated to a strange institution, he finds himself among men who are not only unknown, but for the most part unknowable. His acquaintance is limited to the classroom and perhaps a departmental club which meets at infrequent intervals. If a man stays on at his own university, he finds himself bereft of the main body of his old associates. He lives in a world of strangers, with whom he has little or nothing in common; and strangers in a strange place are in many ways less appalling than strangers in a place which has hitherto been alive with comrades. In short, at a time when all the instincts of manhood cry out for some real work in the world, the graduate student finds himself caught in the petty web of his own highly specialized studies. It is not strange if the "grad-grind" has been taken as the type of all that is thin-blooded and anemic.

From the merely professional point of view the situation is quite as bad. Scientific culture and research being the order of the day, the tendency of the candidate for the doctorate in philosophy is to neglect the broader outlines even of his own specialty. Yet even the philologist needs to keep in touch with workers in neighboring fields; and if he wishes to gain a true perspective on the world as a whole, he will do well to have some knowledge of the harvest in distant vineyards. As the man withers in the friendless world of the graduate school, so the scholar dries in the bud.

In the postgraduate college at Princeton Dean West is creating an institution in all respects similar to the English college, except, of course, that it is composed of more advanced and serious students. It is a Gothic structure, very beautiful, and about its quadrangles are students' rooms, common-room, dining-hall, and the residence of the dean. Over the whole rises a stately tower, pinnacled like the tower of Magdalen. One has only to open his eyes to be back in Oxford.

For the last decade Dean West has been busy organizing the graduate school on a residential basis, creating traditions of humanistic culture and social solidarity. In their new home the members will live as a close community within walls that beautifully symbolize the spirit of academic order and decorum—the order and decorum which make one free to expand in all the interests and activities natural to the scholar who is still a man.

Residence in a compact community makes friendliness easy and natural at any hour, and at meals the graduate school will gather as a whole in the spacious and dignified hall. In the common-room there will be current periodicals, and easy-chairs for reading and talk. There is probably no place in America where the life of learning is likely to be one half as stimulating to the scholar and to the man. The specialist cannot fail to gain breadth of vision, the humanist some touch of the spirit of modern science.

As I have said, the college crowns a hill. It looks down upon the neighboring university and the distant valley beyond. It is characteristic of President Wilson that he fought against this isolation. It is one of the fixed ideas of our people, and it explains, perhaps, why of all modern nations we are most lacking in variety of life and distinction of character. Our tradition is for the mechanical plane, the dead level.

Thus, in founding the University of Chicago, President Harper saw the value of residence in groups, and was the first to make actual progress in the matter. If he had lived, he would possibly have developed a thorough system of residential halls. His successor, President Judson, follows him in believing in residence in groups, but deprecates the plan of permitting any group to develop an individual character. "It seems to me advisable," he says, "that a given residential hall shall contain students of all sorts, graduates and undergraduates alike." Is it possible that at Chicago freshmen discuss divinity with theologs, that graduates discuss literature with sophomores? Elsewhere, as far as I have been able to find, both parties refuse to place themselves at so great a disadvantage. They may mingle, but cannot mix.

In "The Promise of American Life," Mr. Herbert Croly has shown that our traditional conception of democracy had its origin early in the last century, when frontier conditions prevailed and differences of character and of position were few. Obeying the irresistible logic of progress, we have come to a time in which society, and even business, is organized in large units, and in which men succeed in proportion as they become differentiated—specialists. The book marks an epoch in our national thought. The democracy of Jefferson and Jackson is as obsolete as the college of the early nineteenth century, in which a four-year curriculum was supposed to hold the learning of the world in its pint pot. In at least two institutions to-day democracy is expanding by means of varied organization.

23

THE INVASION OF OXFORD

By William C. Crittenden

First Student of the Cecil Rhodes Scholarship from California

IN THE year 1904 there was a call for volunteers to invade Oxford, the stronghold of the classics, mind to mind and brawn to brawn. Some said it was to be an army of brains. It was an earnest whole-souled band but motley. Many carried haughty airs; one a gold headed cane, a few had American editions of the history of the war of the Revolution. Some philanthropic souls were burdened with advice and it hung heavy on them. It was not uncommon to see young heroes wearing all their grey matter on the outside like a peddler with his wares. It was indeed in many ways a formidable throng. Finally without exception all carried lily pots. But this needs explanation.

"Why do you want to take that flower pot," demanded Mr. John of his wife as they started from Ohio on a trip to California. "Why, I couldn't go without it. This is the most beautiful lily in our town, dear, I couldn't leave it. I must take it." And she did. She nursed that lily and pampered it and watered it every day. The porter grew pale, and the husband became thin, but Mrs. John with pride, still clung to her lily pot and for five days and nights she petted that lily. One morning she looked from the car window on the sun-swept lands of California and saw as in a dream whole fields of lilies, great callas, and hers was a mere starveling beside them. She said not a word but picked up the lily and walked with sad measured steps to the rear of the car and leaning over dropped it. And thus these young invaders with even more tenacity clung to their lily pots of prejudice and nursed them and were proud of them.

One good, whole-souled fellow was particularly burdened. "Yes," he said, "when I left home it was very sad. I went out on the farm for the last time and I said: 'Good-bye, old farm, I'm going to Oxford,' and I patted 'Bossy' on the neck and said, 'Good-bye 'Bossy,' I'm going to Oxford,' and then," he said: "I looked up to the bright blue sky and murmured 'Good-bye, God, I'm going to Oxford.'" And when he arrived and found God over here, I really believe he was disappointed.

And others in the same way found Oxford milder than they had anticipated. The *Avernia* on which about thirty of America's ornaments were transported was the scene of a great contest. One party was for "Do as the Romans do;" the other flaunted the banner of the righteous, "We shall reform Oxford." Hot waged the factions and all on account of those famous wine breakfasts, reports of which had stirred many hearts—but in different ways. "No wine for breakfast" was the war cry and with tense muscles and set teeth and minds alert for the contest the worthy band advanced upon poor old Oxford with the firm determination to reform a development of thirteen centuries. The summons came to each. "Come to breker" (breakfast). With teeth set tighter, with the glory of battle in the blood, with their lily pots under their arms, these "nasal-twanged Americans" went to "breker!" Course by course went by but no sparkling bottles of the wily juice beamed proud of their years and no glasses clinked. Verily, great was the disappointment even of the reformers who were loudest in their complaints of "weak tea, bad coffee, always got better at home," and finally one poor fellow went so far as to admit "he would just like to get a smell of all that good grape juice he had heard so much about."

So, one by one we dropped our lily pots, relaxed our muscles and calmed down to normal. Then it was, that we began to wonder what the difference really was between the English youth and ourselves. The veneer or better crust of time was rather thick, but this conservativeness, the ready manner of the American, soon broke through and beneath it all, there were found genial companions and loyal friends. When an Englishman comes up to one before a vacation, and begs your pardon for asking you to telegraph him if by ill luck you run short of money, and ends by inviting you to spend a fortnight at his home if you get lonesome—after a few such experiences one forgets everything except this big-heartedness and it warms your heart to have the privilege of knowing such men. And when they see that any sojourner in a strange land, is looking gloomy over the prospect of a Christmas dinner on a patriarch and a fake plum pudding, before one knows it there is a kind invitation from the

IN THE QUADRANGLE OF ORIEL—MERTON TOWER AT THE RIGHT

"mater" of one of your friends and you are given a chance of bursting your heart through the remembrance of the hospitality that has been shown you.

It is this heart and hand friendship, the friendship which goes to the bottom of the purse and the center of the heart which all Americans most admire, but thought they had left behind when they sailed from the "States." The Americans here will soon be saying what John Beerbarrel said to his devoted spouse who seeing him in a very dilapidated condition of mind and body began, "Now John, ain't yer coming 'ome! Won't yer please come 'ome? If yer don't come 'ome I'll beat you." "Well," says John, "I'll do anything yer likes, in reason, M'ria, but I won't come 'ome!"

And now it is a familiar sight to see two broad shouldered fellows walking down "The High," arm in arm, with cap and gown and turned-up trousers and one will be English and the other American but no one will know it. They are always mingled. The Britisher and the "men from the States" are cursed by the same coach on the river, advance the same football on the gridiron; are chased by the same proctors and plow (fail) in the same examinations. But with all this we are not becoming Anglomaniacs. Far from it. We respect the Englishmen too much to characterize

A SHADED CORNER OF MAGDALEN QUADRANGLE
SHOWING THE STATELY COLLEGE TOWER

them. With the exception of one of our band we have too little time even for the essentials to waste over cultivating thoraxal feats. There seems to be unanimity of opinion on this one point that when anything tends to make us unfitted to perform the duties of citizens of the United States in after years it is to be avoided. We don't wish to be like the American actor who was seeking employment of a London manager:

"No, I don't think I require your services, you have too many Americanisms, too much of the American accent."

"What am I to do?" replied the actor. "In the 'States' they say I have the British accent and you say I have the American. And you can't expect me to give recitations on a transatlantic liner can you?"

But the Rhodes men have done more than avoid the pitfalls. They have gained many positive advantages and in general made a success of their sojourns here, although many recent publications in the United States have declared to the contrary. Even a comparison between the Americans and Colonials would be favorable to the "men from the States," judging from articles on Rhodes scholars published in England, although some of the eastern dailies have stated the contrary, basing their opinion on the fact that the two best prize scholarships were

THE INVASION OF OXFORD

A SUMMER-TIME "BUMPING RACE" BETWEEN THE COLLEGE EIGHTS—ON THE LEFT ARE THE COLLEGE BARGES WITH
THEIR FLAGS

taken by the Colonials. Both of these men were educated from their childhood on the English system, fitting them for Oxford and particular courses of study. The one, before he came to England, had spent seven years on English law, the other had studied classics since he was ten years old. It has often been remarked how admirably the Americans have done considering the disadvantages they are placed under.

The consensus of opinion the first year was that our work here was a waste of time. To some extent that was due to the fact that few worked the first year. One man was only going to remain one year, now he intends to stay four. There are several others with similar intentions. It is now generally admitted that the courses of study here and the methods of work are most satisfactory, especially for those who intend to practice law or become professors. In a debate a few weeks ago among Americans it was moved:

That the Oxford system of examinations and instruction is more advantageous than that in an American university. The affirmative won the debate by a vote of about two to one.

Besides, the Americans especially have taken advantage of the opportunities to travel on the continent and study French and German or even Italian and Spanish in these countries. A great admirer of Oxford not long ago asked a Rhodes scholar what in his opinion was the greatest advantage the scholarship afforded. "Why," was the careless reply, "the opportunity it gives one to travel on the continent." There is a certain amount of truth in this thoughtless answer. It has even been suggested that a joke in *Punch* was called forth by the traveling propensities of Rhodes men. A band of tourists was standing looking into the fiery crater of Vesuvius.

"This does remind me of hell," remarked an American.

A young lady near by whispered to her mother: "How these Americans do travel!"

The Rhodes scholars have succeeded not only from their own standpoint but also from that of the English student. They have fulfilled the purpose of Rhodes and mixed with the British youth. In athletics, the American has readily adapted himself to the beau ideal of the English, that is to attempt many sports and do one or two well. The Oxford student admires a man who is "sporting" as they call him, one who will help his college out when a man happens to be needed in any game. The question is not how well he can play but will he have the spirit to attempt for the sake of his college. An American is always ready to attempt and what is more to do it successfully. There are some Rhodes men who have played for their college in four or five sports. These men come in contact with many more students and are naturally the most popular.

But athletic ability is not all that is needed to fit a man for life at an

A TYPICAL COLLEGE GROUP TAKEN IN A CORNER OF THE QUAD. THOSE IN WHITE TIES AND GOWNS AND "MORTAR BOARD" HATS ARE TAKING FINAL EXAMINATIONS; THOSE IN STRAW HATS WITH STRIPED BANDS MARK THE MEN ROWING IN "THE EIGHT." MR. CRITTENDEN, THE FIRST RHODES SCHOLAR FROM CALIFORNIA, AND THE WRITER OF THIS ARTICLE, IS IN THE FOURTH ROW FROM THE BOTTOM AND WEARS A STRIPED BAND HAT

English university, as is sometimes supposed. The British youth is a study at first; an American doesn't know how to take him exactly. The first side of an Englishman you see will make you think him an idler and an overgrown boy—irresponsible and thoughtless. That is the side that presents itself at a dinner or a "smoker." Then some night you will be sitting by your fire and a young Britisher will come in, light his bulldog pipe, pull an easy chair so that his feet will reach the fender and ask you whether you think the Constitution of the United States is going to be amended to enlarge the power of the Federal Government, or some similar poser with regard to European politics. A couple of hours later he will leave you with a firm determination on your part to learn more about your own country at least. Or perhaps he will advance a crude theory of life—a sort of philosophy of his own and will wait for you to knock it in the head. If you do he will return perhaps a week later with a better constructed theory and a pouch full of tobacco. Then one begins to see the Britisher in a different light.

It is a strange inconsistency, the youthful, boyish hilarity and the deep workings of a thoughtful well-poised mind. This is what the American must understand and he must adapt himself to this apparent inconsistency. A scatter-brain will fail here and so will a very sober-minded student. But the average American, being adaptable and somewhat of an actor by instinct, is soon one with the rest, for he is never adverse to a good time and can usually hold his own in discussing politics and government even if he doesn't knock in the head many theories of life, or give a visitor a vigorous discussion of Kant.

One might say that the first test is athletic ability, the next, sociability and the final, scholastic ability. When you have passed the first two you are the admiration of your friends; when you have shown yourself a scholar besides you are the admiration of your college.

One is a scholar at Oxford, only if to all appearances he does little work and takes "honors" in his examinations. It is a peculiar distinction. A man who is unsociable and "sports his oak" (shuts and locks his door) and takes "honors" is not a "scholar" in Oxford—he is a "dig," "smug," "outsider"—anything but a scholar. "Of course he doses well" they say, "for he does nothing else but work." The man who plays for his college, whose door is always open emitting odorous streams of good smoke, who will always make up a four at bridge and then likes "honors"—he is the "scholar." When one studies at college he must do it on the sly as it were. If anyone comes in he must make that man feel that he would not work if he were eternally alone. He must fill a pipe and discuss the Triple Alliance or a football match, perhaps both. He must never look at his watch; the best timekeeper is the fact that the "baccy" has run short.

This in general is the attitude towards one another when the examinations are a year or so off. But as every man in a college knows what the other two hundred men are doing there is a sort of understanding that when "schools" (examinations) are only a few months or weeks off, those who are to try for degrees must be left alone and they generally are visited only after twelve for a half hour or so to cheer them up, but the oak must not be sported.

At first it seemed to the American that every man had to be a genius to take honors under these conditions, but when the intermittent vacation began to come and he found that half of the year he was free to go off and work far from tobacco smoke, then he began to understand. But it is not "sporting" to work more than half of each vacation, and the Americans are "sporting" as well as the Englishman, and often more so for the continent is a great temptation, but he works longer hours and harder than the Britisher when he does study.

The interesting point now is, do the Americans pass this last test and prove themselves "scholars" in the Oxford sense of the word? It is fair to say that the majority do. It is taken for granted that the Rhodes scholars have scholastic ability and that is an incentive to live up to their reputation.

Of the forty-three invaders who came over three years ago and returned to the United States this summer, several will not attempt to take degrees. The remaining may be divided into two classes; those who are graduates of some American colleges and those who have not taken a degree in the United States. The former, numbering thirty-seven, were given advanced standing and excused from all preliminary examinations; the latter had to spend the first year in passing preliminaries. Of those who were given advanced standing, four took Oxford honor degrees at the end of their second year, i. e., June, 1906, as follows:

R. H. Beven, of Rhode Island, degree of Bachelor of Civil Law, Third Class.

C. F. Tucker-Brook, of West Virginia, degree in English Literature, First Class.

H. A. Hinds, of North Dakota, degree in Natural Science, First Class.

J. A. Brown, of New Hampshire, degree of Bachelor of Science, First Class.

Of the seven who were required to pass the preliminary examinations, all have now done so and two of this class obtained final honor degrees at the end of their second year:

W. C. Crittenden, of California, Second Class, Final Honor, School of Jurisprudence.

D. R. Porter, of Maine, Fourth Class, Final Honor, School of History.

And now one can say that like the band of Ulysses of old, we have left Scylla on the one hand and Charybdis on the other—we have secretly dropped our lily pots, the spiders haunt, the histories of the Revolution and through necessity, or in most cases through choice, we have escaped Anglomaniacism. We are not less staunch and patriotic Americans but better and more enthusiastic Anglo-Saxons.

From the English standpoint a quotation from *Punch* to Artemus Ward best expresses the progress of the invasion. It was handed to a Rhodes scholar by an Englishman whom he had visited:

"This North American has been a inmate of my 'ouse over two weeks, yit he hasn't made no attempts to scalp any member of my family. He hasn't broke no cup or sassers, or furniture of any kind (Hear, Hear) I find I can trust him with lited candles. He eats his wittles with a knife and a fork. People of this kind should be encurridged. I purpose 'is 'elth (loud 'plaws)."

OLD CHRIST CHURCH AND ITS SURROUNDINGS

THE FIRST CONTINGENT OF CECIL RHODES SCHOLARS (1905) AT THE UNIVERSITY OF OXFORD—THESE STUDENTS WERE FROM THE UNITED STATES, GERMANY, AND THE COLONIES OF THE BRITISH EMPIRE. (See "The Invasion of Oxford")

FRONTISPIECE, SUNSET MAGAZINE, SEPTEMBER, 1907

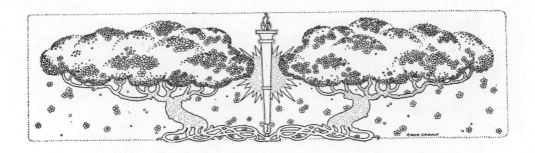

24

DEMOCRACY AND MANNERS

APROPOS OF AN INQUIRY INTO THE TEACHING OF MANNERS IN THE PUBLIC SCHOOLS

BY CHARLES W. ELIOT

President Emeritus of Harvard University

THE effects of democracy on manners interest both the friends and the foes of democracy. On one side it is alleged that the tendency of a democracy, which makes much of universal education, is to improve the average manners without injuring the manners of the most refined class. On the other side it is alleged that, although the manners of the lower classes may be a little improved by popular education and by the contacts of all classes in public conveyances and places of public entertainment, those of the higher classes are necessarily coarsened and roughened by association on terms of equality with persons of inferior breeding. The general interest in the subject has been heightened in the United States by the great changes in the conditions of American life within the last fifty years in consequence of the congestion of population in cities and the advent of millions of immigrants of non-Teutonic stocks, with political, religious, and industrial histories very different from those of the earlier settlers on the Atlantic border. The question whether home, school, and church, and particularly the democratic school, can teach good manners is all-important under the new conditions of American society; and this question THE CENTURY MAGAZINE has been trying to study and deal with.

The feudal system had several sorts of manners, each appropriate to one of the fixed classes into which society was divided. Armies and navies, which are by no means democratic institutions, have always been schools of certain sorts of manners, and they still are. But manners in democratic society ought to be, and are, much more homogeneous than in feudal or military society; and if the fundamental principles of democracy are sound, the combined influences of home, school, church, and government ought gradually to produce in a democracy a high average of civility based on freedom and equality before the law, and in the well-educated classes the common possession of excellent manners. Before taking up the specific question of the contribution to the cultivation of good manners which democratic schools can make, it will be well to consider what the foundations of good manners are, and what part manners play in the social education of mankind and in the individual's pursuit of happiness and success.

THE IMPORTANCE OF GOOD MANNERS

MANNERS affect for good or ill the daily happiness of every human being and the fortune and destiny of every tribe or nation. Their influence on human existence is profound and incessant. Good manners are founded on reason or common-sense, and good-will. They put people at ease in social intercourse, welcome graciously the stranger and the friend, dismiss pleasantly the lingering visitor who does not know how to withdraw, express alert sympathy with others, and prompt to helpful coöperation with others. They enable people to dwell together in peace and concord; whereas bad manners cause friction, strife, and discord. Inasmuch as good manners smooth the rough places and make things pleasant in human intercourse, some candid and combative persons who see many proper occasions for righteous indignation, hot strife, and unyielding pertinacity, are inclined to think that good manners may easily slip into insincerity, dissimulation, and a habit of easy compromising. They imagine that well-mannered people express in their habitual greetings warmer affections than they really feel, conceal their aversions or condemnations, moderate their heats in argument, make little use of superlatives, and in general repress passion in both speech and action. Hence they suspect that good manners are a drag on moral earnestness, or at least inconsistent with a prophet's or a reformer's zeal. Such an apprehension may naturally be felt about manners which are merely a superficial polish, with no groundwork in genuine good-will and sympathy, or an habitual conformity to conventional rules of behavior; but, nevertheless, long experience among civilized men has proved that good manners are compatible with holding strong convictions and expressing them firmly on fit occasion. They cannot and should not prevent earnest contentions, but they can take the bitterness out of strife, and prevent personal animosities between sincere and strenuous opponents.

GOOD MANNERS A FINE ART

IT is obvious that good manners involve not only habitual good-will and kindness, but also no little personal skill. They are, indeed, a fine art; for their means of expression are generally mere tones, inflections, quick glances, momentary gestures or postures, or other slight gradations of sound or movement; and they need at their best a quick imagination and a ready wit.

In agreeable intercourse neither party will be on the one hand rough and forthputting, or on the other bashful and constrained. A rough indifference is not much more disagreeable in social intercourse than an embarrassed sheepishness. A bashful person is always annoying in company, and a superior who is not serene and confident in the presence of subordinates is as uncomfortable for them as he is for himself. Any exhibition of want of respect or of consideration for others is destructive of pleasant intercourse, and this lack of respect need not go so far as contempt or insolence in order to cause uneasiness and aversion. Habitual expression of a tendency to find fault, blame, or censure is of course fatal to agreeable converse and a habit of criticizing or contradicting on the spot the statements of others is unpleasant even in a comrade or friend, and more so in casual acquaintances. Engrossing the conversation is another ill-mannered practice to which even the possession of a remarkable wit in the speaker will fail to reconcile the aggrieved listeners. An opposite source of offense is a continuous silence, which implies lack of interest in the conversation or inattention to it. An eager talker with a story to tell in which he is much interested may often find very exasperating the mere silence of his imperturbable, though amiable listener. No ceremoniousness is agreeable except as it is obviously intended to show respect or deference, and there is nothing more disagreeable in the intercourse of civil people than the deference which descends to flattery and obsequiousness.

GOOD MANNERS AS A PERSONAL INFLUENCE

EMERSON in his admirable essay on "Manners" points out that underneath the best manners must lie some spiritual power or ascendancy, perceived by every observer, although held in reserve. The gentleman or the lady ought to possess a personal influence distinct, though often unconscious, as well as beauty of form or feature and grace in action, and to that end should be manifestly a truthful, straightforward, and self-reliant person. It is impossible for a lying, insincere, fawning man to have the best manners, although he may be polite in the ordinary sense. Every exclusive set of people, like a royal court, or a group of county families, or the fashionable set in a great city, or the leading group in a lodge or grange, is based on the possession of some kind of power, political, magisterial, financial, or industrial. The advantages won by the valor or virtue or capacity which distinguished one generation will carry over to another generation which may not possess the natural or acquired powers of the preceding, imparting to these descendants some distinction, cultivation, or excellence which they could not have secured for themselves.

The often-mentioned difference between good manners and good breeding, namely, that the latter involves a long education and the acquisition of much knowledge and skill, whereas the former do not, is quite as important in democratic society as in aristocratic. Peasants, barbarians, and illiterate persons often exhibit some of the best elements of good manners, but their experience of life has not given them access to good breeding.

Selfishness, ignorance, stupidity, and habitual inattention to the desires and claims of others are the chief causes of bad manners; and since these qualities are rather common among mankind and some admixture of them often exists in meritorious characters, bad manners are not uncommon.

Like good manners, bad manners have a universal quality, since they are due to the absence of sound moral qualities, or of fine perceptions, or of the indispensable conditions of a refined and beautiful life. Savage or barbarous peoples often exhibit in their finest specimens personal dignity, composure, and a grave decorum; but they also exhibit in general a lack of cleanliness, slovenly or hasty ways of eating and drinking, and lack of consideration for the weak, and they often manifest their individual emotions with the *abandon* of children.

Although good manners are based in all societies and all nations on character and the possession of good sense and good feeling, it cannot be alleged that there is any universal ritual of good manners. To be sure, there are many obvious "don'ts" or prohibitions and a few positive, universal affirmations. Thus deference is expressed in different postures or gestures in different nations, and even in different groups within the same nation. Persons of good sense can exercise great freedom in adapting their manners to their surroundings and their companions of the moment, provided they exhibit composure, gentleness, and disinterestedness. Nevertheless, there is, on the whole, a remarkable agreement about certain points of good manners among peoples that exhibit strong differences in other respects. Thus, the soldier's attitude of respect is common to many peoples. He stands erect, with his heels together, and touches his cap or fez with his right hand. In religious ceremonies many of the same postures are used by Christian and Moslem peoples. During religious service the people sit, stand, bow, and kneel in succession. The Moslem and the Buddhist, however, add one posture of worship which comparatively few Christians use, namely, prostration with the forehead on the ground. Gentle speech is the same thing in all languages, since it is a matter of tone and inflection. Everywhere the gentleman or lady listens attentively to the narrator, petitioner, or dealer who is speaking, since this attention is an inevitable manifestation under the circumstances of interest and good-will. Emerson's remark that "a gentleman makes no noise; a lady is serene" is of universal application.

THE CONTAGION OF GOOD AND BAD MANNERS

IN respect to manners, most men and women, and particularly young people, are highly imitative; so that both good manners and bad are contagious. Hence the strong influence of family groups and school groups on the manners of their members, and hence also the deplorable influence of the objectionable social groups in large variety which American urban society has developed, such as the street "gang" of boys; the group of the season's "buds," with their boy comrades, in keen pursuit, without any measure, of their own pleasures and excitements; the "smart set" of fashionable society, with its selfishness and luxury; the base-ball nine, with its vulgar chatter; and the foot-ball eleven, with its secret practice, surprises, and imitation in sport of the barbarous ethics inevitable in combat to the death. The more public the operations of these groups are, the more wide-spread their effects as schools of bad manners. The street-railway companies in American cities maintain active schools of bad manners wherever they fail to provide a number of vehicles adequate to carry in a decent manner the throngs that are compelled to use them. Any crowd which is in a hurry is apt to afford practice in bad manners.

WOMAN'S RESPONSIBILITY FOR MANNERS

IN Christian society, where the women are tolerably free, it is they who are largely responsible for the condition of manners. In the absence of the severe physical restraints imposed on women in Moslem society and in much heathen society, tenderness and protection are due from men to women, and for a considerable proportion of their lives a measure of privacy or "touch-me-not" reserve is their right. Every gentleman recognizes these natural rights of women, and every man who is not absolutely brutal recognizes the woman's claim on him because of her relative weakness and delicacy of body. On these chivalrous sentiments toward women the manners of civilized men are in large part formed; so that men are liable to lose all standards in manners whenever any considerable proportion of the women who come within their field of observation show themselves unworthy of these sentiments in men by becoming themselves coarse, combative, rude, and lacking in modesty, or by ceasing to condemn in their male companions insolence, violence, selfishness, and the ungenerous use of strength or power.

The sentiments on which good manners depend being by no means universal, and the real art difficult of attainment, cultivated people have agreed on certain elementary rules of behavior which anybody who wishes to can learn and put in practice; so that multitudes not specially distinguished for good sense or good will may, by taking a little pains, avoid social friction and troublesome breaches of good manners. Many people who do not possess in any large measure the spiritual qualities on which good manners are based do, as a fact, observe these minor rules of behavior, to the great advantage of society. This fact encourages the belief that useful instruction on many details of manners can be given to children in the home and the school, which happily are also just the places where the sentiments and affections of which good manners are the expression can best be fostered.

PERSONALITY IN MANNERS

LITERATURE abounds in statements that manners are to be learned by example rather than by the study of rules, from good company rather than from books. This unquestionable fact makes clear in what consists the high privilege of gentle birth. Such birth secures to children constant examples of gentle manners in both men and women. Republicans are glad to remember that this very precious privilege of gentle birth is not confined to monarchies or aristocracies, or to social systems built on caste or hereditary privileges. It is obviously commoner under republican institutions, which secure widely diffused education in childhood and encourage continuous education throughout life by means of social and industrial freedom, than under any other governmental institutions. Indeed, one of the best ultimate tests of the success of republican institutions will be the relative diffusion of good manners and bad among the people. Locke, in his "Thoughts on Education," gives very sensible directions "how to form a young gentleman as he should be. . . . It is fit his governor should be himself well bred, understanding the ways of carriage and measure of civility in all the variety of persons, times, and places, and keep his pupil, as much as his age requires, constantly to the observation of them. This is an art not to be learnt or taught by books. Nothing can give it but good company and observation joined together." These excellent directions for the bringing-up of a young gentleman by a well-bred governor suggest one explanation of the great difficulty which day schools have, even in the best urban school systems, in improving the manners of children who come from rude or coarse environments, and spend in school only a quarter of their time even during school-terms, and no time at all during rather more than one quarter of the year. They point also to the importance of securing, for all schools, teachers whose speech and manners are gentle, kindly, and refined.

WHAT THE PUBLIC SCHOOLS ARE DOING

IN order to ascertain how much attention is now directed to instruction in manners in American public schools, THE

CENTURY MAGAZINE sent to 1400 superintendents of public instruction two questions, to which 740 answers were received, with the following results: in 519 school systems there is incidental and discretionary instruction in manners; in 155, there is regular, systematic, and somewhat extensive instruction, for which definite periods are assigned in the school programs during several years; in 50, the teachers are required to give some instruction in manners, but the instruction is only partly systematic, no provision for it being made in the programs; in 16, there is virtually no instruction. The success of the incidental and discretionary instruction depends of course on the capacity of the individual teacher to draw lessons in manners from the happenings in the schoolroom, the reading assigned to the children, and the current events of the day. The regular, systematic instruction is carried on by means of primers or elementary manuals of ethics and manners, supplemented by the explanations and comments of the teacher. In some cities the superintendent had prepared for the use of the teachers a syllabus on manners and the ethics of manners, with numerous references to passages in recommended textbooks, these books being provided for the teachers, but not for the pupils. In some schools instruction has been given by means of lantern-illustrations, with running comments from the teacher. One superintendent reported through the principal of a large school in which more than half of the children came from bare homes, with only elementary notions of manners, and were destined to leave school by fourteen years of age or even earlier, a dramatic or representative method of teaching good manners which was used in addition to a ten-minute daily discussion in each room of the rules of politeness toward elders, teachers, visitors, and strangers, and of behavior at table and in the street, streetcar, shop, and school. Periodically all the children from the different rooms were called together in the assembly-hall, on the stage of which representations of correct behavior were given. This method takes advantage of most children's pleasure in "making believe" and acting. Selected children illustrate on the stage the proper way to speak to a lady or an old gentleman, and how to perform and acknowledge an introduction. Little table scenes are enacted, and a boy helps a lady from a carriage or a car. This is all done in an earnest, serious way; but the children are interested in the performance, and both actors and spectators enjoy it. Much instruction in manners can be given in schools by acting plays and charades which illustrate both good manners and bad. Although children often fail to discern or be interested in the real plot or subtle motives in dramas, they usually apprehend perfectly the manners depicted on the stage. The members of the school and their parents will always provide an interested audience for such plays, and by having several different casts for each play, the number of children who get the benefit of acting may be made considerable, and the number of interested relatives will be so great as to require several representations of each play. There are plenty of plays adapted to this school use; but the selection of those to be presented requires care on the part of the teacher and an understanding of both the capacities and incapacities of the children.[1]

MANNERS AND MORALS

SCHOOL instruction in manners necessarily mixes manners with morals and ethics, and this combination of teaching rules and the moral reasons for rules at the same time is in practice the inevitable way. To teach mere cleanliness and neatness of the body, clothes, and implements for individual use, it is necessary to go beyond the motive of personal hygiene to the altruistic motive of caring for the health and comfort of others. We cannot teach or illustrate gentleness or serenity in manners and speech without inculcating the duty of kindness. We cannot teach children to show deference to elders, parents, and teachers without explaining the debt of each succeeding generation to the preceding. One can hardly teach children who come from coarse environments to avoid profanity, obscenity, gossip, and slander, without expounding the moral principles on which social purity and justice are

[1] It is an incidental advantage of teaching school-children to act, recite, read aloud, and declaim, that such exercises give the teachers opportunity to insist on agreeable tones of voice and distinct enunciation, points in good manners hard to inculcate in any walk of life, and not infrequently lacking in well-to-do families.

based. The teaching of good manners in school, whether from manuals or by example and oral exhortation, whether systematically in assigned periods or incidentally at the discretion of the teacher, involves giving ethical instruction on the authority of the teacher.

It should be no surprise, therefore, to find that in many public-school programs the heading "manners and morals" appears, and in the time assigned to this instruction the affirmative duties of kindness, truthfulness, fidelity to duty, honesty, and self-control are actively inculcated, and civic duties and patriotism are subjects of discussion and exhortation. Such a course of instruction is intended to lead the child gradually from its natural egoism to a reasonable altruism, and the measure of its success is the degree in which this object is attained in regard first to manners, and then to morals. Of course all well-conducted schools inculcate punctuality, order, quietness, and mutual accommodation, and these are all elements of good manners; but they can do much more than this. They can teach thoughtfulness for others, and the sense of obligation to make others comfortable or happy. They can train in many of their pupils some individual faculty or skill which will enable them to give pleasure to other people, such as a faculty or skill in reading aloud, reciting, singing, playing on some musical instrument, acting, story-telling, or playing sociable games. They can teach all their pupils that the surest way to enjoy oneself is to contribute to the enjoyments of other people. They can teach cooperation in sports or recreations, a kind of coöperation which later leads easily to coöperation in more serious matters. They can utilize emulation and competition as incitements not only to individual improvement, but to social progress.

There can be no doubt that the great majority of American public schools are actively contributing to-day to the diffusion and development of good manners among the people, and hence to the improvement of social conduct. Whoever learns to observe and respect, through manners firmly based on ethics, the lesser rights of others is likely to acquire increased respect for the larger rights of the neighbor and the citizen.

Since the safe conduct of democratic society on its bold voyage of philanthropic discovery depends on an unprecedented development of mutual good-will, manifested kindliness, and hearty coöperation, the function of the common schools in teaching manners and morals is plainly one of the most important parts of public education and the main reliance of democratic optimism.

THIRD

LEARNING
and the
INTERCOLLEGIATE LIFE

The university today idyllically says that its primary interests are educated people (including trained professional manpower), basic and applied research findings, and a variety of specialized services to the public. These are generated by three major programs: instruction, research, and public service—individually and in combination. Yet, in an age of radical activists, concerned liberals, hippies and yippies, amoral hostiles, the uncommitted, and so on, these objectives seem incongruous. The perplexing and disturbing argument for general education has been disputed for generations. As university leaders have weighed the changing values of their society by observing the manner in which the younger generation relates to the tasks of growing up and achieving identity, they have attempted to form systems which aid young people in becoming effective carriers of new values in a democratic, highly productive society. In a sense, the collegiate structure has always been experimental—that is, attempting to find how best through learning and the intercollegiate life to accomplish its missions.

Continuing to disinter the past, we see in Part Three an augury of the future. Students, then as now, were experimenting widely with a variety of expressive activities as a means of discovering new values. Although many of these academic and social activities appear to be naive or simple, they nonetheless were challenging the educational systems of the day. Students were exploring unknown territory which might lead to important esthetic discoveries. Movements of ecumenical cooperation and charity were common. Today we refer to them as the Peace Corps, VISTA, and the hundred other volunteer activities. With feeling, students believed in loyalty, probity, and the significance of instruction.

Part Three is an exploration into the social, psychological, and physical environment of learning at the turn of the century, documenting well the American penchant for higher education. In sometimes raucous, good-natured odes to the undergraduate, writers spin mellow and sometimes serious tales about long-lost life styles and adventures. The narrations are insightful, especially to those who were to be born thirty to seventy years later. For the nostalgic and reverent educator, more so than the serious student, the section is a pleasant, sometimes melancholy, reading experience. From ten major selections one will be able to reconstruct the values of youth and the varieties of their intercollegiate activities, with all their subtleties and half-measures. If the reconstruction is a bit inflated, a shade out of focus, too pastel, one must remember these are precisely characteristics of an emerging system. The writings are excellent, especially "College Fraternities," "Undergraduate Life at Wellesley," and "Football: Battle or Sport." Others are authoritative and readable; a few may even seem recalcitrant, sometimes condescending. Yet all were selected because of their warmth and genuine affection. Each narration forces us to quarrel and to become involved, and heightens our sensitivity to one of the most exciting periods in undergraduate history.

25

Blasting at the Rock of Ages

By Harold Bolce

The very hopes of man, the thoughts of his heart, the religion of nations, the manners and morals of mankind are all at the mercy of a new generalization.—*Emerson.*

Editor's Note.—This is the first of a series of three articles by Mr. Bolce, who has now completed a study of American colleges extending over two years. What Mr. Bolce sets down here is of the most astounding character. Out of the curricula of American colleges a dynamic movement is upheaving ancient foundations and promising a way for revolutionary thought and life. Those who are not in close touch with the great colleges of the country will be astonished to learn the creeds being fostered by the faculties of our great universities. In hundreds of class-rooms it is being taught daily that the decalogue is no more sacred than a syllabus; that the home as an institution is doomed; that there are no absolute evils; that immorality is simply an act in contravention of society's accepted standards; that democracy is a failure and the Declaration of Independence only spectacular rhetoric; that the change from one religion to another is like getting a new hat; that moral precepts are passing shibboleths; that conceptions of right and wrong are as unstable as styles of dress; that wide stairways are open between social levels, but that to the climber children are incumbrances; that the sole effect of prolificacy is to fill tiny graves; and that there can be and are holier alliances without the marriage bond than within it. These are some of the revolutionary and sensational teachings submitted with academic warrant to the minds of hundreds of thousands of students in the United States. It is time that the public realized what is being taught to the youth of this country. "The social question of to-day," said Disraeli, "is only a zephyr which rustles the leaves, but will soon become a hurricane." It is a dull ear that cannot hear the mutterings of the coming storm.

TO discover the scope and daring of college teaching in the United States to-day I have undertaken an itinerary of class-rooms from Cambridge to California. Some of the institutions I have entered as a special student. In others I have attended lectures as a visitor, or interviewed members of the faculty, or consulted the typewritten or printed records of what they teach. In these ways my course has included Harvard, Yale, Princeton, the University of Pennsylvania, George Washington University, William and Mary College (where Thomas Jefferson and other founders of the Republic studied), the University of Chicago, Columbia University, Syracuse University, and the University of California. What I have come upon in the teachings of these universities, with what I have obtained additionally from presidents, deans, and professors of Northwestern University, New York University, the University of Iowa, the University of Wisconsin, the University of Nebraska, Union College, Cornell, Brown University, and Leland Stanford, Jr., University, constitutes a profound surprise—a series, in fact, of increasing surprises—absorbing and sensational.

In my course I have heard all the multiplex issues of morality and all the pressing problems of political economy—marriage, divorce, the home, religion, and democracy—put through merciless processes of examination, as if these things were fossils, gastropods, vertebrates, equations, chemical elements, or chimeras.

There is scholarly repudiation of all solemn authority. The decalogue is no more sacred than a syllabus. Everything is subjected to searching analysis. The past has lost its grip on the professor. The ancient prophet is less potent than the new political economy. Nothing is accepted on the *ipse dixit* of tradition. Olympus and Mount Sinai are twin peaks beautified but not made sacred by mythology. From the college standpoint there are no God-established covenants. What happens at the primaries is more to the point than what took place in Palestine. Time is a laboratory wherein reactions are eternally producing new phases of civilization having changing forms and hues.

From Boston to Berkeley I found the universities curiously alive and alert. The professors believe that they are in the forefront of progress. Whether the subject be a god or a gas, a matter of morals or volcanic mud, a syllogism or a star, the professor approaches it impersonally, critically determined to know the truth. A government is great, but so is a gnat—either may afflict the land. There is nothing *ex cathedra* in the professor's curriculum, save as he expresses it himself.

And this new dogmatism has stirred up some of his familiars. The preacher to Harvard University, a clergyman of the Unitarian faith, is arrayed against the "specialist who, fired with the ambition for wide generalization, becomes an intellectual tyrant." This Harvard pastor calls the college despot "a veritable Tamerlane who, if he rears no pyramid of skulls, leaves behind him a multitude of muddled brains."

Contemporary college teaching, as I find it, may be likened to an exploring expedition over a sea that has not been charted or across unknown continents. Everything encountered is new. The lectures take you along a course lined with none of the immemorial landmarks. The church does not count. To accept the teachings of any hierarchy is like looking for life and light in the grave. And conscience cannot show the way: in one age it approved burnings at the stake. Democracy has been the mirage of modern nations. It is a theme for suave, declamatory statesmanship, but, in reality, does not exist. And the home, once the cradle of the race, has become the breeding-place of woe, ignorance, inefficiency, and debt. The professors even suggest and outline a substitute for the modern home.

NEW CONCEPTIONS OF MORALITY

They teach young men and women, plainly, that an immoral act is merely one contrary to the prevailing conceptions of society; and that

the daring who defy the code do not offend any Deity, but simply arouse the venom of the majority—the majority that has not yet grasped the new idea. Out of Harvard comes the teaching that "there are no absolute evils" and that the "highest ethical life consists at all times in the breaking of rules which have grown too narrow for the actual case."

"Every man's mind," says Prof. Charles H. Cooley, of Michigan, "is the theater of a conflict of standards," and that warfare is made intense by the current college course. Frank W. Blackmar, professor of sociology and economics in the University of Kansas, teaches that the "standards of right perpetually change in social life, these varying standards being found not only in different races but in the same race from age to age."

And out of Yale comes an almost cynical devotion to science that would eliminate God from the commandments. Prof. William Graham Sumner teaches that there have been all kinds of forces in history except ethical forces. "Let us recognize this fact," he contends, "and its consequences." Ethics, he explains, grow out of customs, and are not antecedent to them. He regards ethical notions as mere "figments of speculation" and as "unrealities that ought to be discarded altogether." In this connection Prof. William James, of Harvard, insists that it is possible to "spoil the merit of a teaching by mixing with it that dogmatic temper which by unconditional thou-shalt-nots changes a growing, elastic, and continuous life into a system of relics and dry bones."

Summarizing the teachings of American colleges, they may be said to group themselves into three principal divisions:

First, the remarkable doctrines regarding morality, marriage, divorce, plural marriages, the home, and religion. This includes the teaching that marriage is a transitory standard and that the home as an institution is doomed.

Second, the scholastic conception of politics and political economy, the citation of democracy as a failure, and the academic labeling of the Declaration of Independence as "a work in spectacular rhetoric." The surprises in this division of the general subject of college teaching—which includes such doctrines as the one promulgated by Prof. E. L. Bogart, of Princeton, who said that the public is benefited when an inefficient competitor is forced out of business by the superior trust—are no less absorbing than the new preachment on morality. Formerly the best man in the community was the good Samaritan, but now, as Professor Patten, of the University of Pennsylvania, contends, "society owes its debt to the wealthy and far-seeing citizenry that paves and lights and polices the road to Jericho."

Third, the college forecast of what is in store for America. Despite the unemotional tone of much of the scholarly teaching, most of it is unequivocal in its optimism. A few of the professors lament that society does not advance, but merely travels in a circle and arrives, after all its effort, at the starting-point. But the majority by far of our twenty-one thousand professors protest against the looking back regretfully to a Golden Age. The Land of Promise lies beyond. There are many evils under our system, but there is visible progress. As Frank S. Hoffman, professor of philosophy at Union College, tells in his teaching, Colbert, minister of finance for Louis XIV, cynically defined taxation to be the process of plucking the greatest quantity of feathers from the goose while provoking the least possible amount of hissing. Society has escaped many of the former phases of bondage, and the professors believe that a new emancipation is at hand.

LATEST INNOVATIONS IN RELIGIOUS THOUGHT AND PRACTICE

In this section of college teaching there is a transition into the metaphysical and spiritual fields, the lecturers lending unexpected support to some of the latest innovations in religious thought and practice. A doctrine proclaimed as "psychophysical idealism," and curiously akin to current spiritual sciences, has established itself at Columbia University and other institutions. Just one illustration, as given by Prof. C. A. Strong, of Columbia, at the head of the department of psychology there, discloses that the denial of matter is not confined to outside cults.

"Suppose," said he, "I am looking at a candle; the candle I am looking at and am conscious of is a mental modification. How can I convince myself of the fact? By the simple process of closing my eyes. Something then ceases to exist. Is it the real candle? Certainly not. Then it must be the mental duplicate. By successively opening and closing my eyes I can create and annihilate the perceived candle, but the real candle continues unchanged. Then what I am immediately conscious of when I open my eyes must be the mental duplicate."

In presenting this I am trenching upon later disclosures. I cite it now to indicate the scope and ambition of college teaching. Most of the university philosophers subscribe to a belief in "the spiritual unity of all life," and in the confidence that "good will be the final goal of ill" they are trying to convince American college youth that the things that are seen are temporal, but that the unseen things are vital and permanent. It is a novel departure for hard-headed men of science.

The professors are sanguine that their metaphysical science will illumine humanity. Theology, they believe, is breaking down. At Syracuse University, whose chancellor is a clergyman, I heard it stated that *to change from one religion to another is like getting a new hat!*

These articles will follow the divisions already indicated; *viz.*, first the social, next the economic and political, and third the prophetic, dealing with possible reforms. I have recorded merely what I learned, not clouding it with my own opinions.

It was with no preconception of what the teachings of the colleges are that I started on my student's pilgrimage. I realized, of course, that the volcanic transformations being wrought in current thought and conduct had not come through chance, and that back of the economic and moral upheavals of the time might be found the men giving first expression to the new ideas. But I did not expect to find academic warrant, as some have already construed it, for departure from conjugal restraint. Nor did I count on hearing the home decried as too archaic and narrow a channel for the transmission of progress to the race to come. It was, too, a shock to learn that college professors claim that conscience is a false guide and that there are no abiding standards of right and wrong; that moral precepts are merely passing shibboleths; that the conceptions of right and wrong are as unstable as the styles of dress, and no more significant; and that society, by its approval, can make any kind of conduct right. These teachers therefore claim that their doctrines, which may now shock the conservative, will probably be the gospel of to-morrow.

Let me make it plain at the outset that when I quote a professor of Syracuse University, or of Harvard, or the University of Pennsylvania, or any other institution, it does not necessarily commit the rest of the faculty to that belief. What a man in a chair of sociology thinks and says is likely to be at variance with what the dean, the chancellor, or the president believes. There is, perhaps, no body of thinkers in America freer from dominance of any sort than college professors. So much freedom, in fact, is given them that the few, beginning with Prof. George D. Herron, who have been forced from the class-room, charged with poisoning the minds of youth, were banished, not for their teachings alone, for the doctrines ultimately condemned had been given to the classes for an indefinite period, but because the outside world protested against their life or creed.

SOCIETY AND MORALS

In other words, it appears that students may absorb ad libitum *what conventional society condemns as tainted ethics unless the professor, seeking publicity or inexpert in dodging it, arouses the wrath of the community.* At no time, however, has it been my conviction that the professors were teaching their startling doctrines in any covert way. It was merely, as I readily discovered, that the professors, defending, or exalting as new ideals, what the orthodox condemn, have been addressing young men and young women who have been receiving without outcry what the outside world, mature in its convictions and with inherited bias, denounces as unfit.

Most of what is said to the classes is new. A doctrine which, universally applied, might overturn religion, society, and the civil law is accepted as placidly as a demonstration in geometry or algebra. The student takes in ethics as he absorbs Euclid and equations. Automatically the teachings of the professor sink into the student mind. What the scholar in the chair of authority says is gospel. He is usually a man of force and genius, and often magnetic. He has a following. Some of the class-rooms are so crowded that seating-room is at a premium. That is why, if the teachings of

the professor are wrong, they are unusually dangerous.

THE COLLEGE A FACTOR IN AMERICAN LIFE

A glance at the statistical strength of American universities and colleges shows that what they teach is vital to the interests of the nation. There are 493 institutions of higher learning in the United States. In their class-rooms 229,000 students daily listen to instruction from more than twenty-one thousand professors and assistants. Thus a quarter of a million people are busy with new ideas — doctrines which, translated into the realities of American life, are potent in transforming the standards of society.

We are sending out annually a mass of enthusiastic students comprising a population greater than that of Minneapolis, and at every matriculation a similar army enters the universities. The proportions of such an educational movement are continental and national.

Every detail of higher education reveals its significance. The students annually pay $13,347,000 in tuition fees; and this does not fully gage the earnestness of the classes, for in many of the Western universities, as, for example, the University of California with its three thousand students, education is free. More than forty million dollars is the aggregate income of American colleges, while the value of university grounds and buildings, plus the total of productive funds and endowments, raises the material worth of these temples of learning to half a billion dollars.

The college is obviously one of the mighty factors in fashioning American life. For good or bad results, professors in these institutions have been shaping modern thought. The colleges will be the first to admit that they exert a powerful influence upon current thought and conduct.

Some who review this record will be convinced that out of the curriculum new movements are revolutionizing current thought and social standards. Others who cannot believe that college teaching is far-reaching enough to effect these changes will realize at least this, that the doctrines taught to the more than two hundred thousand students in America interpret and not infrequently justify the conspicuous tendency of the day.

Among the important institutions of learning I entered was Syracuse University. I was to meet many surprises here. In the first place, it is a far more important university than is generally believed. Success is conspicuous in the splendid college structures that look down on Syracuse from more than seven hills. The university has thousands of students drawn from many parts of the continent. Some of the paths to this temple of learning may be worn by struggling feet, but what is

EDWIN L. EARP
(Syracuse University)
"It is unscientific and absurd to imagine that God ever turned stonemason and chiseled commandments on a rock"

vard is commonplace in comparison.

Syracuse University is a religious institution tempered by secular subsidies. Chime bells ring out fine old hymns at the morning chapel hour, and in the sporting hours of the afternoon these same bells are vibrant with popular melodies.

These incidental details are not significant, unless perhaps they may be some-

CHARLES ZUEBLIN
(University of Chicago)
"There can be and are holier alliances without the marriage bond than within it"

FRANKLIN H. GIDDINGS
(Columbia University)
"It is not right to set up a technical legal relationship . . . as morally superior to the spontaneous preference of a man and woman"

SIMON N. PATTEN
(Univ. of Pennsylvania)
"Society owes its debt to the citizenry that paves and polices the road to Jericho"

more in evidence are automobiles carrying students and professors there. Cut in a great amphitheater of the hills is a stadium which, in its architectural beauty and its capacity is not eclipsed on the continent. Even the Greek Theater at Berkeley does not overshadow it, and the stadium at Har-

what symbolic of the spirit of the university, which is at least up to date, and by some may be considered as traveling fast beyond the conventional pace of progress.

It was my good fortune to enter as a special student, taking a course in sociology under Prof. Edwin L. Earp. The lectures included important social questions, such as the family, relations between labor and capital, immigration, social welfare, and the social basis of ethics. Professor Earp, who was formerly a clergyman, is one of the most original and forceful lecturers it has been my pleasure to hear. It seemed to me that if anywhere among the colleges of America old-time doctrines would find valiant defense it would be here, in the teachings of this doctor of philosophy and divinity, in an institution presided over by one of the foremost leaders of a great evangelical denomination.

RIGHT AND WRONG THE PRODUCT OF EXPERIENCE

Early in the course Professor Earp touched upon the doctrine of the origin of morals. He was expounding the scientific interpretation of conduct, and explaining that our standards of right and wrong are the product of experience. I had heard a number of other professors in other colleges dwell upon this same theme, saying that our conceptions of what we should do are not sent to us from heaven, but are the development of the centuries. Mankind, they asserted, had tried many things from age to age, and out of all the stumblings and successes of the race had selected whatever was best for any particular period.

I wanted to know what this capable sociologist, who had obviously thought himself out from old-time tradition, would say in reply to a direct question. So from my seat in the class-room I addressed him.

"*Do you not believe, Professor,*" *I asked,* "*that Moses got the ten commandments in the way the Scriptures tell?*"

The professor smiled. "*I do not,*" *said he.* "*It is unscientific and absurd to imagine that God ever turned stone-mason and chiseled commandments on a rock.*"

What gives piquant emphasis to Professor Earp's scholastic denial of the divine origin of the decalogue is that even now, in addition to his busy and successful labors in Syracuse University among many classes of young men and young women, he frequently speaks from the orthodox pulpit.

It will be apparent as this record proceeds that Professor Earp is by no means a solitary pioneer among the modern college authorities in the scientific handling of the sacred story. Syracuse University, at least

in this department, is merely proclaiming the same character of latter-day criticism and belief that caused the suspension by the General Assembly of the Presbyterian Church of Dr. Charles A. Briggs, now of Union Theological Seminary, and in more recent times the retirement of his colleague, Doctor Crapsey. I shall show, when I have occasion to quote Prof. George H. Howison, of the University of California; Pres. David Starr Jordan, of Leland Stanford University; Dr. Herbert L. Willett, of the University of Chicago; and Prof. George A. Coe, of Northwestern University, which is governed by a religious denomination, that the reverend academician of Syracuse is really a conservative among his contemporary iconoclasts.

Professor Earp's course embraces many topics. His survey of contemporary affairs is unique. He is a man of liberal outlook. "Out in Milwaukee," said he one day to his class, "the leading citizens are brewers because that city has the right kind of beer."

In discussing plural marriages he arrayed himself against polygamy, but explained that under certain economic conditions it would be easily accepted by society. "When there is an unequal division of the sexes," said he, "monogamy is not consistent. It is a scientific truth that in cold climates there are more men than women, and so, as among the Esquimaux, polyandry exists."

RACE SUICIDE

This earnest thinker takes sharp issue with Mr. Roosevelt regarding the alarm about race suicide. Frequently in his lectures he dwelt upon the fearful mortality among infants, and said that what society needs to preserve itself is not more births but fewer deaths. And he endorsed a doctrine set forth in the *American Journal of Sociology* that if the world could discourage or prevent the breeding of the unfit it would result in diminishing the temptation to drunkenness and betting. In treating of marriage he said, "*Prolong celibacy and you increase immorality, and yet many men by marriage involve themselves in debt and never get out except through the poorhouse or the grave!*"

The professor delivered some interesting lectures in regard to the home. "The servant problem," said he, "is every year growing more difficult to solve. The modern home is in myriads of instances inefficiently run. Unless some great change comes to solve the question of obtaining expert and earnest domestic labor society must inevitably turn to the central kitchen and the institutional home. It would be far better for the people of one block to share a common cuisine, conducted scientifically, than to struggle along as at present, contracting debts and dyspepsia. An expert French cook to-day gets infinitely more wages than a teacher of romance French. It is impossible for an ordinary family to secure the services of such a chef, but it would be easy enough for the people of a block, where everyone is now spending money on an inefficient cook, to combine and get the services of a master of the culinary art."

Prof. Simon N. Patten, of the University of Pennsylvania, teaches a similar doctrine regarding the home. Instead of being conservative, as might be supposed, the department of political economy in this old institution of learning, set in the heart of Philadelphia, is radical and suggestive of startling changes in society. Professor Patten says that while modern ideas of efficiency characterize the administration of churches, humane institutions, factories, and nations to-day, the family is "kept back by poverty, inexpert management, and inherited prejudice."

Poverty in the rural family, he says, is not the degrading thing that the lack of money produces in the city home. So long as the homes of the poor were set down in fields and at the edge of forests the battle with fate was picturesque and even glorious. It developed strong and splendid traits of character. And while there was much poverty, it was intermittent; there were times when everyone enjoyed plenty.

NECESSITY FOR THE HOME NO LONGER EXISTS

In pointing out what he believes to be the doom of the home as a civilized unit, Professor Patten shows that the growth of great cities has transplanted the poor into the midst of a doleful poverty that is perpetual. There is a deadly round of monotony in the daily work. And the professor dwells upon the fact that the poor in cities are segregated, because of high rents and the limit of space, with the criminal and depraved classes. Formerly the poorer a family the farther it went into the frontier, but to-day, in the great cities, the poorer a family the more

crowded the quarter in which it has to live. Millions of worthy working people have to live amid a disreputable environment because they cannot pay the rent in better sections. Under such conditions the home as the unit and source of society, Professor Patten insists, is an unfortunate survival which cannot last.

Family life as we now practise it has been idealized, but it was not founded in sentiment, says Professor Patten. When the whole known world was a battle-field the poor were immune from the conflicts of kings and feudal knights, because the conqueror found that the poor man's life was valuable to him. An invader, therefore, spared the poor and put them to work. Thus the poor became a sort of recognized order, and the comparative security of this class made possible the preservation of the race. Formerly, too, industries were carried on in the home. This gave it added economic strength. To-day the workers leave the home and go into the factory. Thus the family unit is a product of conditions which do not now exist.

The professor further insists that society is reaching the stage when a change is inevitable from the present home to a more modern economic unit in which municipal or cooperative efficiency will supplant family incompetence and poverty. He claims that society has a right to insist upon some domestic innovation, as he believes that the present family system menaces the life and continuity of the race. There should be adequate nutrition, leisure, and hygiene in the home, and these the modern industrial family cannot supply.

In summing up what he believes to be a menace to society growing out of the modern city homes of the poor, Professor Patten teaches that "the ideals of a personal morality may be no loftier in the agricultural districts of England or in the hamlets of Scotland than they are in the slums of New York," but "the vital point of difference is that living under the old régime does not interrupt physical continuity, while the newer transgressions bring sterility with them." "The difficulties of those who do not give way to vicious associations are equally serious. The factory system, displacing home industries, takes the woman out of the house, where formerly she could be both a mother and a maker of commodities, and postpones marriage to a later and later period of the woman's youth. . . . Provision for the future should be made henceforth from the current body of society's riches rather than out of the weakness of mothers; the human being must cease to be the frail yet all-important vessel upon whose capacity depends the progress of the type. . . . We are at the stage of development in which conditions independent of us and scarcely recognized by us are forcing a change from the primitive type of family to some modern or economic form."

Along the same lines, in other courses of his teaching, Professor Patten has said: "The martyr is a useless type under whose influence we have made an art of wretchedness. The mothers in tenements must have the aid of the city in guaranteeing sanitary conditions."

Edward A. Ross, professor of sociology in the University of Wisconsin, approaches this subject from another angle. "*Wide stairways,*" he says, "*are opened between the social levels, and men are expected to climb, if they can. But to the climber children are encumbrances.*"

CHILDREN ARE ENCUMBRANCES

To gratify newly awakened wants men learn, Professor Ross points out, "to economize in offspring, as the little strangers trench on raiment, bric-à-brac, upholstery, travel, and entertainment." Another factor making the home unproductive of children is the "moral emancipation of women." Every child "taxes the father's purse, but the mother's body." The decay of religious beliefs he cites as another secret of childless hearths; yet he does not lament the passing of these beliefs. He quotes Luther's serene saying, "God makes children and he will provide for them," as a sentiment rightly repudiated by contemporary wives, and further fortifies his position with the quotation from Matthew Arnold that "a man's children are not 'sent' any more than the paintings on his wall or the horses in his stable are sent." Moreover, the struggle of woman to realize an individuality "has obliged her to rebel against the Bible status of woman," with the result that many American women "have broken the scepter of Ishtar."

"*The sole effect of prolificacy is to fill the cemeteries with tiny graves —sacrifices of the innocents to the Moloch of immoderate maternity,*" insists Professor Ross, and he pro-

tests against the "dwarfing of women and the cheapening of men" and regards the restriction of the birth-rate as a "movement at bottom salutary, and its evils minor, transient, and curable."

This is virile gospel, and particularly significant coming from the teacher who invented the term "race suicide," which many have erroneously attributed to Mr. Roosevelt.

STRANGE VIEWS ON MARRIAGE

It is taught by many college sociologists that marriage, under conceivable conditions, will pass away, like medieval institutions. Prof. William Graham Sumner, of Yale, teaches that "both pair marriage and democracy are produced by the conditions of society, and both are transitory"; and that "when life becomes harder it will become aristocratic, and concubinage may be expected to rise again." Moreover, this professor joins with a number of his colleagues in maintaining that marriage as now contracted and protected is a form of monopoly, interwoven with capital, conducive to exclusive families and the culture-ground of family pride and ambition.

Prof. Frank A. Fetter, of Cornell, does not hold a high opinion of modern marriage. "In barbaric times," he teaches, "the stronger and swifter conquered and survived; and the early social institutions of polygamy, patriarchal concubinage, war, and the capture of women favored the survival of ability. But to-day intellectual and economic power contributes not to offspring but to sterilized scholarship, barren selfishness, and social display." And he calls attention to the epigrammatic fact, as pointed out originally by a visiting economist from France, that "all the big families live in little houses, and all the little families live in big houses."

Out of George Washington University, at the national capital, where was lately preached the virtue of big families, comes the dictum of Prof. C. W. A. Veditz that "if society is to reap the benefit of large families society should bear a large part of the burden involved by large families."

Prof. Franklin H. Giddings, of Columbia, one of the world's foremost sociologists, has taken daring ground regarding marriage and unconventional alliances between the sexes. He endorses the beliefs of those who insist that "it is not right to set up a technical

SHAILER MATHEWS
(University of Chicago)
"We go into family relations with the same *sang-froid* that we go on a picnic"

CHARLES H. COOLEY
(University of Michigan)
"Every man's mind is the theater of a conflict of standards"

WILLIAM G. SUMNER
(Yale University)
Ethical notions are "mere figments of speculation" and "unrealities that ought to be discarded altogether"

legal relationship, an economic convenience, or a circumstance of social conventionality as morally superior to the spontaneous preference of a man and woman who know, and whose friends know, that they love each other."

"The whole or a part of this doctrine," Professor Giddings teaches, "has been held and taught by some of the best men and women that have yet lived. Dante foretold it in his 'Vita Nuova.' Petrarch proclaimed it in his fidelity to Laura. John Milton, the sanest, as he was the greatest, of Puritans, iterated and reiterated it in his famous tract on divorce, which no ecclesiastic with a self-respecting regard for his own intellectual reputation has ever dared try to answer. Shelley and Goethe preached it in both their words and deeds. Richard Wagner stood for it unflinchingly throughout life, and gave it expression in the imperishable music of 'Tristan and Isolde.' John Stuart Mill, a calm-minded philosopher, held fast to it through his relations with Mrs. Taylor, when his cherished friends cut him dead because

of it. George Eliot proclaimed her loyalty to it by a life of very quiet but effective defiance of Mrs. Grundy and all her British matrons. And Herbert Spencer carefully formulated it in his autobiography."

Going back to Syracuse University, I heard the timely question of affinities discussed in the class-room there. Like many other lectures, this would have afforded first-class material for a newspaper story, but the young men and women taking notes with hurried precision did not dream that the theme was sensational. It was all given, and accepted, in the scientific spirit.

Professor Earp did not condone the movement away from conventional altars, but his citation of the various theories accounting for the contemporary defiance of the sacredness of marriage was sufficiently interesting to arouse in the students a toleration for, or at least a catholic understanding of, the choosing of "soul-mates." It should be kept in mind in this connection that Syracuse University is co-educational—a number of young women listened to the exposition of affinities. The professor, with considerable enthusiasm, went into the subject of reincarnation, saying that the affinity people might justify their course by believing that the person one meets and finds irresistibly alluring was simply a friend or sweetheart of some ancient yesterday.

He said that there would be far more cases of clinging to affinities if people followed their natural impulses, but made it plain that society, as now constituted, does not warrant the system.

What Chancellor Day thought of this and other questions could not be learned. The chancellor, who is a fighting man, said that he was willing to write magazine articles on all questions, but did not wish to be interviewed on any subject.

The University of Chicago bristles with progressive new thought. Everyone is familiar with the character of this institution's endowment. It has been enabled with its vast funds to engage the services of world-renowned scholars. It stands to-day not only great as an American university, but is recognized throughout Europe as one of the world's centers of higher learning. In fact Professor Michelson of its faculty added to his own honors and to the reputation of the university by winning the Nobel Prize in 1907.

This institution is nominally a religious seat of learning, but if it were dedicated to free thought and agnosticism it could not be more outspoken in its arraignment of many things in our orthodox theology. Some of the professors, too, go much farther than Professor Earp in uttering daring ideas regarding marriage and the home. Prof. Charles Zueblin in particular takes advanced or at least new ground in his attitude toward marriage. Here are the texts of some of his teaching: "*There can be and are holier alliances without the marriage bond than within it.*" "*Every normal man or woman has room for more than one person in his heart.*" "*Like politics and religion we have taken it for granted that the marriage relationship is right and have not questioned it.*"

Prof. Shailer Mathews declares that society is abandoning many of its old standards. This is the way he sums up the tendency of the age: "Much of our current literature shows a certain deterioration of the Christian idea of the family. Our literature is becoming anti-family; it minimizes its

sanctity. We go into family relations with the same *sang-froid* that we go on a picnic."

It must be kept in mind, as pointed out above, that the members of any American university's faculty are not a unit in believing what may be taught in its class-rooms. If the professors were assembled in convention to discuss any of the matters touched upon in this review, the debate would doubtless be as spirited and as many sided as it would be if the outside world took issue publicly with the schoolmen.

BLOOD-RELATIONSHIP BETWEEN HEALTHY PARENTS NOT INJURIOUS TO OFFSPRING

Prof. George B. Louis Arner, university fellow in sociology, has just prepared for Columbia University a monograph on consanguineous marriages, taking the startling ground that "it is not proved that even the closest blood-relationship between parents is directly injurious to offspring." Even "the horror of incest," he announces, "is based upon a myth." He believes that with proper restrictions, prohibiting the marriage of the diseased and degenerate, consanguineous unions might be valuable to the state. His deduction is that the reason such marriages now result so frequently in abnormal offspring is that under the ban on such alliances only the defective contract them, but that if such conjugal daring had the approval of the world, worthy and normal relatives would mate, and the children would be blessed with the genius and virtue of both parents. He quotes Prof. Karl Pearson in support of the daring doctrine that "homogamy is a factor of fertility."

Clearly, college teaching defies all traditional ideas!

Outspoken as all these professors are on subjects that challenge most of our cherished religious, ethical, and economic standards, they are all merely hinting at the complexities involved, if we compare their utterances with the fearless and comprehensive teachings of Prof. William Graham Sumner, of Yale. Hundreds of professors share his beliefs, but few have been equally daring in expressing them. He takes the view that the majority can make anything right. He has coined a new word, or rather resurrected an old one from its Latin grave, to take the place of the Bible as an authority. This word is "mores," and by it he means popular usage and tradition exerting a dominating influence on individuals. The "mores," he teaches, cover all the habits of society with "the mantle of current custom and give them regulation and limits within which they become unquestionable." He thus takes the daring ground that *anything tolerated by the world in general is right*.

Professor Sumner's

C. W. A. VEDITZ
Professor of Economics
in George Washington
University

FRANK W. BLACKMAR

(University of Kansas)
"Standards of right perpetually change in social life . . . in the same race from age to age"

views are worth considering, because they are a clear expression of a great deal of the college teaching constituting the body of doctrine which is taken advantage of by many free-livers to justify their departure from conventional standards. He has devoted a large part of his university career to proving that there

FRANK A. FETTER
(Cornell University)
"Intellectual and economic power contributes not to offspring, but to sterilized scholarship and social display"

is no such thing as God-given and unchanging morality.

"The crimes of Clapham," Kipling says, "are chaste in Martaban," and this Yale professor cites numberless things to emphasize that philosophy. He says, for instance, that the line of decency in dress is always paradoxical. "No matter where it may be drawn, decency is close to it on

EDWARD A. ROSS

(University of Wisconsin)
"Wide stairways are opened between the social levels. But to the climber children are encumbrances"

one side, and indecency on the other. A Moslem woman on the street looks like a bundle of bed-clothes. Where all women look so, one woman who left off her mantle would seem indecent, and the comparative display of the outline of the figure would seem shameless. Where men and women wear only a string around the waist, their dress is decent, but it is indecent to leave off the string. A Moslem woman with her veil, a Spanish woman with her mantilla or fan, a Quakeress with her neckerchief, can be as indecent as a barbarian with her petticoat of dried grass."

These and other racial differences in dress are used by the professor to demonstrate that no human standards of propriety are fixed or universal. "It would be difficult," he says, "to mention anything in Oriental 'mores' which we regard with such horror as Orientals feel for low-necked dresses and round dances. Orientals use dress to conceal the contour of the form. The waist of a woman is made to disappear by a girdle. To an Oriental a corset which reveals the waist-line and the plasticity of the figure is the extreme of indecency." Among some native tribes the people who paint the body are ashamed to be seen unpainted, and among tribes that practised tattooing any individual who might appear without the tattoo marks would be disgraced. Thus it is not modesty that makes men and women wear clothes; the basis of the custom is vanity. It is not a question of morality at all, but purely a matter of custom.

"The notion," he says, "that there is anything fundamentally correct implies the existence of a standard outside and above usage, and no such standard exists." Religion and philosophy are created by custom and usage, and are not, as is popularly believed, "the sources and regulators of conduct." "A people sometimes adopts an ideal of national vanity which includes ambition, but an ethical ideal no group ever has. If it pretended to have one it would be a humbug." His teaching is that after a community has established its habits "it creates the philosophy and religion to grace or justify its acts."

STARTLING CONCLUSIONS

The college teaching that all our standards of right and wrong are derived from experience leads to startling conclusions. We have not yet approved trial marriages, but trial morality, these professors say, is the only kind the world has known. Morals, like all methods of living, merely fit the times. Believing this, they claim that many of our institutions and standards (such as the conventional home) have outlived their service to civilization and are scheduled to disappear.

These professors, in justifying the new morality, the new ideas regarding marriage, the insistence upon a scientific or possibly a communal home, and the daring teachings in regard to the substitutions in store for democracy, agree with Prof. James Quale Dealey, who, from Brown University, has taught that "race morality and individual morality are both exclusively human attributes, having their strict analogues in the animal world." It is all a matter of evolution: heaven has nothing to do with humanity. "As the passage from animality to humanity," it is taught, "was wholly the result of brain-development and consequent dawn of intelligence, so both kinds of morality have been the products of the rational faculty." Religion, as explained by Lester Frank Ward, merely invents supernatural penalties to dragoon men into following the adopted plan.

The new morality based only upon what is expedient has its parallel, so some teach, in the transformations wrought in every phase of material advance. The whole tangible world has broken ancient fetters and is utilizing methods up to date. And morality should be at least as modern as machinery! The reformer no longer shouts from the housetops; he gives his message to the Associated Press. And now, discarding copper wire as a track, we are sending despatches across the void. So, too, aeronauts are sailing the empyrean in ships much heavier than the air, and the schoolmen produce with relish a thesis by Sir Isaac Newton "proving" that aerial flight is beyond the possibilities of the race.

Similarly it is taught that antique authority can no longer hold in the fields of economics, religion, and philosophy. The old ideas, Dr. Samuel M. Crothers, preacher to Harvard University, teaches, have "held their own as squatters," but now the new science is evicting them. Some people will see in the scholastic repudiation of former gospels and dogmas a surrender of their dearest hopes, but why cling to the oar, the schoolmen ask, when the turbine will take you to your port in another world?

26

ACADEMICAL DEGREES:
ESPECIALLY HONORARY DEGREES

By Theodore D. Woolsey

OUR system of learned and higher education in the United States has been borrowed, with some changes, from that of England; and the English universities were themselves built on the plan which was originated in continental Europe in the fourteenth century. One feature of the university system was the degrees, given on satisfactory evidence of proficiency to such as offered themselves, after a certain term of study, for examination. In process of time, to these literary honors earned by study, others, purporting to be of the same value, were added, which did not necessarily imply previous study or examination, or even residence at a learned school, and were often bestowed apart from any evidence of learning or literary merit. These degrees, conferred *honoris causâ*,—honorary degrees, as they were styled,—were not very uncommon, by the side of such as were conferred on examination, at the time when our earliest colleges were founded. But our earliest colleges themselves did not give to their graduates, or to any distinguished persons not educated within their halls, any such honorary testimonials for quite a number of years after their foundation. A person who may have the curiosity to satisfy himself on this point has only need to look at the first pages of the catalogues containing the names of graduates of Harvard or Yale to see that this is true; he will find there doctorates in theology, and a few in law, conferred by the universities of Scotland, by one or two of those of Holland, and by Oxford and Cambridge — the latter, however, conferring their honors principally on those in the colonies who had forsaken the Puritan plans of church government, and had gone over to the Church of England. That the right to confer such honorary degrees existed in the new colleges of the colonies was a matter of doubt at first will be made to appear in the sequel. But these doubts gave way after a long interval, and a precedent was established for the action of every new college, which, for a little more than a century, has been freely and constantly followed. The multiplication of colleges, which are generally schools of philosophy and the arts only, has led to an increase of honorary degrees even in law and theology, to say nothing of degrees in other branches; so that at present many friends of sound learning are inquiring whether this conferring of the highest degrees without examination is not a cause of harm to the whole system of education, and whether it might not be better to give up altogether such degrees so conferred, or, if that be impracticable, in some way greatly to diminish their number. To this and other points relating to honorary degrees the present article will be devoted. But since a judgment on this matter cannot well be formed without some historical statements, our aim will be, first of all, to take a brief look at the degrees given in the early universities on examination, and at the honorary degrees as they crept in, both before and since the time when the earliest colleges in the English colonies were founded. We shall confine ourselves chiefly to degrees in law and theology.

The word "university," as a term of Roman law, denoted a *corporation* or *commune*, whether of a civic or a social kind; and in its mediæval acceptation, when used of a community of teachers and scholars, it was readily applied to such as were engaged in the studies of a single department of knowledge, or even to teachers and scholars from a particular part or country of Europe so united together. Thus at Bologna, where law was first studied on a large scale, there was early in the twelfth century a university of citramontanes or Italians, and another of ultramontanes or students from beyond the Alps. Not long afterward a third such institution, called the *universitas artium*, arose, where the study of the liberal arts was pursued; and to this that of medicine was added about A. D. 1316. In the same fourteenth century a fourth or theological university was added, and at length these corporations were united together. Canon law was taught in connection with civil law, and not in connection with theology. About the same time that Bologna became a school of law, at Salerno, in southern Italy, there arose a school of medical art, which, however, after some time, ceased to flourish, and gave way to other medical schools, especially to one founded at Montpellier in southern France. The theological school of Paris grew, at an early date, out of a monastic school into what may be called a theological university. In process of time the liberal arts, including philosophy and the science of medicine, were here taught with theology; but by the management of the popes, who directed matters relating to learned studies in the interests of the Bologna law faculty, this important department of instruction was kept out of the curriculum in the University of Paris.

From these three centers universities, with minor differences and peculiarities, yet adhering on the whole to a single general form and idea, spread over Europe. We must omit to speak of the *nations*, as they were called, or groups of students from the same quarter or country united together, of the relations of the universities to the popes, and of the internal constitutions of the universities themselves.*

At first the *personnel* of these institutions consisted of teachers, quite independent in their instructions, and of students freely attending their lectures; but afterward usage and law determined who should teach, and prevented collisions which might arise between the teachers in the same departments. The end of the course, for each student who desired to become a teacher or to enter into some position in practical life, was an examination conducted by a faculty of promotion according to the statutes or usages of the university. If the examination was satisfactory, it was signified by the title which he acquired of bachelor, as in law, or theology, or arts. The bachelor seems to have acquired his name first in Provence and France, where *bachalar* was used to signify an owner of a peasant's estate of considerable size, which ranked below a knight's property, just as this first degree was below that of a fully qualified teacher. The term *licentiate*, although not properly denoting a distinct degree, was used of a person who was permitted to teach in the interval between his first and second or higher examination.

The titles for persons admitted to the higher degrees were drawn from the simple Latin words *magister*, in its relation to the scholar or pupil, and *doctor* or teacher. They meant nothing more than the right of teaching: the first, of teaching in the liberal arts; the second, of teaching in law, civil or canon or both, or in theology or medicine. Sometimes the student in law might offer himself for both civil and canon law, in which case his degree would be J. U. D., *juris utriusque doctor*, or for one of the two, as J. C. D., *juris civilis doctor*, etc., other terms being D. C. L., LL. D., etc. The candidate for the office of Doctor of Law in the early times, as at Bologna, was first subject to a private examination, for

which two texts were put into his hands, both from Roman or both from canon law; or one from each of these branches of law if he sought for graduation in both. He exhibited his work the same day on which it was laid before him; the doctor who presented him conducting the examination, and others, if they saw fit, making objections to his expositions. If when his trial was over he was accepted, he was called a *licentiate*, and might remain in this intermediate condition for some time; or, if he wished, he might appear at an early day in the cathedral, where after a discourse and a juristic prelection, at which students might dispute against him, he was proclaimed a doctor amid appropriate formalities.†

There were in different countries, in the course of time, different practices which it would be beyond our limits to speak of, or which we are not acquainted with. In regard to a usage which dispensed with final examinations, although not with attendance on lectures and a stated time of study, we beg leave to cite a passage from Ersch and Gruber's Encyclopedia, vol. XVI., *voce Doctorat:*

" The honor of a doctorate was bestowed ordinarily by special promotion, on application of a candidate made to the proper faculty; and it was an exception when distinguished men were graduated by free movement of a faculty, in order to give them a public proof of respect. The opposite state of things took place only among the theologians [where and to what extent?], who got their promotions regularly *causâ honoris*. Many faculties granted a diploma at once [*i. e.*, without examination] after the proper fees were paid, and a scientific [or scholastic] treatise had been handed in. Such doctors were wont to be treated with some want of respect, and were called *doctores bullati* [in allusion probably to the Roman boys who wore the *bulla*], as contrasted with those who had passed through a full examination. In reference to those, the saying was in use, *Sumimus pecuniam et mittimus asinum in patriam.* In most of the faculties the candidates were promoted only after a complete and rigorous examination. First, the aspirant had to undergo a trial of his fitness before the appropriate officer, as, for instance, before the archdeacon of the cathedral church at Bologna, or at Paris before the superintendent of the cathedral school, out of which, in part, the University of Paris was developed. If the candidate was, on examination, found worthy of a further test, there was set before him a problem or question to be solved in Latin. When this was laid before the faculty of promotion and was found satisfactory, the examination, properly so called, began; after which, if he had passed through it successfully, there remained for him to hold a disputation; and then the dean went through the ceremony of promotion, and the candidate took an oath that he would fulfill the duties of the doctorate."

He thus had a right to remain and lecture at the university, in the department where he

---

* An article entitled " The Rise of Universities," drawn chiefly from Savigny's " History of Roman Law in the Middle Age," and written by the author of this article, appeared in the " New Englander," vol. X., No. 1, 1852, from which much here is drawn.
† Compare the article in the " New Englander " already cited, vol. XI., p. 31.

had been found to be a proficient; or he might be called to some office in the state or in the ecclesiastical system, which must have had great need of canon lawyers. The rules and usages of Bologna prevailed more or less in southern Europe; those of France in France, Germany, England, and other northern countries.

Hitherto we have found no higher degrees which were not won without some previous study; and probably the degree of bachelor was never given without examination, even where the theologians got their doctorates on the easier terms above described. But a practice began of promoting distinguished men to the higher degrees, we know not when; and such honors were given not only to those who had had them in their own universities, but also to others who were without liberal education, or whose life at the university had been interrupted. This usage has existed for a long time, and, if we are not in an error, through all the countries of Europe, wherever there are universities. Sometimes degrees are given in the way of honor to persons who have acquired special distinction out of their own department. Thus, not many years since, a military officer in Germany received the degree of Doctor in Theology on account of an extensive and learned biography of Calvin.

The English universities, so far as pertains to the conditions for being admitted to the higher degrees, have not materially departed from the practice of the mediæval times. They have in substance the same system of graduation and interval of time between a lower and a higher degree, and the same examinations before a public officer of the university and others, which were in use centuries ago; but for the higher honors study at the university is not strictly required. For the rules we must refer to the calendars, which, however, will show some considerable departures from the early usage, especially in recent times. It is enough if a formal connection is kept up with the university. As we have no space for details, we give here only the rules which regulate the granting of the degrees in theology. At Oxford the degree of Doctor of Divinity may be obtained four years after admission to that of Bachelor in Divinity, and this again, if we understand the rule, three years after taking the degree of Master of Arts. As the degree of Master of Arts cannot be taken until in the twenty-seventh term from matriculation, the whole

time, there being four terms in the year, from the beginning to the D. D. is nearly fourteen years. A candidate for the degree of B. D. is required to read two dissertations before the Regius Professor of Divinity, and a candidate for the degree of D. D. to read three exegetical lectures on parts of Scripture. At Cambridge a master of arts or law may be admitted to the degree of Bachelor of Divinity in the seventh year from his graduation, and the candidate for D. D. must be a B. D. of not less than five years' standing. The rules in regard to the proceedings require the candidate for the lower degree to keep an "act," or read a dissertation in English or Latin on some subject connected with Scriptural exegesis or theology, and the candidate for the higher to prepare a similar dissertation in Latin or English, his particular subject having been approved beforehand by a majority of the professors of divinity. The dissertation must be printed before the degree can be obtained. We must omit the regulations for degrees and examinations of bachelors and doctors in law.

If the lists of the highest degrees on examination in theology and law to which we have access can be any guide for forming a general judgment, few proceed so far in their course. At Oxford, in 1879, we find seven doctorates in theology and one in law to have been thus given; and at Cambridge, in 1882, one in divinity and five in law.

How far the higher degrees are held in estimation, and how far they fulfill the end for which they were originally designed, may be questionable points. All are not of one opinion in this respect. Archbishop Whately, in his very entertaining evidence before the Oxford Commission, does not hold them in very high repute (Report, etc., Lond., 1852). He says that "if any Oxford man were asked whether the degree of M. A., and those in law and divinity, do not convey, at least to *some* of our countrymen, *some* notion of merit or proficiency, more or less, of some kind, and whether, therefore, a university *so* conferring these degrees as to create or keep up a false impression is not guilty of a kind of fraud on the public, I do not know what he could answer." And again he says: "I can think of but one remedy—to limit the number of these degrees, allowing only a certain proportion of the whole number of members of the university to obtain them, or so many annually." * Whately, be it observed,

* An appendix to Newman's translation of Huber's "History of the English Universities" is instructive, as showing how canon law ceased to be taught and candidates for degrees in this branch of law fell off as the Reformation prevailed; and also how degrees in civil law became gradually fewer in the sixteenth century. After 1533 there were no doctorates in canon law given at Cambridge, of which there had been 54 between 1500 and that year. There was, indeed, no use for them after appeals to the Pope had been prohibited. From 1500 to 1662 the doctorates of civil law, conferred on examination, were in all 184.

refers here to degrees given on examination. It is probable that, since he wrote, a great improvement for the better has taken place. But is there really any difficulty in making the examinations hard enough to deter or reject those who are not real scholars? Could a body of learned men fail of coming to the conclusion that the examinations must be severe enough to frighten away those who are unqualified? And may not the number of honorary doctorates disincline some persons to offer themselves for an examination who otherwise would pass it with honor?

The practice of granting honorary degrees has long prevailed in England, and was in full blast when the earliest colleges in the English colonies were founded. These are given for a variety of reasons besides scholarship—as to persons of rank, foreign envoys in Great Britain, distinguished writers, political leaders, and so on. Confining ourselves to the statistics of the present time, we find that at Oxford, between 1848 and 1879, the honorary doctorates in civil law (D. C. L.) and in theology conferred were 307 of the former and 39 of the latter, besides 23 degrees of Master of Arts. These were published chiefly at the "Encænia," or days of commemoration of founders and benefactors, which are held annually in June. At Cambridge a distinction is made between honorary and *titular* degrees. The latter, answering to honorary degrees as ordinarily understood, were, in twenty-four years, between 1859 and 1883 inclusive, 143 LL. D.'s and 12 M. A.'s. No doctorates in theology are found among degrees of this class. The honorary degrees, so called, which seem to be confined to persons of rank or official station, are conferred on privy councilors, bishops, or bishops designate or elect, judges of the Supreme Court, deans of cathedrals, heads of colleges, and peers and sons of peers, unless they come as *juvenes* to the university, when they can have only the degree of B. A.

We now pass over to a very important feature of the English universities, as forming the original model after which the places of higher learning and science in the United States took their first form. We refer, of course, to the colleges, which, although not peculiar to England, have had a prominence given to them there which they attained and retained nowhere else. These colleges were somewhat monastic, and consisted of students who were, especially at first, from the same part of the country, gathered around a master (for whom the titles were various, such as master, president, provost, principal, dean) and his assistants, who were called *socii* or *fellows*—that

is, fellow-teachers and governors of the college or school. It shows the connection and tradition followed in the New England colleges, that at Harvard and at Yale the corporations, although not teachers, are in the first acts relating to the foundations styled presidents (or rectors) and fellows. These officers led a common life with their students in a building, the property in which did not necessarily at first belong to the university, but might, with all the original endowments, have been contributed by friends of religion and learning to the earliest founder, or might have been given by the founder himself. The principal work of the president and his fellows, besides that of watching over the life and character of the pupils, was to aid them in understanding the prelections of the professors, who were, as such, university officers, but might be connected with some college also. The common life, the moral and religious training, the preparation for university duties, were a very good work, but not a work essential to the existence nor to the earliest form of the universities. The professors, the lecturers, the examinations, the degrees, the honors, all belonged to the universities. After the invention of printing and the easier access to books and to texts (which at first, in civil law at least, were written out by copyists and sold to students), lectures declined in importance, and the fellows and others in the colleges became the principal instructors in study; and thus the college side of education, which now chiefly consisted in Greek, Latin, logic, and mathematics, prevailed to a great degree over the oral instruction by public lecturers. Meanwhile some of the most important sciences, such as law and medicine, were transported to the city of London; and to a great extent that which was the original work of the professors and of the faculties was taken from the officers of the old university system, the examinations and the conferring of degrees remaining in their hands as their exclusive, as it had been their original, province. As for degrees, and honorary ones in particular, a change of the old plan, committing these into the hands of the college authorities, would have been most injurious to the whole system by introducing into it rivalry and disharmony in their worst shapes. And, on the other hand, to take away the power of conferring degrees from the universities would have been still more disastrous — if, for instance, a plan could have been adopted of transferring the power to grant them to officers appointed by the state. The removal of the studies of law and medicine to a great extent from the old centers of study, although it abridged and lowered the importance of those institutions, was perhaps inevitable, and may never be repaired; but the new sciences, and the enlargement of the field of study in metaphysics, philology, and history, if earnestly taken advantage of, as they now seem to be, may make up for the loss of branches which have found a more convenient home in the great capital. Certainly it does not look at present as if the English universities would be necessarily injured and be obliged to fall behind by any new advances of human knowledge.

When the first New England colonies were founded it was nothing strange that the Puritan ministers, who were chiefly graduates of the two universities, should copy the college system, which was the most living part of the university system. It was the part of the education which admitted of immediate application in the circumstances of the new settlements, and one which would open to the heads and fellows an influence religious and moral over the undergraduates. It is also evident that the poverty of the new colonies was quite unequal to the great burden of erecting so vast a structure as that of an English university.

That degrees in arts, as well the degree of bachelor as that of master, should be felt to be essential in the newly founded institution at Cambridge is quite natural. Rules made during President Dunster's administration, in 1642,— the year of the foundation of the college,—contain forms relating to the conferring of degrees in arts *pro more academiarum in Anglia.* In the act of June 27, 1692, it was enacted (in section four) that "the president and fellows of said college shall have power from time to time to grant and admit to academical degrees, as in the universities in England, such as in respect of learning and good manners they shall find worthy to be promoted thereunto." Under this act Increase Mather received the degree of S. T. D., being then president. The reason given for this shows that higher degrees in the several branches taught in universities were thought of: " And whereas it is a laudable custom in universities . . . to confer academical degrees or titles on those who by their proficiency as to knowledge in theology, law, physic, mathematics, or philosophy have

been judged worthy thereof, it is hereby enacted," etc. Under this act Increase Mather, as we said above, was created a Doctor of Theology, and two others, John Leverett, afterward president of the college, and William Brattle, both graduates of 1680, received the honor of Bachelors of Theology. But the Privy Council in England, having rejected this act in 1695, practically denied also any right under the original charter to the conferring of such honorary degrees; although what was done between 1692 and 1695 remained in force, because neither the legislature of the colony nor the Privy Council disallowed it. Things continued thus until 1771, when Nathaniel Appleton, a graduate of 1712, was honored with the degree of S. T. D. with no intervening precedent after the degree given to Increase Mather spoken of above. The first degree of Doctor of Laws ever granted in Harvard College was given to Washington in 1776. The Constitution of Massachusetts, framed in 1781, gave the first undoubted authority that existed to confer any degrees whatever, if indeed we can go so far as to find this right granted even there in undoubted terms. *

The act for liberty "to erect a collegiate school" in his Majesty's colony of Connecticut, October 9, 1701, gives express power to the undertakers, partners, etc., " . . . to grant degrees or licenses, as they or those deputed by them shall see cause to order or appoint." And the charter of 1745, which was substituted for the earlier one at the instance of the President and Fellows of Yale College, provides that said corporation "shall have power to give and confer all such honors, degrees, or licenses as are usually given in colleges and universities to such as they shall think worthy of them." This charter remains until now, except so far as it has been altered by the president and fellows' own consent and request.

In neither of these institutions, with the exceptions already mentioned, was any higher honorary degree conferred until the near approach of the Revolution, although quite a number of graduates of both received academical honors from abroad. Cotton Mather was honored in this way in 1710, and Benjamin Colman in 1731, both of them by the Univer-

* The reprint of this Constitution in Poor's edition of the " Federal and State Constitutions " (i. 969) contains the following provision : " The president and fellows of Harvard College in their corporate capacity, etc., shall have, hold, etc., all the powers, authorities, rights, etc., which they now have or are entitled to have, hold, etc., and the same are confirmed unto them, etc., forever." It may be still asked whether they then had, and so whether they now have or are entitled to have, the right of conferring degrees or higher degrees under this charter. The question, however, is not of any practical moment.

It deserves remark that the term "university" is here made synonymous with "college." " Our wise ancestors laid the foundation of Harvard College, in which university," etc. We may add that Cotton Mather in his " Magnalia " (IV., pp. 132 *et seq.*) uses the word in the same way: " I see not why such marks of honor may not be properly given by an American University as by an European," etc.

sity of Glasgow; and Rector Cutler of Yale College, a graduate of Harvard, received the same honor from Oxford in 1723, but not until he had conformed to the Church of England and had been deposed from his rectorate. In the course of years a number of other ministers of the gospel, graduated at Yale, who followed Cutler in his movement, were in like manner rewarded; as Johnson, afterward president of King's College — now Columbia — in New York, Caner, Chandler in 1745, and somewhat later Seabury, subsequently bishop of the Episcopal Church in Connecticut, and first prelate of the Church of England in America. Many others from both institutions, and from other colleges in the colonies, had such degrees from Scotch or Dutch universities, the motive for which must have been to honor prominent men of non-Episcopal churches. As for honorary degrees given by American institutions themselves in the eighteenth century, we have room only for one or two particulars in addition to what has been said of Harvard. Yale College gave the degree of S. T. D. for the first time, in 1774, to Benjamin Lord, a graduate of 1717, and of LL. D., in 1787, to Chief Justice Dyer, first of all its graduates. During and after the Revolution this practice extended, so that every newly founded college exercised this power without scruple; and a person who could take the trouble to search the charters given in the last century, as well as the vastly greater number given in this, would probably find that they all received the power to grant such degrees as were then in use, if they did not acquire a wider privilege. Thus Dartmouth College, under a charter of 1769, honored with the degree of S. T. D. Benjamin Pomeroy, who had been at Yale a classmate with Wheelock, Dartmouth's first president; and Princeton College, founded in 1746, and opened in 1757, exercised this power before the Revolution, as in the case of a president of Yale in 1774.

It is perhaps deserving of remark that the frequency of honorary degrees in theology during the latter part of the century had no perceptible effect in calling forth talent and learning. The speculations in theology and metaphysics proceeded from the followers of Jonathan Edwards more than from any other source; but this eminent man did not live into the time when the theological honors were freely dispensed by places of learning in the colonies, nor was he as highly estimated in his life-time as he has been since his death. As the century proceeded in its course, however, and especially after the Declaration of Independence, the colleges then existing took the providing for academical honors into their own hands, and the youngest of them started in this career at not far from the same point of time with the oldest. The habit thus fastened on the United States began by a kind of necessity, if we would follow the same path which had been pursued in Great Britain and on the Continent. Yet in so doing we adopted not the original plan of conferring the highest degrees on examination upon those who offered themselves for that purpose, but the plan of selecting men of age and prominence, who rather conferred honor on the colleges than acquired honor for themselves. As the country spread, the demand for new colleges and for what began to be styled universities * spread *pari passu*, and the names of the new institutions grew larger the more humble was their origin. All of these acquired by charter, it would appear, the same right of conferring degrees, honorary or other, which the oldest had been permitted to exercise, with no limitation of their power in this respect. The extent to which this power has been exercised it is not easy to ascertain with accuracy; yet statistics in this matter are needed to test our opinions. To these statistics we now come, and shall endeavor in all brevity to show first, by a statement of the higher honorary degrees conferred by the two oldest colleges (which are selected as being fair representatives of the rest), what the condition of things has heretofore been; and then, by other statements, what the number of such degrees is at the present time.

The degrees conferred *honoris causâ*, without examination, are S. T. D. and LL. D. These may be placed under two heads, one of which includes such as are given to graduates of these two institutions, whether by the Alma Mater herself or by some other seat of learning; the other includes the same kinds of honorary degrees given to other persons, whether graduates of other institutions or not graduated at all. The honorary degree finds its place on the catalogue of graduates, whenever it is conferred on them, after the person's name, and under the year of graduation. For instance, the literary honors of John Adams, President of the United States, will be found in the cat-

---

* The confusion of college and university appears as early as 1701, in "proposals for erecting a university in the renowned colony of Connecticut." So the writer afterward speaks of a Synod being gathered for settling a university, etc.; and again says: "There have been many famous universities without colleges." The writer may have been a Massachusetts minister who was not in sympathy with the leading persons at Harvard.

alogue of Harvard graduates under the year 1755, when he received his degree of Bachelor in Arts, although his academical honors were given to him long afterward—between 1780 and 1797.

The degrees of Doctor in Law and in Theology conferred on graduates of Harvard by their Alma Mater or by other places of learning before 1801 were in all, if our count is right, 179, of which 108 were conferred by Harvard itself, and 71 came from other quarters. Between 1801 and 1879, 206 graduates of Harvard received honorary degrees, 91 in law and 115 in theology. Of the degrees in law 56 came from Harvard itself and 36 from other sources. Of the degrees in theology 64 were conferred by Harvard and 51 proceeded from other sources.

The honorary degrees of a similar rank granted by Harvard to non-graduates or to persons graduated at other institutions were in all 218 in number, of which 55 were in theology and 163 in law. The first honorary doctorate in law, if Increase Mather's in 1692 is not counted, was conferred on General Washington in 1776.

The higher degrees conferred on the graduates of Yale College down to 1801 (between 1702 and 1800) were in all 144, of which 55 were in law and 89 in theology. Of these 90, 22 in law and 68 in theology were conferred by other institutions, and 33 in law and 21 in theology by Yale College itself. From 1800 to 1880 the higher degrees were in all 360, in theology 220, in law 140. Of the honorary degrees in theology, Yale conferred 15 and other institutions 205; of those in law, Yale conferred 50, and other institutions conferred the doctorate in law upon 90.

The higher honorary degrees given by Yale to persons not there graduated were in the second period in all 91, 37 in theology and 54 in law. The first of these degrees was given in 1766.

We beg leave to make two remarks on the lists pertaining to the last period, one of which is that the degrees received by graduates of Yale were very numerous, exceeding by about 150 those conferred by other colleges on graduates of Harvard, while Yale itself conferred only 15 on its graduates. The causes which brought this state of things about were the great number of students at Yale then having the ministry in view and their dispersion over a large part of the United States. This of late years has in a measure ceased. And, again, the reason why only 15 honorary doctorates in theology were bestowed by Yale on its graduates out of 220 was chiefly owing to the feeling which some of the "fellows" or corporation had in respect to honorary degrees, and especially to degrees in theology. From 1835 to 1869 there were no such degrees given, we believe, either to its own alumni or to any other persons. Not long after this feeling had given way to some extent, a rule of the corporation made a limit to the number of such honorary degrees which could be given in any one year, and a committee, consisting of professors from the several faculties or departments, was appointed, whose annual duty it was to examine a report made on names proposed for such honors. It is worthy of mention that the policy of the college authorities did no harm, apparently, to the graduates or to the college. The doctorates in theology were more numerous than before, from the opening of other channels, yet the feeling against higher degrees was not confined to the place of learning spoken of.

These statements will show what the older colleges have been doing in the way of bestowing academical honors since the time of the Revolution. As for the annual number of such honors conferred by all the institutions in the United States exercising this power, our materials are scanty, and are chiefly drawn from Commissioner Eaton's reports for 1879, 1880, and 1881. In the first of these years the doings of 281 places of learning with degree-conferring powers are published; in the second there are reports from 285 such institutions. There were created in 1879 150 doctors in divinity and 85 in law, and in 1881 128 of the former and 65 of the latter—in all for two years 428. For 1881 we have had no complete account until this article was all but furnished. We now learn from Mr. Eaton's report for this year that the honorary degrees of D. D. or S. T. D. conferred in that year were 165, and of LL. D. 86. The reports come from 306 institutions, many of which, described as agricultural colleges or industrial universities, etc., would not think of conferring the degrees with which we have to do.

An article in the "Independent" of August 17, 1882, throws light on the number of ministers then living who had had the degree of D. D. or S. T. D. conferred upon them. Among the Congregationalist ministers in Massachusetts, one out of eleven was found to bear the title, but if the retired ministers were reckoned in, the ratio would be as 1 to 8. In the Presbyterian Church (of the Northern States?) there were, according to the same authority, 610 Doctors of Divinity, or 1 to about 8.3 of the 5086 then belonging to the denomination. In the Episcopal Church there were in 1882 545 clergymen who had received doctorates, or 1 out of 6.5. The proportionate number among the Methodists and Baptists must be much less, but is sure to increase with the learning and zeal which are putting the ministers of these bodies on a level with their compeers belonging to denominations formerly stronger.

Of the doctorates of law, which are far from being few, we have but meager statistics; and as our main object in this essay is the value and estimation of degrees in theology, we feel less interest in hunting doctorates of law out from college catalogues and other documents. We may, however, mention here a single fact which shows how the tendency to use new degrees in awarding scientific honors has begun to show itself. The degree of Ph. D., which in Germany is what M. A. has been in England and the United States, has been used for a few years among us as a degree conferred on examination upon students in science. There certainly can be no objection to this novelty, if the examination is severe and thorough. But some colleges, chiefly if not entirely seated in the Western States, went beyond this, and gave the degree to some who, without an examination for it, had gained some distinction in physical sciences. It was according to logic and analogy so to do; but a convention of scientific men, more than a year since, protested against this extension of the field of honors, and their protest has been received, we judge, with no dissatisfaction by the country.

From what has been said thus far in regard to honorary degrees, we may safely draw the conclusion that by ancient usage the *colleges* of the United States have no right to confer any degrees whatever, whether honorary or as the reward of scholarship determined by examination. If we depart from the precedent of earlier times, it may fairly be pleaded that in the circumstances in which the early colonists found themselves the conferring of degrees on examination was a necessity, whether supported by precedent or not; but the giving of higher degrees never was in the hands of colleges properly so called, and only pertained to bodies properly styled universities, where faculties of instruction were united together in one corporation. To the university alone it belonged to make laws in regard to examination, to prescribe what studies should be required for degrees, to fix the length of residence before a student could offer himself for a degree; nor, so far as we are aware, had the single colleges, in those universities where they existed, the least right of interfering in the general system of education so far as to put one study in the place of another prescribed by the general statutes: the governing board alone, however it might be called, could or-

dain what criterions and tests for scholarship should be made use of. Still less could a college in the university, if there were any colleges there, give degrees *honoris causá*. The king might express his wish to have such and such honors conferred on particular persons; but the wish had no effect until complied with by the university acting through its officers or senate. The university, perhaps, might introduce new degrees by its inherent power; but the whole subject of degrees was outside of the province of a college, whose business was to train up persons who could have degrees from the university, if they were found worthy on examination. Hence, to confer the power of giving degrees, such as are usually given in universities, on an infant college in a new colony, seems to imply some ignorance of what universities were, or a strong hope that one faculty would expand into three or four.

But another point deserves consideration. The degrees on examination followed the approval of the particular faculties, or of committees from their members. This implies that the universities, for their own credit or even self-preservation, committed the examinations in a department of study to professors or instructors in that department; nor can we suppose that teachers belonging to other departments interfered with their office. This, we presume, is the case in all respectable colleges; the corporation or fellows or supreme authorities, by whatever name called, will not give degrees, unless to those students whom the teachers pronounce worthy of such honor. Some universities did not have the full complement of four departments or faculties; thus that of Paris had for a long time, as we have already said, no faculty of law. Now, suppose that such a university, with the faculty of law wanting, should have undertaken to give degrees in law, common or civil or both, without examination, would that have been endured? If the University of Paris, in its earlier times, had taken this license, would there not have been a general outcry, and would not the Pope have considered it an indirect attack on his authority? This is but acting according to the very fair rule that neither examinations nor degrees ought to be permitted in any branch of an institution, where there is no corps of instructors in that branch competent to decide on the merit of a candidate to receive such a degree. According to this principle, where in a place of learning a certain branch of study is not taught, there ought to be no degrees given in it. If, for instance, law or theology is not taught, there should be no degrees in law or theology. As well might a medical school give degrees in the arts or in theology, or a theological school make doctors of medicine; as well, we mean, so far as analogy is concerned; for in matter of fact such a passing over into another department of study would be unauthorized, complained of, and condemned. And yet among us, small colleges, where there is only a faculty of arts, are, as we find from year to year, in the constant exercise of such power, even to the using of new degrees unknown before.

But there is a ready reply to what we have said, drawn from established usage. The distinctive characteristic of the American colleges has been, it will be said, growth, without legislation, both in the colonial and in the national form of our existence. In answer, we say that the progress of the American higher education has indeed been, in most respects, more rapid and more satisfactory than could have been anticipated. But if there are excrescences in the system, such as seem to be hurtful to the advance of real study, every educated man ought to desire that they should disappear. Such we hold to be honorary degrees, especially doctorates in law and in theology; and we believe them to be so little in accord with solid learning that we could wish them to be suppressed, or, if that is impossible, checked and regulated. We intend, however, in this article to go no further than to urge the propriety of going back to the original system of granting such degrees, like all others, to persons who, on their own responsibility, offer themselves for examination. As for the present system of high degrees without examination, we intend to do no more than to show what its evils are, and to inquire whether a return to the old plan, still pursued, we believe, in all the universities of Christendom where faculties of law and theology are found, may not have a good influence on the standard of learning and on the value of the higher degrees themselves in all parts of the country.

The higher honorary degrees, as it has been made to appear, were not conceived to be within the competence of the earliest colleges in the colonies to bestow; and with one exception they were not conferred by them between the founding of Harvard and the years just before the Revolution, or nearly a century and a half. If, at that time, a plan could have been introduced of granting such degrees on examination, it might have been preventive of much evil; but the Revolution cut off to a great extent the former sources of supply, and it is remarkable how all the colleges within a few years provided for themselves in this respect. From this time onward the stream of honorary degrees has run in a smooth channel, nor has the supply ever failed. But the abundant supply has brought with it a sense of the evil which attends such a way of helping ourselves to honors. Some of the evils are the following:

In the first place, these honorary degrees are bestowed on no evidence of thorough learning in theology or in law, and thus are in no way certificates of deserving the honors, saving that, for some reason or other, the corporation of a college regards the person thus honored as a man worthy of notice beyond most of his fellows. But whether he was a scholar or not, whether he was a theologian or an accomplished lawyer or not, in the estimate of the board governing a college, does not appear. There are so many causes for a man's taking rank above his fellows in the same profession, so much ambition for notoriety in some persons, and so much shrinking from it in others of equal abilities and learning, that, as an actual distinction between those who deserve a degree and those who do not deserve it, such honors are of very little worth. Add to this that the ways of obtaining them often take away what would otherwise be their value. By this we do not mean to intimate that a person eager for such an honor will use unworthy means to secure it, or that his friends, understanding his wishes, will so act in his stead; but we mean that the trustees of a college have no sure means of judging of the relative, and still less of the absolute, merit of names brought before them; that the trustees themselves are not a body capable, in the time which they can afford, of forming a judgment in such a case; and that, if the object in view is to find among its own graduates or in the body of graduates of all the colleges the man who ought to be honored before all others, this is by no means an easy problem to solve. We are acquainted with the method which one of the largest institutions in the land has for a dozen years or more acted upon, which in substance is this: The number of honorary degrees is limited by a standing rule, and a committee from all the departments or faculties is called together to act on names submitted to them, without which no honor can by ordinary rules come before the corporation. This shows a conscientious desire to do a duty fairly and deliberately; but whether the committees from the faculties would pronounce the plan to be satisfactory we very much doubt.

We have also a right to say that this distribution of honorary degrees is to a great extent unmeaning. It fails of selecting the most worthy; it disappoints many, as is probable, and gratifies a few, and those few not, of course, the best fitted to fill the place; it by no means selects the most learned and useful scholars, but rather those who have an artificial or undeserved prominence. The desire to obtain the honor is a desire which no man should indulge, and yet the uncertainty and unreasonableness of the rules of selection provoke such a desire especially in persons who have no good claims by which it can be justified. If the honor of a doctorate in theology is given to ministers of one denomination, it will in the end be given to those of another,—not in order to encourage a learned ministry, but owing, in part, to the sway of the spirit of equality, and because, in part, it gives a title which is as good as if the largest university had conferred it, as well as a standing in the upper section of one's fellow ministers. Perhaps, too, it may help him in getting a good parish. The social distinction conferred on a man by an academical honor, whether deserved or not, is not an inconsiderable motive for desiring and even for seeking it; and the value of titles is perhaps nowhere more highly estimated than in a democratic country like ours. Thus the official title which attaches itself to a person in a civil, military, judicial, or political sphere is commonly given rather than the christian name, not merely because it is shorter to say Colonel or Major or Mr. Smith, but also because it is supposed to afford pleasure to the person so addressed. It is owing to these causes that addresses by word of mouth, or on the covers of letters, have gradually fallen down from their original honorary meaning, so as to be open to almost all men,—such titles, we mean, as Esquire, Master or Mr., and Honorable. In this widening of the use of titles, they come to mean at length little or nothing, and instead of distinctions are bestowed on all men. Who that adds the title of *Esquire* to a name on a letter ever thinks of the aristocratic employment which it once denoted? It is getting to be very much the same in regard to doctorates in theology. They carry with them no evidence of learning, but only a certain indefinite superiority above others in the same sacred calling.

The estimate of the value of honorary degrees will be, of course, affected by the number of institutions which have the authority to confer them. There are more than three hundred colleges which can confer honorary degrees, and over their trustees there is no control. As it is generally unknown from what source these honors in each particular case proceed, those who wear the honors will pass on an equality, and the number of the institutions will only diminish the respect for the title when it accompanies the name of a minister of the gospel; for men will be slow to believe that the opinion of so many unknown boards of trustees, giving the highest distinction in learning, is to be greatly respected, any more than they can trust as many mints throwing out coin over the country with no general board of control, or banks issuing paper at discretion. In England the small number and great size of the universities make their judgments to be respected over the literary world; but even there the honorary degrees can do very little good to the system. It is rather the system which in a measure supports this excrescence of literary honors conferred without examination.

What we have said thus far of honorary doctorates in theology will apply to the same honors in law, only that the latter are honors in a more exclusive sense. They are used with less frequency than the theological ones, either as suffixed to individual names on the title-pages of books or in addresses. Thus a judge who had the title would hardly choose to have it attached to his name in court, or, indeed, anywhere else, since his official name commands respect. Add to this that, as an honorary degree, it is more frequently bestowed on men of political distinction, on distinguished writers or other men of mark, than on lawyers; so that it is given to a very miscellaneous class of important men, and thus indicates no special kind of talent or proficiency. It is thus more a compliment than anything else; it might be spared without being missed, and is not very much valued when it is conferred. But why should compliments invade places dedicated to the realities of learning and science?

It is somewhat humiliating to have to mention here the forged degrees which have within a few years been detected and exposed in the United States; and yet, as they bear upon our subject, they deserve mention, because but for honorary degrees such forgeries would hardly have been attempted. The most notorious of these dealers in *bogus* degrees, nearly all of which were pretended degrees in medicine, was one Buchanan, of Pennsylvania, whose career is exposed by Mr. Eaton in his Report on Education for 1880, pages 157–165. To his purchases of charters as early as 1858, his opening a market for certificates of doctorates in medicine, his detection and pretended death by drowning, his subsequent arrest and confinement for trial, we can only allude. One remarkable circumstance attending his career was that a commerce was opened between him and a man in Great Britain, who was without doubt aware of the fraud. This person writes from London to ascertain whether he could "grant him a degree, honorary or otherwise," for gentlemen to be introduced by him, " they proving themselves proficient to write a suitable petition in Latin, and forwarding their testimonials and manuscripts and printed works, or to pass an examination in this college (at London), the questions to be proposed by yourself. If you would oblige me by doing this, I will guarantee you £1000 a year, or £8 or £10 for each degree."

The detection of this fraud did not put an end to the species to which it belongs. One Stickney obtained a charter from the Legislature of New Hampshire, and sold degrees of the Nova-Anglica (!) Universitas Artium et Scientiæ, which had no real existence ; and in the winter of 1882–3 the managers of a medical college, which, if we mistake not, had procured a charter, and was removed from its original place of work to Boston, were entering on the same career, when the law put a stop to further proceedings. We are aware that the responsibility for such frauds is not wholly to be imputed to the bestowal of honorary degrees, and that the medical art is that one which especially offers a chance of successful imposture, since the pretenders in it well know how easily the poor and the ignorant are exposed to the deceptions of quacks; but this much may be said at least: that honorary degrees, although they have lost their repute to some extent, are yet held in esteem by very many, and carry with them an impression that other degrees also, somewhat resembling them, proceed from respectable sources.

If, now, honorary degrees in the very important departments of theology and law are liable to the charges which we have made against them, and especially to that of doing harm to thoroughness and honesty in learning, what is the cure for this ? Either they should be thrown aside altogether or be retained under restrictions; while the old system, in use since the foundation of modern universities, of degrees given on examination in law and theology, which still exists all over Europe, ought to be restored. To abandon honorary doctorates altogether may be found impracticable, and cases may occur in which a study begun in all fidelity is interrupted by sickness or poverty. In such cases, which are not very numerous, where the lower degrees of various kinds had been sought for by earnest study, but were not regularly attainable owing to the misfortune of the student, it has been not unfrequently the practice to give the degree at a subsequent time, even without examination. This comes near to an honorary degree, yet the intimate knowledge of the student's ac-

quisitions, until illness or poverty blocked the way, places this on a different ground from those degrees which are simply honorary. It might be well, also, to reward discoverers of important principles in science, who had had, perhaps, no public education whatever, with the honors which incorporate them among those who rose by regular stages to the higher platform of learning; but if this should be found desirable, let such rewards be reserved for cases which would be rare and of distinguished merit. As for the rest, let the way be opened to any graduate, if he feels it important, to prepare by the study of years for the highest degree within his reach, and that whether he resides within the college walls or outside of them. This is the bravest course for the individual himself. He offers himself, we will suppose, for the lower degree or baccalaureate in law or theology. The time when this first degree after graduation could take place should be not so very early; it might be at the end of four years from his graduation. Then the higher examination for his doctorate should be long enough afterward to give him time to become a proficient in the science which he pursues — eight years, perhaps, from his graduation as a bachelor in law or theology. The tests of his fitness for this higher degree, which would generally demand a separate examination, might be selected as they have been hitherto, and the examiner or examiners would naturally belong to the faculty within which the studies are included. In theology, for instance, exegesis of the Hebrew and Greek Scriptures would naturally be one of the most important subjects, then the history of the church and of theological science, together with some essay, selected by the candidate but approved by the examiners, on some branch of theological study. In law the examination would naturally take the same course, with an essay as before. If the essay offered by any candidate were thought to be of peculiar value, it might be published by order of the examiners at the expense of the university. The faculties concerned in the examination ought to be remunerated at the candidate's cost, since it was his choice that laid the burden upon them.

For a time at least, faculties of law, theology, medicine, or natural science, having no connection with a group of other faculties, might exercise this power of conducting the higher examinations by themselves; but the healthy rivalry of different branches of learning would probably be found so stimulating that no experienced instructor could wish to have them pursued apart. Residence at some place of study other than those which have faculties capable of examining candidates ought to be encouraged, but at first not required. This concession, if found hurtful, could be withdrawn, and, at all events, certificates of good character ought to be demanded. Other provisions would be suggested when the system was put into operation.

These remarks are suggested in part by a difficulty which examinations for the highest degrees must encounter, owing to the number of smaller and feebler places of learning, where there is but one faculty of instruction—not to speak of those professional schools in law, medicine, or theology where honorary degrees are seldom given. The smaller institutions would hardly venture to conduct examinations in anything unless it be philosophy and the arts, although they might give honorary degrees by the score. The difficulty here referred to will in the future be in part removed by the rise, in connection with some of the colleges scattered here and there through the country, of new faculties which will furnish an encyclopedic education. Of course, three hundred or more respectable universities would be out of the question; but if there were twenty, or even fifteen, fully officered, endowed, and furnished with libraries of adequate size and completeness, they could meet the wants of the country for a long time to come. One of their uses would be to open their doors to the graduates of colleges having but a single faculty of instruction, who should desire, at no very great distance from their homes, to carry their studies further forward than they could at their own place of graduation. This would be just what is done at those institutions where there are at present schools in theology, law, science, and medicine. There is no distinction there made between students who come to such schools from among the graduates of the institutions themselves and those who come from other quarters.

If such a system could have a fair start, it would probably meet with success. The great obstacle to its success would be the practice, which would not cease at once, of honorary degrees which do not reveal the source from which they come, but may be given as readily and freely by the smallest, and feeblest, and newest college in the land as by the oldest and most thorough. If the degrees given on examination and those given without examination should coëxist, one of the two must be driven out of the field to a great and increasing extent. We hope that there may be a trial of strength between the two. Let those who have won honors for themselves by hard and conscientious study put the name of the institution where they earned their degrees on their printed works, let them show how and where they became learned and accomplished scholars, and there will be little doubt that the present plan of giving honors without instruction and without proof of qualification will at length give way.

PEACE.

O Peace! thou swift bird, flying
  Out from the hearts of men,
How is it thou art trying
  Thine empty nest again?
I strove so hard to woo thee,
I told my sorrows to thee,
I sighed to have thee stay,
Yet thou wouldst fly away.

A noise of quick wings whirring
  Along the air at night!
A sound of soft wings stirring,
  And thou wast in from flight.
Too late I would retain thee,
Too soon I would regain thee;
For lo! thou camest still
And wentest at thy will.

By what supreme endeavor
  Shall I insure thy rest?
How shall I hold thee ever,
  Shy bird, my loving guest?
What gift of mine shall win thee?
What longing is within thee
That one so poor as I
May wholly satisfy?

Yet if thy stay is fleeting,
  At least I shall be glad
To dream of future greeting
  And know the joys I had.
From all earth's good I choose thee,
Nor can I wholly lose thee;
When most I feel thy lack
Thy light wings bear thee back.

Isaac O. Rankin.

27

COLLEGE FRATERNITIES

By John Addison Porter

SIGMA DELTA CHI CLOISTERS AND CHAPEL, S. S. S., YALE.

OF college fraternities in the United States one significant fact may pass unquestioned— they have retained the affection and kept the support of a large number of those who knew them best. On their rosters are found not only the names of undergraduates, but also those of men who long since left youth and folly far behind. Indeed, one now and then runs across a name that adds a certain dignity to the catalogue and becomes an inspiration for ambitious youth. Of these many find no small satisfaction in identifying themselves from time to time with the life of the various clubs and societies of which they were members when boys at college; they take a mild, half-melancholy pleasure in reminiscent talk, and delight to meet and wander with half-regretful sadness in halls where youth wears the crown.

The charm of life in the society hall is much easier for one to imagine than for another to relate. A stereotyped phrase, "mere boyishness," fails to explain it; a compendium of dry facts and arguments would be farther still from picturing the life that often masquerades under the thin veil of a half-pretended secrecy.

WHIG HALL, PRINCETON.

More "sweetness and light" seems always to have been the goal towards which the fraternities strove, and the story of their development is a plain tale of natural and steady growth from small beginnings.

Towards the end of the first quarter of the present century the social life of our colleges had become barren— not more barren, perhaps, than it had been for many years, but relatively so in view of the fact that life was becoming richer and the spirit of the times more liberal. Boys from families in which puritanical methods were obsolete naturally hated the puritanism of college discipline; they chafed at the petty decorum of the stuffy class-rooms, and fretted at the deadness of the iron-bound curriculum. Almost the only means of relaxation countenanced by the faculties were open

KAPPA ALPHA LODGE, CORNELL.

debating societies, which met on the college grounds, and to the meetings of which both professor and student might go. In view of the fact that students, from the days of Horace down, were wont to hold their preceptors as their natural enemies, the presence of professors did not increase the popularity of these societies. Indeed, they languished. Here was the opportunity of the typical college fraternity.

Of these societies the first to assume the characteristics that are now recognized as their essential, albeit it soon lost them, had been Phi Beta Kappa. It was founded at Williamsburg, Virginia, December 5, 1776, in the very room where Patrick Henry had voiced the revolutionary spirit of Virginia. The story is a simple one: John Heath, Thomas Smith, Richard Booker, Armistead Smith, and John Jones,

* For friendly assistance in the preparation of this article the writer cordially acknowledges his obligation to Mr. John De Witt Warner, of New York.

HASTY PUDDING CLUB-HOUSE, HARVARD.

students at William and Mary College, then the most wealthy, flourishing, and aristocratic institution of learning in America, believing that there was room for a more effective student organization than the one of a Latin name that then existed there, and recalling that one of their number was the best Greek scholar in college, resolved to found a new society, the proceedings of which were to be secret, to be known by the name of the three Greek letters that formed the initials of its motto — Phi Beta Kappa. The minutes are discouraging to those who would like to consider Phi Beta Kappa as a band of youthful enthusiasts planning a union of the virtuous college youth of this country, who were afterward to reform the world; and even more so to those who have declared infidel philosophy to be its cult. Youths of fine feelings and good digestion, they enjoyed together many a symposium like that on the occasion of Mr. Bowdoin's departure for Europe, when, "after many toasts suitable to the occasion, the evening was spent by the members in a manner which indicated the highest esteem for their departing friend, mixed with sorrow for his intended absence and joy for his future prospects in life." They called themselves a "fraternity." More thoroughly to enjoy the society of congenial associates, to promote refined good-fellowship, was the motive of these hearty young students who founded the first of the true Greek-letter fraternities, with (to quote from its ritual) "friendship as its basis, and

"KEYS" HALL, YALE.

benevolence and literature as its pillars"—one which thrived in their day as its successors on the same basis flourish in ours. So far from being inspirers, or a product, of American national spirit, or of a union of the wise and virtuous to which they invited all known American colleges, the only reference in their record to the Revolution is the single mention of the "confusion of the times" in the record of the final meeting; and the only recognition of the existence of other colleges is the record of the granting of charters for "meetings" at Harvard and Yale, which institutions were never mentioned again.

Meanwhile Cornwallis was coming nearer, and after having chartered additional chap-

"BONES" HALL, YALE.

ters,—Beta, Gamma, Delta, Epsilon, Zeta (Harvard), Eta (Yale), and Theta,—the Alpha, or mother chapter, passed out of existence.

From Epsilon and Zeta have descended the latter-day chapters of Phi Beta Kappa. Of the fate of Beta, Gamma, Delta, Eta, and Theta nothing is known. After a lapse of seventy years, William Short, of the mother chapter, at the age of ninety, traveled from Philadelphia to Williamsburg and revived the Alpha, which, however, soon succumbed to the vicissitudes of its college. It is not known what was its first follower. But of those whose activity have been continuous to date, Kappa Alpha, founded in 1825 at Union College, adopting with its Greek name a badge planned similarly to that of Phi Beta Kappa (except that it was suspended from one corner, instead of from the center of one of its equal sides), and inspired by similar ends, began

BERZELIUS HALL, S. S. S., YALE.

the career that has made it the mother of living Greek letter societies. For Phi Beta Kappa has long since become an honorary, as distinguished from an active, institution, though the reunions of its chapters, especially of the old Zeta, now the "Alpha of Massachusetts," founded at Cambridge in 1779, are still noteworthy events.

Even before Phi Beta Kappa came into existence, Oliver Ellsworth, afterward Chief-Justice of the Supreme Court of the United States, had founded Clio Hall at Princeton, and a few years later, in 1769, Whig Hall arose at the same college with James Madison, afterward twice President of the United States, for its founder; and from that day to this these friendly rivals have never ceased to exert a healthful influence on the intellectual life of Princeton. These were the prototypes, and are the most vigorous survivals, of what, for nearly a century, were the most flourishing and numerous of student societies — the twin literary societies, or "halls," generally secret, and always intense in mutual rivalry, which have been institutions at every leading college in the land.

Another and a third, though less homogeneous, class of student societies may be best described by noting separately its only important examples — at Harvard and Yale. The Hasty Pudding Club of Harvard also took its rise in those interesting and formative years just subsequent to the close of the Revolutionary war, and was founded, as its constitution says, "to cherish the feelings of friendship and patriotism." For the display of the latter virtue the club for many years was wont to celebrate Washington's Birthday with oration and poem, with toasts and punch. Alas, for these degenerate days! Conventional theatricals have taken the place of poem and oration, though, for aught I know, the toasts and punch may yet survive. "Two members in alphabetical order"— so ran the old by-laws — "shall provide a pot of hasty pudding for every meeting," and it is said that this practice is still religiously kept. That the banquet was not lightly considered by the old Harvard clubs may be seen in the tendency to exalt in the name of the club the peculiar feature of the club's fare, the Porcellian taking its name from the roasted pig — classical token of hospitality — that one of its bright young members provided for the entertainment of his fellows on a time when the feast fell to his providing. But the Porcellian has not wholly given itself up to the things that go with banqueting, for no other college society has so fine a library as it possesses. Indeed, its seven thousand well-selected and finely bound volumes might be coveted by many less fortunate small colleges. The A. D. Club is a younger rival of the "Pork," and, in the comfort of its house, the brilliancy of its dinners, and its good-fellowship, is by no means inferior. The development of this species of undergraduate activity has taken a widely different and rather unique form at Yale. The Yale senior societies are the most secret and clannish of college societies. No outsiders ever enter their buildings, and their goings and comings are so locked in mystery that one can only guess what their aims and purposes are. A passion for relic worship and a taste for politics are generally ascribed to both, though the class of men taken by Scroll and Key differs widely from that chosen by Skull

DELTA KAPPA EPSILON HALL, YALE.

295

ALPHA DELTA PHI (EELL'S MEMORIAL) HALL, HAMILTON.

where, and increased in number through almost every imaginable combination of the letters of the Greek alphabet. Many, of course, have vanished from the face of the earth. Of those that still remain, Delta Kappa Epsilon, founded at Yale in 1844, is the largest, and has now above 9000 members, representing 32 active chapters situated in 19 different States; Psi Upsilon, originated at Union in 1833, enrolls some 6600 members, distributed among 19 chapters in 10 States; and Alpha Delta Phi, founded at Hamilton in 1832, has a membership nearly as large. Delta Kappa Epsilon appears to have made good its claim to be recognized as a national institution; and while certain smaller fraternities are favorites in particular parts of the country, all barriers are rapidly disappearing before these three favorite societies in their march towards representation at all the important colleges of the country.

Though fraternities are organized less frequently now than formerly, because of the

DELTA KAPPA EPSILON HALL, ANN ARBOR.

and Bones — the men of the former being selected, it is supposed, for their social position and qualities of good-fellowship, while those of the latter are usually good scholars or prominent athletes.

Thus we have the three classes of student societies — the old literary societies, still flourishing in the older colleges of the South, but languishing elsewhere, except at Princeton, where Clio and Whig are still the great institutions of the student body, and at Lafayette, where the Washington and Jefferson are scarcely less prosperous; the peculiar local institutions of Yale and Harvard, *sui generis* and not to be propagated; and the Greek-letter system of chaptered fraternities, the chartered corporations of which are to-day the most prominent characteristic of American undergraduate social life.

The interval of thirty-five years from the founding of Kappa Alpha to the outbreak of the civil war was the golden age of these fraternities. They sprang up and multiplied with a persistency that should forever make firm the doctrine of the strengthening power of persecution. They were not confined to any one grade of college or to any particular part of the country. They flourished every-

increased difficulty of competing with those that have been long established, still, as the colleges themselves grow, the chapters of the most flourishing fraternities grow with them; so that the increase of the system, as a whole, is both very regular and very considerable. Up to 1883, the date at which the latest general manual of the fraternities appeared, there were enrolled among the 32 general college fraternities of this country, forming an aggregate of 505 active chapters, no less than 67,941 members, representing every possible profession and branch of business, every shade of religious and political opinion, and every State and Territory of the United States. But these figures by no means tell the whole story of

ALPHA TAU OMEGA HALL, SEWANEE.

ALPHA PHI (LADIES') LODGE, SYRACUSE.

the growth and spread of the "little" college fraternities. Many colleges and advanced technical schools in every section of the country, besides welcoming the general fraternities to their privileges, have ambitiously started and preserved local fraternities that are limited or have no branches at other institutions, but nevertheless often enjoy a large share of local patronage. These societies, of which there are 16 now in existence, had a membership of 4077. But this is not all. The female students, not to be outdone, about a dozen years ago began to organize sisterhoods, from which males were ignominiously debarred from membership, and had meantime succeeded in building up 7 prosperous societies, with 16 chapters and 2038 members, situated mostly in co-educational institutions. When to this grand total of 74,056 names are added the large membership of the Princeton halls, the Harvard clubs, and the Yale senior societies, already described, together with the very numerous class organizations in various colleges, it may be seen how firm a hold the spirit of cooperation has taken upon the collegians of the country. The fraternities have grown far away from the persecutions of their early days, when the hands of all men and faculties were raised against them. Because they met in secret, and held themselves free from the intrusion of the faculty for one night in the week, and adorned their poor little badges with Greek letters, all evil and rebellious conduct was charged against them. Though their purposes were sensible enough, and good rather than evil has come from them, a nameless stigma of bad parentage still rests upon the whole system, to live down which, by an overplus of actual and visible good attainment, has not been possible till within recent years. But prejudice has an unequal contest with conviction. Through persecution, and poverty of opportunity, and lack of means the new society men fought their way towards solid ground, finding in their struggles and in their ambitions for the success and honors of their fraternities an incentive and charm college life had till then never yielded.

Whatever may have been the shortcomings of the American college boy of a quarter of a century ago, want of energy was not one of them. To take off his coat and go to work with his hands seemed to him the most natural thing when he needed a society lodge. In this way was built, in 1855, the famous "log-cabin" of Delta Kappa Epsilon at Kenyon College, Gambier, Ohio. The site selected was a deep ravine, far away from any human dwelling. Neighboring farmers were hired to fell the trees and to raise the frame of this ark of a house, forty-five feet in length by ten in height. The entire chapter (including its youngest member, now an orator of national reputation several times elected to Congress) rested not until they had plastered the outside crevices with mud. Inside the room was nicely ceiled, and furnished with good tables and chairs, a carpet, and several pictures. The walls and roof of the building were ingeniously deadened with saw-dust and charcoal, so that not the remotest whispers could reach the ears of curious eavesdroppers, if any such should have the temerity to penetrate to the recesses of this sylvan retreat. " A cooking-stove, with skillet, griddles, and pots complete, was the pride of the premises," writes an old member, " where each hungry boy could roast his own potatoes, or cook his meat on a forked stick, in true bandit style."

DELTA KAPPA EPSILON LOG-CABIN, KENYON.

The building of this lodge gave a great impetus to the owning of society homesteads. Before this the various chapters had been accustomed to rendezvous stealthily in college garrets, at village hotels, or anywhere that circumstances and pursuing faculties made most convenient. But when the assurance was once gained that the fraternities might own their premises and make them permanent abiding-places, the whole system became straightway established on a lasting foundation. In 1861, at Yale, the parent chapter of

ALPHA DELTA PHI LODGE, ANN ARBOR.

the same fraternity, Delta Kappa Epsilon, built for itself a two-story hall in the form of a well-proportioned Greek temple, and this proved to be the beginning of a long epoch of more and more elaborate house-building, the culmination of which has scarcely been reached at the present day.

From the temple-shaped hall with its facilities for the routine work of the chapter, its dramatic and social festivities, the most enterprising fraternities progressed gradually towards ample homesteads, thoroughly equipped for dealing with every phase of student life, including the furnishing of comfortable board and lodging, which, in some features, excelled the average dormitories. The work began in earnest about fifteen years ago, but the past two or three years have excelled all the others combined, both in an intelligent understanding of what was needed to make the houses thoroughly habitable and creditable in appearance, and in the amount of superior work planned in detail or actually accomplished. A critical comparison of the specimens in existence reveals the fact that pretty nearly every kind of known architecture has been tried. At Princeton one may see in the twin temples of Whig and Clio copies of the Ionic architecture; at Cambridge, should he visit the A. D. Club, he could scarcely fail to notice

CHI PSI LODGE, AMHERST.

that this hospitable mansion is the veritable traditional New England homestead, with its air of little pretense and much comfort. At Yale, "Bones Hall" is venerable and picturesque when covered by the foliage of its ivy; the magnificent building of "Keys" is of Moorish pattern; the new "Wolf's Head" society, at the same college, honors our ancestors in the "Old Home" by choosing a corbel-stepped gable, "fretting the sky," to which the English and the Dutch of several centuries ago were noticeably partial; the stone Delta Psi lodges at New Haven and Hartford are veritable castles for strength and ruggedness of outline; no gentleman would need a more tasteful or finely located villa than one of the fraternity houses which he would find at Ithaca; while by Delta Kappa Epsilon at Amherst has been

DELTA PSI HALL, S. S. S., YALE.

introduced, and by Sigma Delta Chi at Yale has been elaborated, what seems probable to become the reigning type — that of "cloisters," in which are lodged the members, joined by gallery or covered way to the "chapel," where are celebrated the rites of the chapter.

If the fraternities as a whole have had a weakness, it has been for what they were pleased to believe was the "Queen Anne style" — a "spread" of red bricks, irregular, very irregular, tile roofs, and an unknown quantity of bowed windows, with the usual accessories of modern stained-glass "Venetian" blinds, and unlimited opportunity for portières. These experiments, as embodied by some amateur architect, most likely a well-meaning but untrained member of the chapter, have not always been successful; but lately the bizarre mode has given way to better taste, and in all probability the next efforts of the fraternities at house-building will be characterized by solidity rather than show, by harmony rather than conspicuousness. Several of the college faculties have, with the consent of their boards of trustees, presented enterprising societies with valuable building-sites on their grounds; and where their invitations have been accepted, they have no cause to regret their generosity.

In interior decoration the houses of the American college fraternities differ no less radically than in external appearance. At a Western lodge the members are often content with, and indeed think themselves fortunate if

SIGMA PHI LODGE, WILLIAMS.

DELTA PSI LODGE, TRINITY.

they have at their command, the bare necessities of life, while not a few of the wealthy chapter-houses of the East are furnished with all the luxury and refined taste of the highest modern art as applied to club life. For instance, the lodge-room of the Delta Psi fraternity in New York City is magnificently furnished in Egyptian designs especially imported from Thebes for this purpose, at a cost of several thousands of dollars; and in the buildings of the Alpha Delta Phi at Wesleyan, the Psi Upsilon at Cornell, the Chi Psi at Amherst, and the Sigma Phi at Williams may be found wood-work, furniture, and objects of art which would be in no wise out of place in the most attractive of modern city homes. Several of the foremost chapters, such as the Sigma Phi, the Alpha Delta Phi, and the Kappa Alpha of Williams College, have been presented with valuable memorials by the friends or relatives of deceased members, which are introduced so as to form conspicuous features of the buildings. Thus the last

of the three societies just named contains a strikingly beautiful emblematic window, designed by Tiffany & Co. of New York. The Samuel Eell's Memorial Hall, at Hamilton College, is itself a tribute to the brilliant young founder of the Alpha Delta Phi fraternity, who died after a short career of great promise at the Cincinnati bar as a law partner of the late Chief-Justice Chase. Other representative lodges have been built or beautified by the generosity of individuals.

With the aid of rich sons and generous parents and friends, the loading down of college lodge-rooms might easily be carried to an unfortunate extreme, especially if a false spirit of rivalry should gain a foothold in our college world. But at present there seems little danger of this. An honorable ambition prevails among the leaders of the best fraternities to make their homes complete and attractive in every particular, but beyond this they do not seek to go. The energies of those who

DELTA PSI HALL, NEW YORK CITY.

DELTA KAPPA EPSILON LODGE AND HALL, AMHERST.

have charge should be directed especially to adorning the chapter-houses with what illustrates and improves student life in general, and with what is of particular importance to the members of the college or university at which the chapter-house is located.

Of the value of the real and personal property belonging to the ten American college fraternities that are represented by at least one chapter-house each, and the leaders by

ALPHA DELTA PHI LODGE, WILLIAMS (MEMORIAL PORCH).

five or more, it may safely be said that the sum is fast approaching a million of dollars; while numerous other fraternities and chapters have well-invested and rapidly accumulating building-funds.

The fraternity literature is another interesting subject. The hideous reptiles and winged monsters, the burning altars and dungeon bars, and other such fantastic symbolism with which the magazines and newspapers of some of the fraternities are decorated, prove to cover interesting and oftentimes useful tables of contents, including reminiscences of college life and literary articles by prominent graduates, news-letters from the chapters at the different colleges, personal gossip concerning alumni, official notices from the officers of the fraternity, editorial comments, and notes from exchanges. Two or three of these society periodicals have attained a large circulation. The fraternities have not confined their energies to current papers, however, but have compiled elaborate record books of their members, in the form of catalogues, which, besides containing the names and occupations of members, give succinct sketches of the chapters and the colleges at which they are situate, interesting tables of residence and relationship, and brief biographical sketches of the most distinguished graduates. But decidedly the freshest and most characteristic literature possessed by the fraternities are their song-books, where, in varied and not always correct verse, the youthful laureates have sung the praises of their clans, comrades, festal nights, the charms of good-fellowship, and many other such tempting themes for the imagination and the heart.

Till about a dozen years ago few or none of the fraternities had a strong executive government, but were managed by the oldest chapter, or by several chapters in turn, and by the hasty edicts of the general conventions of the order. But this system proving inadequate, the leaders conceived and boldly acted on the idea of taking the general executive administration of the college fraternities out of the hands of the undergraduate members, at the same time appealing to the graduate members to assume an active share in their welfare. So far their success has been noteworthy. The graduate councils, which now form the executive department of most of the leading fraternities, are ably managed, and graduate associations of the larger fraternities have been formed in most of the important cities. They hold reunions, banquets, and business meetings, and in most essentials serve as graduate chapters of their orders, cementing old college ties and forming new ones between members of different colleges; and several of the fraternities, such as the Delta Psi, the Delta Phi, the Delta Kappa Epsilon, the Alpha Delta Phi, the Psi Upsilon, the Zeta Psi, and the Delta Upsilon, have lately taken the advanced step of establishing in the large cities regular club-houses, which are well equipped, and well patronized by men of all ages; while at Chautauqua, the "Wooglin" club-house, with its ample accommodations and grounds, is the summer headquarters of the Beta Theta Pi, by a graduate corporation of which it is owned.

The legislative functions of the fraternities still rest with the annual conventions, which are usually held with the different undergraduate chapters in turn, when, be-

FIELD MEMORIAL WINDOW, KAPPA ALPHA LODGE, WILLIAMS.

sides the transaction of routine business, the several hundred students present from all parts of the country are occupied with social courtesies extended to them by local residents, and with literary efforts in the form of orations and poems, often delivered by members of the fraternity who have attained eminence in public life.

In view of the facts already presented in the course of this narrative, a defense of the fraternities, a summing-up of all the reasons on which their existence and continuance might be justified, seems altogether superfluous. This one significant feature of the case may however be offered to the dubious without comment, as pointing its own moral — that so far, whenever the majesty of the law has been invoked by still obstinate faculties or trustees to drive the fraternities from their institutions, the law has upheld the continuance of the societies and the free rights of the students to join them, provided that in doing so they do not violate any of the proper functions of the college. It was so in 1879, when the faculty of the University of California tried to disband a society which had been allowed to erect a house on college land, and was met by the hostile criticisms of the entire press of that State; it was so in 1882, when the president of Purdue University, Indiana, striving to compel students entering his university not to join any of the societies, was prevented by a decision of the superior court of that State, and in the end resigned his office. The one notable exception to this rule is the case of the College of New Jersey. Here the faculty succeeded in expelling all the fraternities; but it was before the era of their house-building. All of those chapters

KAPPA ALPHA LODGE, WILLIAMS.

PHI KAPPA PSI (MEMORIAL) LODGE, GETTYSBURG.

which have built houses are now incorporated institutions, paying taxes on their real and personal property, and entitled to the full privileges and protection of local and State laws.

They therefore appear to rest on a more solid basis than mere sufferance; and however ardently certain individuals may wish to see them abolished, it is extremely doubtful if even an organized crusade against them, headed by all the college presidents in the United States and the majority of the faculties under them, could succeed in doing more than to drive the reputable societies into a temporary seclusion, from which, in a few years, they would emerge stronger than ever. Such at least has been the case at many representative institutions.

But the above supposition is relegated to the realms of the impossible when one discovers that a large portion of the educators referred to are themselves members of the fraternities, and in many cases actively associated with their progress. This list includes such men as President Eliot of Harvard, Dwight of Yale, Walker of the Boston Institute of Technology, Seelye of Amherst, White of Cornell, Dwight of the Columbia Law School, Gilman of Johns Hopkins University, Johnston of Tulane, and Northrop of the University of Minnesota. There is not a faculty of any size in the United States that does not contain society members, and few professorial chairs at the largest colleges are not filled by representatives of the leading fraternities. These "little societies" have supplied forty governors to most of the largest States of the Union; and had in the last administration the President of the United States and the majority of his Cabinet. On the Supreme Bench of the United States the fraternities are now represented by five of the associate justices. A summary, published in 1885, showed Alpha Delta Phi, Psi Upsilon, and Delta Kappa Epsilon to have furnished of United States senators and representatives 39, 25, and 36

respectively; while in the last Congress 13 representatives and 2 senators were members of the last-named fraternity alone; and in the membership of these 3 fraternities are included 24 bishops of the Protestant Episcopal Church. In the class-room they are represented by Whitney and Marsh; in the pulpit, by R. S. Storrs and Phillips Brooks; in the paths of literature, by James Russell Lowell, George William Curtis, Donald G. Mitchell, Charles Dudley Warner, Edward Everett Hale, and E. C. Stedman; in recent public life, by Presidents Arthur and Garfield, by Wayne Mac-Veagh, Charles S. Fairchild, Robert T. Lincoln, John D. Long, William M. Evarts, Joseph R. Hawley, and William Walter Phelps. These gentlemen were not elected into the fraternities after graduation, but were active supporters of these organizations during their undergraduate days. Whatever, then, may be the shortcomings of college secret societies, it is to their credit that their exponents are men noted for ability and prominence in every useful sphere of life, as well as for mere culture and congeniality, while from end to end of the catalogued chapter-lists run in thick procession the starred names of the most brilliant and lamented of the young officers who fell in the battles of our civil war — in the blue and gray ranks alike. Judging the system by its deeds only, it is difficult to escape the conclusion that the best societies have in reality been groups of picked men among the fortunate few, comparatively speaking, who are able to incur the expense of a college education.

In almost every college where the secret societies have flourished attempts have been made, some of them quite successful, to carry on local anti-secret societies; and there has existed for many years an anti-secret fraternity, with chapters placed in different colleges, which has been patterned very closely after the societies calling themselves secret, both as to means and ends. But in one case only, that of Delta Upsilon, have the anti-secret orders

DELTA PSI LODGE, WILLIAMS.

PSI UPSILON LODGE, HAMILTON.

been able to keep pace with their secret rivals, in either the quality of their membership, their activity in college affairs, or their increase in material resources. Even here this has been the result of assimilation to the secret fraternities, till now, so far as Delta Upsilon can effect it, the distinction between itself and the secret fraternities is simply that the latter exposes somewhat more private business than do they, and, as to the rest, terms "privacy" what they call "secrecy."

Mr. Warner has said:

Notwithstanding their formation is only in obedience to an ancient and universal love in human nature, they are attacked because they are secret. I suppose that some of them are guardians of the occult mysteries of Egypt and India, that they know what once was only known to augurs, flamens, and vestal virgins, and perhaps to the priests of Osiris; others keep some secret knowledge of the formation of the alphabet, or preserve the secret of nature preserved in the Rule of Three, and know why it was not the Rule of Four; while others, in midnight conclave, study the ratio of the cylinder to the inscribed sphere. It matters not. I have never yet met any one who knew these secrets, whatever they are, who thought there was any moral dynamite in them; never one who had shared them who did not acknowledge their wholesome influence in his college life. I mean, of course, the reputable societies; I am acquainted with no other.

The constitutions of many college fraternities are now open to the inspection of faculties; the most vigorous publish detailed accounts of their conventions and social gatherings; nearly all of the homesteads are on occasions opened for the reception of visitors; their rites, ceremonies, and even the appearance of their *sancta sanctorum*, are quite accurately apprehended by rival societies — in short, the old shibboleth of secrecy is a myth rather than a reality.

The shrewdest college presidents have long since discovered that to control undergraduate action with a firm though gentle hand they have only frankly to bespeak the aid and win the confidence and assistance of the fraternities represented at their institutions. It is thus

that we come to see and to realize the importance of such unique departures from the traditional, ever-antagonistic relations between the faculties and the students of large colleges as those lately put into operation at Amherst, Bowdoin, and other colleges; where all matters relating to the privileges and penalties of the students are adjusted to a code of laws which is administered, and from time to time amended, by a council of undergraduates, representing the fraternities, acting in concert with one or more members of the faculty. This simple and amicable relationship between those desiring to obtain knowledge and those desiring to impart it has already been attended with very gratifying results.

Illustrated by such cases as that of Amherst and Bowdoin, and reënforced by the healthy tone of the fraternity press, which has not failed to wage war on what is reprehensible or deficient in our college life, and has labored to inculcate in their members the obligations which they owe to their college and to the members of rival societies as well as of their own, the words of General Stewart L. Woodford, in speaking of the early days of the societies, seem amply justified, and to promise even larger and still more excellent fruit in the near future:

To no one cause more than to the fraternity movement has been due the altered conditions of college culture. . . . In matters of study and discipline each student is now largely guided by his personal predilections, by the advice of those whom he sees fit to consult, by the moral force of his chosen associates. These associations are now determined in many colleges by the Greek-letter societies or fraternities.

PHI NU THETA LODGE, WESLEYAN.

DELTA UPSILON LODGE, MADISON.

That they can use without abusing their privileges was very well expressed by President White, at the dedication of the new Psi Upsilon house at Cornell:

Both theory and experience show us that when a body of young men in a university like this are given a piece of property, a house, its surroundings, its reputation, which for the time being is their own, for which they are responsible, in which they take pride, they will treat it carefully, lovingly, because the honor of the society they love is bound up in it.

He added the following profound observations as the result of his long experience, both here and abroad:

One of the most unpleasant things in college life hitherto has been the fact that the students have considered themselves as practically something more than boys, and therefore not under tutors and governors; but something less than men, and therefore not amenable to the ordinary laws of society. Neither the dormitory nor the students' boarding-house is calculated to better this condition of things, for neither has any influence in developing the sense of manly responsibility in a student. But houses such as I am happy to say this society and its sister societies are to erect on these grounds seem to solve the problem in a far better way. They give excellent accommodations at reasonable prices; they can be arranged in such a manner and governed by such rules as to promote seclusion for study during working-hours; they afford opportunities for the alumni and older students to exercise a good influence upon the younger; they give those provisions for the maintenance of health which can hardly be expected in student barracks, or in the ordinary student boarding-house, and in the long run can be made more economical. But what I prize most of all in a house like this is its educating value; for such a house tends to take those who live in it out of the category of boys and to place them in the category of men. To use an old English phrase, it gives them "a stake in the country."

President Seelye of Amherst College, in an address on June 28, 1887, states, referring to the Greek-letter fraternities:

The aim of these societies is, I say, improvement in literary culture and in manly character, and this aim is reasonably justified by the results. It is not accidental that the foremost men in college, as a rule, belong to some of these societies. That each society should seek for its membership the best scholars, the best writers and speakers, the best men of a class, shows well where its strength is thought to lie. A student entering one of these societies finds a healthy stimulus in the repute which his fraternity shall share from his successful work. The rivalry of individuals loses much of its narrowness, and almost all of its envy, when the prize which the individual seeks is valued chiefly for its benefit to the fellowship to which he belongs. Doubtless members of these societies often remain narrow-minded and laggard in the race, after all the influence of their society has been expended upon them, but the influence is a broadening and a quickening one notwithstanding. Under its power the self-conceit of a young man is more likely to give way to self-control than otherwise. . . .

To represent all the fraternities as standing on anything like the same high plane as to membership, progress in the past, and prospects for the future would be misleading. My thoughts have naturally turned to the standing, the equipment, the aspirations, or perhaps only the pretty dreams of those fraternities which deserve to be ranked as the leaders in the race — that some day all the colleges of the United States will be veritable and acknowledged student democracies; that the fraternity buildings, though smaller than the college halls, will equal the latter in durability and completeness of appointment; that all the large cities will have graduate clubs, where the college fraternity man can renew the old associations that he cherished when a student.

The leading fraternities are fond of affirming the difference in their standard qualifications for membership. Some venerate high scholarship; others pride themselves on the aristocracy of birth or wealth; still others recognize the claims of a heartier and more democratic spirit. This may be true; and yet in all of them there is enough good-fellowship to attract the cultured and enough culture to

PSI UPSILON LODGE, TRINITY.

improve the sociable. They illustrate a law of nature and a law of man, in the tendency of atoms with affinities to form into groups. Having outgrown weaknesses and prejudices, they may be expected to enjoy a career of prosperity.

28

THE QUESTION OF COEDUCATION

BY DAVID STARR JORDAN, LL.D.

PRESIDENT OF LELAND STANFORD JUNIOR UNIVERSITY

DR. JORDAN DENIES THAT COEDUCATION INJURES OUR EDUCATIONAL STANDARDS OR DETERS WOMEN FROM MARRIAGE — HE MAINTAINS THAT IT IS A BENEFIT TO BOTH SEXES AND A DEMONSTRATED SUCCESS

THE essential part of the argument of President Hall's essay is directed, not against coeducation in colleges, but rather against certain abuses, real, half real, or imaginary, in our educational methods in general.

With his contention that we should not give to our girls such an education as will interfere with successful maternity, we may all agree at once. We should not adopt for the fairest and wisest of our maidens methods which will leave them celibate or sterile. No one would favor such a system of education, and no such system exists in fact. Furthermore, such a system is inconceivable as a matter of practical application.

We may also agree with President Hall in deprecating the process by which women and womanish men hold a large majority of the teachers' positions in our high schools and normal schools. This feminization of secondary education has its good sides, but it has been carried much too far, and with serious injury to the effectiveness of these schools.

Dr. Hall cleverly notices the "almost wifely subordination" of the high school to the college, as shown in the "meek acceptance of the prescription of blocks of standardized, shop-worn knowledge," and in the "growing difficulty for any high school or teacher to strike out for anything new." This condition, as he correctly states, reaches a culmination in the normal schools, which illustrate almost the terminal stage of feminization.

We may admit at once that all this is not for the best. These secondary and training schools are controlled by women without being in any sense adapted to women. Still worse, they are adjusted not to woman's best needs, but rather to the ways of feminine crudity.

But this state of affairs has nothing to do with coeducation. Women are chosen as teachers because they will work for lower wages. The classes are large, and the governing boards wish to make the money go as far as it may. Incidentally, too, women teachers are more docile, and, as resignations occur with them more frequently than with men, there are more vacancies for the governing board to fill.

Now that the facts in this connection are becoming clearly seen, our school authorities are finding the remedy. Very many schools are making a conscious effort to replace the surplus of women by men—in some places even by real men, men who could succeed in other professions, and who are able to demand more than a woman's wages.

BOYS AND GIRLS IN THE HIGH SCHOOLS

It is true, too, that there are notable differences in the development of young men and young women. It may be that these differences warrant, or even demand, separate schools and separate

EDITOR'S NOTE—This article is a reply to a paper by G. Stanley Hall, president of Clark University, which appeared in the February number of MUNSEY'S MAGAZINE, and in which Dr. Hall pointed out the dangers of the coeducational system.

treatment in the high school period, although this does not necessarily follow from the known facts of psychology or physiology. That girls, in some stage of their development, are naturally timorous, or gushing, or trivial, is no indication whatever that these traits should be encouraged. Under selection, nature eliminates an undesirable stage of growth as rigidly as she cuts out unfitness among adults. If the callow youth develops metaphoric "pin-feathers" at some stage of his growth, we do not need to encourage these excrescences. Still less do we need to tolerate the equally metaphoric "wild oats" which often grow contemporaneously with "pin-feathers." Nor can we plead the existence of a brutish stage in youth as a reason for encouraging brutishness. The biological law of recapitulation, the law that the development of the individual repeats that of the race—a necessary corollary of the law of heredity—has been made responsible for a multitude of fantasies, psychologic and pedagogic. It is surely bad form to take liberties with biology, unless one is on pretty intimate terms with her and receives her favors at first hand.

There is no doubt that many women suffer for life from causes arising in the grammar school and high school period. It is not evident that coeducation is often a factor in these matters, unless it be through the toleration of social excesses by negligent school officials. These same excesses are far more frequent among young people who are not in school. In general, the fault rests neither with coeducation nor with education, but with unwholesome habits of life—bad air, damp clothing, too much street-car life, late hours, improper food, candies, coffee, starch-indigestion, or lack of exercise and sleep. Of course, boys suffer from the same causes, though usually in a less degree, and to build separate high schools for the two sexes does not necessarily furnish a remedy.

THE BENEFITS OF ASSOCIATION

The essential argument for coeducation in the university is the argument for the university itself. Special subjects can be taught in detached and specialized schools. The university makes better manhood. Its function, in Emerson's words, is to "bring every ray of genius to its hospitable halls, by their combined influence to set the heart of the youth in flame."

For these reasons, it is better for any body of students that they be taught in company with other kinds of students. Culture studies and technical studies gain from mutual association. The man who pursues each gains from contact with other types of mind.

This argument is especially cogent in institutions in which the individuality of the student is recognized and respected. In such schools each man, by his relation to action and realities, becomes a teacher of women in these regards, as, in other ways, each cultivated woman is a teacher of men.

In woman's education, as planned for women alone, the tendency is toward the study of beauty and order. Literature and language take precedence over science. Expression is valued more highly than action. In carrying this to an extreme, the necessary relation of thought to action becomes obscured. The scholarship developed is not effective, because it is not related to success. The educated woman is likely to master technique, rather than art; method, rather than substance. She may know a good deal, but she is not effective in action. Often her views of life must undergo painful changes before she can find her place in the world.

In schools for men alone, the reverse condition often obtains. The sense of reality obscures the elements of beauty and fitness.

It is of great advantage to both men and women to meet on a plane of equality in education. Women are brought into contact with men who can do things—men in whom the sense of reality is strong, and who have definite views of life. This influence affects them for good. It turns them away from sentimentalism. It gives tone to their religious thoughts and impulses. Above all, it tends to encourage action as governed by ideals, as opposed to that resting on caprice. It gives them better standards of what is possible and impossible when the responsibility for action is thrown upon them.

In like manner, the association with

wise, sane, and healthy women has its value for young men. It raises their ideal of womanhood, and the highest manhood must be associated with the possession of an ideal.

THE CHARGES AGAINST COEDUCATION

It is not true that the character of college work has been in any way lowered by coeducation. The reverse is decidedly the case. It is true that untimely zeal of one sort or another has filled the West with a host of so-called colleges. It is true that most of these are weak, and are doing poor work in poor ways. It is true that most of them are coeducational. It is also true that the great majority of their students are not of college grade at all. In such schools low standards rule, both as to scholarship and as to manners. The student fresh from the country, with no preparatory training, will bring the manners of his home. These are not always good manners, as manners are judged. But none of these defects is derived from coeducation; nor are any of these conditions made worse by it.

Very lately it has been urged against coeducation that its social demands cause too much strain both on young men and young women. College men and college women being mutually attractive, the result is that there are too many receptions, dances, and other functions in which they enjoy each other's company. But this is a matter easily regulated. At the most, the average young woman in college spends in social matters less than one-tenth the time she would spend at home.

With the young man, the whole matter represents the difference between high-class and low-class associates and associations. When college men stand in normal relation with college women meeting them in society as well as in the class-room, there is distinctly less of drunkenness, rowdyism, and vice than obtains under other conditions. And no harm comes to the young woman through the good influence she exerts. To meet freely the best young men she will ever know, the wisest, cleanest, and strongest, can surely do no harm to a young woman. The best young men and the best young women, all things considered,

are in our colleges. This always has been and always will be the case.

It is true that coeducation is often attempted under very adverse conditions. Conditions are adverse when the little girls of preparatory schools and schools of music are mingled with college students and allowed to have the same freedom. This is wrong, whatever the kind of discipline offered, lax or strict; the two classes need a different sort of treatment.

Coeducation in the class-room offers no difficulties or embarrassments whatever. The problem, such as it is, is one of proper housing and oversight outside the class-room. When young women have no residence devoted to their use, and are forced to rent parlors and garrets in private houses of an unsympathetic village, evil results sometimes arise. These are not to be charged to coeducation, but to the unfit conditions that make the pursuit of personal culture difficult or impossible. Women are more readily affected by surroundings than men are, and squalid, ill-regulated, Bohemian conditions should not be part of their higher education.

THE "COLLEGE ATMOSPHERE"

Another condition very common and very undesirable is that in which young women live at home and traverse a city twice each day on railway or street-cars to meet their recitations in some college. The greatest instrument of culture in a college is the college atmosphere, the personal influence exerted by its professors and students. This atmosphere develops feebly in the rush of a great city. The *spur-studenten,* or railway students, as the Germans call them—the students who live far from the university—get very little of it.

The young woman who attends the university under these conditions contributes nothing to the university atmosphere, and therefore receives very little from it. She may attend her recitations and pass her examinations, but she is in all essential respects *in absentia.* So far as the best influences of the university are concerned, she is neither coeducated nor educated.

In the English universities the question of where the student should live has been made all-important, almost excluding consideration of methods of study, or even of the relative value or significance of the subject-matter of education. In America we have too much neglected this. We have housed our students in barracks, or, even worse, not housed them at all. We have exposed them, men and women alike, to the vulgarity of the small village or the wear and tear of a great city.

We know that manly men and womanly women are largely made such by association; yet we locate colleges in places where rational association is impossible. We expect great results from the college atmosphere; yet we place our colleges where they can develop no atmosphere of their own. To get the most from a college education, the student, man or woman, should enter into the college atmosphere; and, more than this, he should help to create it. There is a good deal of loose talk about college spirit; but behind it all is a very real thing. The *gemeingeist unter freien geistern,* the comradery of free spirits, is one of the chief elements in all higher education. And this element cannot be developed with men or women under conditions in which real comradery is impossible.

SOME OPPONENTS OF COEDUCATION

We cannot deny that there has arisen in the last few years a reaction against coeducation in our colleges. In so far as this is honest, it is a reaction not against coeducation, but against the lack of provision for wholesome living. It is a protest against turning girls loose unaided and unguarded in college towns, in which adequate safeguards exist neither for them nor for young men. If, for example, Vassar College had no dormitories, and if her students lived as they pleased, in Poughkeepsie or all along the railway to New York, we should have there all the real evils charged to coeducation.

There are about three classes of college boys who seem to object to the presence of college women, and these may be classed as the boorish, the dilettante, and the dissolute. If these are to remain such, the sooner they are out of college the better for others, and often the better for themselves.

I have rarely found opposition to coeducation on the part of really serious students. The majority are strongly in favor of it, but the minority in this as in many other cases make the most noise. The rise of a student movement against coeducation almost always accompanies a general recrudescence of academic vulgarity.

Sometimes, too, the college athlete objects to the presence of women in college. In athletic matters the young women give very little assistance. They cannot play on the teams, they cannot yell, and they are rarely generous with their money in helping those who can. A college of a thousand students, half women, counts for no more athletically than one of five hundred, all men. It is vainly imagined that colleges are ranked by their athletic prowess, and that every woman admitted keeps out a man, and this man a potential punter or sprinter. There is not much truth in all this, and if there were, it is of no consequence. College athletics is in its essence by-play, most worthy and valuable for many reasons, but nevertheless only an adjunct to the real work of the college, which is education.

Of like grade is the feeling that men count for more than women, because they are more likely to be heard from in after life. Therefore their education is of more importance, and the presence of women impedes it.

A certain adverse influence comes from the fact that the oldest and wealthiest of our institutions are for men or for women alone. These send out a body of alumni who know nothing of coeducation, and who judge it with the positiveness of ignorance. Most men filled with the time-honored traditions of Harvard and Yale, of which the most permeating is that of Harvard's or Yale's infallibility, are against coeducation on general principles. Similar influences in favor of the separate education of women go out from the sister institutions of the East. The methods of the experimenting, irreverent, idol-breaking West find no favor in their eyes.

THE FEAR OF FEMINIZATION

The only serious new argument against coeducation is that derived from the fear of the adoption by universities of woman's standards of art and science rather than those of man, the fear that amateurism would take the place of specialization in our higher education. Women take up higher education because they enjoy it; men because their careers depend upon it. Only men, broadly speaking, are capable of objective studies. It is man's province to face fact without flinching, unswayed by feeling or preference. The reality with woman is the way in which the fact affects her. Original investigation, creative art, the "resolute facing of the world as it is"—all these belong to man's world rather than to that of the average woman.

It is quite true, as President Hall has clearly shown, that the work of the woman student in college, in almost all fields except the creative, is better than that of men of the same age. Girls are more docile than boys; they take better care of their time; they see from a nearer viewpoint; they are cleaner, not only in their work, but in their acts; they write better examination papers; they are saved from vice not alone by environment but by instinct. In general, they excel in the conventional courses, especially in those against which the average healthy boy has for generations rebelled.

They excel in others, as President Hall indicates, because these courses appeal to their tastes. The girls compete for outworn prizes, and will complete a useless piece of work with a care and patience which a boy will rarely show on better material. Form is likely to interest women more than substance. On the other hand, women will also do real things with real ability, and perhaps any enumeration of the intellectual differences between men and women as students is likely to exaggerate these differences.

It has been feared that the admission of women to the university would vitiate the masculinity of its standards, that neatness of technique would impair boldness of conception, and delicacy of taste replace soundness of results. It is claimed that the preponderance of high school educated women in ordinary society is showing some such effects in matters of current opinion. For example, it is claimed that the university extension course is no longer of university nature. It is a lyceum course designed to please women who enjoy a little poetry, play, and music, who read the novels of the day, who dabble in theosophy, Christian science, or psychology, who cultivate their astral bodies and think there is something in palmistry, and who are edified by a candy-coated ethics of self-realization. There is nothing ruggedly true, nothing masculine left in it.

Current literature and history are affected by the same influences. Women pay clever actors to teach them, not Shakespeare or Goethe, but how one ought to feel on reading "King Lear" or "Faust." If the women of society do not read a book, it will scarcely pay to publish it. Science is popularized in the same fashion by ceasing to be science and becoming mere sentiment or pleasing information. This is shown by the number of books on how to study a bird, a flower, a tree, or a star, through an operaglass, and without knowing anything about it. Such studies may be good for the feelings or even for the moral nature, but they have no elements of that "fanaticism for veracity" which is the highest attribute of the educated man.

These results of the education of many women and of a few men, by which the half-educated woman becomes a controlling social factor, have been lately set in strong light by Dr. Münsterberg; but they are used by him, not as an argument against coeducation, but for the purpose of urging the better education of more men. They form likewise an argument for the better education of more women. The remedy for feminine dilettanteism is found in more severe training. Current literature reflects the taste of the leisure class. The women with leisure who read and discuss vapid books are not representative of woman's higher education. Most of them have never been educated at all.

In any event, this gives no argument against coeducation. It is thorough training, not separate training, which is indicated as the need of the times. Where this training is taken is a secondary matter, though I believe with the fulness of certainty that better results, mental, moral, and physical, can be obtained in coeducation than in any monastic form of instruction.

COEDUCATION AND MARRIAGE

Finally, does not coeducation lead to marriage? President Hall admits that it furnishes " some gain for each individual in widening his acquaintance with the other sex," but he is also alarmed to find that " the constant association of the two sexes tends to rub off a little of the charm which each feels for the other," and as a presumable result, many otherwise delightful men and women tend to turn with favor to celibacy.

We need not worry over this, because it is. in fact not true, and because if it were, its effects would be of little consequence in the development of the race. Love and marriage and parenthood will' go on normally whatever our scheme of education.

No doubt university training of women, as distinguished from college training, postpones marriage, and probably the majority of the women taking advanced training have in some degree placed some other ideal, at least as a present aim, before that of matrimony. Some of these women are perhaps "agamic" or "agenic" by nature ; and, if so, doubtless they ought not to marry under any circumstances. They do right to cherish the highest aims available to themselves, even if these be not the highest for other more fortunate women. But there is not the slightest evidence that highly educated women are necessarily rendered sterile or celibate by their education. The best wives in the world belong to this class. They bring their husbands not only love and sympathy, but the highest form of personal and professional helpfulness. The difference between a wise woman as a wife and " one who might have been wise and was not " is so great as to outbalance any minor handicap on the part of the well-trained woman.

It is true, no doubt, that cultivated women are more exacting than other women. They are less likely to marry for convenience, and they expect more from their husbands. For these same reasons, their marriages are less likely to prove unhappy.

The woman who finishes creditably the undergraduate course in a well-regulated American college, coeducational or otherwise, has accomplished no *tour de force,* and has performed no dangerous feat of mental gymnastics. She has lived for four years an essentially normal life under wholesome and uplifting conditions. The college girl, normal when her course of study began, is not on her graduation asthenic, anemic, neurotic, or indifferent to matters of love and maternity. The normal girl of seventeen, eighteen, or nineteen has become a normal woman of twenty-one, twenty-two, or twenty-three. Whatever fitness for married life may have been hers by inheritance, she has retained it, with the gain of four years of wholesome exercise, of broadened horizon, and of association with men and women worth knowing.

It is doubtless true that the longer a woman remains in school, the later, on the average, is her date of marriage. But to postpone marriage until the age of twenty-two, twenty-five, or even thirty, is not fatal to love, or maternity, or wisdom, or anything else that is good. Nor is the future of our race dependent on having every woman bear the largest possible number of children. In so far as education is genuine, it helps a woman to rear an increasing proportion of the number she bears.

The mental activity necessary to a successful college course is not intense enough to interfere with fecundity. If it were so in individual cases, there is not a ghost of a reason for believing that such a condition is hereditary. We need not fear that college education on a large scale means progressive race sterility. This is one of the bugaboos which haunt the infancy of the nascent science of genetic psychology.

An Eastern professor, lately visiting a Western State university, asked one of the seniors what he thought of the question of coeducation.

" I beg your pardon," said the student. " What question do you mean? "

" Why, coeducation," said the professor ; " the education of women in colleges for men."

" Oh! " said the student. " Coeducation is not a question here."

And he was right. Coeducation is never a question where it has been fairly tried.

29

THE·LODGE·AND·ENTRANCE·GATES·AT·WELLESLEY····

UNDERGRADUATE LIFE AT WELLESLEY

By Abbe Carter Goodloe

IF you should happen to be going to Wellesley College on a through sleeper of the Pennsylvania or the New York Central line about the time college opens in the fall, you would probably be painfully aware of your destination long before you reached it. The signs are numerous and unmistakable. There is the "express" two hours behind time on account of the appalling number of sleeping-coaches attached, crowded with eager young women feverishly demanding if the train will stop at Wellesley instead of sweeping on into Boston; and there is the conductor majestically walking up and down, assuring the whole coach that the train *will* stop; and the baggage-master rushing around with two assistants to carry the heavy check-rings, and an anxious and despondent look on his face as if he would very much like to change his occupation in life just then; and there is much spasmodic conversation and a forced air of cheerfulness between young girls and their people who are bringing them up to college to matriculate; and finally, a short way before the train draws into the station, there is a little gasp from those who know and are on the lookout, when the turrets of the big main building loom up just visible above the great oaks and tall, slender maples. And then, in a moment, there is a rush for the platforms and an astonishing number of trunks are tumbled out of the baggage-cars, and the station rapidly assumes the look of the New York customs just after the St. Paul or the Paris has got in, and the college coaches fill up in a minute and go dashing off, while the bewildered new-comers weakly allow themselves to be squeezed into cabs and dislocate their necks in a frantic attempt to get a view of the buildings and grounds on their way up to College Hall. And the people who have been left in the sleepers, and who have been grumbling about the crowd and confusion and delay, go on into Boston feeling a little lonely and much more comfortable.

But if you come out sedately from Boston at no particular time during the semester, the quiet instead of the agitation of the place is what most impresses you; and al-

of the few traditions attaching to that institution—that when the college was founded there were but two men in the village, and one was blind and the other was lame. It may have been so, and it was probably a most judicious idea to establish a college for women where masculine attractions were at a minimum; but I am very sure that whatever the conditions may have been at the beginning of the college, they no longer exist, and that, though there are doubtless a lame and a blind man at present in the village, there are besides a great

Photograph by Partridge, Boston.

"The music plays; vouchsafe some motion to it."
From "Love's Labor's Lost." Presented by the Shakespeare Society, June 12, 1897.

though your train is on a sweeping four-track road, with all such a road's possibilities of shrieking engines apparently running into you from before, or insidiously creeping up on you behind, or passing you triumphantly on either side, you arrive in tranquillity and safety at Wellesley, where there is a typical Boston and Albany station, with its striking family resemblance to all the other Boston and Albany railroad-stations, and its tremendous expanse of slate roof utterly out of proportion to the small amount of brown and white stone and creeping vines just showing beneath.

There is a tradition at Wellesley—one

many others who are apparently quite sound physically. Indeed, Wellesley has become absurdly populous and prosperous, for the great development and changes in the college have led to equally important and noticeable changes in the town. There is a big square with a fountain in the centre of it, and a "block" of business-houses set uncompromisingly and defiantly in a most conspicuous place; and there are electric lights, and a great many broughams and traps are to be seen tearing down to the station for the early express into Boston. And even when it is not train-time there is a great deal going

The Main Building from the Lake.

on, and an uninterrupted procession of young women from the college pass and repass you on the street, either hurriedly and with a very business-like aspect, or else with the air of simply walking about for amusement and relaxation ; or they are patronizing the shops, of which there are an astonishing number for such a place. They are of all sorts and are peculiarly adapted to the needs of the students, especially the fruit-shops, and one devoted to miscellaneous articles, of which there is an assortment in the window varying from photographic views and writing-paper to curtain-poles and Japanese fire-crackers.

This shop always struck me as being particularly delightful and un-American, and I used quite to haunt it, in order to hear the little bell on the door jingle cheerfully at my entrance and exit, and to listen to the person who served me use the most correct English with the very broad "a," and in hopes of hearing the young women, who passed in and out in a continual stream and inquired for the most impossible and diverse things, foiled in their attempts to obtain them. But I was always disappointed — the desired articles were

Stone Hall.

inevitably forthcoming. I suppose there must be some underground connection between that shop and all those in Boston, and that the supply and demand will never cease to balance.

Besides the shops and the business "block" and the station and library and churches, there are the long, shady streets, thickly dotted with cottages, the architects of which have all, seemingly, entered into a frantic competition in the way of piazzas and sloping roofs and bow-windows. The effect is very pretty and homelike, and a

great many professors and instructors from the college have taken up their residence in them. Many of the cottages are filled with the girls who have overflowed from the college buildings, and who stroll around the village with a slightly patronizing air and a consciousness of their own worth and attainments, which must be just a trifle aggravating to the townspeople. Indeed, the presence of so many professors and students lends to the village an air of studiousness and learning which is quite impressive, and one would think that the village people would catch the contagion of hard work and mental discipline. One is continually astonished at not seeing all the old ladies and gentlemen starting. off promptly at nine o'clock with books under their arms, and it is rather a shock to discover that there is a shoemaker in the village who does not know Greek, and a grocer who is quite callous about chemistry.

But, pretty and flourishing as the village is, its chief importance—at least, in the estimation of the college people—is that it is where one gets off the train to go to Wellesley College. There is a variety of ways of reaching the college itself, which is quite a distance from the village. I say " quite a distance," because no one has ever been able to decide just how far the college is from the town. If you have been detained by a lecture or recitation and are trying to catch the last afternoon train in Boston, the

Masquerade on the Evening of Tree Day.

Entertainment Given by the Barn Swallows in "The Barn."

distance is about five miles ; but if your friends have been out and are going back, and you will not see them again for quite a while, it is not more than three-quarters of a mile. Or, if one is in a hurry, and knows just how to go, there is a short cut over "the meadow" and then across through the golf-links, up past Norumbega, the prettiest of the cottages, and so to the big entrance. Or you can follow the broad, shaded street until East Lodge is reached, pass around by Stone Hall—which is not stone at all, but very red brick, and named for the founder—with a glimpse of Music Hall across the woods and, every now and then, a bright glint from Lake Waban through the trees, past the beautiful Farnsworth Art Building, and Wood and Freeman Cottages, and so up around the green campus to the big porte-cochère in front of the great doors.

It is doubtless a very fine thing, and a thing to be proud of and to be remembered, to belong to a college which was founded by Cardinal Wolsey, or Henry VI., or Queen Margaret, or the Bishop of Winchester, or some other exalted personage, and which has a wonderful quadrangle, or a famous gate-way, or a chapel with a splendid fan-vaulted roof. But the students of Wellesley College have a still finer thing to be proud of and to remember. They belong to a college founded by an American gentleman, who, crushed by the loss of his only and dearly loved son, turned from the most brilliant legal and social career, to give " his home, his fortune, and ten years of his life " to raising a monument to the God who had so heavily afflicted him.

The story of Henry Fowle Durant and the founding of Wellesley College is so well known that it hardly seems necessary to touch on it here, and yet it is a story that bears infinite repetition, and certainly once a year—the anniversary of his death, the third of October—is not too often to impress upon those who are profiting by his loss the story of his life and death and work. And surely one Sunday in every year—the

A Tree-day Costume.

first Sunday of the fall semester, known as "Flower Sunday"—is not too many to set apart for service from his favorite text, "God is love." And when, in the inevitable course of time, there shall be no reason why we cannot openly honor the woman who is still with us and who helped him to be what he was, and who gives as generously as he did, Wellesley will couple her name with his in her memorial services, and will be proud to recall publicly that it is as it should be, and that a woman helped to found a woman's college.

There is no more striking difference between a man's and a girl's education than the very way in which they start out to get that education. I mean that, in the selection of their colleges, they show wonderfully dissimilar motives. A man decides upon a certain college because his father and his grandfather went there before him, or, more possibly, because he admires the captain of the foot-ball team extravagantly, or because from his preparatory - school record he thinks he will have a chance on the crew. I know small boys of twelve or thirteen who have been proudly wearing a blue-and-silver pin in the lapel of their Norfolk jackets and telling their astonished relatives that they "have decided to go to Yale," ever since last November, and who will promptly and cheerfully put on the orange

Barn Swallows in Stage Costumes.
Sketches by Miss Cowles.

and black of the "Tigers" should Yale happen to be defeated this year in the great contest.

But the girl has no such precedents or ambitions or aims. "Going to college" is yet so new and important a thing with her, and is so frequently for the purpose of studying, that she conscientiously decides upon the institution where she can get the hardest and most thorough course in her most difficult elective. I have known sisters to separate, on going to college, because one was convinced that a certain institution possessed the most advanced electrical apparatus and the other had been assured that the department of history was superior in the college she had decided to enter. While young women continue to select their colleges from such motives, Wellesley, with her faculty of eighty professors and instructors, and her offer of one hundred and ninety-two courses of study, may fear no diminution in numbers, and freshmen classes of two hundred will still continue to present themselves with unabating regularity and cheerfulness, and more cottages will have to be built on the hills surrounding the main building, which was first erected and thought to be absurdly large, with its accommodations for three hundred students! There are over seven hundred now, in spite of the increased requirements for entrance, which include three languages, with a maximum of two and a minimum of the other, or the substitution of a science,

The Tree-day Procession.

"Pan."

Tree-day Costumes.

works—as sometimes happens—and is sent home for a rest, she is daily lectured by him until his shoulder, which he has dislocated in the last foot-ball match, allows him to go back to his own university. It is this extreme conscientiousness which still further differentiates her from her brother. I have known girls who did clerical work for the professors to have in their desks copies of the papers for the examinations which their room-mates were to take the next day, and they were as safe as though locked in the President's private office. Such a state of

and a great deal of mathematics and English and history, and so many other bewildering things that, at first glance, they seem to preclude the idea that there is anything left to learn at the college itself.

But there always is, and the girl goes about it so feverishly and conscientiously as to grieve and astonish her brother at Columbia or Princeton or Harvard; and if she over-things could hardly exist in most colleges where the men make a boast of practising every sort of ingenious device for passing an examination except the very simple one of studying for it, and one cannot help contrasting favorably the standard of morality in a woman's college which would ostracize a girl for taking into class a literal translation of the original, with the cool advertisement of "a first - class Balliol man," as he calls himself, to the effect that he has made a number of word-for-word translations which are peculiarly valuable to the undergraduate for interleaving in his Latin texts ! But it is not with any idea of making the Wellesley undergraduate unduly haughty and proud of her ways of thinking and acting, and of her attainments, that such a contrast is drawn. She is very young and has yet to prove herself. If the next generation of college women are equally high-minded and studiously inclined, then will be the time for congratulations.

Golf Players.
From sketches by Miss Cowles.

he pleases. The university does not consider it incumbent upon itself to look after him personally beyond seeing that he attends chapel and a certain number of recitations, and does not absent himself from college for days at a time, nor haze his undergraduate friends and enemies. These rules, with the general one which requires him to behave like a gentleman, are about all that affect his sojourn at his alma mater. But a girls' college is a very different place. The life is necessarily much more concentrated, because the students cannot live any and everywhere, but must be under the direct care of the college authorities. It rather resembles a large family hotel where the comfort and well-being of the guests are looked after minutely and carefully by a great many people, from the housekeepers who supervise the china and linen, and see that the small army of maids keeps

A large college for girls, such as Wellesley, is a rather curious institution, and is, of course, run on vastly different lines from a college for men. At Harvard or Princeton or Yale a man lives where he pleases and comes and goes pretty much as

the pretty student-rooms in order, down to the laundresses and cooks and the men who look after the furnaces, and the undergardeners who apparently spend their lives raking up dead leaves, and the carpenters who lay the miles of board paths that the young women may always find good walking. Wellesley College especially suggests this idea, for the main building, or College Hall, as it is called, with its palm-filled rotunda, is not unlike a hotel—there is one at Pallanza which strikingly resembles it —and the cottage dormitories scattered throughout the grounds are so many small *dépendances*. The seven hundred students live in these cottages or in College Hall, or in the boarding-places in the village approved of by the college. The expenses of a student who lives in the village vary, of course, with her particular rooms, but if she is in the college proper the cost of board and tuition is the same whether she lives in the main building or in one of the smaller dormitories, which accommodate from thirty to sixty students. Rooms in the cottages are always in demand, owing to the greater quiet of life there, and the little luxuries of open fires and pretty drawing-rooms and dainty table-service, and the general feeling that one has of being in one's own home with a large and pleasant house-party about one. Life at Wood, or Norumbega, or Freeman has, in fact, become so popular that the general rule disqualifying an undergraduate from more than one year in a cottage has had to be made. Of course there are exceptions, but the consequence is that generally a student spends three of her four years at college in the main building, and she has the satisfaction of feeling that she is getting a real insight into "college life;" that she is right in the centre of things and that her small world is revolv-

A Senior.

ing about her, even if she does lose the repose and home-like life of the cottage. One can hardly expect repose in a building that is an eighth of a mile long and has rooms in it for three hundred young women, besides thirty or forty lecture-rooms and laboratories, and a post-office and a book-store and a telegraph and telephone bureau and innumerable offices for the different dignitaries of the college, and a library and reception-rooms and a natural history museum, and which is fringed around with paint-shops and repair-shops and electric-light plants and the dozens of other necessary adjuncts to a big building.

As for the rules which govern the daily life of the Wellesley College girl, they are so unobtrusive that one is a little puzzled to discover just what they are. Moreover, the regulations which do obtain are continually being altered to provide for unforeseen exigencies, for, although as a member of Wellesley's faculty once feelingly exclaimed, "Thank God, a woman's college is no longer a curiosity," still it is a new departure even yet, and there must inevitably be many mistakes and many changes. Indeed, the changes are so rapid that in many respects what is true of

Hunnewell.

Drawn by B. J. Rosenmeyer.

Float Day.

Corner of a Student's Room.

nicious, but now no longer frowned upon—have been granted, while on the other hand restrictions, extending from the " credit system" to the rule forbidding an undergraduate to walk to the village or about the grounds alone in the evening, are insisted upon. This last rule, however, would seem superfluous, as it is difficult to believe that any miscreant, no matter how hardened, would not feel properly abashed in the imposing presence of a college girl and would not retire hastily and apologetically.

Perhaps one would best describe the rules which govern a student at Wellesley as those which would naturally govern the actions of any well-bred girl. While at college she is required to have a chaperon to any entertainment in Boston, or to a foot-ball game at Harvard, or to an afternoon tea, just as she would be if she were at home with

Wellesley to-day was not true last year, and probably will not be true next year. Privileges which would have been thought of only in utter hopelessness and awe a few years ago, ranging all the way from the wearing of the cap and gown to a chafing-dish breakfast in one's room—a custom once curiously condemned as most per-

Corridors, commonly called " The Centre."

Drawn by C. Allan Gilbert.

Students' Parlor.

Senior Rolling Hoop.

ifornia, and Mexico, and Colorado, and Canada, and Japan, and India, and the Sandwich Islands. It therefore seems inevitable that these rules should operate differently in different cases and that college life should mean to one a vastly different thing from what it means to another. Also, as after all each girl is a law unto herself when it comes to regulating her own life, the question of individuality steps in, influenced by the particular line of work the student may be pursuing, and the results are as diversified as the colors in a Persian rug.

There are, of course, three typical ways of living at college : the way of the girl who makes her college life one long task, who never has time for anything but work ; the way of the girl—a *rara avis*, fortunately — who does nothing ; and the way of the large majority, who take college sanely, and work when they work and play when it is time to play, and who emerge from their four years' training much better for it, mentally, morally, and physically, with a clear, healthy idea of the meaning of life and a great deal of experience gained from friction with many kinds of girl. It is a curious and profitable study to watch a freshman class and note those who first rise to the surface, so to speak, and the quick judgments formed by one student

her own people. And she is not expected to go to any of these things at the expense of her studies, or to have her friends out so often as to interfere with her work. But when she has leisure to entertain her friends she is at perfect liberty to ask them out to the concerts, or to play golf with her, or tennis, or go boating ; and there are pretty little drawing-rooms provided for her and her guests, and the college with its beautiful grounds is a good show-place to take them over.

Indeed, any girl at Wellesley can see much of social life and lead a healthy, normal existence if she only will. It is a mistake to suppose that because she is at college and hard at work that she is cut off from the world. It is a little difficult to define or describe her life, because, although gathered together under the same institution, and respecting the same rules, there are students who have come from such widely different quarters as New York, and South America, and Cal-

Houghton Memorial Chapel.

of another and the place each takes in her class. Perhaps that intercourse with unfamiliar and widely differing natures, which develops a girl's resources and makes or mars her character, is the most important result of a woman's college education, just as it is of a man's.

There is one law at Wellesley which is universally and cheerfully observed. It is the unwritten law which constitutes every girl a hostess of the college. Nothing impresses the stranger more than the consideration which he receives there. I have seen bewildered visitors walk up to a girl who was feverishly hurrying to catch the coach, or to meet an "appointment" in a building a quarter of a mile away, and ask her where "Miss Smith" or "Miss Brown," as the case be, could be found, and although the hurried student may hastily recall that there are five "Misses Brown" in the senior class and ten in the junior, and an unlimited number among the sophomores and freshmen, yet she will cheerfully inquire the little name of the much-desired individual, and what class she is in, and in which one of the ten college buildings she has her rooms, and will send an office-maid to look her up, or dash after her herself, or set the confused and helpless visitor on the right track ; and she will then miss her coach resignedly, or get to her "lecture" fifteen minutes late, and bear with equanimity the cold glance of the professor.

Possibly, it is the daily appearance of the cap and gown which most distinguishes a senior of to-day from one of a few years ago. She wears them so conscientiously and uninterruptedly, and has such a haughty way of sweeping by you in them, and her

Tupelo Point.

face takes on such an uncompromisingly earnest and severe look under the mortarboard, that you feel quite conscience-stricken, and have an intense desire to go home and look at your sheepskin, to convince yourself that you were once a senior, too, although you are quite sure that you could never have been such an imposing and magnificent one as this young woman. It is rather curious that the students of an institution which so heartily condemns all useless forms, should be so keen for one of the most useless and meaningless. But at present the senior at Wellesley takes an immense pride and delight in her cap and gown ; and they look very well as you catch a glimpse of them on the campus or among the big trees by Longfellow Fountain.

A day at Wellesley passes with alarming rapidity to a student. From the time she goes to chapel at half-after eight, experiencing that moment full of anxiety when the organ stops and she tries to enter a door ten feet wide at the same instant that six or seven hundred other young women are trying to do so too, until she hastily turns off her electric-light a few minutes after ten o'clock, she has an almost uninterrupted series of "appointments," as she euphemistically calls her recitations, and lectures, and laboratory work, and gymnastics, and music or art.

There are some who think her daily routine too full and too inelastic, though when one hears, as I heard a short time ago, the captains of the different athletic teams anxiously beseeching certain young women "not to let study interfere with their practice," one rather doubts that it can be so. But when one looks around on the three hundred and sixty acres of beautiful country which surround Wellesley, it seems rather a pity that one has anything at all to do, except to enjoy them. There are few places in Europe or America which for beauty of woodland, lake, and meadow, can rival Wellesley, and it really does not seem just that one should have to attend biology or literature lectures, or solve original propositions in conic sections, or make temperature-charts, when one might be out in a boat gathering water-lilies, or exploring the lovely nooks about the lake. It is to be feared, though, that some young women allow themselves to get so deplorably engrossed in their studies that they do not realize that "the meadow," for instance, is a very beautiful piece of quiet landscape, and think of it only as a convenient short way to the station, or a particularly stiff bit of ground to be gone over in golf ; and I have known young girls possessed of such overwrought consciences that they sternly refused to occupy rooms which looked out on a too attractive vista of woods and water. It certainly seems a pity that, with such fine natural advantages for having Broad Walks, and Addison Walks, and Peachey Stones, which are so inexpensive and picturesque, and so exactly what all colleges should boast of and show to visitors, that Wellesley is too young to have had many distinguished graduates, and that they have been too busy to haunt any particular spot sufficiently to make it famous. But the college is doing its best, and a great many celebrated visitors are requested to plant trees, and any of them are very welcome to sit down or walk around and make any place famous that may be most comfortable to them. If there is any walk at Wellesley which is famous it is the walk to Tupelo Point, which is very pretty and shaded, and which ends abruptly by the lake and frequently by an engagement.

The Wellesley undergraduate is probably at her best when she is at leisure and has time to think about her gowns. A very good time to take a look at her is on Sunday morning, in chapel, or in the evening, at vespers, when the organ is going softly and the lights are turned down. She is then rested and quiet, and just a little homesick, so that she has rather a spiritual, pensive look, which usually impresses the visiting minister greatly. But, in spite of his finding her individually sufficiently attractive, he looks upon her as rather trying when there are several hundred of her to be confronted. The stoutest hearts have confessed to quailing before such a cruelly young and critical audience. It is told of a celebrated bishop, always ill at ease with women, that after his first sermon at the college, he departed hastily to the village, and was seen shaking hands violently with a porter whom he encountered at the station, as he warmly exclaimed : " How are you? How are you? I am so glad to see a *man!*"

But usually the Wellesley student deals very gently with the visiting minister, and overlooks his little peculiarities and weaknesses, and shows him her best side, and he goes away with an idealized impression of her which would, perhaps, be rudely dispelled could he see her the next evening. Then she is anything but homesick or quiet or spiritual. There is a concert or a reading or reception, and she feels especially light-hearted and wears a particularly nice gown for the benefit of the friends she has invited out for the evening. That is one of the most wonderful things about Wellesley College. It may be situated fifteen miles from Boston—in fact, it *is* fifteen miles from Boston—but, judging by the diversity of college men who find it possible to get out Monday evenings, it is most conveniently near Columbia and Yale and Amherst and a great many other colleges which are geographically rather remote.

But among her many good qualities it is to be noticed that the Wellesley College girl is not dependent for her enjoyment on a dress-suit worn by a man. She would just as soon wear it herself, and the cotillons in the gymnasium, where half the young girls personate their own brothers, are celebrated for their entire success and brilliancy. Indeed, there has never been a time in the history of the college when the students have not shown both special aptitude and great inclination to amuse themselves, and never more so than at present. The different cottages enter into a friendly rivalry, on important occasions, as to which shall get up the most enjoyable entertainment, and the result is most satisfactory to the invited guests, especially when the hours are so considerately arranged that one can go from one "attraction" to the next without missing anything. On Hallowe'en it was particularly pleasant to go to one cottage to see a stirring play in three acts, and then to another cottage for an operetta with bandits, and a lover in black velvet and long plumes, and a *première danseuse;* and then to still another for a dance and ices. As there are seven cottages, the gayeties bore some slight resemblance to a "continuous performance."

It sounds perhaps rather frivolous and familiar to call as dignified and earnest an institution as Wellesley delightfully inconsistent ; and yet that was what one was obliged to call it, in one respect at least, until very recently. Attendance at the theatres—even at the best theatres and for the purpose of seeing the best acting—was forbidden until three years ago, yet once a year a dramatic representation was given by the Shakespeare Society, which was looked forward to and attended by the whole college and throngs of invited guests. It was not quite easy, however, for the average intellect to understand just why it was less reprehensible to see a young girl of moderate histrionic abilities, and the best intentions, assume the rôle of *Katharine* or *Rosalind* or *Viola*, than it was to see it played very well indeed by Hading or Ada Rehan or Julia Marlowe, and the restriction was finally explained by being done away with. Now students are at liberty to go into the theatres if properly chaperoned, and besides the Shakespeare dramatics. at the college, there are those given during Commencement Week by the seniors and those by the juniors to the freshmen in the mid-winter term. Perhaps this delicate attention on the part of the juniors to the freshmen illustrates, as strikingly as anything, the difference between undergraduate life in men's and women's colleges. At Harvard or Princeton the average freshman is regarded with such utter disapprobation as may culminate in an unpleasant and active manifestation of the same, unless he is protected by the college authorities. At best he can only hope for cold scorn and sufferance by upper-classmen. But at Wellesley the young freshman is greeted most hospitably and is made to feel that she has been anxiously awaited, and so she is given a dramatic entertainment by the juniors and a dance by the sophomores to impress upon her just

how welcome she is. The dance is given in "The Barn," and there is frappé, and a band to play two-steps and waltzes, and the young women go in evening-gowns and have their programmes made out and roses sent them by the attentive sophomores.

The Barn, it may be explained, is a sublimated hay-barn, ceiled, and lighted by electricity and heated by steam, and with a very good stage and a fine dancing-floor. It is the floor especially which makes one regret the strict rules against asking one's masculine friends to dance. However, young men are at liberty to come and watch the young women enjoy themselves, although that must be a rather trying diversion, especially if they should happen to enjoy dancing themselves. But when The Barn is profusely decorated with trophies from numberless students' rooms and filled with three or four hundred young girls who seem to be having a tremendously good time, in spite of rules, it strikes one as being a very nice sort of place. This big, delightful hall was given by the college unconditionally to the "Barn-Swallows" (technical name, "*Welleyanæ Consilium Bonis Temporibus Studentæ Communimis*"), a club organized to promote acquaintanceship and good feeling between members of each and all classes in college—a club to be encouraged, when one remembers that, owing to the elective system at Wellesley, it is easily possible for a girl to go through her four years of college life without having ever met many of her own class in the lecture-room, and unless she meets them socially she may graduate without having even a bowing acquaintance with them. Any student can belong to this society by paying a fee, which is merely nominal and utterly out of proportion to the amount of amusement which one gets out of the bi-weekly dramatics and occasional dances. Such clubs have been organized in other colleges, where they are deservedly popular and serve to break up that tendency to exclusiveness which class spirit and smaller clubs engender.

Of the smaller clubs at Wellesley, the Shakespeare Society is one of the oldest and best known. As has been said, it was this society which saved the college from utter histrionic darkness for many years, and membership in it was the ambition of numberless undergraduates with longings for the stage. In the spring of the year the society always presents a play, and very creditable performances of "Twelfth Night," "Love's Labor's Lost," "A Winter's Tale," " As You Like It," and "Midsummer Night's Dream " have been given. The last two have been acted under the big trees on the campus—the first in the afternoon, the last by moonlight — with special success.

Besides the Shakespeare Society, there are at Wellesley the Agora, a debating club, and four Greek-letter societies: Phi Sigma, Zeta Alpha, Tau Zeta Epsilon, and Alpha Kappa Chi. The opportunities for social intercourse which these societies and the class functions offer are supplemented by receptions given at the different cottages or by individual girls to friends, by the Glee Club concerts, and professional musical recitals during the year, and by semi-occasional dinner-dances, where it is rumored that men are to be allowed to take an active share in the dancing. This rumor has only been confirmed on two or three rare and never-to-be-sufficiently-remembered occasions, but it is hoped that the innovation has come to stay.

Commencement Week, with its Senior Dramatics and lawn-party and President's reception and final concert and class-dinner, is a succession of social functions tinged with a good deal of sadness to the departing class. Formerly the greatest social occasion of the year was the Promenade given by the juniors to the seniors. But there were such appalling crowds of guests invited by the large classes, and the expenses and schemes for decoration grew to such proportions, that a conservative element abolished Junior Promenade with its festivities, and twenty thousand lanterns, and harrowing rains, and unfailing eclipses of the moon, and all the other elements that combined to make the life of a junior a burden to her for weeks before and after that important social event. Each junior class now, ignorant of how happy it should be without the anxiety of a Promenade, asks with unfailing regularity that the privilege be granted again, and it is probable that a few years from now will see the revival of that function.

But, perhaps, the social events most enjoyed by the students are those occasions when celebrities are entertained at the college, and it rarely happens that a distinguished personage comes to America that he does not, sooner or later, visit Wellesley. The main building and the Farnsworth Art Building are particularly suited to receiving a great number of guests, and the list of famous people who have been entertained there is already long. It must certainly be a great pleasure and a broadening influence for girls from every quarter of the earth to see and meet such men as John Fiske, or James Lane Allen, or Coquelin, or Ole Bull, or such women as Clara Barton, or Mrs. Henry Stanley, or Lady Henry Somerset. And without exception, I think the "distinguished visitors" depart from Wellesley as much delighted with that institution and the students, as the college and the young women are with them. It must be a pleasant and sufficiently rare experience for celebrated personages to find themselves before such a sympathetic audience, to feel sure that what they have done, or written, or preached, or invented, was fully known and appreciated by those around them, and they can hardly be quite indifferent to the delicate hero-worship, the enthusiasm, and veneration of the young girls who are so proudly handing them tea and chocolate, biscuits and ices, and who so evidently consider it such a privilege and honor to be in their company.

Aside from these modest but enjoyable social events there is not any great amount of " society " life at Wellesley. There is so much hard work done, and so much energy is consumed in doing it, that the majority of girls have very little time or inclination to go about a great deal, or invite their friends out too frequently ; and there is a large class of young women who go to college with a distinct idea of making their own living by what they are able to learn during their four years' course, or who have already earned the money to take them there and to whom life has become very earnest and real. But there is also a large element at Wellesley of young girls who see a great deal of society when they are at home, and who go to college for something more and better than society can offer. Such girls inevitably attract each other and are entertained and go out more than the majority. They do not affect any superior airs, however, and there is the least possible amount of exclusiveness at Wellesley ; and when it comes to class-honors, it is the best girl who is made president or class-orator, or mistress of ceremonies at the Tree, and not the one whose father is a distinguished senator, or who owns her own boat, or brings her dresses with her from Paris in the fall.

There are several purely college functions of the year which are interesting not only to the students but to outsiders, and which give a certain relief to the tension of hard work. Perhaps the most entirely successful one of that sort is the representation of the House of Commons, which is given under the direction of the department of Constitutional History. Each year the debate is held upon a topic of absorbing interest to English constituents, and if there is any flaw in the representation of the scenes and speeches of the Lower House it is that the imitation is more entertaining than the original. Last year the debate was held upon the motion of Mr. Burns, the member from Battersea, to abolish the House of Lords ; and the amount of partisanship aroused and the glittering oratory poured forth by the young imitators of Mr. Balfour, and Sir Michael Hicks-Beach, and Mr. Labouchere, and Mr. Chamberlain would have done credit to those statesmen themselves.

The leader of the House was as imposing as it was possible for a very much frightened young girl in a white wig and black gown to be ; and the *mise en scène* was excellent, the party in power being very properly on her right, the Opposition on her left, while the Irish Nationalists and the Liberals sat and stood and cheered and groaned below the gangway.

In the early days of June, Tree Day is celebrated, a class function which has been observed almost from the founding of the college, and which, since the idea was first suggested to the Class of '79 by Mr. Durant, has been so improved upon and elaborated that it is now one of the prettiest events of undergraduate days at Wellesley. Tree Day is looked forward to with mingled emotions by the different classes. By the seniors with some sadness, because they are there to take leave of the tree which they

planted as freshmen ; by the juniors with indifference, because they have only a small share in the proceedings ; by the sophomores with envious anxiety lest the freshmen should have hit upon a more original and brilliant plan for celebrating the day than they had, and by the freshmen with undisguised and feverish excitement, for they are to show themselves in their true colors, literally and figuratively, for the first time upon that day. They feel that the interest of the whole college is centred upon them, and the sceptical attitude of the sophomores, as to whether they are capable of evolving a sonorous and comprehensive motto and of choosing class-colors with discretion, puts an edge like a razor on their anxiety to do well. Sometimes, in their efforts to eclipse all previous Tree-day celebrations, their imaginations—and the untrained, primitive freshman imagination is a marvellous thing—achieve wonderful results. Last year, when it rained on Tree Day, for the first time in the history of the college, even more wonderful results were achieved than were counted upon, and strange effects in tissue-paper costumes and unheard-of combinations of wet colors resulted, and modest freshmen were seen retiring hastily in every direction. This disaster, however, was nothing in comparison with the tradition which credits one freshman class, serenely ignorant of botany, with having planted and celebrated in song and verse an infant sycamore, under the delusion that it was an elm.

It may be because of the imaginative costumes, or because the college authorities wish to keep Tree Day a purely college function—at any rate, all masculine element is barred from viewing this spectacle, although, as one watches the procession of picturesquely costumed classes winding down East Hill and over the campus, it seems rather a pity that this pretty little addition to the gayety of nations should not be shared by the outside world. The seniors have their exercises first, and usually a masque or dance is given, after which they separate and go to their tree and, as a class, take farewell of it. Then the freshmen, as Amazons, or nuns, or princesses, or carnival revellers, or Canterbury pilgrims, or cards in a game of whist, with the class-colors conspicuously displayed and the newly written class-song singing itself over and over in their excited brains, begin their part of the exercises. This includes the reception of the symbolic spade from the sophomores, and the planting of the class-tree, and songs and speeches and some scenic representation suggested by the costume. And at night, when the speeches and dancing are over, stray knots of the gayly dressed maskers, with mandolins and guitars, go from one cottage to the other and serenade the popular members of the faculty and the sleepy juniors and sophomores, until those irate young ladies come to the windows and throw down all the flowers and sweets they may happen to possess, and implore the serenaders to go away. And so Tree Day is not confined to the day at all, but ends late at night; and next morning there is nothing to show of all the pretty pageant but a very young sapling with a piece of gay ribbon tied around it, which every good undergraduate hopes will grow up one day, to commemorate her class and to blossom each spring and add to the beauty of Wellesley.

It may be personal prejudice, but I do not think the spring comes anywhere else quite so beautifully as at Wellesley, unless it is in the south of England. In the fall there is all the glory of rich autumn coloring, and for sports one has unlimited bicycling, and tennis tournaments, and golf; and in winter the snow stretches white and unbroken over the hills, and there is tobogganing and skating, and hockey in a corner of the frozen lake, which the Skating Club considerately keeps free of snow. But it is in the spring that Wellesley impresses the student and the chance visitor as one of the loveliest places to be seen anywhere. The lake seems to wake up and sparkle more than ever and to turn the true "Wellesley blue," except where the lily-pads spot it white and green. The long stretches of turf put on a mossy color and softness, starred with a thousand wild flowers, and the oaks and elms become masses of dense foliage that throw rich, velvety shadows on the turf, and one comes upon the Farnsworth Art Building, hiding its beautiful façade behind a rampart of great trees, like a Greek temple lost in a wood. The dormitories look like pretty country-places set in some big English park, and here and there one can see groups of students, with their arms about each other's waists, saun-

tering along the shaded paths, the sunshine sifting down through the tender green of the trembling leaves and making flickering white polka-dots on their sombre black caps and gowns. In the college the windows and transoms of the students' rooms stand wide open and the warm air comes in, stirring the muslin curtains and beruffled pillows in the window-seats and sweeping the fragrance of the great bowlfuls of arbutus and snow-drops up and down the long corridors. In the library the students who are unfortunate enough to have briefs or theses or literature papers to prepare, do not trust themselves below, where the temptation to escape would be irresistible, but sternly repair to an upper gallery and barricade themselves in with tables and chairs, and work away gloomily in spite of the seductive breezes that are blowing back the leaves of their note-books, and the glimpses from the windows of the green campus, and the bicyclers and golfers and tennis-players who are heartlessly parading themselves over it. Out on the lake one sees small boats go drifting by, while their occupants snatch at the floating water-lilies, or one comes upon a canoe moored in some shady nook, while the studious owner contentedly sits in it and works. Everyone seems to be busy and happy, from the girls who are playing basket-ball or tennis on the clay courts behind Music Hall, to the conscientious biology student catching polywogs in Longfellow Fountain, or the botany devotee gathering the last flowers for her herbarium. But biology and things of that sort become matters of secondary consideration when spring is fairly installed. Work goes on as usual, perhaps with even more energy as the term nears its close, but other things assume a new and vital importance. The undergraduate feels a sudden and curious affection for the senior class, individually and collectively, and she finds it an absolute necessity to explore the woods and to linger in the students' parlor after dinner, while someone plays on the harp, or piano, or mandolin, and talk goes on in the corners in undertones. And at night groups of bare-headed girls go strolling up and down in the soft air, laughing and singing the funny college songs, which, somehow, do not seem so funny when one is singing them for almost the last time; or they crowd together on the wide piazzas of the cottages and talk of a hundred things, and call to their neighbors across the leafy way. Even the serious and high-minded senior succumbs to the irresistibly happy, *dolce far niente* effect of spring at Wellesley, and on May Day, early in the morning, before chapel, as an outlet for her exuberant spirits, it has been her long-established custom to roll a hoop over the hard, level carriage-road in front of College Hall. Perhaps the whole college-year does not furnish a more unique or pleasing sight than this long procession of dignified seniors in wind-blown cap and gown tearing madly around after their hoops in the fresh morning air. And when they have successfully completed the circuit of the oval they file into "the Centre," and there, around the marble, palm-filled basin, they make a circle by catching hold on each side of the hoops and sing college-songs until the chapel-bell rings, and show themselves to be just what they are—happy young girls who are not at all anxious to put away childish things, and who enjoy a frolic tremendously, in spite of having studied differential calculus and moral philosophy and mathematical astronomy.

I once heard an extremely disagreeable man declare, with a deplorable use of figurative language, that "the country was strewn with wrecks of Wellesley College." I presume that that particular man had a daughter whose constitution had not passed its college examinations and so had to leave. It has been my personal experience that Wellesley young women are exceptionally strong physically, and one's particular friends are apt to be five feet seven or eight inches tall, and to have very broad shoulders, and to be good at tennis and rowing, and to be able to walk into Boston on a wager—and to be extremely tired the next day. One cannot help feeling how unjust are so many of the complaints against the physical sanity of a college education for women. Girls who are not physically strong, or who are not capable of being made so with judicious training, should no more attempt a college course, the demands of which are necessarily trying, than should a consumptive live in a severe climate, or a lame man attempt Alpine climbing, or a victim of chills and fever continue to reside in a place full of malaria. It is distinctly irritating to see parents who have

sent girls to college in an uncertain state of health, deeply surprised and indignant, and inclined to blame "the higher education," because these young women did not return to them vigorous and robust. A serious college is not primarily a health-resort, although everything is being done to balance the strain of mental work with healthy, judicious physical exercise.

Athletics in Wellesley College have received an enthusiastic start under Miss Hill, the director of the gymnasium, with the co-operation of the students and the Committee on Health and Physical Training. Miss Hill does not believe in gymnastics, but in athletics, and practice in the gymnasium is but a means to an end, and is only required of freshmen. But all students are urged to join one of the many organizations of the Athletic Association— the rowing, cycling, tennis, golf, or basketball clubs, which each have a captain and separate regulations, although all are united under the Athletic Association. As a rule, a member of one club cannot belong to another, in order to concentrate energy and insure progress in whatever branch of athletics is chosen.

It certainly seems that when so many people insist on dying and leaving fortunes to colleges which are already vulgarly rich and perfectly equipped, that some wealthy individual might give Wellesley a new gymnasium, especially when Wellesley would not make it a condition of acceptance that he should die, but would take it cheerfully during his life-time, and would ask him out by special invitation to every athletic event of the year in his own gymnasium. It is a very modest gymnasium that Wellesley wants, too. No complicated apparatus, only a big, airy place with room for dancing and bowling and racquets and tennis, and a bicycle-track and a swimming-tank and a basket-ball court. The promoters of athletics at the college, it is true, have visions of some exciting innovations—polo on mature and gentle polo-ponies, and riding and hurdle-jumping, and lacrosse and track athletics; but these would not be insisted upon at first !

Tennis has always had a firm hold on Wellesley students, and tournaments are held in the fall, when some good tennis may be seen. Its popularity has been more than equally shared by golf, perhaps ;

but then what branch of athletics has not had to reckon with golf? There seems to be a large number of young women at Wellesley whose collar-bones are of masculine length, and who can get a remarkably good swing of driver or lofter; and the tam and short golf-skirt are ubiquitous.

It is boating, however, that naturally holds first place in the affections of the Wellesley College girl. Lake Waban is to her what Lake Cayuga is to the Cornell man. But it was not until the last few years that her ambitions and energies were fully aroused, or, to speak more exactly, that her father's ambitions and energies were fully aroused. One may doubt the sincerity and depth of an individual enthusiasm, but when

"Songs of Wellesley."

it has the effect of causing a coldly critical and uninterested parent to build a three-thousand-dollar boat-house and to buy expensive practice-barges, such an enthusiasm must be considered as of a distinct value and genuineness. It is quite easy in a man's college to build a three or a thirty-thousand-dollar boat-house, and the fact would have very little significance, and one would only be mildly astonished that it could be built so cheaply; but fathers are not used to counting in boat-houses and shells for their girls in the annual budget, and it is a mysterious and delightful surprise that young women have succeeded in inserting those little items. It is a wedge. The extent and quality of the interest in boating may be judged of somewhat when one knows that a hundred and twenty-five freshmen cheerfully and confidently presented themselves one year as candidates for a class-crew of eight! For the last few years the crews have been selected on a purely athletic basis, and the physical development and gymnasium-work of the aspirants for crew honors are

carefully watched. In their dark blouses and bloomers the muscular young rowers of to-day present a very different appearance from those of other years, when the formation of a crew was almost a social affair, and those who composed it were elected chiefly for their good looks, and a tight-fitting gown, with an anchor worked on the sailor-collar, was considered a sufficiently nautical costume. There were years, it is even said, when muslin dresses and pink sashes were to be seen on Lake Waban, but no true Wellesley girl of to-day could bring herself to believe such an incredible statement.

Each class has a practice-barge built by Keast, of New Haven, the builder of the Yale crew boats, and costing about four hundred dollars. The boats look alarmingly like shells and have sliding-seats, and are out-riggers, and altogether present a most business-like aspect. And when a muscular young woman, with clear gray eyes and a decided look about her mouth, and hands that are sunburned from handling a cat-boat all summer, tells you of her crew-practice and chest-weight and dumb-bell exercise, and just how many times she goes around the eight-lap running-track, after being out with the crew, you begin to realize how very much in earnest she is and how great a hold rowing has on the student, and you wonder how long it will be before they begin to talk of "making the 'Varsity" and where the training-table is.

These practice-barges are in great contrast to the flat-bottomed, unwieldy boats of a few years ago, which were distressingly safe and which afforded absolutely no chance for romantic adventure. Indeed, the only accident that ever happened on the lake was the going overboard of a young

"O, I am stabb'd with laughter!"

Photograph by Partridge.

From "Love's Labor's Lost."—Presented by the Shakespeare Society.

man who thought he knew how to handle his sail-boat. As he could not swim, he was kindly and quietly fished out by some young women in a passing boat and was lectured for his incompetency—at least he should have been.

The enthusiasm and interest in rowing reaches a climax in "Float," the great aquatic event of the year. On that day the crews are in all their glory, and though it is a very mild and tranquil glory, in comparison with the effulgence of a race at New Haven or Oxford, it is a beautiful and picturesque sight. A great many people seem interested in Float. One year, seven thousand, including the Governor of Massachusetts and the Mayor of Boston, were interested and took the trouble to come out in special cars to see it. The college never puts on so gala an appearance as on Float Day, and the weather is always perfect, and the crowds of people who surge down upon the little beach and into the boat-house seem to enjoy themselves tremendously. Here and there one sees the face of some distinguished man and notes the little wake of silent gazers he leaves as he moves about. At different points knots of college-students are gathered together

so they can give their class-cheer in unison. Groups of visitors stroll farther up the bank, under the big trees, or crowd down nearer the edge of the lake to get a good view of the long, graceful practice-barges as they shoot out swiftly onto the course from the cool darkness of the boat-house. One after the other they come out at a given signal and are rowed with much skill, if not very great speed; and the stroke of each crew is a proud and elated young lady who feels that the interest of the immense crowd is centred in her boat and her crew. Toward the centre of the lake, beyond the course, one can make out the Hunnewell gondola and a whole fleet of sail-boats and canoes and row-boats of every description, decorated with pennants and Chinese lanterns and comfortably rigged up with sofa-pillows, that drift after the competing crews in a leisurely fashion, unlike the feverish anxiety with which the boat containing the coach and the judges follows them up. And after the four class-crews and the two extra freshmen-crews have pulled around the course, the judges pick out the eight young women who seem to handle an oar in the best way, and for half an hour they get into a barge by themselves and form a 'Varsity eight, and are rendered inordinately proud and haughty for the rest of their lives. After that important ceremony is over, and while it is growing quite dusk, the crew-boats get together and form a star that drifts and swims about on the lake. On the lantern-strung little boats, tiny lights suddenly flare out which are swallowed up and changed in the deluge of color from the big calcium-lights on the shore. From the midst of the floating craft comes the sound of mandolins and guitars, and the fresh young voices of the College Glee Club singing the college songs and giving the college cheer, and they never sound so well as they do floating back over the water in the deepening twilight.

The college is very young still. It has no storied past. It is just beginning, and the short years of its existence make Harvard, and Yale, and Princeton seem very venerable and historical in comparison. But after all it is exhilarating to the students of to-day to be able to say, " *We* are the ancients; we are making the college and its history ; and the four years of our life here form not only an epoch in our own existence, but in the existence of the college." It is a good thing to feel that there is no dead weight of years, no old memories, no precedents and traditions, to bind them and to make them other than they would make themselves. But with such privileges come great responsibilities, and the students of to-day must see to it that they build a college which students of future years will be proud to claim.

The Farnsworth Art Gallery.

30

A Scrum. California vs. Stanford. The Ball Is Coming Out.

Football: Battle or Sport?

By David Starr Jordan
President Leland Stanford, Jr., University

"For as concerning footeball playing, I protest unto you that it maie rather bee called a friendly kinde of fight than a plaie or recreation—a bloudie and murtherying practice than a fellolie sporte or pastyme."

(Philip Stubbs; Anatomy of Abuses; about 1550.)

N November, 1905, in *The Woman's Home Companion*, President Eliot of Harvard published a short article full of meat and without a waste word entitled "The Evils of Football." At that time these evils had risen to a very high pitch. The academic authorities in many institutions had lost all control of intercollegiate athletics, normal athletic effort within the colleges had largely disappeared, and expressions of disgust with the game, and with the way it was managed, were heard in every college. It was clear that the game must be purified, moderated, reformed or else that it must be abolished. And the abandonment of the game involved tremendous difficulties so thoroughly was it intrenched by alliance with financial interests outside.

The evils of the game as then played and as then managed were classified by President Eliot as follows:

As lesser objections he gives its publicity, the large proportion of injuries, the obsession of the student-body in the one idea of victory at football, and the disproportionate exaltation of the football hero, who is subjected to "crude and vociferous blame and praise," both "having no relation to rational standards of public approval or disapproval." Another lesser evil is "the state of mental distrust and hostility between colleges, which all too frequently occurs," destroying the value of the broader acquaintance with men, the deprovincializing of college life which is one of the normal virtues of intercollegiate matches. "The carrying into elaborate and highly artificial practice the enfeebling theory that no team can do its best except in the presence of hosts of applauding friends is still one of the lesser evils of football. Worse preparation for the real struggles and contests of life can hardly be imagined. The orator, advocate, preacher, surgeon, engineer, banker, tradesman, craftsman, admiral, general or statesman who cannot do his best except in the presence of a sympathetic crowd is distinctly a second-class man."

Among other minor evils, not mentioned by Dr. Eliot, was the essential stupidity of the game in its most prominent feature, the line-bucking. Its interest lay in the struggle between contending groups of excited students who had no part in the game except as spectators. If one is interested in neither side, no game is more tedious to witness. Almost every time the ball touches the ground the game stops, the masses of armored legs are disentangled and time is given for those who have lost their breath to rise to their feet again. Once in a while a brilliant run stands out as a marked exception, but the interference which makes the run possible is often invisible to spectators. Of course if football were a true sport, this would be no objection, for a sport has its value in the delight of the players themselves and in their improved physical development. That which is played for the benefit of spectators is a spectacle, not a sport. And no man lives who would play the American game of football for pure sport, knowing that nobody would ever be on the bleachers and that neither his name nor that of his adversaries would resound among his fellows or appear in headlines in the newspapers. I honor the scrubs, those who play day after day that the first team may grow strong by running over them. This is the true college spirit, but there is no scrub who would play the American game for fun.

For the American game has never been a sport, but a battle, and the great objections to it are the moral ones which spring from this fact. Mr. Eliot says:

"The game is played under established and recognized rules; but the uniform enforcement of these rules is impossible, and violations of the rules are in many respects highly profitable toward victory. Thus, coaching from the side-lines, off-side play, holding and disabling opponents by kneeing and kicking, and by heavy blows on the head, and particularly about eyes, nose and jaw, are unquestionably profitable toward victory; and no means have been found of preventing these violations of rules by both coaches and players. Some players, to be sure, are never guilty of them, and some

are only guilty when they lose their tempers, but others are habitually guilty of them. The rules forbid unnecessary roughness in play, but there is wide latitude in the construction of unnecessary roughness. To strike a player with the clenched fist is unnecessary roughness; to give him a blow equally severe with the base of the open hand is not unnecessary roughness.

"The common justification offered for these hateful conditions is that football is a fight, and that its strategy and ethics are those of war. One may therefore resort in football to every ruse, stratagem and deceit which would be justifiable in actual fighting. They always try to discover the weakest man in the opponent's line, as for example, the man most recently injured, and attack him again and again. If a man, by repeated blows about the head and particularly on the jaw, has been visibly dazed, he is the man to attack at the next onset. If in the last encounter a player has been obviously lamed in leg or arm or shoulder, the brunt of an early attack should fall on him. As a corollary to this principle, it is justifiable for a player, who is in good order, to pretend that he is seriously hurt, in order that he may draw the opponent's attack to the wrong place. These rules of action are all justifiable, and even necessary, in the consummate savagery called war, in which the immediate object is to kill and disable as many of the enemy as possible. To surprise, ambuscade and deceive the enemy, and invariably to overwhelm a smaller force by a greater one, are the expected methods of war. But there is no justification for such methods in a manly game or sport between friends.

"The general public that witnesses with delight these combats can seldom see or understand these concealed and subtle evils of the game. They witness with pleasurable excitement a combat which displays courage, fortitude and a spirit of self-sacrificing co-operation in the players. The college public, adherents of the contending teams, is stirred profoundly by the sentiment of devotion to the institutions, because they believe that success in football is for the advantage of the institution. All parties welcome the chance to see a strenuous combat, as their ancestors have for unnumbered generations. The respectable people who attend football games—collegians, graduates and others—do not prefer to witness injuries, violations of rules, quarrels and penalties. On the contrary, they always prefer to see skilful, vigorous playing, uninterrupted by such repulsive incidents. The responsible

FOOTBALL: BATTLE OR SPORT

A Line-Out. Stanford vs. California.

heads of secondary schools do not wish to have their pupils taught by college athletes that skill in breaking the rules without being detected is essential to success in playing football. The average college player had much rather play fair than foul. The players have not devised or enjoyed the stupid methods of training which impair the physical condition of most of them before the important game takes place. What then are the sources of the great evils in this sport? They are: (1) The immoderate desire to win intercollegiate games; (2) The frequent collisions in masses which make foul play invisible; (3) The profit from violation of rules; (4) The misleading assimilation of the game to war as regards its strategy and its ethics."

Another objection, not mentioned by President Eliot, is the total unfitness of the game for the use of the secondary schools. The high school boys are too young for such fierce exercise; they have no adequate training, no power to enforce standards, no competent umpires. It is rarely possible for them to play an honest game against honest competitors, and the death rate in these games is appalling. It is criminal, and the crime lies with the public which permits and encourages these dangerous and harmful exercises. The death rate and the list of injuries on college teams is relatively far smaller. This means that the greater age and costly training and rubbing has made them relatively immune to injuries. Quite as likely it means that all athletic youths with fragile bones or weak hearts have been disabled and put out of the running before they reach the college. It is again in the high school or secondary school that the evil of "proselyting" reaches its climax.

Another great evil, only hinted at by President Eliot, is the presence of the professional coach, the promoter of public athletics, who makes his living through winning victories and who goes as far in securing them as a relaxed public opinion in town and in university will let him. The self-respect of the colleges demands a declaration of independence in this regard. A rule that should be adopted, if we must have paid coaches, is that each coach must have been student or alumnus in the institution he represents, and that the academic life of a paid coach like that of an athlete shall be limited to four years.

Still another related evil lies in the immense gate receipts from popular games, and the expenditure of these sums by untried collegians surrounded by the pressure of sympathy and the cold machinations of graft.

The most discreditable feature of the game as it was played in 1905 are set forth in a series of papers entitled "Buying Football Victories," published in *Collier's Magazine* in November and December, 1905, by Edward S. Jordan, of Kenosha, a recent alumnus of the University of Wisconsin. In this paper the demoralization of the student-body by the anything-to-win policy on the part of coaches, and the laxity and apathy of college faculties is vigorously set forth.

The net result of these and many other similar criticisms has been the New Football of 1906. The most important feature of the revised football has been the attempt to clean up the game, to free it from the gross abuses and to conduct the game on the basis of gentlemanly relations. As the worst offenders in the past were such mainly because the students and alumni demanded a winning team and the faculty acquiesced through the suspension of ordinary tests of scholarship in favor of athletic heroes, the change of popular feeling met with a ready response on the part of successful coaches. But the cleaning up has not nearly reached the end of the line and the old moral evils still exist in many colleges and secondary schools.

Besides the moral uplift which in the nature of things cannot be universal nor permanent, certain changes in the game itself were enforced by public opinion. These are, in brief, making the game more interesting by making it more open for observation and by giving greater play to the individual skill, especially that shown in a scattered field. Again, the attacking line is weakened through requiring ten yards' gain instead of five in three downs. This change has made mass play less successful and hence more likely to be set aside in favor of more open plays. At the same time mass play remains the ordinary way of putting the ball in action, however useless it may be with evenly matched teams, while its value for the purpose of breaking down an individual opponent is perhaps relatively enhanced. With this, two additional hazards not germane to the game were introduced. One is the forward pass, perhaps suggested by the passing by the backs in the Rugby football, but under different rules. The other is the onside

kick. Both of these are open to the criticism that they do not naturally rise from the nature of the game. On the other hand they serve as a relief from the line-bucking, a perversion of the Rugby scrum, which by a curious inversion of ideas has come to be known to the public as "straight football."

The new rules have made the game more open, more of a sport, considerably safer and on the whole notably cleaner and more interesting. Shall we be satisfied with this? Is the balance from the academic standpoint in favor of the game or do the evils pointed out by President Eliot and recognized by every college man still outweigh the advantages? If so, are there other modifications still to be made which shall outbalance these evils, and leave a residue in favor of the game as a means of promoting manliness, physical development, courage, quickness of action and the spirit of co-operation?

The writer believes that at present the balance is against the game, a conclusion which he has reached reluctantly, for his natural sympathies are with the struggling athletes. He believes also that most of the present evils would disappear by going back to the British Rugby game of football, a game from which the so-called American game was some thirty years ago gradually modified. If this is true, a change to a better game is an experiment to be preferred to the out-and-out abandonment of intercollegiate football. This is probably the only real

The Ball Being Heeled Out of the Scrum. Stanford Freshmen vs. California Freshmen.

alternative, and outright abolition may be necessary in any event, if the colleges are to maintain their responsibility to the public.

If we test the present revised American game by its relation to the evils enumerated by President Eliot, what do we find?

Taking these criticisms in order, the evils of publicity remain the same. The injuries seem to have been reduced by about ten per cent. It may be noted in passing that many injuries which seem trivial may be of a serious character. In the *Journal of the American Academy of Medicine* it is estimated that in football injuries to the nervous system predominate, these arising mainly from mass plays, and from fierce tackling after long runs. Next come internal injuries, especially to stomach and intestines, arising largely from illegal kicking and "kneeing". Injuries to eyes and head often come from intentional blows, and all these are far more dangerous than the occasional fracture of an arm or leg, which is likely in any strenuous sport. In proportion to the openness of the game, the evils of intentional manslaughter are reduced. But many of the great games and perhaps most of the little ones show that this evil is not abolished. The noise and obsession remain the same. A recent writer claims that football victories cannot be won by institutions in which the student-body does not go wild over it. Harvard is told that she can never win over her traditional opponent so long as the student-body of the former university can endure victory or defeat with equanimity. The evils of artificial training, of dependence on noise, have not been reduced by the change in the rules as to the space to be gained in three downs, nor by the adoption of the forward pass. The coaches do not wish this changed, and curiously enough, while the American game of football has no existence except as an interacademic function, its control has been largely in the hands of unacademic men, who depend on the game for prominence as well as livelihood. To this we may ascribe the mechanizing of the game—the making of the game a matter of "certainty," depending chiefly not on the skill of the men who play, but on the skill of the coaches in arranging their quasi-puppets, and utilizing their muscular strength and their occasional fleetness of foot and accuracy of kicking. The great evils mentioned by Dr. Eliot have been in large degree mini-

mized by closer rules as to eligibility and a greater insistence by college faculties on tests of scholarship. The forward pass gives play for individual skill, for which reason the professional coach, who wants everything certain beforehand, looks on it with disfavor. The players in a losing cause sometimes try it, to increase chances. Being an uncertain element, good luck or quick action may bring its chances in their direction. The essence of a true sport is to offer many chances with victory to the team which has most men ready to seize those chances or to back up their colleagues who have done so.

It is plain, admitting as we may the improvement of the "New Football" of 1906 and 1907 over the old game, its greater interest as a sport, its more rigid limitation as to eligibility and its diminution of danger to life, the greater part of the old count still remains. The evils enumerated by President Eliot are still inherent and with a little less firmness on the part of college faculties the former conditions will again obtain. The balance is against the game. On academic grounds, the only grounds colleges have the right to consider, President Butler is, I think, fully justified in the abolition of football in Columbia University.

It may be remembered that the present American game of football is a modification of the British game of Rugby football, introduced into our colleges by Walter Camp and others in 1876. The chief differences in the two games arise from the legalizing in America of "off-side play," called by us "interference," which is forbidden by the rules of Rugby. In the latter game no player may run ahead of the player on his side who carries the ball. In legalizing interference any number of men on the attacking side may run ahead of the ball, consequently as many of the defense as can be spared must stand in opposition. Hence arises mass play, the ungraceful and unsportsmanlike element, now called "straight football." Secret signals and the fact that the whole attacking side may buck the line together give the attack a marked advantage over the defense. Hence the necessity of holding the ball by the attacking side. In Rugby, when a man is down with the ball the ball is still in play. Only the man who falls is out of the play. The rest goes on. In the American game the play is stopped for him and all the others who may be piled upon him to rise. The held ball renders impossible the particular play which is the glory of Rugby and the prettiest as well as the most sportsmanlike feature of any football game, the passing of the ball from one to another of the "backs," in a scattered field. In the American game, any such passing of the ball involves the too great risk of losing it. In Rugby, a lost ball may be regained by alertness and speed. In Rugby every man plays his own game; each of the backs is "his own quarterback." For these reasons the game is throughout open. The ball can be followed by the spectators; rough play, if present, can be seen by every one. Better still, it is a true sport, not an array of

people on earth, and those of the West are not quite happy unless they play the same games as are played in colleges in the East. This is the only real objection to the restoration of Rugby which the California universities have encountered.

The use of Rugby as an intercollegiate game will doubtless yield evils of its own, as well as repeat some of the evils of its American derivative. The worst possibility is that it will fall into the hands of coaches who will stifle its freedom of play and develop the mechanical battle-like game in which, as now, players would abandon their individuality under the direction of coaches. Foul play in Rugby is plainly visible to

A Dribbling Rush. California vs. Stanford.

battle. As matters are, how does the Rugby game stand related to the evils we have named above? The matters of publicity, of "crude and vociferous public praise and blame" will not be much altered. The huge gate receipts will remain the same. But these invite attack from another quarter. We may make the game free—accessible only on invitation—and an army of evils vanishes at once. But this requires courage and effort and a psychological moment.

There is danger in every manly sport, and there are worse things than physical danger to be faced in college. But the players generally enjoy the Rugby game for its own sake. The student-body enjoys it also for its spectacular qualities and beautiful plays. Boys are, however, the most conservative

spectators, moreover it is ineffective and would lose the game oftener than win it. There is no mass play in Rugby, and a savage tackle is bad play, for to throw the runner and to fall oneself with him does not stop the ball, which has been thrown to some other player. The punting is about the same in the two games, but every man in Rugby must be able to kick quickly and accurately. Punting is not a personal specialty of two or three of the backs as in the American game.

In the two great universities of California, the Rugby game, played under varying but fundamentally identical rules throughout Great Britain, Canada, New Zealand and the northern half of Australia, has been substituted for the American game. The initiative in this matter was due to President Wheeler of the University of California and to Professor Frank Angell, chairman of the committee on athletics of Stanford. The present writer was an early convert to the wisdom of this action. Mr. James Lanagan, the Stanford coach, was a later convert, but a very enthusiastic one. The game has been played for two seasons and with very fair success.

Experience shows that the accidents in Rugby football are much less frequent, less severe, and mainly confined to the limbs. Injuries to the legs are almost as frequent as in the American game. The fact that the game is played in cotton drawers instead of padded coats of mail, indicates at once a

a coach. The most he can do is to give form to individual players. In New Zealand, the especial home of clean, swift, strenuous sport, every player is his own coach, and professionalism of coaches as well as of players, though not unknown, is condemned by universal popular opinion.

To be sure the Rugby game never gives the thrill that follows the shock when masses of men throw themselves against each other. But this sort of thrill is not a thing to encourage. It is psychologically and doubtless ethically bad. At any rate our laws look critically on the value of prizefighting, which shares this feature in common with American football. The obsession and hysteria of the student-bodies are much less

A California Player Breaking Out of the Scrum. Stanford Freshmen vs. California Freshmen.

great difference. The Rugby football is a far swifter game, involving adroitness and co-operation rather than great strength. The giant has the advantage even in Rugby, but he must be a giant whose head and whose feet move quickly. As there are thirty players in a game of Rugby instead of twenty-two, and as it is a sport which men will play even though there is no possible hope of making any team, its introduction tends to revive the life of athletics within the colleges, which the American battle game has done so much to destroy. Men can play Rugby football and carry full work in the class room as well. It is a rare man who can do this and play the American game even as a scrub.

The game of Rugby cannot be planned by

in the Rugby game. It is a sport, not a battle, and the fine play of both sides appeals to the higher instincts of the youth.

For these reasons, the various attendant evils, the building up of a team by proselyting, the immoderate desire to win, and the machinery of intercollegiate war are less likely to arise with Rugby. These evils are wanting in England, in Canada, in New Zealand, in Sydney and Brisbane, and our people in America are of the same nature, the same blood, the same ethics, the same love of sport as these. Doubtless the general adoption of the Rugby game would lead to material modifications. The abolition of interference in the American game, carrying with it the abolition of the held ball and the mass play, would approximate it to Rugby, and a further revision in this direction would perhaps make the game acceptable to college authorities. The outside professional coach should be eliminated in either game. To make him a member of the faculty does not affect the situation. On the other hand, the schoolboyish "scrum" of the Rugby game is sure to be modified in American hands, though not, I trust, by the substitution for it of line-bucking plays. As to these and other matters I am permitted to quote from a personal letter of Walter Camp of Yale, the "Father of American Football," and I do this with the greater pleasure because its expressions are in some degree at variance with opinions I have expressed above. Mr. Camp says:

"Let me correct at once an impression that you seem to have that I am endeavoring to push out Rugby with the American game. If you follow the history of Rugby you will find that wherever it has been transplanted from the home country to one of the colonies, it has undergone some changes and has developed a character of its own. It has never stood still. As you probably know, we ourselves adopted the Rugby Union rules word for word in 1876. It was not long before we came to an *impasse* because the Rugby rule for the scrummage directed that 'each side should endeavor by pushing and kicking to drive the ball in the direction of the opponent's goal.' We soon found that it was a disadvantage to kick the ball through and hence neither side would kick or drive the ball in the direction of the opponent's goal. It was necessary for us to get some outlet and we then began to heel out. At that time I had a very animated discussion through the columns of one of the English papers with Rugby Unionists because I said I thought the final development of their scrummage would be to heel out.

"When I was over in England this Spring I casually remarked to a Rugby man, whom I knew, upon their heeling out. He was greatly astonished when, on looking it up, he found that heeling out had not always prevailed in Rugby. So you see the Englishman changes, but changes more slowly.

"One of the greatest authorities on English football in an article in either *Sportsman* or *Badminton* comes out flatly and says that both heeling out and wheeling the scrum are illegal under the rules, but that no team would stand a chance unless they practiced them. They have seven different kinds of rules in Canada, and, as you are aware, in other places like Australia, they have other varieties.

"Furthermore, the New Zealanders have developed in their own Rugby more of the definiteness of play that characterizes the American game. That is, they have certain planned-out methods of attack.

* * * *

"I had not in any way intentionally advocated the American style at the expense of the Rugby style. In fact, I had brought a team of Englishmen up here to play Rugby with our men in the hope that some good would come of it. . . . I see that the very thing which I objected to has naturally come to pass, and that is, that those who like Rugby seem to believe that it must be built up at the expense of the American game. I doubt if that is necessary. Certainly you are in exactly the same position that I was in 1876—you have adopted the Rugby game. The history of the sport shows that it develops and we have only reached one stage in its development while you are beginning another, and I certainly shall be glad to see how it comes along. I think you, with the greater number of English and Scotch out there on the Coast, can have more of the benefits of Rugby.

* * * *

"I am sure you magnify the element of certainty in the American game. You speak of Rugby being a game in contrast to it where a man is trained to seize chances as they arise and to back up his associates who may do the same. There is hardly an instant in the running game of football, whether it be called Rugby, American, Australian or any other name, where this is not necessary. The only measure of definiteness being that in the American game when the ball is put in play, the side in possession has an opportunity to start on some definite plan. The carrying out of it is another matter, and if you have personally witnessed the game under the rules of the last two years, you must have been convinced that there is plenty of opportunity for independent action.

"I no more believe in endeavoring to lay up an opponent by repeated attacks than do you, and I am sure that such methods are not only bad, but silly. You had an opportunity to see my methods at Stanford and I have not changed. Even those who advocate such a method on the theory that football is like war, must realize that in war if an annihilated battery meant a temporary cessation of hostilities until that battery could be replaced by a new and fresh one, the method would be ineffective.

"As far back as 1894 I advocated the ten-yard rule to bring about just the condition of things which you approve and which I approve. Some four years ago you will remember that I brought up this as the way to correct the evils of our game and set it on the right road. I fought for it as hard as I could, and if you saw clippings from the papers at that time you will probably remember that I was called all over the country 'Ten-Yard Camp' on account of my advocacy of this opening of the game. And yet within a little less than two years they came to it, and it did the work."

I may close this discussion in President Eliot's words, which I am sure will carry the approval of Mr. Camp, and of every other lover of clean and strenuous sport: "If a college or university is primarily a place for training men for honorable, gener-ous and efficient service to the community at large, there ought not to be more than one opinion on the question whether a game, played under the actual conditions of football, and with the barbarous ethics of warfare, can be a useful element in the training of young men for such high service. The essential thing for the youth of our colleges and universities to learn is the difference between practicing generously a liberal art and driving a trade or winning a fight, no matter how. Civilization has been long in possession of much higher ethics than those of war, and experience has abundantly proved that the highest efficiency for service and the finest sort of courage in individual men may be accompanied by, and indeed spring from, unvarying generosity, gentleness and good will."

A *Dribbling Rush. Stanford Freshmen vs. St. Mary's College.*

THE STADIUM ON SOLDIERS' FIELD

The Harvard Stadium

By George P. Morris

HARVARD'S spacious athletic field, given to the University by Major H. L. Higginson as a memorial of his Harvard comrades in the Civil War, and known as Soldiers' Field, now has standing upon it, on a site harmonizing with the scheme for its development outlined by Frederick Law Olmsted, a vast structure of steel-concrete known as the Stadium. In it football and lacrosse are to be played, and track sports carried on. While not entirely finished, it is nearly so. It is usable and already has been the resort of nearly forty thousand spectators at a single game. When completed it may have within its walls dressing-rooms for players, handball courts, a rifle range, and other accessories of sport. Besides furnishing a vast, imposing, fire-proof, durable structure suitable for watching rivalry in sport, this edifice bids fair to be the scene of other academic functions of a less strenuous sort. Class Day exercises were held on the sward near the upper end this year.

Greek in its design, more than any other building in the country it suggests and rivals those stadia built by men in classic times for vast crowds to sit in and watch tests of the strength, speed, and agility of Greeks and Romans. It is a U-shaped structure with a single curved end and two straight sides, and includes within its outer walls an area of 537 x 420 feet. Tier upon tier of concrete seats resting on steel girders and beams of concrete rise to a height of fifty feet, the seats being arranged on three variant angles or slopes. There are thirty-seven sections of seats, with thirty-one rows in a section, each row seating from fourteen to twenty-six persons, according to the position of the section. At the first football game played in the Stadium, that with Yale in the fall of 1903, 23,400 persons occupied seats in the Stadium proper, and 38,400 persons saw the game, the extra attendants being seated on temporary seats or standing on the sward.

The mainspring and chief personality

DURING A YALE-HARVARD FOOTBALL GAME

of the corps of Harvard men responsible for this striking structure has been Professor I. N. Hollis, head of the Department of Engineering of the Lawrence Scientific School. With him have been associated very closely Professor L. J. Johnson, of the same department of the University, and Mr. Joseph R. Worcester, '82, consulting engineer, who are responsible for the work on its engineering and constructive side, and Messrs. C. F. McKim, the well-known architect, and Mr. George B. de Gershoff, '88, who are responsible for the general appearance of the structure and for converting a design guaranteed by engineers into one pleasing to the eye of the critic of architecture and to the average man. Construction was not begun until in Harvard's physical laboratories there had been thorough tests of the concrete-steel type of building, which, because of its first low cost, durability, non-inflammability, and other advantages, is likely to be used more and more.

The Stadium is a memorial of the generosity of the class of '79 and of the thrift of the management of the Athletic Association. The class of '79 gave $100,000 outright, the Athletic Association added $50,000 from an accumulated surplus set aside for this specific purpose, and the balance of the estimated cost ($225,000 to $250,000) will come from money borrowed, to be repaid from future profits of the Association.

Forty thousand people intensely interested in a contest of such importance and such fierce rivalry as a Yale-Harvard football match furnish a spectacle rarely surpassed and very informing for the student of humanity *en masse*. It is a rare place to study the psychology of the mob. The scene visible when this building is crowded with people is unsurpassed for its brilliancy of coloring, intensity of human feeling kept within bounds, and the evidence it furnishes of the hold which intercollegiate sport has on the well-to-do classes of American society. Along with fine sport and exceptional opportunity to witness it with unimpeded view, there now goes assurance of personal safety for the spectators, which was not the case when the former wooden grand stands were in use. Moreover, the structure itself serves as a model, educationally and æsthetically considered ; and it doubtless is but a forerunner of many structures of the kind on academic athletic fields.

32

UNIVERSITY AND PUBLIC LIBRARIES

By Charles Alexander Nelson

"That library of brownstone ruddy,
A structured gem, whose alcoves fill
The treasures scholars come to study,
Guided by kindness crowned with skill."
W. R. Alger.

LIBRARIES have always been the centres around which scholars have gathered since the time when the companions of Xisuthros (Adrahasis) returned to Sippara of the Sun, on the bank of the Euphrates, unearthed the buried tablets on which were recorded all antediluvian knowledge, and opened the school for Babylonian savants, the very house and library of which have but recently been found. Aristotle had his library, and Alexandria, Rome, Cæsarea, and Constantinople were ancient seats of learning because of their large libraries. Books and learning were preserved for us through the Middle Ages in the monasteries, especially those of the Benedictines, who provided in their houses first for a library, next for a *scriptorium* or copy-room, where their books were duplicated for sale or exchange, and lastly for a school open to all comers in search of instruction. To this order England owes her earliest library, and at their abbey of St. Mary's, at York, the learned Alcuin obtained the training which fitted him for the work of establishing the libraries and cloister schools at Aix-la-Chapelle and Tours, to which he was called by Charlemagne. All the great universities of Europe have notable collections of books.

The earliest college library in America was that of Henrico, Va., the so-called college for the education of the natives, in actual operation in 1616, but destroyed in the general massacre of 1622. Harvard was founded in 1636 by an appropriation of one-half the annual rates of the colony, but its active impulse came two years later with the bequest from John Harvard of one-half of his property and his *entire library* of nearly 300 volumes. Yale had its origin in 1700, when its ten trustees, nine of whom were graduates of Harvard, met at Branford, and each laid upon the table his contribution

of books with the words: "I give these books for the founding of a college in Connecticut." In 1757, ten years after the date of its first charter, Princeton had its first building, with a library of 1,200 volumes. King's College, chartered in 1754, received in 1756 by bequest of Dr. Bristow, of London, his library of about 1,500 volumes, the library of Joseph Murray, and other gifts of books.

Eighteen other college libraries were founded between 1700 and 1800, so that the nineteenth century began with twenty-one college libraries; it ended with thirty times as many. In 1790 Harvard College had only 12,000 volumes, and a year later Yale College had only 2,700. The books in these early libraries were largely very learned and serious in character, being designed principally for the use of the professors. "In them theology naturally held the leading place, as the colleges had been founded mainly to educate ministers. So in the Harvard College Library catalogue of 1790, 150 pages out of 350 are filled with theology, 10 with Greek and Latin classics, 4 with books of travel, but only three-fourths of a page with periodicals. In literature, however, one finds Chaucer, Shakespeare, Spenser, Milton, Dryden, Pope, Gay, the *Gentleman's Magazine,* Rabelais, La Fontaine, Voltaire, Boccaccio." Twenty-five years earlier, we are told, the library at Yale College was "well furnished with ancient authors, such as the Fathers, historians, Classics, many and valuable works of divinity, history, philosophy, and mathematics, but not many authors who have written within these thirty years."

In the earliest years of our colleges when students were few in number, and all or nearly all were studying for a special profession and in close contact with their professors, doubtless some use was made by them of the solid books in the college libraries; but as the number of students multiplied and classes increased in numbers, an ever-lessening percentage of students made use of the college library, which in all too many instances

THE HARVARD UNIVERSITY LIBRARY.

was closely guarded against them. Dr. W. F. Poole said in an address ten years ago, "to those of us who graduated thirty, forty, or more years ago, books, outside of the text-books used, had no part in our education; they were never quoted, recommended, nor mentioned by the instructors in the classroom. . . . The college societies, however, supported and managed wholly by the undergraduates, had good libraries, and here was where the students, and the professors besides, found their general reading."

The development of the college into the university was a very slow process covering long years in its accomplishment. Theological, medical, and law schools were early established at the leading institutions. At Harvard it was not until after the election of President Eliot in 1869 that the reorganisation and consolidation of its several semi-independent professional schools began, and it was not until 1890 that the Academic Council was superseded by the University Council. Yale assumed the title of university in 1887, Columbia in 1890, and Princeton in 1896; but prior to these dates real university work in graduate departments had been done at each.

"Americans have always been a bookish people," and the fact that at most of the colleges student societies were organised, which provided their own libraries of books suited to the tastes of their student members, goes far to show that the additions made to the college libraries were not so suited, or that the attractions offered or the privileges granted by these libraries were not sufficient to induce the students to make much use of them. The bulk of the purchases would naturally be of learned books, chiefly for the use of the professors, while the librarian was too often an overworked or broken-down professor, a veritable keeper of books, appointed to the place in order that he might eke out an insufficient income. Occasionally genuine book-lovers like Cogswell, Harris and Sibley were in charge and the library grew apace as did that of Harvard under these master book-collectors.

A new era dawned in the middle of the nineteenth century when the library

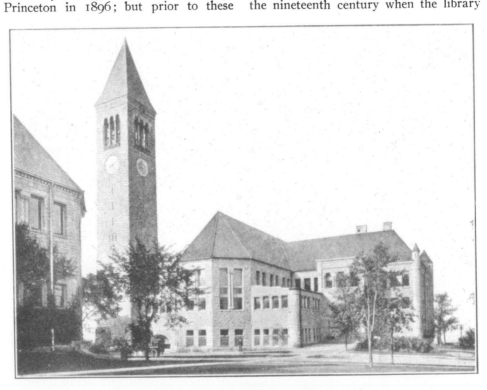

THE CORNELL UNIVERSITY LIBRARY.

OLD YALE LIBRARY.

THE CHITTENDON LIBRARY AT YALE.

spirit moved upon the people, and with the establishment of the Boston Public Library in 1852. "Public opinion in that city," says President D. C. Gilman, "demanded a library free, large, well catalogued, adapted at once to the public and to the scholar, dependent partly on the civic chest, partly upon the private purse, fitted to furnish entertainment and pleasure to the weary workman, and fitted to inspire and satisfy the most gifted writer." Later, C. A. Cutter wrote of the same library, "nowhere yet has the happy combination of private and public liberality made it possible to at once so thoroughly suffice for learned research even of the specialist, gratify cultivated curiosity, please the bibliomaniac and the dilettante, foster idle meditation, or stimulate vigorous thinking, while yet not neglecting to meet every want of the general reader, even the want of amusement and illusion, and, more than this, to attract to itself and to train adults who have never been in the habit of reading at all, and children who have not yet learned to read with profit." Here, in a nutshell, we have expressed the opinions of one of the ablest of university presidents and of one of the most expert of librarians on the scope and work of the first and one of the largest and best of public libraries.

Charles C. Jewett, father of the card catalogue, was its first librarian; Justin Winsor followed from 1868 till 1877, when he was called to the librarianship of Harvard College Library. The same success that attended his administration of the great public library followed his management of that of the great university library.

In 1850, Harvard, which for two centuries had been the largest library in the country, was still in the lead with only 70,000 volumes. The Astor Library had not been founded and the Library of Congress was little known. George Ticknor, a prime mover in the establishment of the Boston Public Library, had been for fifteen years a professor of modern languages and literature at Harvard. In a letter to Edward Everett, in 1851, he gave this expression of his ideal of the new institution: "I would establish a library which differs from all free libraries yet attempted; I mean one in which any popular books, tending to

moral and intellectual improvement, shall be furnished in such numbers of copies that many persons can be reading the same book at the same time; in short, that not only the best books of all sorts, but the pleasant literature of the day, shall be made accessible to the whole people when they most care for it; that is, when it is fresh and new. I would . . . thus, by following the popular taste—unless it should demand something injurious—create a real appetite for healthy reading. This appetite, once formed, will take care of itself. It will, in a great majority of cases, demand better and better books."

Such was the high ideal of this enthusiastic pioneer in the free public library movement, a movement that has been and continues to be so widely endorsed as to prove that the Americans are indeed a bookish people.

The high ideal of the great Panizzi, *facile princeps* of librarians, with the change of a single word, may well be taken as that of the university library: "I would have," said he, "a public [university] library so complete that a scholar, however rich, will find it a more convenient working place than his own study, however well equipped." A university library with such an ideal might well merit the praise bestowed by President Gilman on one where bibliographical "treasures may be enjoyed with abundant light, in an equable temperature, in the atmosphere of repose, with learned and ready teachers near at hand, and with opportunities to enter those glorified cells of the cloister which we call the seminaries of knowledge"; a place where, to quote him again, "the promptness with which any book among a hundred thousand may be identified and summoned, as if it were touched by an electric wire, is an unfailing surprise to those who are wont to spend hours in their own dens looking for some long-lost friend, and an unfailing gratification to every busy student."

But even with such an ideal, with a full collection of books well housed, the university may fail of its purpose. Carlyle said "the true university of these days is a collection of books," but this dictum is true only for the trained scholar, like Carlyle, who knows how to make use of them. The college man is in training

THE COLUMBIA UNIVERSITY LIBRARY.

how to make the best use of his mental faculties, and a most important factor in this training is how to use books. On this point Justin Winsor wrote, in 1880: "I fear we have not discovered what the full functions of a college library should be; we have not reached its ripest effects; we have not organised that instruction which teaches how to work its collections as a placer of treasures. To fulfil its rightful destiny, the library should become the central agency of our college methods. . . . The way to avoid being appalled at the world of books is

sary companions, telling the peculiar value of each, how this assists in such cases, that in others; how this may lead to that, until with practise the student finds that for his work he has almost a new sense." Following lines of instruction like the above there would soon be no place for the complaint so widely made that the great majority of the students of the colleges and universities of the country graduate with very little knowledge of books or of their uses.

Dr. Wm. Fred. Poole in a B. K. address ten years ago on the relations of

LIBRARY OF THE UNIVERSITY OF VIRGINIA.

what the library of the college is commissioned to point out. . . We must build our libraries with class rooms annexed, and we must learn our ways through the wilderness of books until we have the instinct that serves the red man when he knows the north by the thickness of the moss on the tree-boles. . . Take the students by sections and make them acquainted with the bibliographical apparatus, those books that the librarian finds his neces-

the university library to university education, declared "that the study of bibliography and of the scientific methods of using books should have an assured place in the university curriculum; that a wise and professional bibliographer should be a member of the faculty and have a part in training all the students; that the library should be his class room, and that all who go forth into the world as graduates should have an intelligent and practical knowledge of books that will aid

WELLESLEY LIBRARY.

SMITH COLLEGE LIBRARY.

THE PRINCETON UNIVERSITY LIBRARY.

them in their studies through life, and the use of books be to them a perpetual delight and refreshment."

"I do not mean," he adds, "that the university student should learn the contents of the most useful books; but I do mean that he should know of their existence, what they treat of, and what they will do for him. He should know what are the most important general reference books which will answer not only his own questions, but the multitude of inquiries put to him by less favoured associates who regard him as an educated man. . . . He should know the standard writers on a large variety of subjects. He should be familiar with the best method by which the original investigation of any topic may be carried on. When he has found it he appreciates, perhaps for the first time, what books are for, and how to use them. He finds himself a professional literary or scientific worker, and that books are the tools of his profession. . . . No person has any claim to be a scholar until he can conduct such an original investigation with ease and pleasure. This facile proficiency does not come by intuition, nor from the clouds. Where else is it to be taught, if not in the college or university?" . . . John Morley in an address at the dedication of a public library a few years ago declared that the object of libraries and books was to bring sunshine into our hearts and to drive moonshine out of our heads; such a training in the use of libraries as that proposed by Mr. Winsor and Dr. Poole would do very much towards clearing both moonshine and cobwebs out of the heads of those who might take it.

The university library of to-day is a thing of quite recent development; in fact, it is but little more than out of its teens; and yet it is really the ripest fruit of the library movement in America, since it represents and requires the best results in all branches of library economy developed up to the present time. The selection of books to be purchased for a university library is or should be made largely by the faculty, each member of which is interested deeply in some one branch of study. A library thus built up will not only be one of general reference, but will also be an aggregation of special libraries. Such a library is not only the storehouse whence the professor may draw increase of knowledge and inspiration for his work, but by the skillful arrangement of seminar rooms with reference to the books in the several departments of knowledge it becomes the workshop or laboratory of both professors and students, and the very centre of university instruction. And just such libraries our best universities now have. The Low Library at Columbia has a capacity for a million and a half of volumes. It has now 352,000 volumes; a central reading room with an open shelf reference collection of 10,000 volumes; a law library of 36,000 volumes in one wing; the Avery Architectural Library of 18,000 volumes in another; 18 seminar rooms, Mr. Winsor's "libraries with class rooms annexed," 10 with rooms for many more under the same roof, and over twenty department libraries ranging from a few hundred to several thousand volumes each, selected with special reference to their constant use by students in their daily work. Books are loaned to professors and students and the library is open freely to all, properly introduced, for reference and study. Cornell has a general library, a forestry collection, the White historical library, and seven seminars, all under one roof, with law and veterinary libraries in their respective buildings, with a total of over 261,000 volumes, including many very valuable special collections. Primarily a reference library, officers and graduate students may take out books, and undergraduates also over holidays on which the library is closed. There is a free reference library in the reading room, and cards of admission to the shelves in the stacks are issued. Lecture courses on the use of the library and in bibliography are given. The Harvard University Library still holds first place with over 400,000 volumes; has ten departmental libraries, and 29 special reference libraries for the various branches of study pursued under direction of the faculty of arts and sciences; loans books to officers and students, and is freely opened to the use of scholars. "'Tis true 'tis pity, and pity 'tis 'tis true" that the ruthless hand of death should have stayed the signature that would have given the Harvard Library its much needed new home. Princeton, with its two connected library buildings, has capacity for a million and a quarter volumes and more than twenty seminars, nine already organised; has four departmental libraries in proximity to their corresponding laboratories. Its general collection numbers 175,000 volumes, with 90,000 volumes additional in department and special collections. Books may be drawn by all officers and students and by any person properly introduced. The University of Pennsylvania has over 213,000 volumes, with 12 seminar rooms in upper part of library building, open till 11 P.M. Twelve department libraries with over 25,000 volumes in other buildings. Officers and students may take out books, and graduates also on payment of $3.00 a year. Free reference to all. Johns Hopkins has a library, for reference only, of 108,000 volumes, "under ten roofs, and in even more compartments," with over 550,000 volumes, accessible within a radius of one-third of a mile, and all the libraries of Washington within easy reach. Glancing westward we see the University of Chicago with a general library of over 263,000 volumes, several branch libraries, and 27 departmental libraries, all aggregating nearly 370,000 volumes. Books are loaned to officers and students, and nearly 1,300 current periodicals and transactions of societies are received. At Ann Arbor is a general library of over 130,000 volumes, including special medical collections, with law and dental libraries in their respective buildings numbering 35,-000 volumes additional; 1,000 periodicals regularly received. Officers of the university only may draw books; reference to all others; separate study rooms provided for advanced students. And on the Pacific Coast the University of California has a library of 105,000 volumes "selected and arranged with a view to making it especially valuable as a reference library." An introductory lecture is given to students on the use of the library and of books; and there is a summer school course in library economy. These typical libraries have been selected almost at random and without prejudice to others that might well have been named.

33

RECENT AMERICAN COLLEGE ARCHITECTURE

BY A. D. F. HAMLIN

ADJUNCT PROFESSOR OF ARCHITECTURE IN COLUMBIA UNIVERSITY

WITH PICTURES BY CHARLES W. FURLONG
AND DECORATIONS BY EDWARD EDWARDS

A NATION that has many new buildings to erect and plenty of money to spend upon them is sure to develop a characteristic architecture. It may be good or bad or simply commonplace, but nothing can prevent its being clearly expressive of the taste, culture, ideals, and capacities of the Nation. The style of the new buildings will be an index of its artistic taste; the purposes for which they are erected will reveal the dominant interests and illustrate the character of its civilization.

It has been customary to speak of the pervading commercialism of American life. The towering and impressive masses of the business buildings of lower New York seem to give evidence of a triumphant materialism; the more so when we learn that fifty or sixty millions of dollars sometimes go into such structures in a single twelvemonth. But the evidence is fallacious, for when we survey the country at large it is not sky-scrapers that fill our vision, but rather the homes, churches, and schools of the people. We have heard a good deal about our domestic and religious architecture, both from native and foreign critics; but our collegiate architecture has not received the attention it deserves, though not less suggestive than our houses and churches of the National progress and National ideals.

Recent foreign observers have expressed amazement at the magnitude, number, equipment, and endowments of our universities. No one, indeed, who studies the record of recent gifts to education in this country, or the statistics of attendance upon our higher institutions of learning, can fail to be impressed with the increasing popular regard for intellectual culture. We believe that the architectural character of the buildings erected for these institutions within the past ten years indicates an equally rapid advance in the artistic culture of the Nation. It is not without significance that the two most magnificent buildings ever erected in America, with the possible exception of the Capitol at Washington, are public libraries, one built by the Nation at Washington, the other by the municipality at Boston; and that Congress has authorized new buildings to cost fourteen millions of dollars for the two great National schools at Annapolis and West Point. In the very focus of American commercialism, the noblest of recent buildings is the library erected at Columbia University in 1897 by the present Mayor of the city, to be soon, however, surpassed in size and splendor by the city's own new Public Library; and there is in process of gradual erection in Brooklyn a superb museum building for the Brooklyn Institute, an important educational organization—a veritable palace of the arts and sciences, to cost several millions, and to be paid for out of the public funds. Let it also be noted that the people of this same city of New York, with all their reputed devotion to mammon, maintain two great universities, Columbia University and the New York University, both recently equipped with splendid new buildings; and that the city has itself begun upon Washington Heights the erection of a noble and costly group of buildings for its own City College.

The collegiate architecture of the United States represents, therefore, no small or unimportant phase of the National activity. During the past ten years it has fully shared in the general progress and prosperity. In many cases the whole aspect of an institution has been metamorphosed either by a complete reconstruction on a new site, or by notable additions to the buildings on the old site. In the latter case the comparison of the new with the old buildings furnishes an object-lesson in the progress and tendencies of our collegiate architecture. The contrast is sometimes extraordinary. The new edifices are not only more artistic in design, more monumental in effect than the old; they are also better planned, more convenient, more solid and thorough in con-struction, and vastly better furnished and equipped.

The architecture of American colleges has grown up on an essentially different system from the European. The typical American college or university consists of a collection of distinct buildings, grouped more or less regularly about a grassy and shady area called the campus. The original nucleus of the group was usually the chapel, flanked by two dormitories of red brick. A half-dozen lecture-rooms occupied the basement of the chapel. Other dormitories and recitation halls, laboratories, and a library were added as the resources of the institution permitted, and placed as the convenience of the occasion seemed to dictate—in parallel rows, or around a vast square, or in more fortuitous groupings determined by the topography. The successive additions were often wholly unrelated architecturally to their older neighbors, or even in some cases to one another, representing as many diverse styles as there were architects employed. Harvard, Yale, Princeton, Brown, and Wesleyan Universities, Bowdoin and Dartmouth, Amherst and Williams Colleges, and half a hundred others, grew up in this way. The European conception of collegiate architecture was derived from olden monastic traditions; it was that of the cloister or quadrangle, or a series of "quads," each entirely surrounded by a continuous building and entered through an imposing gateway. Such a scheme was not only foreign to our ideas, but wholly impracticable for rural colleges struggling for existence on the slenderest of means; and out of such struggling rural colleges have grown nearly all our great universities.

The newer American college architecture, even in following the traditional American system of isolated buildings, seeks to secure general unity of effect. It is, of course, impossible to correct the chaos of an existing group of heterogeneous buildings, but it is at least possible to establish a definite plan and scheme to which all future additions shall conform. At Harvard the dominant note of the older colonial buildings has been followed in nearly all the more recent erections in and about the "Square." Several colleges and universities have had the good fortune to be able to undertake an entire

NEW DORMITORIES AT THE UNIVERSITY OF PENNSYLVANIA

❧ 359 ❧

THE NEW MEMORIAL GATEWAY AT BOWDOIN

rebuilding on a new site. Trinity College, at Hartford, Connecticut, was the first of these, having as far back as 1875 begun the erection of an imposing block of buildings in four quadrangles, from plans by the late William Burges, of London. Only a small part of this great scheme has been completed, forming a long and imposing stretch of buildings in English Gothic style. About 1890 the Leland Stanford Junior University began in like manner the erection at Palo Alto (California) of new buildings on a comprehensive plan prepared by Shepley, Rutan, and Coolidge, of Boston. This was only in part realized; and the unity of the scheme has been injured by several structures designed by other hands. A few years later the University of New York moved certain of its departments to a new site at Fordham Heights, near the metropolis, and built there, from designs by McKim, Mead, and White, a group of buildings centered around a fine domical library and memorial gallery, which last has become known all over the country as the "Hall of Fame." The new buildings of Columbia University, by the same architects, followed soon after, the noble Low Library forming the center of the group (1895–1897); and in 1898 Mrs.

Phœbe Hearst instituted an international competition for new buildings on a scale of unexampled magnificence for the University of California at Berkeley, in which the prize was won by the French architect Bénard. The first buildings of this vast design—the School of Mines and an open-air "theater"—are now under construction. Washington University at St. Louis has begun the execution of a fine design by Cope and Stewardson, of Philadelphia, on an almost equally ambitious scale. All of these great enterprises betoken abundant confidence in the future of the institutions that have entered upon them, a sublime reliance upon the generous support of the American people, and the determination to plan, not merely for the immediate necessity, but for expected growth, so that order and beauty may reign in increasing perfection as the years roll on. Meanwhile, many other colleges and universities, retaining the old site and buildings, have added new structures of great size, cost, and beauty. There is probably not one among our older institutions of the higher learning that has not received notable architectural additions within the past ten years, and in some cases, as at Harvard, Yale, Princeton, and the University of Penn-

THE LIBRARY OF NEW YORK UNIVERSITY

sylvania, the cost of these additions has run up into the millions. Our medical colleges, theological seminaries, and technological schools have shared in this extension and enrichment.

The causes of this architectural activity are not hard to discover. It is not to be explained merely by any theory of a newly developed passion for expenditure, luxury, or splendor. The trustees of our great educational institutions are almost without exception men of conservative rather than radical ideas; men with a deep sense of their responsibility to the public and to the institution, and they could not command millions for display if they wished it. New buildings have become necessary simply because the new education demands resources and an equipment for which the old provision was utterly inadequate. A chapel and four recitation-rooms were all that was necessary for the

college of 1803. The library was amply accommodated in one or two of the rooms in an adjacent dormitory. For the college of 1903 there must be a modern fireproof library, with stack-room, reading-room, reference-room, seminar-rooms, and staff-rooms; scientific buildings, with laboratories, more varied and complex than our fathers ever dreamed of, with testing rooms and lecture-rooms and instructors' rooms and storerooms; a gymnasium, large and spacious, with running-track, swimming-tank, baths, handball courts, and what not. There must be a suitable administration building for the president, treasurer, and dean, for faculty meetings and trustee meetings, and a hall or auditorium for commencement gatherings and mass-meetings. In some colleges a college "commons," refectory, or dining-hall is required, and the social life of the students must be provided for by a college

THE HARVARD UNION

THE YALE BICENTENNIAL BUILDING

Charles W. Furlong '03

❧ 363 ❧

club-house, or, in connection with their religious life, by a special building for the religious associations and the college Young Men's Christian Association. As the college grows, moreover, the dormitories must be extended or multiplied and new recitation-halls added. Thus architectural expansion and renovation become an absolute necessity wherever there are life and growth in a college, as in any other public institution that partakes of the real life of the community.

Thus made necessary by the main force of circumstances, these new buildings show also the influence of the changes in public taste and in the standards of architectural and structural excellence which have taken place in the past twenty years. Not only have the architects made great progress in their mastery of the resources of design ; their clients, the governing bodies of the colleges, have made an equal advance in their conceptions of what sort of buildings the colleges require. Alike in artistic design, in solidity of construction, and in elegance of finish and equipments, the buildings erected during the past ten years far surpass anything that this country had ever seen before in the way of collegiate architecture.

The cosmopolitan and eclectic quality of our taste is fitly expressed in the variety of architectural style which these modern college buildings display. From 1880 to 1890 the powerful influence of Mr. Richardson showed itself in the general adoption of the Romanesque style, freely treated; but more recently other styles have found favor. The majority of the newer buildings are either "Colonial" (or "Georgian," as some prefer to call it) in style, as at Harvard; or in the late Gothic style of many university buildings in England, to which the name of the English Collegiate style is often given., This style lends itself readily to the treatment of long ranges of buildings of moderate height, and permits of a more picturesque variety of mass and sky-line than the Georgian, and the more stately Classic and Renaissance styles. It has been handled with great skill by Cope and Stewardson in the handsome buildings of the dormitory "Quad" at Pennsylvania University, in Blair Hall at Princeton, and in the new edifices of Washington University at St. Louis. The Vanderbilt

Hall at Yale, by C. C. Haight, and the very picturesque and impressive group of buildings on Washington Heights for the College of the City of New York, by Mr. G. B. Post, are also excellent examples of the style. Mr. Potter's new Library at Princeton approaches closer to the Perpendicular Gothic in style, but is unmistakably scholastic in character.

The Georgian style is less picturesque, more restrained, more domestic perhaps, and better suited for detached buildings than for continuous ranges and quadrangles. It has very naturally been adopted at Harvard for all the newer buildings, which thus harmonize with and emphasize the quaint flavor and historic associations of the older ones. The Harvard Union, the new gymnasium for Radcliffe College, the Randall dining hall, and the new gates are examples of this style ; while the Law School at the University of Pennsylvania, the new Library of the University of Virginia, and Barnard College at New York, represent other applications of it. McKim, Mead, and White's Library and other buildings at Fordham Heights for the New York University are also in a version of the Georgian style, modified by a touch of Italian classical stateliness; and in the more important group at Columbia University these same architects have apparently tried the experiment of establishing a strong contrast between the Low Library—a magnificent Greco-Roman building of creamy Indiana limestone—and the half-Georgian departmental buildings of red brick with stone finishings.

A third style requires notice—the Italian or classic style, not because it is in frequent use, but because of the importance of the few cases in which it has been adopted. The most conspicuous instance is the University of California, where two of the buildings of the vast plan prepared by the architect Bénard are now being erected under the supervision of Mr. J. G. Havard, of New York—the School of Mines and the open-air auditorium. The new buildings for the Naval Academy at Annapolis, by Ernest Flagg, are in this stately and monumental style, which permits of greater majesty of scale and splendor of effect than the other two.

But, whatever the style of the newer college buildings of the United States, they are all in one sense thoroughly

THE NEW COLLEGE OF THE CITY OF NEW YORK

MEMORIAL ARCH AT OBERLIN COLLEGE

Dedicated May 14, 1903, in memory of thirteen American missionaries martyred in China.

American; for their designs have been studied with a special view to meeting American requirements, and the success and merit of the result have depended, not on the style label it wears, but on the ability, skill, and taste with which the architect has solved the specific problem presented to him in each case. In general, this ability, skill, and taste have been of a high order. It is to be regretted that in this respect the Roman Catholic colleges have, as a whole, remained so far in arrears. There is hardly one among these institutions to whose credit can be set down any really notable and highly meritorious work of architecture in recent years.

The complete list of important buildings erected within the past ten years for American colleges, universities, theological seminaries, and other institutions of the higher learning would make an impressive showing. These buildings represent an enormous financial investment; and it must be remembered that this physical growth means also a great increase in expenditure for maintenance and administration. All this is significant of the disposition of the American people to increase their financial investment in the higher education—an investment not only in buildings, which, taken alone, might mean mere luxury, but in all that for which the buildings stand, and to promote which they were built—science, literature, religion, and intellectual culture of every kind. The American scholar may well point to these edifices with pride, assured that a hundred years from now many of them will still be looked upon with admiration, as monuments of the intellectual and artistic enthusiasm of an age too often accounted as wholly given up to a selfish materialism.

34

A MAGNIFICENT HOME OF LEARNING

THE ARCHITECTURAL PLANS FOR THE NEW UNIVERSITY OF CALIFORNIA — THE MOST APPROPRIATE SITE AND THE MOST COMPREHENSIVE DESIGN FOR A GREAT SCHOOL THAT WERE EVER CHOSEN

BY

VICTOR HENDERSON

FOUR years ago Mrs. Phoebe Apperson Hearst invited the architects of the world to enter a competition, the object of which was to obtain permanent plans for the buildings and grounds for the University of California. When she informed the Regents of the University that she proposed to erect two buildings, but that she was unwilling to begin until a worthy general plan had been secured, and that it was her desire to bear all the expense of an international competition to secure a fitting plan, the University was quick to appreciate the far-seeing wisdom of the undertaking.

A board of trustees was appointed consist-ing of James H. Budd, Governor of California, J. B. Reinstein, a Regent of the University, and William Carey Jones, Professor of Jurisprudence in its faculty. After much consultation with architects and university authorities, a programme was prepared, printed in English, German, French and Italian, and widely distributed. An international jury, comprising M. J. L. Pascal of Paris, Herr Paul Wallot of Dresden, Mr. John Belcher of London, Mr. Walter Cook of New York, and Mr. J. B. Reinstein of San Francisco, assembled in the Royal Museum of Fine Arts in Antwerp, September 30, 1898, and after examining the hundred or more

SECTION UPON THE AXIS
OF GYMNASIUMS AND NATURAL HISTORY

THE NEW UNIVERSITY OF

From right to left, on the lower sketch, the buildings are Fine Arts, Library, Philosophy, President's House,

plans submitted, awarded prizes to eleven competitors. The successful architects were invited to visit the University and to prepare revised plans for a second competition.

In September, 1899, the jury met again in San Francisco, and selected the prize-winning plans. When the seals were broken and the names of the authors for the first time learned by the jurors, it was found that the winner of the first prize of $10,000, was M. Emily Bénard, of Paris, and of the lesser prizes of $4,000, $3,000, $2,000 and $1,000, Messrs. Howells, Stokes and Hornbostel, of New York; Messrs. D. Despradelle and Stephen Codman, of Boston; Messrs. Howard and Cauldwell, and Messrs. Lord, Hewlett and Hull, of New York.

M. Bénard, after a long stay in Berkeley and many conferences with the University authorities, undertook a revision of his drawings to fit the plans to the actual necessities of the site and the prospective needs of the University. In December, 1900, he submitted a design which the Regents formally adopted as the permanent plan, from which no important change may be made except with the approval of a self-perpetuating Board of Architectural Advisers, comprising the jurors and other architects of high reputation.

I. GENERAL BIRD'S EYE VIEW

II. BOTANICAL GARDEN

III. COMMEMORATIVE COLUMN

I. BIRD'S EYE VIEW
From the southwest corner of the campus looking toward the hills

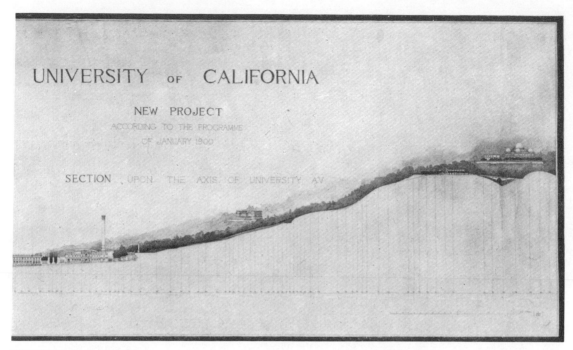

CALIFORNIA AS IT WILL BE

Languages, Botany and Agriculture, Museum, Mining, Mechanical Engineering, a Dormitory, Observatory

The sketches prepared by M. Bénard are not complete working drawings, showing exact grade-lines and details of the construction of individual buildings, but a broad outline, indicating the general character of the architecture, the disposition of the buildings, their relation to one another and to the broad avenues, gardens, and open squares of the admirable composition. The execution of the plans will necessitate surveys and re-surveys, constant checking and correction, arduous study of details, and laborious fitting of parts to the whole. Each building must be planned in its relation to its immediate surroundings and to the whole composition.

To Mr. John Galen Howard of New York has been entrusted the first work of construction. He is now at work on plans for the Mining Building. As soon as the problems of arrangement, form and structure are solved, and the working drawings made, ground will be broken for this, Mrs. Hearst's noble memorial for her husband. By a year's residence in California some years ago, and by exhaustive studies in connection with the Hearst Competition, in which he was a prize-winner, Mr. Howard has familiarized himself

with California conditions and with the site, which he declares the most beautiful university

III. COMMEMORATIVE COLUMN

At the head of University Avenue

II. THE BOTANICAL GARDEN
Looking toward the buildings for Natural History and for Mining and Mechanical Engineering

site he has ever seen. In March, 1901, he spent several weeks in Berkeley studying the grounds and consulting with President Wheeler and with Professor Samuel Christy, Dean of the College of Mining.

Mrs. Hearst's desire is to erect a structure as complete and beautiful as money and thought can build. This building will satisfy a vital need, for the University has to-day more students of mining than are enrolled in the mining course of any other institution in the world.

Other buildings will follow the Mining Building. It is one of the chief merits of the Bénard plan that it is flexible, that it can grow, and that the component parts can in large measure express the individuality of the department sheltered and of the architects who design the single buildings, without thereby losing their harmony with the whole.

The site of the University was selected a good forty years ago as the most beautiful and appropriate spot in all the country round. Berkeley is a village of 15,000 persons, on the eastern shore of San Francisco Bay, some miles by train and ferry from San Francisco, and directly opposite the Golden Gate. It is full of pleasant gardens and well-grown trees and sheltered on the east by a steep range of hills, which rise to their culminating summit of 1,900 feet in Grizzly Peak.

At the eastern edge of the town, and resting on the shoulders of Grizzly Peak, lies the University domain. The campus rises in a gentle, and then in a bolder slope, from a height of 200 feet to one of over 900. Two small streams, issuing from deep, ferny cañons in the hills, flow down across the grounds under noble groves of live-oaks, pines and bays. From November to May the campus is green and flowery, from May to November, a soft brown, save for the never-fading green of the trees. Snow never falls, and the air is sunny and fresh with ocean breezes.

Here on this unrivalled site, with its outlook over plain and bay and mountain, is to rise a picture complete in itself, cut off from all discordant elements, the new city of learning.

From the high hill-summit on the eastern edge of the campus, down the steep hill-slope as a terraced garden, and westward as a broad avenue traversing two great squares, is to run the main axis. The transverse axis is an ex-

ON THE CAMPUS
Strawberry Creek under the bay trees

between the Administration building on the west and the Civil Engineering building on the east, over the conservatory and botanical garden, and past the open stadium, with its flanking tribunes, to the Gymnasium, an imposing edifice whose northern front will descend in stone tribunes to the stadium. At the base of the steep hill-slope will stand the Mechanical Engineering building and central power station, on the north of the main central avenue, and at the south the Chemistry building. On the summit of the hill, 500 feet higher, will stand the Observatory. Habitations for the students, an infirmary, club houses, a restaurant, a military establishment, and various other buildings will be scattered in nooks and corners about the grounds.

To turn the dream city into stone will cost $10,000,000 or $12,000,000. No one expects to see the work near completion in less than a generation. Architectural masterpieces always grow slowly. But the plan is set, and whatever is done will be done right, and the

tensive open space, the northern half a botanical garden, the southern a stadium, linking the natural history group with the monumental gymnasium.

When the plan has been executed, one will enter the grounds at the western end of the main avenue, and advancing eastward toward the hills pass between a fine arts building on the north, and an auditorium and reception building on the south, and out upon the Library Square. The Library will face south, overlooking the finest grove of oaks on the campus. Advancing eastward one will pass between the Philosophy-and-Jurisprudence building on the north, and the building for History, Political Science and Pedagogy on the south, under an eminence crowned by the President's House—a dignified stone mansion now in process of erection—between the Languages building on the north and the Physics building on the south, and out upon an esplanade on the north side of which will be grouped the Natural History buildings, the Museum in the centre, with west and east wings devoted to Zoology and Mineralogy, and flanking buildings for Botany and Agriculture on the south, and Mining on the north. From the Museum one will look south

"THE FOOTBALL PLAYERS"
Bronze statue by Douglass Tilden, offered to the University first winning two Stanford–California games, and won by the University of California

LICK OBSERVATORY
A winter view of the Graduate Astronomical Department Building on Mount Hamilton

material University which is to be will be harmony and not a muddle. Most fortunately the material University of to-day still wears the clothes which were outgrown years ago. The present buildings, with few exceptions, are unworthy of the institution, and so it has been possible to plan the new University without any reference to present encumbrances, and as if the campus were wholly bare. The architect starts unhampered.

This architectural enterprise is of much significance for California. It means that the students of the State's University shall receive the inspiration of noble and beautiful surroundings. It means that a standard will be set for emulation throughout the West. It means that a great training-school for architects will be developed at Berkeley, for in no way can the training of architects be made so efficient as by permitting the student to have a hand in the erection of great and beautiful buildings.

In the past eleven years the number of students has increased fivefold. It is second in academic attendance among American universities, Harvard alone numbering more undergraduates. It is fifth of American universities in total enrollment, the number having passed the 3,000 mark. Its summer session for 1900 counted more students than the summer schools of any other American universities save Harvard and Cornell. Tuition is free, and men and women stand on an equal footing.

The relation of the University to the State is close and mutually helpful. Secondary education has been vitalized by the University's accrediting system. Since 1889–90 the number of California schools deemed worthy of accrediting has risen from thirteen to 110. The farmers' institutes, held in all parts of California, spread wide the latest rule of agricultural science. A system of university extension is developing rapidly in usefulness and scope. A department of irrigation has just been founded, with Elwood Mead, Irrigation Expert of the United States Department of Agriculture, at its head. This action consolidates national and state activity. A department of dairy husbandry has been established, and a dairy school and experimental farm are hopes for the near future. The College of Commerce, the first of its kind established in the United States, promises to put forth trained men for careers in commerce, the consular service, or business. Through the initiative of the University, a Commercial Museum, closely allied with the Philadelphia Commercial Museum, has been organized in San Francisco, and will prove hereafter an invaluable laboratory for the College of Commerce.

An astonishingly large proportion of the students pursue the general or academic course, as distinguished from the technical or professional, last year 70.3 per cent., as compared with 38 per cent. at Cornell, omitting law and medicine. Nearly one-fourth of all the 2,300 students in Berkeley are registered in one or more Latin courses, a very gratifying proportion.

On October 4, 1899, the students gathered around the flagstaff to greet the new president, Dr. Benjamin Ide Wheeler. Since President Wheeler's coming the material university has prospered abundantly. In March, (1901), the State Legislature increased its income by $100,000 per annum, raising the total from all sources, including the income from special funds, such as that for the support of the great Lick Observatory and the Wilmerding Trades School, to $575,000 a year. Mrs. Sather has endowed a chair in classical literature to the extent of $75,000, established two book funds of $10,000 each, and deeded to President Wheeler in trust other property of much value; Mr. D. O.

Mills has given $24,000 to defray the expenses of a two years' expedition from the Lick Observatory to an observing station in the Southern Hemisphere; William H. Crocker has sent an eclipse expedition to Sumatra, and Mrs. Hearst has presented a women's gymnasium worth $45,000, made provision for the annual expenditure of $30,000 or more on excavations and purchases in Egypt, Greece, Peru, New Mexico and the Philippines, for the archæological museum of the University, and in other ways has raised the total of her gifts to the University during the past four years to a figure exceeding $280,000.

No better forecast could be desired of the lines along which the immediate future of the University of California's growth will be than to cite the needs which President Wheeler in his first biennial report declared imperative. Among these are a library building suited to modern demands and capable of extension; library funds to the amount of $500,000; an alumni hall which shall form the centre of the daily social life of the students, alumni and faculty—this the alumni have undertaken to provide—an art building, to furnish shelter for objects illustrative of art, archæology anthropology, etc., schools of forestry, naval architecture and marine engineering, music and architecture; a department of archæology; a department of physical chemistry; a professor of the art of speaking; professors of Spanish, Russian and general linguistics, and lectureships and professorships for the College of Commerce.

And these things will soon come, for California is rich and generous and ambitious for the best in all things.

SUNSET AT THE GOLDEN GATE
As seen from the University of California Campus

INDEX

INDEX